FUGITIVES
OF THE
FOREST

ALSO BY ALLAN LEVINE

NON-FICTION
Scrum Wars: The Prime Ministers and the Media
Your Worship: The Lives of Eight of Canada's Most
Unforgettable Mayors (editor)
The Exchange: 100 Years of Trading Grain in Winnipeg

FICTION
The Blood Libel

FUGITIVES
OF THE
FOREST

ALLAN LEVINE

Stoddart

Published in 1998 by Stoddart Publishing Co. Limited
34 Lesmill road, Toronto, Canada M3B 2T6
180 Varick Street, 9th Floor, New York, New York 10014

Distributed in Canada by:
General Distribution Services Ltd.
325 Humber College Blvd., Toronto, Ontario M9W 7C3
Tel. (416) 213-1919   Fax (416) 213-1917
Email customer.service@ccmailgw.genpub.com

Distributed in the United States by:
General Distribution Services Inc.
85 River Rock Drive, Suite 202, Buffalo, New York 14207
Toll-free Tel. 1-800-805-1083   Toll-free Fax 1-800-481-6207
Email gdsinc@genpub.com

02 01 00 99 98 1 2 3 4 5

Canadian Cataloguing in Publication Data

Levine, Allan Gerald, 1956–
Fugitives of the forest: the heroic story of Jewish resistance
and survival during the Second World War

ISBN 0-7737-3127-X

1. World War, 1939–1945 – Jewish resistance – Europe, Eastern.
I. Title.

D810.J4L456 1998   940.53'089'924047   C98-931460-X

Cover design: Bill Douglas @ The Bang
Text design and page composition: Tannice Goddard

Printed and bound in Canada

*We gratefully acknowledge the Canada Council for the Arts and
the Ontario Arts Council for their support of our publishing program.*

To the Zelkowicz family —
partisans, freedom fighters, survivors:
Gitel Morrison and Simon Zelcovitch;
their parents, Leska (1903–1995)
and Lazer (1901–1982); and their brother,
Yossel (1925–1943), who died in the forest for his people

CONTENTS

Zog nit keynmol az du geyst dem letstn veg. . . .
Never say that you are on your last journey. . . .
— HIRSH GLIK *(1922–1944)*
The Partisan Hymn

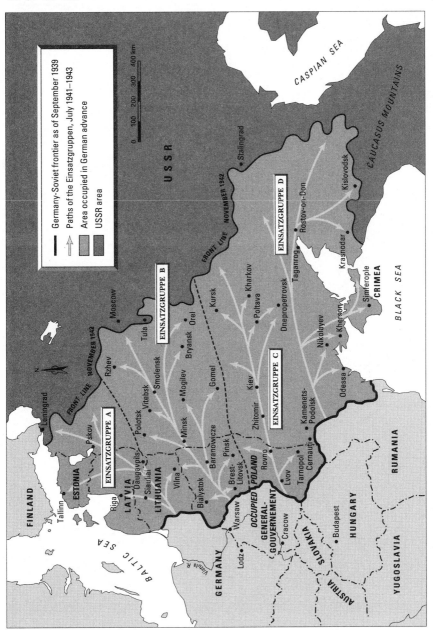

SECOND WORLD WAR EUROPE

Germany-Soviet frontier as of September 1939
Paths of the Einsatzgruppen, July 1941–1943
Area occupied in German advance
USSR area

0   100 200 300 400 km

FINLAND

BALTIC SEA

Tallinn
ESTONIA
Riga
LATVIA
Šiauliai
Daugavpils
LITHUANIA
Vilna

Leningrad
Pskov
Polotsk

EINSATZGRUPPE A

FRONT LINE NOVEMBER 1942

Vitebsk
Smolensk

Rzhev

Moscow

EINSATZGRUPPE B

Tula

GERMANY

Lodz
Vistula R.
Warsaw
OCCUPIED POLAND

Bialystok
Brest-Litovsk

Minsk

Baranowicze
Pinsk

Mogilev
Gomel

Bryansk
Orel

Kursk

GENERAL-GOUVERNEMENT
Cracow

SLOVAKIA

Rovno

Zhitomir

Kiev

Potlava

Kharkov

EINSATZGRUPPE C

AUSTRIA

Budapest

HUNGARY

YUGOSLAVIA

Lvov
Tarnopol
Kamenets-Podolsk
Cernauti

RUMANIA

Odessa

Nikolayev

Dnepropetrovsk

Taganrog

Kherson

EINSATZGRUPPE D

Rostov-on-Don

Simferople
CRIMEA

BLACK SEA

Krasnodar

Kislovodsk

CAUCASUS MOUNTAINS

USSR

Stalingrad

FRONT LINE NOVEMBER 1942

CASPIAN SEA

N

Partisan Camps

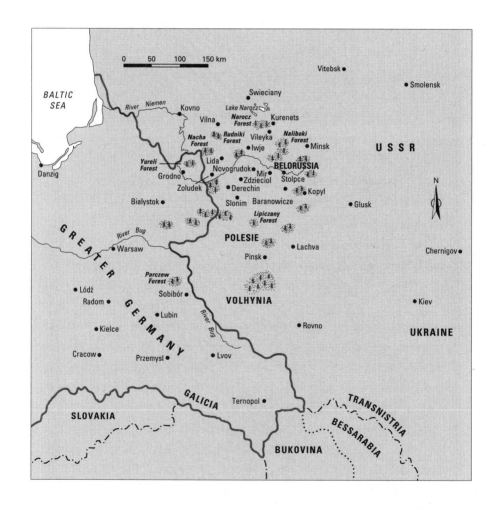

Preface

This book chronicles the heroic resistance and survival of the Jewish fugitives of the forests, from the moment the Nazis began their war against the Jews until Germany was defeated and the mass killing was finally stopped.

Throughout the three years this study was being researched and written, my objective remained simple and straightforward: To tell the story of how and why these Jewish partisans and survivors — fighters and non-combatants alike — managed to stay alive despite the overwhelming forces set against them.

From the very beginning, my research provoked additional questions: How did the Jews escape from the ghettos and become partisans? How did they survive on the run? Where did they find food? What was their relationship with the Soviet partisans who dominated and controlled the forest resistance against Germany? How was it possible for human beings in this century, isolated and sentenced to death by an uncompromising and vicious enemy, to live such a primitive existence in the forests for three years and survive?

Though thousands of Jews participated in partisan resistance in France, Slovakia, Yugoslavia, Bulgaria, and Greece, this book is concerned with the Jews of eastern Poland, Belorussia, the Ukraine, the three Baltic states, and the western part of the Soviet Union. A large portion of European Jews lived in these areas, and this is where this tragic drama was played out to its fullest.

This book is intended for a general audience. Without losing sight of the larger and more complex issues connected with the Holocaust, I have tried to personalize the history of the Jewish partisans and civilians of the forest. As well as many individual stories, I have followed more closely the wartime experiences of several survivors — Gitel Morrison, Ben Lungen, Peter Silverman, Leon Kahn, Faye Schulman, Aron and Lisa Derman, and Jack and Rochelle Sutin, to note only a few — some of whose stories are told for the first time. While I am aware of the obvious limitations of oral history — over time, details are forgotten and some events are exaggerated or placed in improper context — I have, nevertheless, used the survivors' own stories as a guide. Always, though, these remarkable and poignant testimonies of how lives were turned upside down, and how some chose to flee the ghetto for the uncertain refuge of the forest, are placed in the context of harsh ghetto life and the precarious opportunities for resistance and survival in the woods.

I gathered these Holocaust narratives in the course of numerous interviews I conducted in Canada, the United States, and Israel; in testimonies found at libraries and archives in Washington, New York, Los Angeles, at Yale University, and in Jerusalem; and from a dozen or so published memoirs. Despite the flaws in such remembrances, the survivors' recollections are at least (or more, I suggest) as valuable a historical source as any written Nazi or Soviet documents of the era, which were often composed with bias and according to a preconceived agenda. Oral history may be unreliable in some cases, but it is equally true that the passing of years can add a valuable perspective to traumatic events.

Interviewing Holocaust survivors or reading their testimonies and memoirs is an experience you can never forget. To hear a survivor's personal account is traumatic and moving. I am awed by the emotional willpower it must take for survivors to reconstruct, relive, and remember the unique horrors of their past.

■ ■

Like any historian and writer who has tried to tell the tale of eastern Europe's past, I have been faced with the difficult task of getting the names and places right. For instance, because of changing borders, the small town of Eisiskes, as it is known in Lithuanian, has also been called Ejszyszki in Polish. To the Jews, it was Eishyshok. The city of Vilna, as it is known in English and Russian, has been Wilno in Polish and Vilne in Yiddish, and is Vilnius in present-day Lithuania. Surnames are equally problematic, given their Russian, Polish, and Lithuanian variations. For both proper and place names, I have relied whenever possible on the spelling given in the four-volume *Encyclopedia of the Holocaust,* historian Martin Gilbert's authoritative *Dent Atlas of the Holocaust,* and the United States Holocaust Memorial Museum's *Historical Atlas of the Holocaust.*

ACKNOWLEDGMENTS

I was inspired to write this book many years ago as I listened to the astonishing and remarkable stories told to me by some family friends, Gitel Morrison and Ben Lungen. During the Second World War, both had been young and strong and had survived the brutality of the Nazi occupation by hiding and fighting in the forests of Belorussia.

Gitel, only eight years old in September 1939, and her family had fled from the Lida ghetto to become members of a partisan family camp organized by Tuvia Bielski and his brothers. Ben, eighteen when the war started and a soldier in the Red Army, had escaped from a Nazi prisoner-of-war camp and later joined a Soviet partisan detachment. As a guerrilla fighter, he participated in countless combat and sabotage missions and risked his life every day of the conflict. Both lost many family members and friends.

Gitel and Ben were not only inspiring, they also assisted in arranging interviews, tracking down many other survivors, and answering my never-ending queries about life as a wartime Jewish fugitive and fighter.

From the moment my sister Shayla married Jeff Morrison, the son of Gitel and her late husband, Morris, in 1984, his family, including his two sisters, Sheila and Rosie, and their own families, became part of mine (among other things, my two children got a "Boba" Gitel). Both Gitel and her brother, Simon Zelcovitch (originally Zelkowicz), were enthusiastic about this book project, sharing their earliest and often most painful memories with me, particularly those about their older brother, Yossel, who was murdered in the forest in the spring of 1943 while on a reconnaissance mission. It is for their kindness, generosity, encouragement, friendship, dignity, and courage that I dedicate this book to them, their late parents, and their brother. Even after three years of working on this book, I find their tragic ordeal impossible to fathom.

■ ■

A project such as this, which took me across North America and to Europe and Israel, is not accomplished without the generous assistance of many people.

To begin with, research for this book would not have got off the ground without the funds provided by the Canada Council and the Manitoba Arts Council. I am grateful to both organizations, as I am to Mitch McGuigan, headmaster of St. John's–Ravenscourt School, for allowing me to take a leave of absence during 1996 to work full time on this study.

The project proposal eventually landed on the desk of Jennifer Barclay of Westwood Creative Artists, my diligent and talented agent, who led me in the right direction while always taking care of my interests. No writer could ask for better treatment or representation.

At Stoddart, managing editor Don Bastian was a joy to work with. He was enthusiastic about the project from the moment we met, and his fine work is evident throughout the book. I would express my gratitude as well to Jack Stoddart, Jim Gifford, Bill Hanna, Nelson Doucet, and editor Janice Weaver.

For their able assistance, I would also like to thank the archivists and librarians at the United States Holocaust Museum Library and Research Institute, the Fortunoff Video Archive for Holocaust Testimonies (who also granted me permission to quote from several survivor testimonies), and Yad Vashem Library and Archives in Jerusalem; the staff of Beit Lohamei Haghetaot (Ghetto Fighters' House) on a kibbutz not far from Nahariya in Israel; the YIVO Research Center in New York; the Simon Wiesenthal Center in Los Angeles; Nina Thompson, the former librarian at the Jewish Public Library in Winnipeg; and Mona Fargey, the librarian at St. John's–Ravenscourt, for permitting me to keep several books as long as I needed them. I promise to return them soon.

Ian Reifowitz, a talented Ph.D. history student at Georgetown University, was an enormous help in Washington, researching and translating hundreds of Nazi documents that I put to good use, especially in Chapter Eleven. In Winnipeg, David Timms, my colleague at SJR, also helped with German documents, while Esther Nisenholt and Philip Weiss aided me with Yiddish and Polish translation respectively. Ruth Mamon assisted me with my Hebrew interviews from Israel, and Prof. Myroslav Shkandrij, of the University of Manitoba's Department of German and Slavic Studies, provided me with much-needed guidance with Russian words and phrases used by the inhabitants of the forest.

On my various travels, many individuals offered me hospitality that made these trips all the more enjoyable. I would like to express my sincere thanks to my cousins Ian and Reeva Shaffer, for a great time in Washington; Sheila and Danny Rother, for opening their house to me on my visits to Toronto; Brian and Sharon Earn (my young aunt) and my cousins Seth and Josh, for always having room for me at their home in Guelph; my brother- and sister-in-law Aaron and Marian Tenenebein and their family, for an enjoyable time in New York; David and Sigal Earn, for their companionship in Jerusalem; and last but certainly not least, Mel Kliman, my uncle, for accompanying me in May 1996 from his temporary home in Paris on a journey to Warsaw and on an excursion into the Polish countryside. Both Mel and his wife, Eve, have always supported my literary endeavours with interest and enthusiasm and for that I am most fortunate.

As I was researching and writing this book, many people took the time to share their experiences with me and to read and comment on portions of the manuscript. A complete list of interviews can be found in the bibliography, but I would like to single out (besides Gitel Morrison and Ben Lungen) Peter Silverman of Toronto for his tremendous help in arranging interviews, for permitting me to quote from his memoirs, and for taking the time to read several chapters. Peter introduced me to Sandor Kowarski of Toronto and Tel Aviv, a man with an encyclopedic knowledge of the partisan movement, who was a great source of information and ensured that I spoke to the right people while I was in Israel.

Others whose assistance and advice I would like to acknowledge include: my colleague and friend Wendy Owen; Dr. Yitzhak Arad, a historian of the Holocaust and the former chairman of Yad Vashem; Moshe Bairach of Tel Aviv; Jack and Rochelle Sutin of Minneapolis; Leon Kahn in Vancouver; Faye Schulman in Waterloo, Ontario; Lisa and Aron Derman of Chicago; and Evita Smordin, a Holocaust educator in Winnipeg (who once taught me more years ago than I am certain she cares to remember). All shared their knowledge of the Holocaust with me. The writing of this book would have been impossible, as well, without the pioneering efforts of a generation of Holocaust historians, several of whom are former partisans and survivors themselves. Special mention is owed (in addittition to Yitzhak Arad) to Yisrael Gutman; Shmuel Krakowski; Dov Levin; Nechama Tec; Martin Gilbert; Shmuel Spector; Shalom Cholawski; Chaim Lazar; Isaac Kowalski, for his three-volume compilation of partisan articles; and above all, Reuben Ainsztein, for his voluminous and richly detailed 1974 study, *Jewish Resistance in Nazi-Occupied Eastern Europe*. The work of each of these historians has contributed immeasurably to my understanding of forest life and the resistance movement. Of course, all omissions, misinterpretations, and errors of fact and judgment are solely my own.

Often while I am working on various literary projects (which is almost always), I can be difficult to live with. My wife, Angie, and our two children, Alexander and Mia, put up with an awful lot from me. Despite it all, they remain my most loyal and enthusiastic supporters, and for that I am, indeed, a most fortunate husband and father. I can honestly say that without them in my life, my writing and work would have little, if any, meaning. A mere thank-you is hardly enough, but for now it will have to suffice. I know they will understand — as they always do.

Grateful acknowledgment is made to the following for permission to use extended quotations from copyrighted works: *Ghetto in Flames: The Struggle and Destruction of the Jews in Vilna in the Holocaust*, copyright

Allan Levine
Winnipeg, March 1998

Introduction
THE FUGITIVES

The forest was white and we sought protection from it. A forest of hikes and summer camps is nowhere like a forest where one lives permanently and which serves as a refuge and a source of hope and security as well. Every tree became a fortress, every thicket a stronghold, the whole forest a constant friend, kind to all of us without awaiting any reward. If only I could sing a song of praise to the forest, our loyal friend.

— LIZA ETTINGER

More than fifty years ago, as the Second World War and the Nazi assault on Europe ended, approximately 25,000 Jews, entire families in some instances, walked out of the forests of Poland, Belorussia, Lithuania, the Ukraine, and Russia. For three years, these men, women, and children had miraculously survived, eluding Nazi hunts and Soviet, Polish, and Ukrainian partisans who often killed first and asked questions later. In many cases these fugitives fought against the Nazis, in armed combat and through the sabotage of railway tracks and bridges. Some lived on the run, others built camps. The partisan camps housed guerrilla soldiers exclusively, while in the family camps, families and partisans lived together, creating a semblance of daily routine. In the swamp-filled forests, the most resourceful built *shtetlach*, or small villages, which were complete with water facilities, huts with stoves, schools, and people practising their trades.

The fugitives emerging from the forests had harrowing stories to tell.

THE ZELKOWICZ FAMILY

The reconnaissance party returned without Yossel Zelkowicz, and his family never found his body. The Zelkowiczes were told that a group of local farmers had buried Yossel, but they could never be certain.

For three years, Yossel's mother, Leska, had resisted and adapted. She had followed her husband, Lazer, from Lodz to Lida, and from Lida to the forest. She had become a fugitive to save the lives of her two youngest children, Gitel and Simon. Yossel, her oldest child, was only fifteen when the war began; he grew up quickly after that. A partisan fighter at seventeen, he guided Jews, including his own family, from the ghettos to makeshift camps in the woods where, against enormous odds, they defied the forces of nature and evil that had been unleashed upon them.

Something in Leska Zelkowicz snapped the day the Nazis shot Yossel, who was only eighteen. For weeks, in a daze, she muttered to herself, oblivious to her family. Gitel, then age twelve, was angry with her mother for abandoning her. For a time, Gitel had no choice but to assume total responsibility for the care of her younger brother, Simon.

Simon, though not even seven years old when the war ended, also has vivid memories of his childhood in the forest and of the family camp commanded by the legendary Tuvia Bielski. Images of his father carrying him from the ghetto, of sitting in Yossel's arms high on a horse, and of being hungry and covered in lice still invade his sleep.

Simon remembers that at meal times, he always sat beside his mother. "No matter how slowly I ate, and I ate slowly to make it last longer, my mother would eat ten times slower, passing on to me her food when I finished my own," he related in his mother's eulogy, five decades later.

In case of emergency, Simon kept a piece of bread in his pocket. It was his protection against starvation. As the weeks passed, the bread turned mouldy and pale. Simon remembers:

> One day a woman approached his family and told them that she had learned her husband was alive in another part of the forest, fifty kilometres away. She wanted to go to him.
>
> "Does anyone have any food?" she asked. I put my hand in my pocket, pulled out this piece of bread, and offered it to her. She looked at me and began to cry. "I can't take this from you," she said.
>
> My mother went to her and said, "If my son offers you a piece of bread, you should take it." With tears, she accepted my food.

LEON KAHN

Half a lifetime later, the distinctive image of the eagle on the Polish soldiers' cap is as clear in Leon Kahn's mind as it was on that fateful day in October 1943. Leon Kahn, or Leibke Kaganowicz as he was known then, was a young Jewish partisan fighter allowed a few days leave to visit his father, Shael, and his sixteen-year-old sister, Freidke, at their camp in the nearby Yureli Forest, north of Grodno. He brought food with him. The family talked late into the night of their plans for surviving another winter.

At about ten o'clock the next morning, sentries discovered a Polish farmer named Nowicki wandering near the forest retreat. The sentries brought Nowicki to the camp, where he pleaded with the suspicious Jews that he had only become lost while searching for a stray cow. Despite Shael Kaganowicz's apprehension, Nowicki was allowed to go on his way. The farmer assured the Jews that he could be trusted and promised to return with vodka.

A few hours later, as Leon and his family ate lunch, a group of Polish soldiers of the Armia Krajowa (AK), the Home Army, surrounded the Jews. The eagles on the soldiers' caps were clearly visible. The AK made little distinction between Nazis, Soviets, and Jews. They were all occupiers, enemies, and interlopers, a triple threat to a separate and independent Poland.

As guns blared, the Kaganowicz family and the rest of the partisans defended themselves, but their lone machine gun and few rifles were no match for the more sophisticated arsenal of the Poles.

Shael crouched behind his son. "Hold them back!" he shouted to Leon. "Hold them back!" It was hopeless to stay and fight, so the partisans ran deeper into the forest. The Poles chased after them. Suddenly there were no more trees — only a barren field of stubble rye lay before the Jews. This moment is forever etched in Leon Kahn's memory:

We had no alternative but to try to cross the field and outrun them to the next patch of forest . . . I burst from the shelter of the trees, raced into the open field, and began firing at random to cover the flight of the others. Inching forward on my belly I fired, then ran a few yards and dropped to my belly again. Behind me my father burst from the forest and fled across the field.

"Run, papa, run! Run, Freidke, run! No! No! Crawl on your bellies close to the ground where they cannot aim at you! Like me, papa! Like me!"

He didn't listen to me, or perhaps he didn't hear me. I can still see him racing across that field as I carefully inched my way to the protection of the trees on the opposite side.

I looked up for a moment and saw him falter slightly in flight. He's been hit, I thought. Oh, God, he's been hit! But then as he continued on, I thought, it's only just a flesh wound.

I looked for Freidke and saw her trailing behind the others, her pursuers inexorably closing in on her. Poor frightened sister of mine, try a little harder! Hurry! I thought. And slowly I came into the wooded area where my wounded father awaited me . . . He undid his shirt and I almost fainted at the sight. The wound was enormous. I could put my fist into it and his lifeblood poured out of him in a river before my horrified eyes.

"It's nothing, papa," I said. "You'll be all right. Sit by the tree for a moment and rest. Where is Freidke? Where is Freidke?" I looked out and saw her. Three of her pursuers were almost upon her, bayonets poised as she fled in front of them.

I raised my rifle, aimed, and fired. "One down, Freidke!" I shouted. Then I fired again and as the next one fell, I screamed, "One more, Freidke! Run, Freidke, run!" Again I fired, but this time I missed. Her attacker was closer. I tried to fire again and my gun jammed!

As in a slow motion movie, I saw her fall as her pursuer poised his blade over her. I cursed my gun and its impotence as the bayonet entered my poor sister's defenseless body.

As in a dream, I heard my father shouting over and over. "Hold them back . . . Hold them back!" But it was too late for Freidke. Too late for my little sister. She fell to earth like a wounded bird, and as her life ebbed away, I wept with sorrow. "Goodbye, Freidke . . . Goodbye, my little sister . . ."

Three days later, Shael Kaganowicz died as he lay in his son's arms on the edge of the woods. Leon was now truly alone, the last survivor of his family.

THE PARTISANS

It is all too easy to make sweeping generalizations about the war and the behaviour of those whose lives were affected by it. Certainly it is difficult to measure or define the development of forest life in partisan and family camps, or the relationship between Gentile and Jew, or even to gauge the role the partisan resistance actually played in the outcome of the conflict.

Given the tremendous forces pitted against them, it is a miracle that so many Jews were able to avenge the murders of their families and survive to protect their children and parents in partisan and civilian camps. True, millions of Jews still perished in spite of their efforts. But those who dismiss as inconsequential the Jewish partisans' resistance work fail to appreciate the immensity of the struggle. The question should not be, why did more Jews not resist? But rather, how, under the circumstances, was any resistance possible at all?

During 1942 and 1943 in Poland, as the Nazis were liquidating the ghettos and the difficult decision to flee could no longer be delayed, more than 100,000 Jewish fugitives were likely on the run. Most were later killed by Nazi police patrols or by Soviet or Polish partisans (who also resisted the Nazis but cared little about the Jews' plight). Israeli historians Yisrael Gutman and Shmuel Krakowski estimate that in the district around Lublin alone, approximately 20,000 Jews were caught and killed during this two-year period.

By 1944, in this vast area stretching from eastern Poland into Russia and south into the Ukraine, at least 200,000 to 250,000 Soviet partisans (perhaps even as many as 350,000) were operating in hundreds of brigades. Approximately 20,000 to 25,000 of these partisans were Jewish, fighting with and supporting the Soviets. Another estimated 10,000 Jews survived in family camps, usually attached to a fighting unit.*

From the Parczew Forest in eastern Poland to the Naliboki Forest, a vast wilderness west of Minsk known in Polish as a *puszcza* because of its size and its jungle-like topography, to the Rudniki Forest farther north in Lithuania, Jews took up arms. Under the direction of such famous Jewish partisans as Misha Gildenman (codenamed Diadia Misha, "Uncle Misha"), young Chil Grynszpan, and Josef Glazman, who escaped from the Vilna ghetto to form the Jewish battalion Nekamah (revenge), the partisans conducted daring raids and sabotage operations. More notably, they acted as protectors for Jewish refugees who joined the family camps of such dynamic leaders as Tuvia Bielski and Shalom Zorin.

---

*I stress that the statistics on Jewish fighters, civilians, and especially survivors in the forests of eastern Europe and the Soviet Union during the war are only general estimates. As Israeli historian Yitzhak Arad, a former partisan and an authority on Holocaust studies and on the Jewish partisan movement, explains: "There will never be 'accurate' numbers, because in no place do such lists exist. In Soviet archives there are partial lists, mainly of those partisans who were in Soviet partisan units in the last stages of the war, but they are not complete. Many Jewish partisans perished in the forests before the organized Soviet formations took over control in the specific area where they operated, and they don't appear on these lists . . . . There were [also] Jewish partisans who did not belong to [Soviet] units. In addition, quite a substantial number of Jews in partisan units did not identify themselves as Jews, because of anti-Semitism that existed in the forests among Soviet, and even much more among Polish, partisans." (*Letter to author*, February 8, 1998.)

SEPARATE AND APART

In hindsight, it is not surprising that the Jews had only themselves to depend on once they fled into the woods. Since being "imprisoned" in the Pale of Settlement by Russian autocrats at the end of the eighteenth century, they had lived side by side with Poles, Belorussians, and Ukrainians but led very separate lives. The Jews spoke their own language (Yiddish), practised a different religion, and were caught up in their own brand of nationalism (Zionism), in all its many forms and factions. To fight for their rights in the factory, Jewish workers also created a union of their own design, the socialist-oriented Bund. This is not to say that Jews did not participate fully in Polish society. Indeed, there was a strong Jewish presence in many Polish professions and cultural pursuits — journalism, teaching, politics, theatre, and music. But the vast majority, sometimes by choice, led segregated lives.

On the eve of the Second World War, owing in large part to the magnanimous actions of world leaders at Versailles in 1919 (and later confirmed in the Treaty of Riga, following the Polish–Soviet War of 1919–21), the new independent country of Poland stretched from Katowice in the west to Pinsk and Rovno in the east. Thirty-five million people lived within Poland's borders, including 5 million Ukrainians, 1.5 million Belorussians, 700,000 Germans, 80,000 Lithuanians, and more than 3 million Jews, still mainly living in the bounds of the Pale of Settlement established by Catherine the Great of Russia in 1791. In all, about one-third of the population was non-Polish.

Though the Poles cherished the agricultural way of life, most did not own the land they worked. Approximately 75 percent were peasants, and any land they had access to was the property of the elite aristocracy. Still, the vast countryside, despite its economic backwardness and poverty, gave the country its soul and personality.

The majority of Polish Jews, on the other hand, by virtue of age-old laws that did not permit them to own land, resided in the cities, towns, and villages. According to the 1931 census, close to one million Jews lived in the large urban centres of Warsaw, Lodz, Cracow, Lvov, Vilna, and Lublin, where they represented anywhere from 28 to 35 percent of each city's population. In the numerous towns, villages, and *shtetlach* that dotted the Polish landscape, Jews eked out livings as merchants, shopkeepers, cattle buyers, and peddlers. While a minority of Jews felt at home and comfortable in the rural regions, they were truly an urban people. In short, Jews were people of the town, which was home to their synagogues, schools, and kosher shops.

Centuries of legal restrictions and unequal treatment before the law compelled the Jews to withdraw into their own communities, which only reinforced the argument of right-wing Polish leaders such as Roman Dmowski that Jews were a threat because they would never assimilate. "The Jew treats with aversion the entire past of European nations," the head of Endecja, the right-wing National Democratic Party, declared in 1914. "He harbors hatred toward their religions and looks upon all the hierarchies that have arisen in these societies as he does upon the usurpers who have taken the place due his 'chosen people.'" Dmowski's solution to this problem, clearly articulated during the interwar period, was the "de-Judaizing of Poland." His goal was nothing less than to drive Polish Jews from the economic life of the country. The National Democrats supported boycotts of Jewish businesses, the implementation of a quota system (*numerus clausus*) at Polish universities, and the use of separate seating, or "ghetto benches," in university classrooms.

Successive Polish governments, including the popular semi-dictatorship led by the charismatic military leader Marshal Jozef Pilsudski from 1926 until his death in 1935, refused to reform educational institutions as much as the Endecja demanded. Nonetheless, the Endecja mounted pressure on university officials, and Jews continually faced discrimination, harassment, and, ultimately, violence. Jewish enrolment in Polish universities dropped from 24 percent in 1923–24, to 17 percent by 1933, to only 8 percent in 1938. In the classrooms, Jewish students refused to sit on the segregated benches at the back of the halls, but in doing so faced the wrath of young right-wing nationalists. One professor at the University of Lvov who supported the stand taken by the Jewish students had his classroom bombed in the fall of 1938.*

---

*The extent of this anti-Jewish agitation was astonishing. As Szymon Rudnicki relates in his survey of university politics: "On June 26, 1926, the director of the anatomy department at the Warsaw University sent out a circular stating that because of a shortage of cadavers, Jewish

Following Pilsudski's death, the anti-Semitism that was flourishing under Hitler in neighbouring Germany enflamed Polish conservatives as well, and the last Polish government before the war took a decided turn to the right. An official government study released in 1937, one of many on the "Jewish Question," defined the situation as follows: "The effect of [Jews'] separate political aspirations and the effect of their numbers, plus their major influence over many areas of social and national life, is to make the Jews, in the present state of affairs, an element that weakens the normal development of national and state strength that is currently being achieved in Poland."

In the streets, often violent anti-Semitic incidents became part of daily life for Jews, wealthy or poor. From the perspective of Lucy Dawidowicz in 1938, then a young American student on a visit to Vilna, the anti-Semitism she encountered in Poland was unique. "It wasn't so much an ideology or a racist philosophy," she later recalled, "as it was raw and ungovernable hatred, different from what was happening in Germany." Dawidowicz, who would later become an eminent historian and chronicler of the Holocaust, observed that in Germany, the anti-Semitism of the Nazis had been "orchestrated from above," while in Poland it "erupted spontaneously [and] volcanically." In any event, random violence ("hooliganism," as Dawidowicz called it) became an unwanted aspect of Jewish life.

Jack Sutin, who grew up in the town of Mir, south-west of Minsk, claims that by the time he was three years old, he had a "sense" that Jews were hated in Poland. "By that age," states Sutin, who survived the war as a partisan, "you knew that you were not the same as all the other kids, that you were discriminated against in the subtlest ways, as well as in the most overt and painful ways. I remember once, while I was a young student, I boarded a crowded train. I went through several cars and finally found a passenger compartment with a single empty seat. But the man sitting next to it stared at me and then spat out the words, 'No Jews

---

students wishing to attend lectures and demonstrations would only be admitted if the Jewish community provided corpses. It was claimed that the reason for this dispute was not political but the result of the objection to Jews 'profaning consecrated corpses.' The Jewish community could not provide the requisite number of corpses since Orthodox Judaism forbade dissection." (See Rudnicki, "From 'Numerus Clausus' to 'Numerus Nullus,'" in *Polin*, vol. 2 [1987]:253)

allowed!' I remember that moment because it made me realize, more than anything that had come before, that in Poland I would never be allowed to live a normal and peaceful life."

Jewish children were chased home from school as young gangs of hooligans taunted and threw stones at them. "Dirty Jew," they yelled. "Go back to Palestine." Jona Fuks (now John Fox), only twelve years old when the war began, remembers that in the Polish school he attended in Tuszyn, a small town near Lodz, there were only three Jewish students in his class of forty-three children. "When the teacher walked out of the classroom the Poles would throw things at us, curse, and spit on us," he told Martin Gilbert. "When the teacher returned he would pretend that nothing had happened. We wouldn't complain because nothing would be done about it. . . . Many days I would come from school with a bloody nose or a swollen lip from getting beaten up in school."

Like that teacher, the police and courts generally did little to stop this behaviour. Violent acts against Jews were rarely punished. Moreover, according to Dawidowicz, "in instances when the Jewish victim of a hooligan attack fought back and injured his assailant, the Jew was likely to be arrested and charged with disturbing the peace, even if he himself had been badly wounded."

With few countries willing to take them, Jews could not leave Poland even if they wanted to, so they endured the insults, attacks, boycotts, and discrimination. "The overwhelming majority of Jews in the cities and [villages] in central and eastern Poland, including those registered as independent wage earners and merchants, lived under conditions of dire and deepening poverty," Holocaust historian Yisrael Gutman has written. "Their income lagged behind the average income of an industrial worker."

The year before the war began, an independent member of the Polish parliament, the Sejm, introduced legislation aimed at abolishing the practice of *shchitah*, the Jewish ritual method of slaughtering and koshering animals. Beginning in 1935, the meat industry had been severely regulated; now the intent was to drive Jewish butchers out of business altogether. The Jews of Vilna responded with a boycott of all meat; overnight thousands who consumed large quantities of meat and poultry became vegetarians. But this bold response did not stop the Sejm from approving the bill and passing it on to the Polish senate for ratification. Before the senate could vote on the issue, however, the war intervened.

Just as Jewish adults attempted to deal with the various obstacles caused by their minority status — actively participating, for example, in Polish political life through their own political organizations, such as the religious Agudat Yisrael or the more secular Folkist party, the Yiddishe folk-partey in poyln — so too did Jewish youth. They joined Zionist and socialist clubs, where they not only developed life-long friendships and a love for Yiddish and Hebrew culture, but also prepared themselves for either the eventual move to Palestine or a future socialist Utopia. Debates raged over the most minute of details. Young members of Betar (the followers of the right-wing and more militant Revisionism Zionism and its charismatic leader, Vladimir Jabotinsky) clashed with the left-wing Ha-Shomer Hatsair and Hechalutz factions.

Young socialists of the Bund and Zionists of every political orientation could, however, unite on the issue of self-defence and confronting the anti-Semitic hooligans with force. The Bundists, in particular, organized their own self-defence units and pledged themselves to defend Jews, "their livelihood, dignity, honor, and often their very lives." When they heard rumours of an impending attack in one village or another, they would travel there in an attempt to thwart it. They patrolled the streets and intervened in beatings whenever it was possible.

This spirit of defiance would soon be challenged in ways these young Jewish men and women could never have imagined. With displays of courage and fearlessness well beyond their years, they rose to face the greatest challenge and tragedy of their young lives, and provided the leadership for the resistance in the ghettos and the forests.

The pages that follow are an account of a group of ordinary people whose lives were altered forever during six years that have stained the history of civilization. Theirs is a story that testifies to the strength and fortitude of the human spirit. This tragic tale deserves to be told and told again.

PART ONE

■

OCCUPATION
AND
DEATH

NAZIS AND SOVIETS

They came like a cloud of green locusts, a horde of brutes in human form; masses of flesh and steel, a stream of thunderous terror in dawn, heavy with foreboding. Even the smallest child among us could feel the abysmal evil and disaster that descended upon us. We were enveloped, as doomed to destruction as the sinful generation of the Flood.

— *Anna Eilenberg-Eibeshitz*

"When the Jewish blood spurts from the knife / then all goes doubly well"

Before the war, before Hitler and the Nazis, the forests that surrounded the cities and towns of eastern Europe played a minimal part in the lives of the vast majority of Jews. They were a place to conduct business with local peasants, to obtain lumber, and for children, an adventurous wilderness for hikes. The woods and the surrounding countryside were for camping in the summer and skiing and other sports in the winter. On nearby farms, Zionist groups established agricultural-training projects in order to prepare for life on a Palestine *kibbutz*.

If you had told most Jews in 1939 that in order to stay alive during the ensuing four or five years, they would have to live in the woods in holes in the ground, they would have thought you were mad. But by about early 1942, the forest emerged as the Jews' final haven, their last chance for survival. Reaching that hopeless conclusion, however, was not easy; it was a life-and-death decision filled with much sorrow and pain.

Indeed, as the Holocaust advanced along its systematic path of destruction, at each horrible phase — from the Nazi invasion, through the incarceration in ghettos, and finally to the deportations to death camps — many Jews refused to surrender, albeit often reluctantly, to their hopeless fate. Still, it was in such boldness, courage, and a refusal to submit to the evil which had engulfed their lives that the partisan movement was ultimately born.

■ ■

For fifteen-year-old Anna (Landman) Eilenberg-Eibeshitz, the Second World War started in Lodz on September 5, 1939, the day the Nazis arrived. A week later, standing side by side with other frightened and dazed Polish and Jewish residents of the city, she witnessed a parade of German soldiers. As they passed, she could hear their strong voices singing. *"Wenn Judenblut von messer spritzte / Dann geht's nochmal so gut!"* they chanted. She knew enough German to understand the song: "When the Jewish blood spurts from the knife / Then all goes doubly well."

"Then I noticed our neighbour, Mr. Schultz," she recalled. "He was one of the few men among the spectators wearing a German militia uniform, with a shiny black swastika on the armband, and he was singing lustily along with the soldiers. A frightening tremor seized my whole body. For the first time in my life, I knew the meaning of utter despair."

Who could blame young Anna and many others for feeling so helpless? The Nazi assault on Poland had been swift and harsh. With a devastating display of air and land power, the German army had swept through Poland in a matter of days. By the end of September, Warsaw had been captured and the last remaining Polish military units were forced to capitulate. The occupation was immediately characterized by terror and brutality — distinctive Nazi trademarks that the world would never forget.

■ ■

Like a "master chess player" (to use the words of Sir Neville Henderson, the British ambassador to Berlin in the summer of 1939), Hitler had methodically put his policy of *Lebensraum* into action. More living space for Germany was the goal, claimed the Führer. First came Austria, then Czechoslovakia, and finally, in the early hours of September 1, 1939, the attack on Poland commenced.

In a strategic maneuver, Hitler had already neutralized the Soviet Union by negotiating a non-aggression pact with Stalin in mid-August. The pact, including the secret protocol that determined how Poland was to be divided, required that both dictators turn their backs on political and philosophical crusades they had carried on for years.* Stalin had denounced Nazi ideology as much as Hitler had condemned Bolshevism. But such were the opportunities of the day; for the moment, neither wanted to fight the other, and dividing Poland between them seemed like the most sensible thing to do.

In late August, at his retreat in the Alps near Berchtesgaden, Hitler had advised his generals of the pact with the Soviets and emphasized again that the moment was at hand for eastern expansion. His destiny, he declared, was intertwined with that of Germany. "There will probably never again in the future be a man with more authority than I have," he told his military commanders. "My existence is therefore a factor of great value."

According to the notes of the meeting, taken by Adm. Wilhelm Canaris, Hitler concluded his speech with a message that would echo throughout Europe for the next four and half years: "When starting and waging a war it is not right that matters, but victory. Close your heart to pity. Act brutally. Eighty million people must obtain what is their right. Their existence must be made secure. The stronger man is right. The

---

*As British historian Alan Bullock notes, "The existence of the secret protocol, long known in the West from captured German documents, was only admitted by the Soviet Union fifty years later, in 1989." (Bullock, *Hitler and Stalin*, 619).

greatest harshness. Swiftness in making decisions is necessary. Firm faith in the German soldier. Crises are due solely to leaders having lost their nerve."

The Führer's orders were followed to the letter. As the German soldiers marched through Poland, they left a wake of destruction behind them. Towns were burned and civilians murdered. In the town of Bydgoszcz, on the German-Polish border, Nazi soldiers rounded up a group of boy scouts, ages twelve to sixteen. They stood them in front of a wall in the town's marketplace and killed them. "No reason was given," remembered one witness. "A devoted priest who rushed to administer the Last Sacrament was shot too."

Farther south, in the border town of Wieruszow on September 3, 1939, the day Britain and France declared war on Germany, soldiers of the dreaded SS (or Schutzstaffel, Hitler's protection squad) ordered twenty Jews to the centre of the town. They were to be shot. One of the men was sixty-four-year-old Israel Lewi. "When his daughter, Liebe Lewi, ran up to her father to say farewell," relates Martin Gilbert, "a German ordered her to open her mouth for her 'impudence,' and then fired a bullet into it. Liebe Lewi fell dead on the spot. The twenty men were then executed."

From the beginning of the occupation, it was the orthodox Jews, with their easily recognizable beards and long black coats and hats, who received the worst of Nazi brutality. Tormenting these Jews, by cutting or burning their beards and forcing them to desecrate religious artifacts, quickly became a favourite Nazi pastime.

On Yom Kippur (September 23), Nazis in the town of Wegrow, north of Warsaw, amused themselves by making the rabbi sweep the streets and pick up garbage in his fur hat. As he bent over, they stabbed him with their bayonets. In several cities and towns, Jews were locked in synagogues and burned alive. Fifteen-year-old Mary Berg, an American Jew visiting Poland in the fall of 1939, recalled in her diary that in Lodz, the Germans "forbade the Jews to remove the sacred books, and the 'shames,' or beadle, who wanted to save the holy relics was locked up inside the temple and died in the flames." In Lublin, in November, the Nazis took great delight in destroying the city's Talmudic Academy. It took twenty-four hours to burn its precious and voluminous library, while the city's Jews watched helplessly. Such looting, murder, and arbitrary beatings continued unabated throughout the fall of 1939. In Poland, no Jew was safe.

■ ■

No one was more stunned by the German advance into Poland than Stalin. Nevertheless, to consolidate his position, he moved his troops westward with little trouble, on the grounds that he was only protecting the interests of the Ukrainians and Belorussians, his "kindred" people. On September 28, some last-minute negotiations between the Russians and the Germans moved the dividing line from the Vistula River farther east to the Bug River. As compensation for giving up this territory, Stalin acquired the right to control Lithuania, as well as Estonia and Latvia. For the moment, he agreed to allow the three Baltic states to remain independent, although the Soviets did establish a military presence in each territory. Much to the delight of local nationalists, Lithuania took back the city of Vilna, its former capital, which had been under Polish rule since 1919 and was home to more than 55,000 Jews.

Under this new arrangement, approximately 12 million Poles, Ukrainians, Belorussians, and Jews (1.3 million of the total) became citizens of the Soviet Union, while 21 million, of which 2 million were Jews, came under the heavy hand of Nazi Germany. A western portion of this territory, including the city of Lodz with its 223,000 Jews (34 percent of the city's population), immediately was annexed into Greater Germany; the remainder, which incorporated Warsaw's Jewish population of 375,000 (29.1 percent of the total), became a part of an area designated by the Nazis as the *Generalgouvernement*.

It was in the *Generalgouvernement*, under the command of Gov. Hans Frank but subject to the arbitrary dictates of the SS and the Reich Security Main Office, led by Reinhard Heydrich, that the destruction of Polish Jewry began in earnest. "We won't waste much time on the Jews," declared Frank at a meeting in the district of Radom on November 25 to discuss the deportation of Jews from the west to the *Generalgouvernement*. "It's great to get to grips with the Jewish race at last. The more that die the better; hitting them represents a victory for our Reich. The Jews should feel that we've arrived."

Methodically, the Nazis went about making Frank's words a reality. First, large numbers of Jews from western Poland and the rural area of the *Generalgouvernement* were brought to the urban centres around Warsaw and Lublin. In time, they were isolated in ghetto prisons, and cut off from the rest of the world by walls and barbed wire.

The first ghetto was established in the town of Piotrkow in early October 1939. By the spring of 1940, Jews had been sealed in a ghetto in Lodz and later in the year the same fate befell the large Jewish population of Warsaw. From the start, the residents of the ghettos were faced with abysmal living conditions: food shortages, no running water, no coal or fuel, limited or no provisions for sanitation, and tremendous overcrowding. In the Lodz ghetto, for instance, a population of about 164,000 (which increased to more than 200,000 by 1942 through deportations and births) was crowded into a dilapidated area of the city meant for no more than 40,000 people.

During late 1939 and throughout 1940, each day brought more restrictions and further hardship. Jewish councils, or Judenrate, were established in each city and town to deal directly with the Nazis and ensure that their orders and regulations were carried out. By a decree of December 1, 1939, "all Jews and Jewesses, resident in the *Generalgouvernement* and more than ten years old" were required to "wear on the right sleeve of their clothes and outer garments a white strip at least 10 cm wide with a [blue] star of David upon it." In the area around Lodz, Jews had already been ordered to wear a yellow armband, which was later altered to the distinctive yellow badge worn on the front and back of their clothes.

Failure to comply resulted in a variety of harsh penalties, including beatings, death, and fines. Adam Czerniakow, the fifty-nine-year-old chemical engineer and politician appointed the first head of the Warsaw Judenrat, recorded in his diary that he was often forced to pay fines of 50 and 100 zlotys for armband infractions.

Large exactions, as Czerniakow called them, were regularly delivered to the SS on the threat of death for a variety of charges. "We must collect 30,000 zlotys for the Labour Battalion," he wrote on November 17, 1939. "In the evening I am called to the SS. An exaction of 300,000 by Monday. Five hostages from the Council in jeopardy: drawing lots . . ." The latter amount, demanded because of accusations that a Jew had fired a shot at a Polish policeman, was dutifully paid on time.

Again, in late January 1940, Czerniakow was forced to pay a fine of 100,000 zlotys as a penalty for an apparent Jewish attack on a German-Polish woman. The Nazis had threatened to kill one hundred Jews if the money was not delivered. Somehow Czerniakow, who suffered both physically and mentally from his onerous responsibilities, was able to raise or borrow enough money to save members of the community.*

Life in Warsaw and other Polish cities became an ordeal of pain and punishment. Worst were the home invasions. Suddenly, without warning, at any time of the day or night, a group of German soldiers would drive up to an apartment complex in a truck. They would storm a Jewish home, beat and whip its occupants, and then order the helpless owners to load their furniture and belongings on to the Nazis' vehicle. During one such raid in Warsaw, Nazi officers humiliated several Jewish women by forcing them to undress, and then, at gunpoint, recalled David Wdowinski, "they performed gynecological examinations on each one of them. And even this was not enough. They forced the women and girls to get up on the tables and jump to the floor with legs straddled. 'Maybe something will fall out. One never knows how deep the Jewish swindlers can hide their jewels.'"

Within a month or so of the occupation, Jews were also forced into slave labour, where the beatings were meted out mercilessly. Eleven-year-old Arek Hersh was conscripted into a railway labour gang and required to work fourteen-hour days. The Jews were whipped, beaten, and even hanged for the most minor of infractions, such as begging for food or urinating without seeking the guard's permission. "One guard

---

*Czerniakow committed suicide on July 23, 1942, after the Nazis ordered him to assist them in collecting Jews for deportation to the death camps. He also may have been ordered to kill Jewish children with his own hands. (See "Adam Czerniakow," *Encyclopedia of the Holocaust* [hereafter EH], vol. 1; 334–36; and Hilberg, Staron, and Kermisz, eds., *The Warsaw Diary of Adam Czerniakow.*)

called Rudi was in charge," remembered Hersh. "He came from the Sudetenland and was particularly brutal. I remember he was blond, of medium build, and he wore glasses. He killed prisoners by hacking them to death with a spade."

Similarly, on December 16, 1939, Chaim Kaplan, a Warsaw Hebrew school principal who was later murdered at Treblinka, recorded in his diary (which was discovered after the war in a kerosene can on a farm near Warsaw) this episode about a group of young girls in Lodz: "These girls were compelled to clean a latrine — to remove the excrement and clean it. But they received no utensils. To their question: 'With what?' the Nazis replied: 'With your blouses.' The girls removed their blouses and cleaned the excrement with them. When the job was done they received their reward: the Nazis wrapped their faces in the blouses, filthy with the remains of excrement, and laughed uproariously. And all this because 'Jewish England' is fighting against the Führer with the help of the *Juden*."

"I'D RATHER DIE ON RUSSIAN SOIL"

It took Lazer Zelkowicz only a few months under Nazi rule to realize that if he did not immediately find a way to transport his family from their home in Lodz to the eastern territory under Soviet control, they would all soon be dead. It was not an easy decision to make.

At thirty-nine, Lazer, whose family had lived and prospered in Lodz for generations, was a successful wholesale butcher. He owned an apartment and happily provided all the comforts of life for his wife, Leska, and their three children, Yossel, age fifteen, Gitel, nine, and Simon, only an infant when the war broke out. To save his family, Lazer was forced to abandon everything he had worked so hard for and leave behind his parents and siblings, who for a variety of reasons chose to stay and wait out the Nazi occupation. They were all to perish.

Lazer and Yossel fled first, taking only what they could carry. Lazer promised his wife that he would return for her and the younger children as soon as was possible. From Lodz, the Russian border was about 230 kilometres away. Since Jews were not permitted to travel, Lazer and his oldest son, who was tall, blond, and blue-eyed, had to pass themselves off as Poles. They rode a farmer's wagon part of the way and were able to take a train the remainder of the journey.

Crossing the Russian border, however, was as dangerous as getting to it. By the time the Zelkowiczes arrived in December 1939, the border was already closed. For a brief period, during September, October, and part of November, Ukrainians and Belorussians were allowed to enter the Soviet zone, while Germans on the east side of the Bug River travelled freely to German territory. The Soviets and Germans also had permitted Jewish refugees to flee east. Estimates put the number of Polish Jews who were able to escape into Soviet territory at between 300,000 and 350,000. Still, some Jews didn't know where to go, fearing both the Communists and the Nazis.

In his memoirs, Moishe Grossman relates how at the Biala Podlaska train station, the first stop on the German side of the frontier, "a train filled with Jews going east met a train going west: When the Jews coming from Brisk saw Jews going there, they shouted: 'You are mad, where are you going?' Those coming from Warsaw answered with equal astonishment: 'You are mad, where are you going?'" Many Jews fled to Vilna, thinking that under Lithuanian control they would be safe. But to many Lithuanian nationalists, Jews were Communist sympathizers. Indeed, anti-Jewish riots broke out there at the end of October, the moment the Soviets left.

Once the border was sealed at the end of November, Jews were forced either to smuggle themselves over or to bribe Russian guards who cared little about the plight of Polish Jews. Nahum Kohn, a twenty-one-year-old Jew from Sieradz, west of Warsaw, for example, spent several harrowing days in a neutral zone near the border trying to figure out how to get to the other side. As he was attempting to sneak through a wooded area, he was robbed and stabbed by two local peasants and was found the next morning by Red Army soldiers. One of them happened to be Jewish and fortunately took Kohn to a nearby clinic, where his wounds were cared for.

In Warsaw, in November 1939, Yitzhak Rudnicki (hereafter known as Yitzhak Arad) celebrated his bar mitzvah while the Nazis stormed the streets outside. A month later, as the situation worsened in the city, his parents paid two Poles 250 zlotys to take young Yitzhak and his fifteen-year-old sister, Rachel, to the first railway station in Russian territory. From there, they were to travel to relatives in Swieciany, a Lithuanian town north of Vilna. But after Yitzhak and Rachel had arrived by train at Siedlce, not far from the Bug River, the two Poles deserted them, as well as a young Jewish couple and their fifteen-year-old son who had accompanied them. Together, the five refugees walked across the frozen Bug, avoiding Russian patrols, and successfully reached Soviet-occupied territory.

Unable to return to Lodz for his family, Lazer Zelkowicz arranged for a Polish farmer to assist his wife and children. In early January 1940, the farmer took Leska, Gitel, and Simon Zelkowicz to a nearby train station. Posing as Poles, they travelled four hours to a town near the border (most likely Siedlce). At a stop along the way, however, Gitel recalls that there was an inspection conducted by the SS. With the help of a friendly German railway worker, they managed to avoid detection and continued with their dangerous journey.

Lazer and Yossel were waiting for them in a small village on the German side of the border. With the aid of local farmers, who were paid about 1,000 zlotys, the Zelkowiczes were guided through the country-side to the Soviet checkpoint. "When they saw us," Gitel remembers, "the Russians were going to send us back. They did not want any more Jews. But my mother spoke perfect Russian and began pleading with them that she was a good Communist."

Leska Zelkowicz, a determined and charming woman, convinced the Soviet guards that she had previously been arrested in Poland for her political beliefs. When that still did not have the desired effect, she offered them jewellery and began to cry. "If you want to send me back to the Germans," she told them, "I'd rather die on Russian soil." Reluc-tantly, the guards allowed the Zelkowiczes to pass and gladly accepted Leska's gold ring as a border fee.

The family's first stop was the city of Bialystok, but it was overflow-ing with refugees. After a few sleepless and uncomfortable nights in a crowded synagogue, Lazer and Leska took their children to relatives in the town of Lida, farther north. Their plan was to travel to Vilna, where

Leska had been born, but the Russians would not permit it. So the Zelkowiczes stayed in Lida. Lazer rented a house and found a job, while Yossel and Gitel went to school to learn Russian and become worthy citizens of the Soviet Union.

"STALIN IS THE MESSIAH HIMSELF"

The day the Russians marched into Slonim, in September 1939, many of the town's 22,000 Jews lined the streets and cheered. Some of the younger people waved red flags. Farther south, in the village of Torczyn, Jews gave the Soviet soldiers flowers while they shouted, "Long live the redeemers!"

It was the same story in cities and towns throughout the region east of the Bug River. Jews welcomed the Soviets as though the Messiah himself had arrived. "These are Messiah's times," an elderly Jewish man was overheard saying in one *shtetl*, "and Stalin is the Messiah himself." Other Jews were a little more sceptical about their new Soviet masters. "We had been sentenced to death," a popular joke among the Jews of Luck went, "but now our sentence has been commuted — to life imprisonment."

But who could blame those Jews who breathed a sigh of relief? With their rigid economic dogma, authoritarian government, and secret police (the NKVD), the Soviets were hardly regarded without suspicion or trepidation, but they were not Nazis. And for the Jews of eastern Poland, this was obviously an important distinction. Any trouble the Jews had from the Soviets resulted from their livelihoods and political beliefs, not their religion. Shalom Hamiel of Rovno recalls one of his Jewish neighbours remarking when the Red Army entered the town, "I know who the Bolsheviks are. I know they take all my property. But they will spare my life."

There is no denying that the Russians were ruthless. A frequently repeated Russian saying in occupied Poland, for instance, "divided the whole population into three categories: 'Those who were in prison; those who are in prison; and those who will be in prison.'"

Soon after the Soviets arrived, the NKVD targeted members of the Polish intelligentsia — lawyers, judges, teachers, doctors, landowners, and politicians. Property was expropriated and Polish currency rendered useless. Businesses were seized and merchants thrown in jail. Historian Jan Gross points out that under the Soviet regime, prisons were filled, on the average, "to about five times their original capacity." During the twenty-one months of the Russian occupation, approximately 500,000 people, mostly men, were incarcerated. Torture and beatings were common, and at least 1.5 million Poles were deported to Siberia in unheated cattle cars. Half of them died en route. Once they assumed control of the three Baltic states in the spring of 1940 — on the pretext of defending "provocative acts" against Russians — the Soviets followed the same pattern of terror. Nationalist leaders were arrested, and thousands, including many Jews, were deported.

In one of the worst incidents of the Soviet occupation, the Red Army massacred 15,000 Polish army officers in late May 1940. Later the Russians maintained that the Nazis had committed this atrocity. In 1989, however, the Soviet Union finally conceded the truth: its forces had killed all 15,000 men.

Such harsh Soviet treatment of the Poles, coupled with the Jewish outpouring of affection and support, led to a widely held belief among the local Gentile population that most Jews were Communists who could not be trusted to fight for an independent Poland. (It should be noted that many Ukrainians and Belorussians also cheered the arrival of the Red Army.) The fact that during the previous five years there had been a rise in anti-Semitism at all levels of Polish society was clearly beside the point. For many Poles this was a black-and-white issue. Forget the extenuating circumstances and the few days of Nazi rule in some border towns, where hundreds of Jews were murdered before the Germans were forced to vacate. Jews were traitors to the Polish cause, pure and simple — and they would pay the price in the future.

That was the conclusion offered by Jan Karski, a twenty-five-year-old Polish courier who travelled throughout occupied Poland in November 1939. In his extensive report of February 1940 on life in the *Generalgouvernement* and the Soviet zone, secretly prepared for the Polish government-in-exile in London, Karski observed that "[Jews] are entering political cells; in many of them they have taken over the most critical political-administrative positions. They have played quite a large role in factory unions, in higher education, and most of all in commerce; but, above and beyond even all of this, they are involved in loansharking and profiteering, in illegal trade, contraband, foreign currency exchange, liquor, immoral interests, pimping, and procurement."

He further added, "It is generally believed that the Jews betrayed Poland and Poles, that they are basically communists [sic], that they crossed over to the Bolsheviks with flags unfurled. . . . The Jews have created here a situation in which the Poles regard them as devoted to the Bolsheviks and — one can safely say — wait for the moment when they will be able simply to take revenge upon the Jews. Virtually all Poles are bitter and disappointed in relation to the Jews; the overwhelming majority . . . literally look forward to an opportunity for 'repayment in blood.' "

As Karski predicted, many Poles did later take their revenge on the Jews for mistreatment by the Soviets — the image of the Jew as a Communist was accepted as fact and further perpetuated by Nazi propaganda — but the issue was more complex than he acknowledged. Were some Jews members of the Communist Party? The answer is yes. Of course, so were many Poles.

In reality, during the interwar years membership in the Polish Communist Party, its youth wing, and all other Communist factions was never that high. At Communism's peak in the mid-thirties, there may have been as many as 40,000 committed Polish Communists, of which perhaps 6,500 to 10,000 were Jews. Still, Richard Lukas, an American historian, is correct when he argues that "Jews constituted 25 percent of the membership [in the Polish Communist Party]; in urban areas in central Poland, the percentage rose to 50 percent." Seeing no future for themselves in an independent and nationalistic Poland, many younger Jewish adults and teenagers gravitated towards Communism. (On the other hand, even given Lukas's high percentages, this means only that, at most, about .33 percent of all Polish Jews were active in Communist organizations.)

To suggest, however, that Jews embraced the Soviets out of a political and economic affinity is a misreading of the situation. "Who cared about Communism?" one Jewish elder in Slonim asked. "Who paid any attention to theoretical problems of national economy, when one faced an immediate danger to life? The question of whether the regime was good or bad was irrelevant. There could hardly be any doubt that the entire Jewish population, poor and rich, workers and factory owners, was relieved when the Red Army entered our town."

It was true, as Karski noted, that some Jews were appointed to government positions, something that was impossible under the earlier Polish regime, and that young Jewish adults had an opportunity to attend university. But it was equally true that the Russians arrested prominent Jewish leaders like Dr. Emil Sommerstein, a former member of the Polish Sejm, and Viktor Alter and Henryk Erlich of the Bund. Thousands more were harassed by the NKVD for being "enemies of the state." Soviet authorities closed Jewish newspapers, synagogues, and schools, and outlawed Zionist clubs. *Yeshivot* (Jewish religious academies of higher learning) in Mir and Volozhin were shut down, as were kosher butcher shops throughout the region. Overnight, school curriculums changed, and Jewish children were now required to learn the Russian language and Communist doctrine.

Many Jews lost everything. "If you had ten to fifteen people working for you, you were a capitalist," says Saul Ihilchik, who watched Soviet officials seize his father's mill in the town of Glebokie. Leo Raber, who at age twenty-one ran his family's grocery store, was forced to sell off all his merchandise. And in Kovno, after the Soviets arrived in June 1940, not only did Sara Ginaite's father lose his well-paying job as a salesman with the DuPont Company, but the military evicted the family from its apartment. Such stories of Soviet expropriations are endless.

In short, when it came to Jews, the goal of Soviet policy was, as Israeli historian Ben-Cion Pinchuk has pointed out, the "complete assimilation and abolition of a distinct Jewish existence." But before the Soviets could finish the job, Hitler turned his guns east and the lives of Russians, Poles, Ukrainians, and Jews were never the same again.

JUNE 1941

The struggle against Bolshevism demands ruthless and energetic measures above all against Jews, the main carriers of Bolshevism.
— Directive from Field Marshal Wilhelm Keitel,
September 12, 1941

Barbarossa

It took a mass murder perpetrated by the Einsatzgruppen death squads, a slaughter that marked the real beginning of Germany's policy of genocide, for many east European Jews to begin to grasp the incomprehensible. In these initial dark days of the eastern occupation, the forests still remained primarily the site of annihilation — "unknown destinations" in the nearby woods from which there was no return — rather than a refuge for resistance and survival.

■ ■

For the good of the Fatherland and the future of European civilization, the rules of war were not going to be observed in the destruction of the Bolshevik menace. On June 6, 1941, two weeks before Operation Barbarossa began and the Nazis declared war on the Soviet Union, the

German High Command issued a top-level directive advising army officers that in the ensuing struggle, "respect for international law" would jeopardize the security of the Reich and the success of the military operation. In this and subsequent directives, the message was clear: The destruction of Bolshevism required "ruthless and energetic" measures. Resistance, whether active or passive, was to be eliminated at all costs.

To Hitler, Russian Bolshevism in all of its manifestations was dangerous but weak. The Führer believed it would take five months at best to defeat Soviet forces, and he then planned to turn his full attention to the conquest of Britain. Many of his generals and party officials — including Deputy-Führer Rudolf Hess, who without Hitler's authorization flew to Scotland on May 10 to negotiate a peace settlement — disagreed and regarded Barbarossa as a grave error of military strategy.*

Not surprisingly, this opposition fell on deaf ears. Years earlier, Hitler had committed himself to wiping the so-called Communist-Jewish menace from the face of the earth. Indeed, in Nazi ideology, there had long been a strong link between Jews and the theories of Karl Marx. "The Jewish doctrine of Marxism rejects the aristocratic principle of Nature and replaces the eternal privilege of power and strength by the mass of numbers and their dead weight," Hitler wrote in *Mein Kampf.* "If, with the help of his Marxist creed, the Jew is victorious over the other peoples of the world, his crown will be the funeral wreath of humanity and this planet will, as it did thousands of years ago, move through the ether devoid of men."

In order to halt this conspiracy, the Nazi plan called for employing all methods available, no matter how brutal or ruthless. (Later, after thousands of innocent people had been slaughtered, Field Marshal Walter Von Reichnau explained official policy in this way: "The essential aim of

---

*Hess flew to Scotland on May 10, 1941, apparently to arrange a peace settlement with the British using his connections with the Duke of Hamilton. Hess's trip proved very embarrassing for Hitler, and his former second-in-command was declared to be "a deluded, deranged and muddled idealist with hallucinations traceable to World War I injuries." According to William Shirer, Hitler "ordered to have Hess shot at once if he returned." Of course, he did not. He parachuted into Scotland, was promptly arrested, and spent the rest of the war in British custody. At the Nuremberg trials, he was sentenced to life in prison. Hess committed suicide in Berlin's Spandau Prison in 1987. (See Shirer, *The Rise and Fall of the Third Reich*, 1094–99.)

the campaign against the Jewish Bolshevik system is the complete crushing of its means and power and the extermination of Asiatic influence in the European cultural region.") In preparation for the coming battle against the two million or so Jews who then resided in the Soviet-controlled eastern territory, the soldiers of the SS, under the command of Heinrich Himmler, were to have "special tasks," in the words of Field Marshal Wilhelm Keitel. In such vague orders lay the foundation for the Einsatzgruppen, the sadistic death squads given the job of murdering hundreds of thousands of Jewish men, women, and children.

The first wave of German soldiers — 3.2 million men in all — marched into Soviet territory before dawn on the morning of June 22 in a line of attack that stretched 1,600 kilometres from the Baltic to the Black seas. On the first day alone, the Soviets lost 1,200 planes; most had not even taken off and were bombed from the air.* For months, Hitler had been amassing troops along the eastern front, but Soviet leader Josef Stalin and his generals refused to believe that their Nazi allies would break the pact that had been signed two years earlier. So ill-prepared was the Red Army for the eventual onslaught that, by the end of July 1941, the Germans were 320 kilometres from Moscow. While Hitler basked in his latest conquest, the lives of millions of east Europeans, especially Jews, were about to take a tragic turn.

"WE DID NOT BELIEVE IN COLD-BLOODED MURDER"

Sixteen-year-old Leibke Kaganowicz was eagerly anticipating his summer holidays. It was June 1941, and he had just returned from his second year of school in Vilna, the major Jewish centre (then under Soviet control), which was not far from Eisiskes, the small town where his family lived and where he had grown up. Eisiskes was a *shtetl* like any other. Most Jews eked out livings as small tradesmen or shopkeepers. They dedicated themselves to their families and preserved the Sabbath.

---

*The massive German forces were divided into three main sections in the east: Army Group North, which swept into the Baltics; Army Group Centre, which fought in Belorussia and western Russia; and Army Group South, which took over the Ukraine. (See Chant, et al., *Land, Sea and Air Battles, 1939–1945*, 57–58.)

For the most part, they got along fairly well with their Christian neighbours.

Like other Jewish children, Leibke revered his parents, was fascinated with the jungle adventures of Tarzan, and suffered the occasional humiliation at the hands of Polish-Catholic bullies who blamed him for murdering Jesus Christ. His father, Shael, was a cattle and grain buyer, and Leibke would often accompany him on trips into the countryside. One day in 1936, Polish authorities arrived to arrest Shael Kaganowicz, accusing him of being a spy for Lithuanian nationalist freedom fighters. He was forced to endure three months in jail until the Poles decided to release him.

The Kaganowicz family, like the other Jews of Eisiskes, was relieved when the town fell under Soviet control after the German invasion of Poland in September 1939. Though their knowledge of Nazism was limited, they had heard stories. At least with the Red Army, they knew what they were getting. But the few Soviet soldiers who arrived in Eisiskes didn't stay long; a month after the occupation began, the area around Vilna, including Eisiskes, was ceded to Lithuania. In July 1940, however, the Soviets altered their plans and much to the dissatisfaction of the local population, reestablished their complete authority over the three Baltic states.

As a result of his past connections with the Lithuanians, Shael Kaganowicz managed to obtain a valuable liquor vendor's licence and the family opened a new store. Leibke returned to Vilna to attend high school and live with his great-aunt. The war had yet to intrude on their lives.

The first German soldiers marched into Eisiskes on June 23, 1941. It was quiet. Fearful of the unknown, the town's Jews remained in their homes behind "drawn blinds and locked doors." They had been surprised by the attack, as had most of the region's population. News on the radio and in the papers had contained no hint that Hitler was about to break his pact with the Soviets. Nevertheless, most Jews were certain that the powerful Red Army would repulse the German enemy. When that did not come to pass, and the townspeople witnessed the massive Soviet retreat, there was nothing to do but wait.

Even if escape to the east was contemplated, the opportunities were limited. The only modes of transportation available to most Jews were bicycles and horse-pulled wagons. Walking to safety was an unrealistic option, although some younger Jewish men and dedicated Communists tagged along with the retreating Soviet soldiers. Still, even if they made it to the border, the former Polish and Lithuanian Jews were not welcomed by Soviet authorities. Many were denied access. Others who fought alongside Red Army soldiers, often hiding their Jewish identities, were later captured and suffered atrocities in Nazi POW camps.

By the evening of June 24, the Germans had cut off the main highways from Vilna to the east. The last train had left Vilna a day earlier, with about 3,000 Jews on board. At least for the moment, the Kaganowiczes and many other Jewish families were trapped.

Even before the Nazis had officially installed themselves, local nationalist thugs began to abuse Jews. The quick departure of the Soviets left a legal and political vacuum, and a vicious anti-Semitism surfaced once again. In Vilna, for example, on the night of June 25, as many as one thousand Jews were killed and several synagogues burned to the ground. Eighty kilometres away, in Kovno, the former Lithuanian capital and home to more than 30,000 Jews, an edict issued by Jurgis Bobelis, a colonel in the Lithuanian army, declared that "for every German killed by a Jew, a hundred Jews would be killed in return." Rioting in Jewish neighbourhoods led by local city officials followed. Sara Ginaite, then seventeen years old and hiding out in a Kovno apartment block, remembers that Jewish survival was dependent on the whims of the building's caretaker. "If he closed the gates, helped people and did not participate in the pogroms, you could avoid the violence," she says.

In surrounding towns, similar outbreaks occurred as young men, often aided by local police, raped Jews and pillaged Jewish neighbourhoods. Nationalist spokesmen, if they bothered to explain their actions at all, claimed that this was just retribution for those who were overly sympathetic to the Communists. Indeed, it was true that in 1939 many Jews living east of the Bug River had quite logically preferred occupation by the Russians, though this was hardly adequate justification for such overt violence.

Such pogroms, though harsher than usual, were not unheard of in the history of Jewish-Gentile relations in the east. Most Jews resigned themselves to the fact that this was merely an unfortunate reality of life. How much worse could it become under a Nazi regime?

Schifre Z.'s* family thought about running away from their home in Dolhinov, not far from Vilna, but ultimately rejected the idea. "How do you abandon a house you have lived in all your life?" she asked many years later. "We did not [in June 1941] realize the whole tragedy. We could not have foreseen it. We did not believe in cold-blooded murder."

Sonia Ostrinsky was only twelve years old in 1939. She vividly remembers a cousin, a young rabbi from Warsaw, who arrived at her home in a Belorussian village soon after the war began. His wife and children had been murdered by the Nazis. "No one believed him," she recalls. "They were sure that nothing like that would happen to them."

More telling was the attitude of Rochelle Sutin's father, Lazar Schleiff, a businessman in Stolpce, a small community south-west of Minsk. "He actually believed that things would be better if the Germans invaded eastern Poland and drove the Communists out," writes Sutin in her memoirs. "He didn't understand who the Nazis were, what they believed in. When Lazar thought of Germany, he thought of World War I, when his father was still alive and was able to do business with the Kaiser's army."

Beyond plain ignorance about the Nazis and an unwillingness to believe the horror stories related by refugees from western Poland, there was the issue of strong family ties that linked one Jewish generation to the next. With elderly parents and grandparents to care for, Jewish families equated escape from the Nazis with abandonment, something unheard of both then and now. As Ernie Tessler, who in 1941 was an eleven-year-old boy in Mezerich, a town near Rovno, puts it: "In those days, you didn't leave a grandmother behind." As events unfolded for

---

*The Fortunoff Video Archive for Holocaust Testimonies at Yale University in New Haven, Connecticut, does not permit researchers to use the last names of witnesses in any publications. Unless otherwise noted, readers can assume that if a last name is not provided for a survivor reference or comment, it has been taken from the Fortunoff Archive Testimonies. (See *Guide to Yale University Library Holocaust Video Testimonies* [New Haven, Conn., 1994].)

the worse, this notable characteristic of eastern European Jewish life proved to be critical and perilous. Leaving the ghetto while parents, young children, and loved ones often remained behind to face a certain death was not a decision made lightly.

"RAUS, RAUS, JUDEN"

The soldiers of the Wehrmacht, on their way to Moscow and points east, were first to arrive. Most were friendly and polite, hardly the monsters the Jews were expecting. They shared their food and threw chocolate bars to the children. In Slonim, Nazi soldiers stayed for a few nights at Gershon (Jerry) Seigel's large house, sharing sardines and bread with his family. Similarly, in Kovno, Nazi officers assured Sara Ginaite's mother that they would not harm her family. "They took our radio and a few other goods," Ginaite recalls, "and like the Germans, gave us a receipt." The Jews started to relax.

Not far behind the Wehrmacht soldiers were the elaborate and multilayered Nazi SS police units, which established the German presence. These units included the Security Police (Sicherheitspolizei, or Sipo), comprising the Secret State Police, or Gestapo (Geheime Staatspolizei), and the Criminal Police, or Kripo (Kriminalpolizei); and the Order Police, or Orpo (Ordungspolizei), divided into the Shutzpolizei for urban areas and the gendarmerie for the countryside. As well, and more important, with the German occupation came the four divisions of the Einsatzgruppen (A,B,C, and D), the mobile death squads specifically trained to cleanse the region of Jews, or in the language of the German bureaucrats, to make it *Judenrein*. (*Judenfrei* or "free of Jews" was another favourite Nazi term to denote "the absence of Jews from a given area as a result of deportation and extermination operations.")

The men of the Einsatzgruppen had been given vague instructions about their grisly mission at a special military school in Pretzsch about a month before the invasion into Soviet territory. They had been recruited from the ranks of the SS, specifically from the Security Service (SD), Sipo, and the Waffen-SS (the military arm). Additional men, many of them middle-class reservists with little military training, were taken from the Order Police and were joined later by hundreds of local collaborators, eager to slaughter their Jewish neighbours.

In all, the Einsatzgruppen consisted of about 3,000 men. Each group was responsible for a section of the area stretching from Leningrad in the north to Kislovodsk in the southern Ukraine. For example, the one thousand men of Einsatzgruppe A, under the command of SS-Standartenführer Dr. Franz Walter Stahlecker, were attached to Army Group North and operated in the three Baltic states of Lithuania, Latvia, and Estonia. To cover such a large area, Einsatzgruppe A, like the three other groups, was divided into small sub-units known as Einsatzkommandos and Sonderkommandos.

The Einsatzgruppen were directly answerable to the three Higher SS and Police Leaders, who had been appointed to co-ordinate the Soviet occupation. But in fact, all lines of command flowed back to the Reich Security Main Office (RSHA); to its head, Reinhard Heydrich; and ultimately to the supreme architect of the Nazi police system, Reichsführer Heinrich Himmler, second in power only to Hitler. Yet due to the unique nature of their task — few among the Einsatzgruppen had ever participated in such large-scale mass murder before — the four division commanders and their subordinates did have some latitude in carrying out their orders. This would explain the "haphazard" pattern of the Einsatzgruppen killing during July 1941.

At first, only Communist Party officials and "Jews in the service of the Party or State" were to be targeted. Exactly when the order was given for an all-encompassing extermination is a matter of academic debate. In his affidavit given at the Nuremberg trials after the war, SS-Standartenführer Prof. Otto Ohlendorf, head of Einsatzgruppe D, declared that prior to the invasion of the Soviet Union, "Himmler stated that an important task consisted of the extermination of Jews — women, men, and children — and of Communist functionaries." At any rate, within a short time the slaughtering took on a life of its own. All Jews, young and old, became expendable, even such skilled artisans as shoemakers and tailors, who had provided the Nazis with much-needed services.

Because the German troops advanced so rapidly once the battle with the Red Army began, the Einsatzgruppen were able to move into cities and towns with little delay. The murder squads, for example, arrived in Vilna on July 2 and the killing started two days later. Order Police Battalion 309, operating on its own, was in Bialystok on June 27. Under the command of Maj. Ernest Weis, the police rounded up a large number of male Jews and went on a rampage. "The unit had barely driven into the city when the soldiers swarmed out and, without any sensible cause, shot up the entire city, apparently also in order to frighten the people," recalled one Jewish survivor several years later. "The incessant shooting was utterly horrible. They shot blindly, in fact, into houses and windows, without regard for whether they hit anyone. The shooting lasted the entire day."

Elderly Jews were dragged out of their homes and ordered to dance in the street. Then their beards were set on fire. As the beatings and humiliations continued, several Jewish leaders begged for mercy and protection from a German general. Seeing this, one member of Police Battalion 309 "unzipped his fly and urinated on them while the general turned his back." Hundreds of Jews were collected at the marketplace and shot on the spot. When this did not produce the desired results for Major Weis, about 800 Jews were driven into the city's main synagogue and it was set on fire using gasoline and grenades. Jews trying to escape the inferno were shot immediately. By the time the smoke cleared in Bialystok, 2,200 Jewish men, women, and children had been murdered. In Kovno, between June 25 and July 7, about 80 to 100 Jews were killed each day. Farther south in Lvov, thousands of Jews were also massacred in the same two-week period.

Initially, the Nazis had hoped that the local population would do most of the work for them. Indeed thousands of Jews were killed in brutal pogroms across eastern Poland, Belorussia, the Ukraine, and the Baltic states, often with the Germans happily supervising, but such actions were not going to make the vast region free of Jews. In large urban centres like Vilna, gangs of Lithuanian hoodlums were paid ten rubles for each Jew caught in Nazi round-ups, or *Aktionen*, terrorist assaults on Jewish areas conducted to inflict the utmost fear and compliance. No Holocaust survivor who lived through an *Aktion* has ever forgotten it. "Just their screams killed you, '*Raus, Raus, Juden*.' You didn't know what to do," says Rachel Szternfeld Goldstein, who was only twelve years old in 1941.

■ ■

Jewish life no longer had any value. Community leaders and anyone else liable to create trouble were rounded up and shot first. In several instances, Nazis arrived with lists of Jewish names prepared for them by local police and politicians. Such was the case in the Belorussian town of Novogrudok when, within a few weeks of their arrival, the SS ordered a group of fifty men to report to the marketplace for a work detail. "They were the strongest and most intelligent men in the town," remembers Frances B., then twenty-three years old. "The men were locked up in a synagogue overnight. The next day, they were led out into the street and publicly executed."

In Stolpce, Rochelle Sutin's father, Lazar, was taken away by the SS and Polish police, forced to dig his own grave, and then stoned to death. The Nazis and local police did not want to waste their bullets. Disobedience meant endless humiliations, beatings, or death. As had been their practice in the west, the Nazis rigidly enforced collective responsibility and punishment as a way to deter resistance. One escaped Jew or one German soldier harmed resulted in the death of hundreds or more innocent people. After a Nazi policeman was killed in a fight near Pinsk, for example, the Einsatzkommando unit in the area gathered together 4,500 Jews and killed them all.*

Assisted by local collaborators, the Nazis quickly implemented the same series of rules that had been successfully imposed in the west, rules that were designed to intimidate and isolate those Jews that were still alive after the first wave of terror. From one end of the east to the other, Jews ten years of age and older were required to wear yellow stars of David on their clothes or paint stars on their homes; they were

---

*Nazi punishment reached levels of absurdity. One day in the ghetto in Lida (north-east of Bialystok), Gitel Zelkowicz (now Morrison) recalled, someone took the food belonging to the German shepherd owned by the local head of the SS. The dog became ill, and his distraught owner warned that if the dog did not recover within twenty-four hours, the families of those who worked in his office — ten in all — would be shot. All day and night, the Jews prayed that the dog would recover. Their prayers were answered the next morning.

forbidden to purchase food in the same stores patronized by Germans and were forbidden to walk on sidewalks; they were required to remove their hats when passing a German or a local resident. The rules changed daily — one day the yellow star had to be worn on the front, the next day on the back — and those caught unaware were brutalized. Soon, Jews had to surrender all jewellery, gold, fur coats, pillows, bicycles, and copper pots and pans. Some gave their belongings to Gentile friends for safekeeping.

■ ■

Such harsh conditions quickly took a toll, both physical and psychological. Yitzhok Rudashevski — "Itsele" to his family — was a teenager in Vilna who was later killed in the death pits at Ponary by the Einsatzgruppen. The few surviving photographs of him show that he was a small boy for his age. His capacity for learning and life, however, knew no bounds. He was, like Anne Frank, that most famous of Holocaust child chroniclers, an astute and passionate observer of the times.*

His diary for June 28, 1941, composed about a week after the German occupation, captures the hopelessness of the situation confronting Vilna's Jews: "I stand at the window and feel a sense of rage. Tears come to my eyes: all our helplessness, all our loneliness lies in the streets. There is no one to take our part. And we ourselves are so helpless. . . . Life becomes more and more difficult. People do not go out anywhere. . . . We are so sad, we are exposed to mockery and humiliation. . . . Our hearts are crushed witnessing the shameful scenes where women and older people are kicked in the middle of the street. . . ."

---

*Yitzhok Rudashevski was born in Vilna on December 10, 1927. His mother, Rose, was a seamstress and his father, Eliahu, worked as a typesetter for the Yiddish newspaper, *Vilner Tog* (*Vilna Day*). During the final liquidation of the Vilna ghetto, which began on September 23, 1943, Rudashevski (fifteen years old), his parents, and other family members — including his teenage cousin, Sore Voloshin — went into hiding to avoid capture. They lasted only a few weeks. The Germans found them in early October and dispatched them to the Ponary, where they were killed. But Sore Voloshin was able to escape and join the partisans in the forest. After the war, she returned to Vilna and the family's hiding place and discovered Yitzhok's 204-page Yiddish diary covered in dirt. It made its way into the hands of the YIVO Institute for Jewish Research in New York City where it is presently preserved. (See Rudashevski, *The Diary of the Vilna Ghetto*, and Holliday, *Children in the Holocaust and World War II*, 137–83.)

Rabbis and other community officials who had escaped the first
Aktionen were ordered to form councils, or Judenrate, so that all Nazi
directives could be channelled through these organizations. Reluctantly,
the Jews complied. Next, they were relocated into older and often
dilapidated neighbourhoods that were transformed into ghettos.

During the night of September 5, 1941, Yitzhok Rudashevski, like
most Jews of Vilna, was restless. "[It] is a sleepless, desperate night,
people like shadows. People sit in helpless, painful expectation with
their bundles," he recorded in his diary. "Tomorrow we shall be led to
the ghetto."

No official announcement was made or posted about the relocation
to two designated areas in the old Jewish quarter in the middle of the
city, but Vilna's Jews had heard the rumours. Early in the morning of
September 6, 1941, Nazi and Lithuanian police evicted Jews from their
homes and herded them into one of two adjacent ghettos (separated by
a street) or to the Lukiszki prison (from which they would be taken to
Ponary and killed). The Jews were given less than thirty minutes notice
and were ordered to take only as much as they could carry.

By nine o'clock that morning, the air was already hot. Some people
wore two and three coats; others hauled their meagre belongings in
baby carriages and wheelbarrows. The procession along the streets was
a pathetic sight. "The street streamed with Jews carrying bundles. . . .
People fall, bundles scatter," wrote Rudashevski. "Before me a woman
bends under her bundle. From the bundle a thin string of rice keeps
pouring over the street. I walk burdened and irritated. The Lithuanians
drive us on, do not let us rest. I think of nothing: not what I am losing,
not what I have just lost, not what is in store for me. I do not see the
street before me, the people passing by. . . . Here is the ghetto gate. I feel
that I have been robbed, my freedom is being robbed from me, my
home, and the familiar Vilna streets I love so much . . ."

The move took twenty-four hours. By the next morning, about
30,000 Jews had been imprisoned behind the wooden fence of Ghetto
No. 1, 10,000 in Ghetto No. 2, and another 6,000 were locked in the
Lukiszki prison. Yitzhok Rudashevski was sent to Ghetto No. 1 with his
parents and grandmother. The evening of September 6 was the first of

many unbearable nights he was to endure. "Besides the four of us there are eleven persons in the room. The room is a dirty and stuffy one. . . . The first ghetto night. We lie three together on two doors. I do not sleep. In my ears resounds the lamentation of this day. I hear the restless breathing of people with whom I have been suddenly thrown together, people who just like me have been suddenly thrown together, people who just like me have suddenly been uprooted from their homes." Liza Ettinger, from Lida, who was trapped in Vilna that September, echoed similar sentiments. "The first night was hell on earth," she remembered. "Only the tongues of fire were missing. Crying of babies and groaning of sick people filled the air."

In some ghettos, this massive and chaotic movement of people into the ghettos was often preceded by a *Selektion*, as the Germans called it: those deemed capable of work or possessing skills the Nazis regarded as necessary were herded to the left, those deemed expendable to the right. If a *Selektion* did not occur before the ghetto was created, it took place — not in all cases — within the first six months of the ghetto's existence as the Jews were gradually liquidated. In Kovno, for instance, the ghetto was established in mid-July 1941, and sealed on August 15, 1941, and the first major *Selektion* took place on October 28, 1941, This is how Avraham Tory, a survivor of the Kovno ghetto, describes the ordeal in his diary:

The [Demokratu, or Democracy] square was surrounded by machine-gun emplacements. [SS Master Sergeant Helmut] Rauca positioned himself on top of a little mound from which he could watch the great crowd that waited in the square in tense and anxious anticipation. His glance ranged briefly over the column of the Council members and the Jewish Ghetto Police, and by a movement of his hand he motioned them to the left, which, as it became clear later was the "good" side. . . . The Gestapo man fixed his gaze on each pair of eyes and with a flick of the finger of this right hand passed sentence on individuals, families, or even whole groups. Elderly and sick persons, families with children, single women, and persons whose physique did not impress him in terms of labor power, were directed to the right. There they immediately fell into the hands of the German policemen and the Lithuanian partisans, who showered them with shouts and blows. . . . From time to time, Rauca feasted on a sandwich — wrapped in wax paper lest his blood-stained hands get greasy — or enjoyed a cigarette, all the while performing his fiendish work without interruption.

Two ghettos were established in each of several locales, including Kovno, Vilna and Ludmir in the southern Volhynia district: one for the remaining Jews to work in, the other a temporary holding cell for the elderly, women, and children destined for immediate death. In Vilna, the two ghettos had been initially organized according to a geographic division. But within a few weeks of their creation, those holding work permits or possessing desirable skills were sent with their families (one spouse and two children under the age of sixteen) into Ghetto No. 1, which became the "productive ghetto"; those without essential skills, as well as women, children, and the elderly, were ordered into Ghetto No. 2, known as the "unproductive ghetto."

Jews imprisoned in the "productive" ghettos were immediately forced into labour, becoming slaves of the Third Reich. They were tormented day and night, working in fear. Most often, the work began and ended with severe beatings. In Lenin, a *shtetl* in the Polesie district in eastern Poland, eighteen-year-old Faye Schulman (*née* Lazebnik) was forced to clean Nazi quarters. "When the light of day arrived, we begged for night, when we could go home to rest," she remembers. "At night, we prayed to go to work the next day, so frightened were we of being killed during the night."

As terrified as they were of the SS, many survivors today insist that the treatment they received at the hands of local collaborators was often worse. From the start of the German occupation, there were large numbers among the local population who were more than willing to undertake the Nazis' dirty work. Police and officials assisted the Germans in identifying Jewish victims, and Jew-baiting again became a popular form of entertainment. Crowds gathered in the streets to watch the Nazis beat Jews with truncheons. David Kahane, who lived in the ghetto in

Lvov, recalled one Ukrainian explaining the situation to another: "One must not waste one's hand to beat a Jew; the Jew must be kicked."

Holocaust historian Philip Friedman has shown that members of the intelligentsia — teachers, judges, and municipal officials — were among those leading anti-Jewish pogroms in the Ukraine in 1941, for example. In one Ukrainian town, local schoolchildren were enlisted to damage grave stones at a Jewish cemetery. As the slaughter began, anti-Semitic collaborators defiled synagogues and former neighbours looted Jewish homes. This type of activity occurred particularly in the chaos that preceded relocations to ghettos.

Faye Druk, a survivor of the Lida ghetto, remembers. "When we had to move out of our house, this friend approached me. She was a young blond Polish girl I had grown up with. 'Faigie,' she said, 'you know that you're going to die, why not give me your clothes?' But I refused." Similarly, Eugene Katz, who eventually escaped from the ghetto in Dzisna in the Vilna region and joined the partisans, recalls shovelling snow while Polish friends he had grown up with spat on him as they passed by. "These were the same friends who had sat beside me for five years in school," he says. "People turned into animals. It was unbelievable." In time, informers betrayed Jews in hiding for a few kilograms of salt and willingly participated in mass murder.

Many Poles, Ukrainians, Belorussians, and Lithuanians paid with their lives for helping their Jewish friends escape, or for smuggling food into the ghettos. Later, many were murdered for hiding Jews in their barns and attics, a "crime" that meant instant death for the peasant's whole family. (Since 1953, more than 2,000 Poles have been recognized by the Yad Vashem Remembrance Authority in Jerusalem as "Righteous Among the Nations" for their acts of rescue during the Holocaust. This has included the former members of Zegota, a Polish underground organization with links to the Home Army, which hid and assisted thousands of Jewish fugitives.)

In some cases, as for Adam Goszer in Korets, past friendships with Ukrainian school chums who volunteered to become collaborationist policemen often meant the difference between life and death. "I saw them kill my [Jewish] neighbour," says Goszer, "but they did not touch me." Indeed, the Nazi terror affected each and every life it touched, whether Jewish or Gentile. But making generalizations about east European behaviour is admittedly dangerous.

"To ask why the Poles did little to help the Jews," argues British historian Norman Davies, "is rather like asking why the Jews did nothing to assist the Poles. Stories of individual gallantry, though real enough, vastly exaggerated the opportunities for chivalry that actually existed. In a world where immediate death awaited anyone who contravened Nazi regulations, the Nazi could always exact a measure of co-operation from the terrified populace."

Fair enough. But can the abnormal and horrific circumstances of the Nazi occupation also explain numerous incidents of blackmail, looting, informing, and participation in raids and murders? Consider two typical examples. In September 1941, near the town of Eisiskes, sixteen-year-old Zvi Michalowski miraculously escaped the death pits. Leaving the dead body of his father beside him, he crawled out of the pit naked, covered in blood, and ran to a nearby Lithuanian farmhouse. He pleaded for the peasant to let him in. "The peasant lifted [his] lamp [which he had looted earlier in the day from a Jewish home] and examined the boy closely. 'Jew, go back to the grave where you belong!' he shouted at Zvi and slammed the door in his face." He received the same response at another half-dozen farms, until he convinced a peasant woman that he was her Lord, Jesus Christ, who had arrived for a special visit. She allowed him to come into her house and gave him food and clothes.

Willy Moll was only eleven years old when the Nazis murdered most members of his immediate family in December 1941. Two years later, having survived with relatives in the Lida ghetto, he was captured in an *Aktion*. As the group of fifty Jews he was with was being marched out of town to face a certain death, he managed to escape. "I had run down an alley about half a block," he recalls, "when a Polish woman looking out her kitchen window started to shout, '*Jude, Jude.*' I was a small thirteen-year-old boy, what had I done to her? I'm not saying she should have saved me or other Jews. I don't know if I would risk my life and that of my family today to save a stranger. But to bring a Jew to the Germans, why did she have to do that?"

Both Michalowski and Moll barely succeeded in eluding the Nazis and death. These stories and similar (or worse) ones are difficult to ignore. Israeli historians Yisrael Gutman and Shmuel Krakowski, in their extensive study of Polish actions and attitudes towards Jewish fugitives, examined 10,000 events that occurred in 765 different locales throughout occupied Poland, west and east (the city of Warsaw was excluded and was studied on its own). They concluded that "the overall balance between the acts of crime and acts of help, as described in the available sources, is disproportionally negative. The acts of crime outnumbered the acts of help. . . . The overwhelming majority of Jews who approached Poles for help fell prey either to Nazi police or gendarmerie, or to rabid anti-Semites in the Polish society and in the Polish underground."

How can we account for this hateful and often sadistic behaviour of such a large segment of the eastern European population during the war? There was, as noted, the fresh memory of how some Jews had cheered the Soviet occupation, an affront not tolerated by locals with nationalist aspirations. In some cases, writes Philip Friedman, displays of anti-Jewish behaviour and collaboration with the Germans was simply a quick way of "acquiring wealth, prestige and power in the new political constellation."

The complex and deep-seated anti-Semitism propagated for generations by Catholic and Orthodox Eastern clergy and passed down as gospel by uneducated peasants to their children was most damaging. They believed that Jews were the killers of Christ, that they were different. Jews lived apart, spoke their own language, and voluntarily segregated themselves. And the peasants owed Jewish merchants money.

Sam Gruber, a Polish Jew who distinguished himself as a partisan leader during the war, recalls one meeting he had with the wife of a Polish peasant. (Gruber had been captured by the Germans in 1939 while serving in the Polish army but was later able to escape to the forest.) The woman, who did not know that Gruber was Jewish, provided him with some food and began talking about how Jews were evil and had horns sprouting from their heads.

"Did you ever see a Jew?" Gruber asked her, trying to maintain his composure.

"No, never," replied the woman.

"So how come you know everything about Jews?"

"I read, I know what Hitler says."

"And you believe everything?"

"Of course."

"Listen, I am a Jew," Gruber declared.

The Polish woman turned white and ran out of the farmhouse in horror. When she returned, Gruber removed his hat.

"Look, I have no horns. We don't want wars. What you believe is untrue."

His reasoning was to no avail. The woman ran from her house, afraid.

Such were the backward attitudes that confronted east European Jews. And the horror and tragedy of the Nazis' "war against the Jews," whether in the ghetto, concentration camps, countryside, or forests, was magnified by the actions of superstitious peasants and opportunistic collaborators like the 15,000 or so members of the *Polnische Polizei* (Polish police). They collaborated with the Nazis and informed on Jewish fugitives, which enabled the mass murder and destruction to proceed as efficiently as it did. Without Hitler and German complicity, the Holocaust would not have happened. But at the same time, the attitude and behaviour of far too many Poles, Ukrainians, Lithuanians, and Belorussians made the Nazis' evil work all the easier to accomplish.

■ ■

By the beginning of the summer of 1941, the brutality and murder were nearly in full force. There were no limits to how violent the German soldiers and local police could be. In Riga, a group of storm-troopers amused themselves by throwing Jewish children from the roof of a six-storey building. A German officer approached them and asked them what they were doing.

"We're carrying on scientific work here. We're testing the validity of Newton's law of universal gravity!" they yelled from the top of the roof.

"*Donnerswetter*! Well said! Continue gentleman!" shouted back the officer. "Science requires sacrifices."

In the same city, a nineteen-year-old Jewish girl named Lina Gottschalk was apprehended by several German soldiers who discussed the best way to kill her for several minutes. As is related in *The Black Book* (a collection of eyewitness testimonies and documents about Nazi atrocities in the Soviet Union, parts of which were first published in 1946): "After a lengthy debate the Germans came to a decision — to convert the girl into a being without bones. She was tied up inside a sack and beaten methodically with ramrods. The beating lasted two hours. The girl was already dead and all her bones were broken. The Germans would not leave their venture until they were convinced that every last bone was broken. So they rolled up the body of Lina Gottschalk into a bloody ball of flesh and ordered a soldier to throw it onto the boulevard near the opera theater."

Meanwhile in Eisiskes, Leibke Kaganowicz (Leon Kahn) volunteered for work detail with twenty other young Jewish men. He was marched to the gendarmerie headquarters and was forced to work in the garden, clean the grounds, and chop wood. The abuse soon began. The German police ordered the men to crawl on the road and clubbed those who did not crawl properly. After that, the Jews had to wade into the river up to their chins. Finally, Leibke and one of his father's friends were told to clean the outhouse pits used by the police.

"For our task we each needed a bucket fastened to the end of a pole, but the Germans had a better idea," recalled Kahn in his memoirs. "They tossed us into the pit full of excrement where we stood in it up to our waists. Then they handed us pails and ordered us to go to work. We were wearing light summer clothes and open sandals, and this disgusting slime sucked at our bodies. . . . After a half hour of this work, two Lithuanians who were passing by decided to investigate the source of the Germans' laughter. When they discovered what was happening, they took down their pants and sat down in the outhouse directly over the place where I was working. I attempted to get out of the way, but the Germans ordered me to stand where I was and in a little while my face and hair and shoulders were covered in excrement."

When he returned home, his mother helped him wash and he laughed while telling his family about what had happened. His parents tried to look on the bright side.

"If this is all the Germans intend to do to us, it won't harm us that badly," said his mother. "Leibke," began his father, "we have too much faith in God and in ourselves to let this destroy us! We'll outlive them, you'll see!" And young Leibke Kaganowicz believed them.

In Novogrudok in western Belorussia, near Minsk, Tuvia and Zus Bielski, after a day of beatings and humiliation at the hands of Germans and Poles, swore to each other that they never again would be caught by Nazis. "This decision contained no special plans," writes Nechama Tec in her biography of the Bielskis, "no specific steps, but it was firm."

WHEN THE GROUND BLED

October 6 was the first day of Sukkot, the Festival of the Tabernacles, an annual holiday both to commemorate the journey of the Israelites through the desert and to welcome the harvest season. For nine days, Jewish families gather in the *sukkah* for prayers, festive meals, and fun. It is usually a time for rejoicing and thanksgiving. But for the Jews of Swieciany, a town north of Vilna, the Sukkot of 1941 was filled with only horror and death.

A day earlier, the police had recruited local peasants to dig huge pits — "two meters wide, three meters deep and twenty-five meters long" — in an area about 4 kilometres from where a large number of the town's Jews had been locked up in a compound known as the Polygon. The few who remained behind in the ghetto were selected by the Nazis and deemed necessary to serve Nazi interests.

On the second day of Sukkot, the men, who had been separated from their wives and children, were brought out first, fifty at a time. They boarded trucks.

> The Jews could not see the pits until they emerged from among the trees, but the moment they saw them they knew what was waiting for them. Encircling them in a radius of several kilometers were strong patrols to make certain no one would escape. The police, without exception, were drunk; only the German officer who stood beside a movie camera and filmed the scene was sober. The Jews were ordered off the trucks and led to the edge of the pits. No one screamed or

wept. After a moment the German officer signaled with his hand, and the machine guns opened fire. The fifty Jews fell into the pit, some dead, some wounded. The trucks returned to the camp to load the next shipment. The shots were not heard at the Polygon. By noon all the men had been killed. When the women were brought to the mass grave, many were numbed by despair and almost indifferent to their fate. But the worst horror was when the children were snatched from the women: mothers fought for their children with amazing strength, marks of their fingernails remaining on the policemen's faces. Children and infants were flung into the pit alive; when it was full the police threw a number of hand grenades in after them. Only some of the children were killed. . . . The police covered the mass graves with earth, but the following morning cracks appeared in the blood-soaked soil. Peasants were hired to bring wagon loads of earth from a distance and another layer was dumped on the pits. But the ground continued to swell. Layer after layer of earth was added, until after several weeks the blood was finally absorbed.

Such horrific scenes of a *shchitah*, or slaughter, were repeated throughout the fall of 1941 and the spring and summer of 1942. The special mobile killing squads, the Einsatzgruppen, worked their way across eastern Europe leaving a trail of blood and carnage not witnessed before or since.

In the words of a secret German military memo dated October 10, 1941, there were two main tasks for Nazi soldiers in the eastern campaign: "total annihilation of the false Bolshevist doctrine of the Soviet State, and of its armed forces," and "the pitiless extermination of the alien treachery and cruelty and thus the protection of the lives of the German forces in Russia."

The first to feel the effects of these harsh policies were the 3.5 million Russian prisoners of war who had been captured by December 1941. Regularly condemned in Nazi propaganda as "sub-humans," the Soviet POWs (many Jews among them) were starved and beaten into submission in overcrowded concentration camps. "There was no food and we received water only once a day," recalls Ben Lungen, who was captured in September 1941. Then twenty years old, he had joined the Red Army when the war started. "Sometimes the locals would throw us some food over the fence."

In a POW camp near Kiev, Lungen successfully hid the fact that he was Jewish and was able to escape when the Germans decided to release prisoners under the age of sixteen. "I took a chance," Lungen says. "I knew there was no future there. I started in the line at nine o'clock in the evening to go through the SS checkpoint. They looked at your face. If they thought you were older than sixteen, they pushed you to the side, where you were beaten to death. I wasn't scared but it took until the next day at two o'clock in the afternoon until I reached the front. I got through by telling them my name was Boris Lungeki and I was a Pole. They believed me."

Lungen survived the war fighting in the forests as a partisan in a Russian unit. In fact, the German brutality of Soviet prisoners played a major factor in the formation of the Soviet partisan movement after many POWs were able to escape from the camps and take vengeance on their enemy. These forest fighters would play a major role in the defeat of Nazi Germany.

■ ■

A tremendous sense of hopelessness and panic gripped the ghettoized Jewish communities of the east. Some Jews were beaten or shot to death the moment they stepped out of their homes. Others, like the Jews of Swieciany, were isolated in crowded detention camps or ghettos and then moved to vast graves outside the city or town where they lived. The death pits at Vilna were located about 10 kilometres from the city at a site on the edge of the Ponary Forest, where the Soviets had previously dug deep holes for fuel tanks. There, beginning in October 1941 and for two months, approximately 33,500 of Vilna's Jews (of a total population of 57,000 in June 1941) were methodically slaughtered by Lithuanians and Germans.

Some Jews attempted to evade capture by concealing themselves in makeshift hiding places, known in Yiddish as *malines*. *Malines* were holes dug into basements and false walls built behind closets. People hid in ovens, attics, and chimneys. They were, in the words of one Jewish youth hiding in Vilna, like "animals surrounded by hunters." How long could they survive with a limited amount of food, little water, and no provision for sanitary needs?

Mina Rosner, a survivor who hid with her family in a basement bunker 15-feet long and 8-feet wide, likened the experience in her *maline* to that of twenty people stuffed "like sardines in a can." "We all had to lie next to each other with no space between," she writes in her memoirs. "The extent of the movement available to us was to sit up or lie down, and for most people there was not enough room to extend their bodies fully. In the very front of the basement, at the foot of the stairs, was a pail that served as our toilet. The bunker opening had a hatch on top, with clothes and other debris secured to it. It was virtually impossible to detect."

Still, as Rosner admits, this was a temporary situation at best. Two or three days in a *maline* were unbearable, the tension and desperation impossible to comprehend. In some cases, young children were suffocated to death so that their cries would not give away the location of the hiding place. "It was a slow death the Nazis were dealing out to us," writes Rosner, "sapping us of our energy and vitality and keeping us in a state of perpetual anxiety and fear."

Forced to leave their *malines* to find food and water, most Jews in hiding were inevitably caught and executed, either on the spot or at the mass graves. Evading capture during an *Aktion* was often a matter of pure luck and unimaginable desperation. When a major *Aktion* began in Novogrudok in August 1942, Frances B. and her sister-in-law lowered themselves into an outhouse cesspool. The human waste reached as high as their chests. They found two other women hiding in the cesspool as well. There they remained for six horrible days without food or water. Worms crawled all over their bodies. They could hear machine-gun fire, barking dogs, and the screams of children, unabated.

At last, on the sixth night, when Frances decided she could take no more, a man with a yellow patch entered the outhouse. She yelled to him and he eventually brought her brother, who rescued her. "I could not stand on my feet and no one could be near me," she relates. "We tried to wash up. My hair was cut." When Frances was clean, the surviving members of her family contemplated their escape.

Other Jews throughout the eastern area faced a torturous and humiliating death. Initially, as in Swieciany, the victims were ordered to strip and to line up on the edge of the pits in small groups, and the men of the Einsatzgruppen and locally recruited killers shot them at point-blank range. Sometimes elderly religious Jews were ordered to crawl and were humiliated until the moment they were killed. Blood and body parts splattered everywhere, even onto the clothes of the murderers. Dissatisfied with the inefficiency of this method, SS and Polizeiführer Friedrich Jecklin, who worked with the Einsatzgruppe A in Latvia and Lithuania, invented the *Sarindenpackung* (sardine pack), in which victims were forced to lie head to toe in graves and were then executed from above. Children were often beaten to death, or were flung crying into the pits, still alive.

From his hiding place on a farm near Kovno, Aba Gefen, twenty-one years old, wrote in his diary on October 30, 1941, about the brutal execution of Jews in one nearby Lithuanian village.

The [Jewish] men were assembled in the synagogue and murdered; the women and children were given a day's grace. When they were brought next day to the death pit, the girls were raped, then killed. The women were forced to undress, pushed into the pit, then shot. Only the little children were left. Even the most hardened killers shirked the task of murdering the infants. But one volunteer, the Lithuanian chief of police, covered his nice uniform with a white smock and methodically smashed the heads of Jewish babies against the stone wall of the Christian cemetery, adjacent to the killing site. Then calmly he returned home to his wife and four little children. On Sunday he attended chapel in the friendly company of the parish priest.

Concerned that the work might be too difficult for his men, Einsatz-gruppe D commander Ohlendorf ensured that executions were done as group shootings. In this way, he later argued, "direct [and] personal responsibility" was avoided. In fact, postwar testimonies and pictures taken at the time confirm just the opposite: the executions were quite personal acts of violence. "I had to shoot an old [Jewish] woman, who was over sixty years old," reported one former member of Police Battalion 101. "I can still remember, that the old woman said to me, will you make it short or about the same. . . . Next to me was Policeman Koch. . . . He had to shoot a small boy of perhaps twelve years. We had been expressly told that we should hold the gun's barrel eight inches from the head. Koch had apparently not done this, because while leaving the execution site, the other comrades laughed at me, because pieces of the child's brains had spattered onto my sidearm and had stuck there."

Often plied with liquor and pep talks, most of the men, like Koch, had little difficulty carrying out their gruesome tasks. Those who did were allowed to opt out, though few asked to be transferred to other units. Himmler, who attended a mass execution near Minsk, found the scene he witnessed quite disturbing. As SS Gen. Karl Wolff, who stood beside the SS chief at the death pit, later remembered, "While he was looking in, Himmler had the deserved bad luck that from one or other of the people who had been shot in the head he got a splash of brains on his coat . . . and he went very green and pale. . . . After the shooting was over, Himmler gathered the shooting squad in a semi-circle around him and, standing up in his car, so that he would be a little higher and be able to see the whole unit, he made a speech. He had seen for himself how hard the task which they had to fulfill for Germany in the occupied areas was, but however terrible it all might be, even for him as a mere spectator, and how much worse it must be for them, the people who had to carry it out, he could not see any way round it. They must be hard and stand firm. He could not relieve them of this duty."

Many Jews accepted their fate without tears. On one occasion, outside Riga in the Bikernieki Forest, one person shivering in the pit began to cry. A woman jumped up and shouted: "Why are you crying, Jews? Do you really think these monsters will be moved by tears? Let's be calm! Let's be proud! We are Jews! . . . We are Soviet Jews!" And the Jews in the pit heeded the woman's advice. For a few moments, the forest was silent. Then the SS men began to laugh.

This incident was reported by a seamstress named Frida Frid (later Michelson), who was struck by a German officer with a pistol before the shooting began. For hours, she lay as still as she could under a pile of shoes that had been dumped on top of her. Then, miraculously, she crawled away in the snow to elude Nazi guards posted around the pits. She was ready to run when she heard the cry of a child pleading to her dead mother to get up: "Mama, I'm cold. . . . Why are you just lying there, Mama?" She thought she could rescue the child, but the Germans were a step ahead. "They walked up to the pit," she recalled in her memoirs many years later, "found the child with their bayonets, and stabbed him. One of the Germans said, laughing: 'From our kettle nobody escapes alive.'"

Among the most notorious acts of the Einsatzgruppen was the killing at Babi Yar, the massive death pit outside Kiev. Over a two-day period in late September 1941, 33,711 Jews (of a total Jewish population of about 175,000) were executed. Here the Jews "were ordered to lie face down on the dead bodies while the SS men walked on the mounds shooting them at close range with pistols."* As efficient as the entire operation was, the massive killing at Babi Yar and other places still remained too personal an experience for some of the murderers. Eventually, nerves were frayed. Within time, the use of gas vans and deportation to death camps would rectify such problems.

■ ■

After all these years, questions persist about Jewish compliance in their own liquidation. Why didn't they resist more? How could so many people have marched to their deaths? Why didn't they flee to the forest sooner?

---

*In the cold language of the Nazi bureaucracy, the slaughter at Babi Yar was reported by the chief of Einsatzgruppe C on October 7, 1941, as follows: "All Jews of Kiev were ordered, in agreement with the city commander, to appear on Monday, September 29, by 8 a.m., at the designated place. These announcements were posted throughout the city by members of the Ukrainian militia. At the same time it was announced orally that all Jews were to be resettled. In collaboration with the Einsatzgruppe staff and 2 commandos of the Police Regiment South, the Sonderkommando 4a [a special commando assigned to police and political tasks] executed 33,771 Jews on September 29 and 30. Money, valuables, underwear and clothing were confiscated. . . . It was accomplished without interference. No incidents occurred. . . ." (See Dawidowicz, A Holocaust Reader, 90.)

Many, as astonishing as it now seems, simply refused to believe the unbelievable. As late as October 1941, Jews in Baranowicze, a town in Belorussia, could not be convinced by Yehuda Szymszonicz, a survivor of a massacre at a nearby village, that the stories of the executions were true. After Szymszonicz told the Baranowicze Judenrat what he knew, "they shrugged in disbelief and advised him not to spread such horrible rumours." The Jews in Jody, a *shtetl* east of Vilna, hoped that the Einsatzgruppen would pass them by. "We were horrified; it was unbelievable but the evidence was there before us," explains Peter Silverman, who survived as a partisan. "The human psyche, being what it is, always responds to tragedy with hope. It was our hope that this wholesale slaughter was contained. . . ."

Even those marching to the pits could not comprehend their own demise. "The people who were seized did not believe they were being led to their death, that guiltless people would be killed," recorded one resident of Vilna in his diary. "They thought there would be interrogations and those found to be Communists would be punished, but ordinary people would never be killed. They went to the Ponar with these thoughts in mind."

Given the Jews' previous experiences, their limited knowledge of the Nazis' potential for evil, and their relative isolation from centres of political power, such attitudes are not hard to understand. As historian Isaiah Trunk has observed, "The paramount importance of the Jewish factor in the theory and practical implementation of the overall Nazi strategy of world domination was generally underestimated, as was the Nazis' fierce determination to destroy the Jewish people."

Beyond this, what type of resistance was available for a Jewish tailor, shoemaker, or housewife already facing the guns of the Einsatzgruppen? "To say that when a Jew was told to dig a hole in the ground for a grave, he should have hit the German with the shovel because he was going to be shot anyway is completely wrong," argues Peter Silverman. "In most cases, this kind of resistance did not succeed. If he chose this type of action, the Jew was open to torture and indescribable pain. Before he attempted to hit the German, the Jew had to be sure that he would kill him with the first blow, and that other Germans would shoot him rather than try to capture him alive. Many tens of thousands of Jews were inhumanely tortured."

With the local police at the disposal of the Nazis and informers ready to hand over Jews without giving it a second thought, there was nothing for them to do, nowhere for them to run. In the summer and fall of 1941, the forest seemed an unlikely place for anyone to hide, let alone survive.

PARTISAN BEGINNINGS AND COLLECTIVE INTERESTS

We must show [the Germans] that we are very useful. . . . Work, especially work for the military, is the order of the day. . . . Jewish workers must give up easy, convenient jobs and take on more difficult work, in order to increase their usefulness. . . . This is essential for the collective interest of the ghetto.

— JACOB GENS

CALL TO ARMS

The voice on the radio that summer evening in early July 1941 was clear, distinct, and strong. At sixty-two, Josef Stalin, his black hair speckled with white and a large paunch bulging under his military uniform, had lost none of his edge. True, he had been depressed and miserable in the first few days after the German attack on June 22. He may have even suffered a nervous breakdown. He had terribly miscalculated Hitler's strategy and the ability of his own soldiers to fend off such a massive onslaught.

Slowly, the besieged Soviet army began to regroup and fight back. But the Nazi battalions were not easily intimidated, and it would take more than a year and half — until the hard-fought battle of Stalingrad was won by the Red Army in February 1943 — for the tide of the war in the east to turn. The cost in lives was enormous. "The war on the eastern front that . . . lasted four years," British historian Alan Bullock has observed, "was the longest, most intensive, and brutal conflict between two nations in history, costing them in combatants alone between three and four times as many dead as all those killed on all fronts in the First World War, without counting the millions of civilians, refugees, and deported prisoners caught up and destroyed in the maelstrom."

Stalin, too, regained his confidence and called his people to arms. "Comrades! Citizens! Fighting men of our army and navy! Brothers and sisters!" his radio broadcast of July 3 began. "I turn to you, my friends. . . . Our country is in serious danger." He urged all citizens of the Soviet Union to join his campaign against the Hitlerites and "to destroy everything, if forced to retreat."

To the countless number of Red Army soldiers trapped or captured behind enemy lines, the Soviet dictator called for the formation of "guerrilla units . . . to blow up bridges and roads, damage telephone and telegraph lines, set fire to forests, stores, transports." He further declared that "In the occupied regions, conditions must be made unbearable for the enemy and all his accomplices. They must be hounded and annihilated at every step and all their measures frustrated."

It was a powerful appeal for action, heard by millions of east Europeans and Russians, including Soviet prisoners of war and officials of the Communist Party caught in occupied territory. In Kiev, Stalin's radio address prompted Nikita Khrushchev, then the first secretary of the Communist Party in the Ukraine, to enlist Aleksei Fyodorov, a local Party official, to begin preparations for an underground partisan movement. There was, Khrushchev told Fyodorov, no time to lose.

The Soviet leader's message of resistance and sabotage also inspired many young Jewish boys, such as fifteen-year-old Yitzhak Arad and his friends Moshe Shutan and Yeshike Gerten, who were then under Nazi attack in the Lithuanian town of Swieciany. Shutan and Gerten had hidden a radio in the attic of Moshe's house. That July evening, the three teenage boys, covered in blankets to mask the sound, listened intently to Stalin's words. "In the darkness, under the blanket, I could not see

Yeshike," Yitzhak Arad remembered, "but I felt his body tremble close to mine. This broadcast inflamed our imaginations and set us thinking. For the first time in this war I heard of 'partisan warfare' as a call to immediate action."

With Stalin's appeal, there emerged within Arad and his friends, as well as many other Jewish men and women, a strong desire to retaliate against their oppressors. The only question was *how*. For Soviet soldiers either interned or in hiding, and particularly for young, idealistic, and courageous Jews in the ghettos, translating Stalin's words into action was not easy.

Soviet officials meeting in Moscow two weeks after Stalin's broadcast recognized immediately that a successful partisan operation was dependent on centralized control, loyalty, discipline, effective leadership, and access to weapons, ammunition, and explosives. It would take more than a year of intense planning before all of these various factors were addressed.

More than 3 million Red Army soldiers had been captured by the Germans during the first six months of the war. Imprisoned in concentration camps, starved, and forced to live under the most deplorable of conditions, hundreds of thousands died; others escaped when it was possible. A German report of February 19, 1942, indicated that by that date, 4 million Soviet soldiers had been taken prisoner and close to 3 million had died. Some were lucky enough (or so it seemed then) to be released by the Germans. These included Jews, who were told to return to their homes, and Ukrainians, who were regarded by the Nazis as being anti-Soviet.

Other Red Army soldiers either blended in with the local population or hid in the nearby forests in such regions as Belorussia and Bryansk. (Only about one-third of the eastern territory occupied by the Germans was capable of sustaining partisan warfare. In the Ukraine, for example, only the northern part, with its large forests, was suitable.) They joined thousands of their comrades: Red Army "stragglers" who had avoided capture, Communist Party loyalists, members of the NKVD (or People's Commissariat of Internal Affairs), and in some cases, actual military units that had been separated from their brigades but had remained hidden and intact. By the end of 1941, the evidence suggests that there were about 30,000 Soviet partisans living in and fighting from the forests in Bryansk in the east to the region near Brest-Litovsk in the west, a number that increased to more than 150,000 by the summer of 1942.

Initially cut off from the Soviet command in Moscow, these men, hungry and often without weapons, were less concerned with restoring the tarnished glory of the mother country and more interested in basic survival. What local peasants would not give them, they took by force — behaviour that did not endear them to the region's agrarian population. And they were not interested in risking their lives to save Jews, nor to help those who managed to escape to the forests. More often than not, they shot strangers, and rape and murder were not beneath some of them.

It would be wrong to conclude that all Soviet partisans were anti-Semitic. But considering the tenuous position of the Jew in Russian society from the time of the czars — a history of oppression, restrictions, and pogroms — negative feelings against Jews existed among officers and the lower ranks and, as will be seen, were a fact of partisan life that Jews in the forests had to deal with.

Jews made up less than 2 percent of the Red Army, and most Jewish soldiers felt it necessary to hide their identity from their comrades. According to many of them, the common view among the rank and file was that Jews evaded military duty, had too much power, were active in the NKVD, and most important, were cowards. "Jews shoot with crooked guns," a popular saying among Soviet soldiers went, "so that they can hide behind walls."

Despite Stalin's order to engage the enemy, these first Soviet partisans confronted the Germans only if it was absolutely necessary. Indeed, the term *partisan* hardly suited many of them. The Nazis called them "stragglers" and "bandits." "Bands of marauders," to use Yitzhak Arad's phrase, would be more accurate. They were an undisciplined and uneducated bunch, mostly low-ranking Soviet soldiers who, by the coincidences of war, found themselves at the vanguard of what would become one of the greatest guerrilla operations in modern history.

Yet the effectiveness of these early groups rested on individual feelings about patriotic duty and ties to the Communist Party. With its vast forests, Belorussia was, from the beginning of the conflict, the area of the Soviet Union most adequate for partisan activities. The German army swept through western Belorussia in a matter of weeks. But by mid-July 1941, Communist Party officials had already organized a few detachments, and Nazi reports mention some minor trouble with "partisans" and mined roads as early as July 20. That September, a small group of parachutists — including David Keymakh, a Jewish political commissar who later was involved in plotting the assassination of Wilhelm Kube, the Nazi governor of Belorussia — led by Comdr. Grigorii Linkov were dropped into the area with the goal of organizing local opposition. This proved difficult. The peasant population, whose lives had been turned upside down by the war, were hardly interested in assisting the Soviets while the Germans were clearly winning on the battlefields. Moreover, these simple Belorussian farmers had already witnessed for themselves how the Nazis punished those who challenged their authority.

Prior to Linkov's arrival in the village of Lukoml, north of Minsk, a German officer, who'd been seriously wounded by a knife stuck in his neck, was brought by wagon into the town. Just before he died, he whispered, "A *Jude* killed me." That was enough reason for the Nazi commander in the area to gather together 150 Jewish families — men, women, and children — and execute them on the spot. It was also enough of a warning that resistance of any kind was an extremely dangerous undertaking that was better avoided. Hostility towards the Soviets further increased each time a group raided a farm for food or destroyed a village in a confrontation with the Nazis. Within time, when the peasants were forced to choose between the Germans and the Soviets, they chose the latter only because they were the "lesser evil."

The reorganization of the Soviet partisan system occurred during the winter of 1941–42. By early October 1941, the German forces had reached the outskirts of Moscow; it was the closest they ever got. Two months later, the Soviet counter-offensive began and slowly pushed the Nazis back west. Red Army victories west of Moscow, near Velizh, boded well for the future of Soviet partisans, as did the establishment of the "Vitebsk Corridor." This narrow route, protected by the Soviets for the next year, allowed men and supplies to get through to join partisans well behind the German front lines.

Beyond the shift in Soviet military fortunes, the other significant development was the organization in Moscow of the Central Staff for Partisan Warfare at the end of May 1942. This was a joint operation between the Red Army, represented by the Soviet minister of Defence, Marshal Klimentii Voroshilov, and Pateleymon Ponomarenko, the first secretary of the Belorussian Communist Party and a confidant of Stalin, who was appointed chief of staff. From this point on, partisan activities were co-ordinated and stabilized. Airdrops of supplies, weapons, communication equipment, and specially trained commandos greatly strengthened the movement. Within a few months, strict discipline and party loyalty among the partisan detachments, or *otriady*, were enforced by brigade commanders and political commissars. (A Soviet partisan brigade could have as few as 300 fighters and as many as 2,000. Each usually consisted of four or five detachments, each ranging from 50 to 200 partisans.) Sabotage operations and other rear actions started to make a dent in the Nazis' armour. Soon large bands of Soviet partisans were a force to be reckoned with throughout Belorussia, and in parts of Lithuania, the Ukraine, and the *Generalgouvernement*. As Hitler was forced to concede on August 8, 1942, "The [partisan] bands in the East have become an unbearable menace during the last few months and are seriously threatening supply lines to the front."

Farther west, across the Bug River in the *Generalgouvernement*, Soviet partisans found willing allies in a small contingent of Polish Communists, who in January 1942 established the Gwardia Ludowa, or GL, (two years later, the GL was renamed the Armia Ludowa, or AL). Unlike the Armia Krajowa (AK, or Home Army), the far more popular underground movement linked to the Polish government-in-exile headquartered in London, the GL wanted to immediately engage the Germans in battle. They were also prepared to work together with Soviets and Jews to accomplish their chief objective of ridding Poland of the Nazi occupiers. But the GL's numbers remained small during 1942, around 1,500 men, and as a result its effectiveness as a partisan operation was limited.

The AK, on the other hand, born in December 1939 as the Zwiazek Walki Zbrojnej (Union for Armed Struggle) and reorganized in February 1942 under the command of Stefan Rowecki, was virulently anti-Communist and argued that real resistance could not begin until the population was adequately prepared and the enemy sufficiently weakened. "Active warfare against the Nazis can take place in our country only when the German people will be broken by military defeats, hunger, and propaganda," General Rowecki wrote in a dispatch to London in early February 1941. "Any attempt by us to take action while the German army is at full strength ... will be drowned in a terrible bloodshed." A general Polish uprising did not occur until 1944, though the AK carried out extensive sabotage operations in late 1942 and throughout 1943.

While the prime minister of the government-in-exile, Gen. Wladyslaw Sikorski, did much to publicize among the Allies the tragic fate of Polish Jews at the hands of the Nazis, the relationship between the AK, Jewish escapees from the ghettos, and partisans back in Poland was complex and not easily defined.* Its official policy towards Jews, who were generally regarded by the organization's leaders and partisans alike as Communists and an unassimilated minority, was, as will be demonstrated, more admirable than its actual treatment of Jews in the forests of eastern Poland. Moreover, its alliance with the right-wing and anti-Semitic underground group Narodowe Sily Zbrojne (NSZ, or National Armed Forces, established in September 1942) complicated matters further.

---

*In 1942, General Sikorski visited Washington twice to advise the Americans about German atrocities and convened a major meeting in London to discuss the fate of Jews. Later that year, news about Jews being gassed at the Chelmno concentration camp was made public by the London office of the government-in-exile. It also published a more comprehensive report of the atrocities sent to it by representatives of the Jewish socialist Bund. As American historian Richard Lukas points out, "The Polish government-in-exile was the first official body to propose Allied bombing of railroad lines leading to and including the German death camps." But as is now well known, British and American military and political leaders were sceptical of the reports they read about Auschwitz and other death camps and did not consider bombing them (or the rail lines leading to them) a military priority. (See Lukas, *The Forgotten Holocaust*, 166–67, and Laqueur, *The Terrible Secret*, 111.)

IN THE GHETTO

Fear, despair, starvation, and isolation. These were only a few of the more prominent characteristics that defined life in the ghettos of eastern Europe. Jacob Greenstein, who survived the war fighting as a partisan in a Soviet unit, could well have been describing every ghetto in Europe when he remembered that the ghetto in Minsk "was a death camp. Hunger, cold, blood every day."

Few Jews knew anything of the intricate details and strategic planning of the Soviet and Polish partisan movements. To them, rumours of fighters in the forests were like a tree branch to a drowning man. Stories of Soviet soldiers resisting Nazis and surviving were the lifeline they needed.

"We were desperate," recalled Ester Marchwinska of her time in the Belorussian ghetto in the town of Mir. "We were like someone who is about to drown and tries to cling to anything that promises life. The idea of joining the partisans gave us hope. In reality, we had no contacts. None whatsoever. What we heard came from peasants who would tell us that there were partisans. We Jews exaggerated their presence and their power. We know now that at the time, in 1942, their numbers were insignificant. For us, however, the dream was important and not the reality. This dream told some of us that our salvation depended on the partisans."

■ ■

In quick order, the Einsatzgruppen and their many helpers had murdered and disposed of more than 700,000 Jews in the massive area formerly under Soviet control. This included the death of about 10,000 Jews in the liquidation of Vilna Ghetto No. 2, which occurred between September 15 and October 21, 1941, in three separate *Aktionen*.

By the New Year, following the initial wave of terror, about 600,000 Jews were still alive, trapped in ghetto prisons. Some, as noted, had evaded capture by hiding in *malines*, others because they possessed skills that could serve the Third Reich. In Vilna and other ghettos, the *schein*, or work permit, as historian Lucy Dawidowicz put it, "became the sole guarantee of security, the admission ticket to life."

But such security was fleeting. As the Nazis continued to reduce the size of the ghetto populations, more and more Jews became expendable. In Vilna, for instance, at the end of October 1941, new yellow work permits were issued with an expiry date of March 31, 1942. German officials responsible for forced labour distributed the majority of the cards (3,000 in total) to the ghetto's workers, but 400 were given to the Judenrat to be allocated as its members saw fit. Demand for the permits well exceeded supply — "as precious as a yellow permit" became a common Yiddish colloquialism in Vilna — and the members of the ghetto's Jewish council were placed in the unenviable position of deciding who should live and who should die.

"Fate suddenly split the people of the ghetto into two parts," recorded young Yitzhok Rudashevski in his diary. "One part possesses the yellow certificate. They believe in the power of this little piece of paper. It bestows the right to life. The second part — lost, despairing people — people who sense their doom, and do not know where to go."

Jacob Gens, commander of Vilna's Jewish ghetto police and later the controversial head of the Judenrat, appealed to German officials for additional permits, but they refused his request. By all accounts, however, he did attempt to save as many Jews as he could. In the end, the "Yellow Schein Aktion " and subsequent *Aktionen* during November and December 1941 resulted in the murder of more than 5,500 people. This left approximately 20,000 — at least 7,500 without the proper passes — inside the Vilna ghetto. (Yitzhak Arad estimates that another 3,500 fled to nearby cities and towns or were hiding in other parts of Vilna.)

For a brief period during the early winter of 1942, the *Aktionen* and killings slowed down in eastern regions and the Baltic states, as the Nazis reassessed their labour needs. Meanwhile, on January 20 at a villa in Wannsee, Berlin, Reinhard Heydrich (head of the RSHA), Adolf Eichmann (his associate and recognized "Jewish expert"), and other members of the Nazi high command met to discuss their strategy for "the final solution to the Jewish problem." Heydrich's master plan (presumably ordered by Hitler) called for the eventual elimination of 11 million Jews in Europe and Britain. As Eichmann later testified at his trial in Jerusalem, "These gentlemen [in attendance] were standing together, or sitting together, and were discussing the subject quite bluntly, quite differently from the language that I had to use later in the record. During the conversation, they minced no words about it at all. . . . They spoke about methods of killing, about liquidation, about extermination."*

Gas vans were already in use at the concentration camp in Chelmno, 70 kilometres from Lodz, and experiments with Zyklon B gas pellets were being conducted at the then prison camp beside the Polish town of Oswiecim. The Germans called it Auschwitz.

As deportations and liquidations of western Polish ghettos continued, *Aktionen* resumed in the east in time for the Purim celebrations of March 1942. Since the war began, the Nazis took a special delight in carrying out their massacres on Jewish holidays. In the large ghetto at Minsk, about 25,000 of the 100,000 or so Jews had been murdered by early 1942. Now the Nazis used Purim, a holiday that commemorates the victory over the anti-Semite Haman in Persia during the reign of King Ahasuerus, to inflict more pain and death.

The Jews of Minsk hoped that their Nazi tormentors would suffer the same fate as Haman, but this time there was to be no miracle. "We did not know then," writes Hersh Smolar, a leader of the Minsk underground who survived the war as a partisan, "that the [SS] had deliberately chosen Purim for their massacre in order to show the Jews that they had nothing left to hope for." The killing started at about ten o'clock in the morning on March 2, and within one hour, Jacob Greenstein later recalled, "the streets and houses wherever you threw a glance were filled with dead people, men, women, and children." That day, Greenstein and his wife, Bela, watched as their baby was murdered when Nazi police started shooting into a crowd.

The mass murder of more than 5,000 Jews in Minsk also included a group of young children from the Shpalerna Street orphanage who were

---

*After researching documents discovered in previously secret Soviet archives, German historian Christian Gerlach has concluded that there is evidence that Hitler decided as early as December 12, 1941, that all European Jews must die. The real purpose of the Wannsee conference, he suggests, was to determine the fate of German Jews in particular. (See "Historian finds 'proof' that Hitler ordered Holocaust," *Globe and Mail*, January 22, 1998).

buried alive in deep sand pits. Wilhelm Kube, an SS officer, threw them candy while they cried in terror. (According to Smolar, Adolf Eichmann was in the car with Kube.) The story was similar in many other ghettos during the spring of 1942, as a new wave of terror struck such Jewish communities as Baranowicze, Skala, Radun, Dvinsk, and Lida — to name only a few.

■ ■

Life in the ghettos was extremely difficult, a daily regimen of forced labour, starvation, arbitrary punishments, death for minor transgressions, public executions, disease, and unsanitary conditions. And degradation, always degradation.

With the help of a young German soldier, who she paid with her wedding ring, Liza Ettinger was able to escape from the Vilna ghetto and return to her family in the Lida ghetto in the fall of 1941. She later remembered one Sunday in the winter of 1942, when the Jews in Lida were ordered to clean the streets of snow. "It was a hair-raising sight — thousands of men, women, and children at work clearing the snow in a bitter cold while the [military] governor of the town and his retinue gallop along on their horses the length of the road lashing the workers on both sides of the road, their laughter echoing through the air. They rode back and forth until they tired. Towards evening the people were freed and sent back to the deserted ghetto both hurt and degraded."

Almost always located in old parts of cities or towns, the typical eastern European ghetto consisted of several narrow streets with rows of wooden houses in an area surrounded by barbed wire or a wall. Thousands of Jewish families tried to survive in an area where only hundreds had once lived. The conditions were abysmal. "The congestion is unbearable," wrote seventeen-year-old Sara Fishkin about life in the Wolozyn ghetto, south-east of Vilna. "In each apartment, shelves are put up for sitting and sleeping. Bundles lie in each corner. Hungry children cry for bread. Jewish homes behind the ghetto stand forsaken and empty. In the ghetto Jews walk around depressed. They do not laugh and they do not smile."

Rochelle Sutin has similar memories about the ghetto in Stolpce.

"You had only as much space as you needed to sleep. . . . There was no place to bathe, so you couldn't keep clean. At night you couldn't sleep well, no matter how tired you were, because the mattresses were filled with bedbugs that sucked the blood out of you. When you woke up in the morning, your sheets were red with blood from the bugs you had squashed while rolling over in your sleep. During the day, the lice took the bedbugs' place. They were in our hair, in every crevice of our bodies. We itched, we had rashes that were as red and thick as welts."

In Vilna, according to Yitzhak Arad, "the congested conditions were indescribable. The sewers, the water supply, toilets, and showers were not meant for so many people. The drains clogged and were severely damaged and became a source of pollution. Pipes burst in many houses, leading to water shortages; garbage piled up in the courtyards. These sanitary defects, along with the shortages of food, clothing, and firewood, the damp and mouldiness in the rooms, the bugs and lice, created ideal conditions for disease and epidemics."

Most ghettos had hospitals, but they were understaffed and short of supplies. The most common ghetto epidemic was typhus, spread by infected lice (also prevalent were typhoid fever, dysentery, infectious hepatitis, and scarlet fever). But having a disease made one incapable of work and was therefore a death sentence. Hence, ghetto residents often hid their ailments as long as was possible. In Kovno an underground hospital operated undetected by the Nazis. In Vilna a secret gynecology ward was created, since, by an order of February 1942, Jews were not permitted to have children. Nevertheless, babies were born and hidden with their mothers in a *maline* inside the hospital.

Part of the German master plan was to starve the Jews out of existence, so hunger was constant. Each day, the search for food stretched from the moment the sun rose until it set. "A slice of bread was everything," remembered Lisa Derman about her time in the ghetto in Slonim. In the Lida ghetto, bread rations were distributed early each morning. Young Gitel Zelkowicz would rise at dawn and race to line up at five in the morning. One day, several Nazi soldiers amused themselves by randomly shooting those Jews in line. Gitel quickly ran away and saved herself by jumping into an open toilet pit. After this incident, her mother, Leska, would not permit her to go for food.

The official food ration distributed by Nazi administrators was about 40 to 60 percent of the normal calories necessary for human survival. In Vilna, for instance, a Jew was given approximately 650 grams of bread each week, enough for one loaf, and small amounts of sugar and flour. Whatever meat there was to eat was usually smuggled into the ghetto illegally — a dangerous undertaking.* Often the smuggling was done by young children, who were able to squeeze through holes in ghetto fences and walls and trade with locals on the black market. In most ghettos, searches were conducted each time a Jew exited or entered. This was often done by Jewish members of the ghetto police under the watchful eye of the Nazis. Jews caught smuggling were almost always beaten (sometimes by the Jewish police), but more often shot on the spot by Nazis or local collaborators.

In Piotrkow, in central Poland, nine-year-old Hanka Ziegler and her fourteen-year-old brother, Zigmund, successfully snuck out of the ghetto on numerous occasions and were always able to return with potatoes and bread. But one day in October 1942, while they were scavenging for food, the ghetto was sealed and surrounded by troops and police preparing themselves for the final *Aktion*. "We were two children, freezing cold, begging potatoes. We came to the ghetto and they wouldn't let us in," Hanka later remembered. "A German soldier at the barrier shouted at us, 'What are you doing, you children? Go home. Tonight we are sending the Jews out of here.' He thought we were non-Jewish children going in to get money from the Jews. We had a sack of potatoes and some flour. We were both very blond children. We spoke good Polish. I was crying. I knew my mother was hungry. We walked away from the ghetto." Hanka and her brother never saw their family again. After months of wandering, begging, and hiding, they were taken in by a Polish woman who later sold them to farmers. They were forced to work as slave labourers for two more years.

---

*Nearly all of the meat available in the ghettos was not kosher. Horse meat was most common. As Lucy Dawidowicz has explained, even with the rabbi's permission, "for most observant Jews the suspension of *kashrut* [kosher rules and rituals] was no easy accommodation. A sense of guilt and self-denigration pursued those who yielded to the demands of their hunger." (See Dawidowicz, *War against the Jews*, 338.)

The lack of food had both physical and psychological side effects. Hunger not only weakened the ability of ghetto Jews to work and function, it also, over time, impaired their power to think. And yet, against tremendous odds, they persevered. The ghetto experience, however, did take its toll. As Pessia Bairach, of Zoludek, a town near Lida, later explained, "The dread of disaster which depressed most people usually contributed to make them more tolerant, less possessive, and willing to make concessions. They were satisfied with very little, willing to share their meagre possessions with the others. Since what value could have those trivialities compared to the dangers that we were constantly exposed to? But on the other hand, fights would start out of nothing and that was the result of the never-ending tension, [nervousness,] and of the disequilibrium of the emotional balance."

On one level, Jews attempted to make the best of a horrific situation. Even after the various *Aktionen* that took mothers, siblings, and children, those still alive either failed to understand or refused to accept that life in the ghetto was not intended by the Germans to be permanent. Yet how else could these Jews have continued living? So they tried, as difficult as it was, to normalize things. They overlooked the dead bodies in the street and the daily brutalities that they were forced to endure.

Despite the ban on all Jewish rituals and celebrations, they defied the Nazi edicts in any way they could. Sonia Ostrinsky, for example, remembers her father attending synagogue services every day in the small Belorussian ghetto in Sharkovshchina, north of Glebokie. And in the Baranowicze ghetto, says Irving F., "you didn't have to look too far for a *minyan*." Before they were transported to the Bialystok ghetto and eventually to Auschwitz, the Jews in the town of Goworowa performed the melodic Kol Nidre service on the eve of Yom Kippur in October 1940. "Heavy drapes were drawn across the window," recalled Chava Burstyn-Berenstein, whose father was the town's rabbi, "and the Sefer Torah, which had been saved from the fires and which had thus eluded the hands of the Germans, was placed on the table. Because there was no cantor, my father recited Kol Nidre himself. In a choking voice he started the prayer, his eyes moist, his face radiating an inner nobility. . . . Suddenly, before we had a chance to react, a military vehicle pulled up in front of the house and a number of SS men jumped out. They had a movie camera, and amidst riotous shouting, they began filming the trembling Jews in the household, who had been caught in the act of praying. After they left, we had no more strength for tears, for we knew our time was limited."

As late as June 1943, Willy Moll, whose parents had been murdered in an earlier *Aktion*, celebrated his bar mitzvah in the Lida ghetto. His uncle taught him the portion of the Torah he was to read, and his aunt prepared whatever food she could find. He remembers wearing a prayer shawl and reading from one of the few Torahs that had been hidden and preserved. There was no rabbi, remembers Moll, because the rabbi of his family's synagogue had been killed in the large *Aktion* of May 8, 1942, when 6,000 Jews were massacred. But in front of a small group of relatives and friends, Willy Moll took an important step towards adulthood.

Education was also forbidden, but secret schools operated in Vilna and Kovno, as they did in Warsaw, Lublin, and Lodz. For Yitzhok Rudashevski, this was an important part of each day. "I think to myself: what would be the case if we did not go to school, to the club, did not read books," he wrote in his diary on October 17, 1942. "We would die of dejection inside the ghetto walls." Five months later, he added, "I often reflect, this is supposedly the ghetto yet I have such a rich life of intellectual work: I study, I read, I visit club circles. Time runs so quickly and there is so much work to be done. . . . I often forget that I am in a ghetto."

The thirst for literature and culture could also not be quenched. An orchestra performed at least once a week in the Kovno ghetto, and in Vilna there were book exhibits and theatre performances. But these were not without dispute. Members of the Socialist Bund disapproved of plans for the dramatic productions and posted Yiddish signs throughout the ghetto that read: *Oyf a besoylem shpilt men nit keyn teater* (In a cemetery no theatre ought to be performed). Later, after the war, the director of the Ghetto Theatre, Israel Segal, in testimony at the Nuremberg trials and in a Yiddish journal article, blamed both the Germans and the head of the Judenrat, Jacob Gens, whom he claimed forced him to put on the productions. According to Solon Beinfeld, however, Segal was probably more in favour of the theatre than he admitted.

In any event, the first performance in Vilna took place on January 18, 1942, in a former school auditorium. Jewish poetry was read and a dramatization of a short story by Austrian playwright and novelist Stefan Zweig was presented. By all accounts, the evening was a great success. "People laughed and cried," wrote Dr. Lazar Epstein in his diary. "They cast off the depression that had been weighing on their spirits. The alienation that had hitherto existed among the ghetto population seemed to have been thrown off. . . . people awoke from a long difficult dream."

Jewish libraries were as busy as ever. Even after all of the destruction and pillaging, the Vilna Jewish library's large historic collection, known as the Mefitsei haskalah, still had more than two-thirds of its 45,000 books available for loan. And they were popular. Herman Kruk, head librarian in Vilna, reported in October 1941, at the time of the Yom Kippur *Aktion* that killed thousands, "October 1, 1941 — Yom Kippur, some 3,000 Jews taken away. And on the morrow, 390 books changed hands."

Such activities generally had the full support of the various Judenrate, who wanted to maintain a calm daily routine. Believing, wrongly as it turned out, that they could bargain for Jewish lives with the Nazis, many Judenrat members reinforced the message that if the Jews obeyed the rules, worked hard, and served the German war effort, they would survive. In most cases, talk about resistance and escape was strongly discouraged.

Ralph F., then age twelve, was present at a meeting of the Kobylnik Judenrat held in late 1941 when a heated discussion took place about the amount of gold the Nazis had ordered the Jews to deliver to them. Young Ralph spoke up and suggested that instead of handing over the gold, they should attack the dozen or so policemen guarding the ghetto, disarm them, and run into the forest. Without saying a word, the chairman of the council smashed Ralph's nose, then yelled at him in Yiddish to "never come out with such a comment again" or he would kill him. Ralph left the meeting with his nose bleeding.

For a brief time, in such ghettos as Bialystok, this positive though misguided approach seem to work. Located in north-eastern Poland, Bialystok was an important German supply centre during the occupation and many of the ghetto's 50,000 to 60,000 Jews were kept alive to labour in a variety of the city's factories. For more than two years, Ephraim Barash, the head of the Judenrat, supported an expansion of the ghetto's industrial output and stubbornly insisted on negotiating with the Nazis. "I would like to declare that we have one sole objective," he announced in March 1942, "to preserve ourselves until the war is over." This was to be achieved, Barash explained, by:

a. 100 percent compliance with orders;
b. proving useful — this will provide those who champion us [the Germans] with material that can be used to our advantage;
c. conduct that will satisfy the German authorities in the manner in which Jews behave in their Diaspora lives.

Despite Barash's limited success in bargaining with Nazis over gold and money deliveries, relocations, and transports, his strategy ultimately failed. Deportations of Bialystok's Jews to the death camps at Treblinka and Majdanek began in November 1942 and continued until the ghetto was liquidated in August 1943. (Barash and his wife were deported to Majdanek and killed there.)

From the perspective of the Nazis, Barash's noble but futile efforts kept the majority of Jews outwardly co-operative. But the ghetto was, in fact, a place of many moods and competing emotions. Stress was constant and the hardship brought out the best and the worst among its incarcerated inhabitants.*

---

*Remarkably, some Jews in the ghettos did not lose their senses of humour. According to the diary of Herman Kruk, from Vilna, common jokes from the late winter of 1943 — following the Soviet victory at Stalingrad on February 2 — included: "A German approaches a Jew and asks him for a loan of twenty rubles. The Jew opens his wallet and hands him the requested sum. The German is surprised: 'Why, you don't know me at all and trust me?'

'I have the fullest measure of confidence in the Germans,' says the Jew. 'They had taken Stalingrad and gave it back. They had taken Kharkov and gave it back. I am therefore sure that you will give me back my twenty rubles.'"

Or, "What is the difference between the Germans and the sun? The sun rises in the East and goes down in the West. The Germans rose in the West and go down in the East." (See Kruk, "Diary of the Vilna Ghetto," in *YIVO Annual of Jewish Social Science*, 13 (1965), 51–52.)

As more relatives and friends vanished, Jews began to live each day as if it was their last. Leon Kahn recalls that by early 1942, Jews in Radun took turns watching the street, day and night, for any trouble. "The smallest change in the ghetto's routine was passed from house to house," he writes, "with everyone trying to interpret the change and decide whether danger had increased."

Some, too, were more willing than others to take risks and to exercise a subtle form of resistance. An act of defiance could be as minor as not wearing an armband and violating curfew to smuggling food and hiding in a *maline* during an *Aktion* or labour round-up. There was, however, no question about the intent. "Lacking weapons and military organization, [Jews in the ghettos] learned to use tricks of intelligence and manipulation to prevail against their persecutors," observed Lucy Dawidowicz. "They learned not only to invent, but to circumvent; not only to obey, but to evade; not only to submit, but to outwit. Their tradition of defiance was devious rather than direct, employing nerve instead of force."

Even young children faced with imminent danger displayed resourcefulness and shrewdness beyond their years. Each day in the Lida ghetto, eleven-year-old Gitel Zelkowicz would be left alone to care for her younger brother, Simon, when her parents and her older brother, Yossel, went off to work. Often the Nazis would use this opportunity to clear the ghetto of children, the elderly, and the sick. But each time Gitel heard trouble in the streets, she would run with Simon into the fields behind their house. She was also astute enough to put a dress on her four-year-old brother. With her blonde hair and fluency in Polish, she reasoned that in the event that they were caught, she might be able to pass herself as a Pole and Simon as a young Polish girl. "I didn't want anyone looking under Simon's clothes to see if he was a Jewish boy," she recalls.

One day, an *Aktion* began before she had a chance to run. She grabbed Simon and together they hid in a small dark greasy hole at the bottom of the large clay oven used to keep chickens. There they remained for the next twelve hours. Even when she heard her parents' voices, Gitel stayed put. Finally, around midnight, she and Simon crawled out of their hiding place. She found her mother, Leska, crying in a corner, believing that her two children were dead.

"Why didn't you come out when I called?" Leska asked her.

"I thought that the Germans might be making you call for your children," responded Gitel. "I thought it was a trick."

As the *Aktionen* in the eastern ghettos resumed with a vengeance in mid-1942 and 1943, the options open to Jews for survival became fewer and fewer. For older children and young adults imbued with the spirit of Zionism, Socialism, or Communism, an uprising was one choice, escape to the forest another. Neither route seemed likely to succeed. Moreover, Judenrat officials often condemned both options as reckless and dangerous. And indeed, the Nazis showed no mercy to either ghetto escapees or resisters who were apprehended. In the end, none of this mattered. Some Jews simply refused to go like sheep to the slaughter.

JUDENRATE

Much like a Nazi commander, Jacob Gens, then head of the Jewish police in the Vilna ghetto, stood directing the long line of people. With a wave of his cane, some went to the right, others to the left. Children separated from their parents cried; women who were forced to abandon their elderly parents wept. "Gens is a Jewish murderer. Gens is a traitor," someone said. The words quickly flowed from one person to the next and down the long line.

A family of five came before him, a mother, a father, and their three children. They patiently awaited his decision. In a matter of seconds, Gens decided to reward the man with a life-sustaining work permit. But there was a problem. According to Nazi regulations, those receiving a yellow *schein* were allowed to keep with them a spouse and no more than two children. Without hesitation, Gens sent the man, his wife, and two of their children to the side reserved for the labourers. The couple's third child, a boy of twelve, was pushed to the other side, the side for the dead. The mother cried in agony as her son was led away.

Behind them another family of three made their way before the tall and imposing police chief. Gens stared at them and began to count.

"One, the father; two, the mother; three, the child! You scoundrel," he yelled at the father, "where have you left your second child?"

"I have no other child," said the bewildered man.

Without warning, Gens struck the man with his cane and then reached for the young boy belonging to the first family. He pushed him towards the man, declaring in a loud voice: "Here, scoundrel. Here is your second son. Next time don't abandon him, you fool!"

Immediately, these few tense moments were relayed from person to person throughout the crowd. "Gens saved the boy's life," they whispered to each other. "Gens is a Jew after all. Two souls struggle within him. Gens is a riddle."

Jacob Gens was indeed a riddle. He was equally a tragic and controversial figure of that most tragic and controversial of all ghetto institutions, the Judenrat. We will never know for certain what drove him, or if he genuinely believed that he could make a difference. What is certain, however, is that in his efforts to save the lives of Vilna's Jews, he became a pawn who was ultimately manipulated by the Nazis for their own evil purposes.

Gens was born in 1905 in the small Lithuanian village of Illovieciai. When he was fourteen years old, he joined the Lithuanian army and served until 1924. Later, he attended university in Kovno, where he studied law and economics. By 1927, Gens had a government job as an accountant with the ministry of Justice. He married a Lithuanian woman and together they had a daughter. But Gens maintained his link with the Jewish community through his involvement with the right-wing Revisionist Zionism movement led by Vladimir Jabotinsky.

Following the occupation of Kovno by the Soviets in July 1940, Gens was dismissed from his government position. Fearing that his political views would lead to his arrest, he fled with his family to Vilna, where an acquaintance got him work as an accountant with the city health department.

A year later, after the Nazi invasion, Gens, through his Lithuanian connections, was made director of the Jewish hospital. There he met Anatol Fried, the first chairman of the Vilna Judenrat. Once the Vilna ghetto was created, in early September 1941, Fried appointed Gens head of the ghetto Jewish police force. Gens's wife and daughter did not join him in the ghetto, and he could have hidden with Lithuanian friends.

But he believed that as a Jew, he had an obligation to serve the community. "This is the first time in my life that I have to engage in such duties," he explained to his wife in a letter written from the ghetto. "My heart is broken. But I shall always do what is necessary for the sake of the Jews in the ghetto."

As head of the police, Gens became a power unto himself. The Nazis cleverly made ghetto police forces (in Vilna and Kovno, the ghetto police numbered about 200 men; in Warsaw, the figure was as high as 2,000) responsible for much of their dirty work. Jewish policemen, usually armed with wooden truncheons, carried out inspections at the gate, collected booty for the Nazis, and eventually helped in rounding up Jews for selektionen — as Gens did during the Yellow Schein Aktion of November 1941. In some ghettos, like Kovno, Jewish policemen assisted underground movements, but in most they were despised.

Yitzhok Rudashevski wrote that each time he saw the ghetto policemen in Vilna wearing their official dark blue hats adorned with a golden star of David, "an unpleasant feeling" came over him. "I hate them from the bottom of my heart, ghetto Jews in uniforms, and how arrogantly they stride in the boots they have plundered," he noted in his diary in mid-October 1942. "Everyone feels the same way about them and they have somehow become such strangers to the ghetto. In me they arouse a feeling compounded of ridicule, disgust and fear."

Dissatisfied with the Vilna Judenrat, the Nazis reorganized it in July 1942 and appointed Gens its new chairman. To the Jews of Vilna, Gens was known as the "Commandant" and "*der stolzer Jude*" — the proud Jew who could deal directly with the Nazis. So fragile and volatile was life in the ghetto that Gens's moods and facial expressions were widely and variously interpreted. "He is smiling," they would say, "therefore all is well." Or, "Gens is depressed. A bad sign. Danger awaits the ghetto." Regardless of the death, destruction, and brutality around them, the majority of Vilna's surviving Jews wanted to believe, indeed they needed to believe, that Jacob Gens would somehow save them.

Gens accepted the role bestowed on him, as he did his elevated status. He enjoyed the attention, adulation, and power. In return, he attempted to introduce a degree of normalcy into ghetto life, as impossible as that was. Gens supported all cultural activities — at performances of the Vilna theatre, Gens and his Judenrat executive naturally obtained the best seats — and education for children, and tried to negotiate with the Germans for additional food and fuel.

Like several other controversial Judenrat chairmen, including Ephraim Barash in Bialystok, Chaim Rumkowski in Lodz, and Moshe Merin of Sosnowiec in south-west Poland, Gens believed that he could save Jews by making them into workers and an essential part of the Nazi war machine. Jewish survival, in Gens's view, was dependent on obeying the rules and demonstrating to the Germans that Jews were "useful" to them. For this reason, he was wary of Jews who hid in *malines*, disapproved of attempted escapes from the ghettos, and strongly opposed any form of resistance. Within time, these firm convictions pitted him against the young Zionists and Communists who were determined to challenge the Nazis in any way open to them. But events demonstrated to him and other Vilna Jews that his cautious and pragmatic attitude towards escape and resistance was justified.

A group of young resisters, for example, left the Vilna ghetto at dawn on July 24, 1943. They were led by Josef Glazman, the serious thirty-year-old former head of the Betar Zionist movement and one of the founders of the Vilna underground. Glazman's group already had an invitation to join a Soviet and Lithuanian partisan unit in the Narocz Forest, some 150 kilometres to the east of the city. Posing as labourers on a wood-chopping team, they marched out of the ghetto with their weapons hidden in their coats. Gens knew of their plans and had reluctantly agreed to allow them to leave. When Glazman and his men reached the nearby labour camp at Novy Vileyka, they were joined by another fourteen Jewish men.

Trouble began two days later on a bridge over the Vileyka River, close to the village of Laboriszki. Earlier, one of the men had snuck into Laboriszki to find some food, but he was seen by local peasants, who notified the Nazi police. The police quickly set up an ambush and attacked the Jewish fighters near the bridge. In the ensuing battle, nine men were killed; the others managed to reached the forest and the Soviet partisans a short time later.

Back in Vilna, their escape had tragic consequences. The Gestapo chief in the city, Rolf Neugebauer, ordered the arrest of thirty-two Jews identified as family members, relatives, or friends of those who had escaped. They were taken to the Ponary and murdered. New and more restrictive rules were also introduced for work details leaving the ghetto. The labour camp at Novy Vileyka was closed down and another forty-eight Jews who had been associated with the fourteen escapees were killed as well.

Devastated by what had transpired, Gens thereafter more stringently opposed any attempts to escape. He explained his position — a position that had the support of many Jews in the Vilna ghetto — in the Yiddish weekly newspaper, *Geto Yedies* (*Ghetto News*), the official Judenrat organ. Under the headline "*Tsar un tsorn*" ("Wrath and Grief"), the escape was condemned. It was pointed out that Vilna Jews had already lost thousands of people from "outside forces" over which they had no control, but "such was not the case with the thirty-two souls uprooted from our midst last Monday. . . . It is clear that the sacrifices were unnecessary, their deaths lie on the consciences of those who, by their irresponsible behavior, made innocent people pay with their lives for a crime not of their making. . . . May the blood that has been spilled be a last warning to us all, that we have but one way — the way of labor."

The fear of Nazi retribution was so great that the Judenrate reacted in different ways to the establishment of underground movements or escape plans. In Kovno, Dr. Elhanan Elkes, the sixty-two-year-old head of the council, was much more willing to assist the underground with supplies and weapons. He also forged identity cards for those planning to escape, and provided them with warm clothing and boots.

More of the Judenrat chairmen in the larger towns and cities, however, followed Gens's indifferent or negative approach. In Glebokie, the ghetto police often patrolled the fence in order to prevent Jews from escaping. In nearby Stolpce, in November 1942, a young partisan named Abraham Zaretski, who had come to the ghetto to lead a group of Jews out, was betrayed by the Judenrat chairman. Zaretski was arrested by the Gestapo and tortured to death. Similarly, Yitzhak Kac, head of the

Judenrat in Brody, a town near Lvov in the Ukraine, sent any partisans he caught in the ghetto to labour camps.

Worse still were the actions of the Judenrat head in Kurzeniec, a town near Vilna. He threatened the parents of children known to be associated with the ghetto underground, declaring that if their sons and daughters did not cease their activities, he would report the parents to the Gestapo. In Novogrudok, survivor Pinkos Novaredok remembered that "the Judenrat and Ghetto police did all they could to prevent escapes from the ghetto. When the Jewish policemen found out that someone was making ready to leave the ghetto, they would take him to the Judenrat cellar, beat him up severely, and leave him there. People who had to go out to special jobs had their boots taken from them in the evening and returned the next morning." And in Sosnowiec, Moshe Merin, who ran the Jewish Council like a dictator, waged a bitter battle with the ghetto's resistance movement. In 1943, he had the Jewish police arrest and deliver two young resistance leaders, Zvi Dunski and Lipek Mintz, to the Gestapo. Both were shot.

Most controversial, however, then and now, was the position of Gens, Merin, and other Judenrat leaders that sacrificing 1,000 Jews to save 5,000 was a necessary and acceptable trade-off. Gens explained his views in a passionate speech delivered at the presentation of a literary prize in 1942. It is a good example of his state of mind and the power of his rhetoric:

> Many of you think of me as a traitor, and wonder what I am doing here among you. . . . I, Gens, order you to uncover your hiding places; I, Gens, struggle to obtain work certificates, jobs, and benefits for the ghetto. I take count of Jewish blood, not Jewish honor. When the Germans ask me for a thousand persons, I hand them over, for if we Jews will not give them on our own, the Germans will come and take them by force. Then they will take not one thousand but thousands, and the whole ghetto will be at their mercy. With hundreds, I save a thousand; with the thousands that I hand over, I save ten thousands. . . . If I survive, I shall come out of here unclean, my hands dripping with blood. Nevertheless, I shall willingly declare before a Jewish

court: I did my best to rescue as many Jews as I could to bring them to the gates of redemption. I was forced to lead some to their death in order that a small remnant may survive; in order to have others emerge with a clear conscience, I had to befoul myself and act without conscience.

Desperate, some Jews truly believed in Gens's power. He offered them the one ray of hope in a world of darkness. They came, one survivor of the ghetto later recalled, to the Judenrat offices "and wept and begged for mercy to save their relatives. The members of the Judenrat, too, were no less naive than the remainder of the Jews and believed they could do something by interceding."

In fact, the Nazis allowed Gens to use his so-called power as long as it suited their needs. In October 1942, for example, Gens and his police force were ordered to conduct a selection in the nearby town of Oszmiana. The Germans wanted to execute about 1,400 women and children. Gens delivered instead 400 elderly and ill people and believed he had achieved success, though, as he conceded after the fact, it "wrenched" his heart. (It should be pointed out that Gens's decision was supported by the town's rabbi.) Later, Gens was tricked into collecting 5,000 Vilna Jews, whom he was told by the Germans were being relocated to the Kovno ghetto. Instead, the transport headed directly for the killing pits at the Ponary, where all 5,000 were murdered. Gens took this terrible deception very hard.

The truth was that Gens and other Judenrat chairmen were in an impossible and devastating position. There was no way they could win, no matter what they did. If they did not supply the required labour or Jews for transports and deportations, they themselves were executed. (This was the fate, for instance, of Dr. Joseph Parnes, the head of the Judenrat in Lvov, who was murdered when he would not comply with the Gestapo's orders to round up workers for the nearby Janowska labour camp.) Each Judenrat head attempted to deal with this life-and-death dilemma in his own unique way. Some complied, others refused and were killed. A small number committed suicide rather than turn over Jewish women and children to the Nazis. A few, like Gens and

Chaim Rumkowski in the Lodz ghetto, were swept away with their own self-importance.

At the same time, it can be argued that Judenrate did fulfill certain necessary functions. Germans could have imprisoned Jews behind ghetto walls without the help of the councils, but they did ensure, as much as possible, that there was food, water, and shelter available for every Jew trapped in the ghetto. More than fifty years later, it is easy to condemn many of these Jewish community leaders for being foolish and naive. Some, like Merin, may even have been guilty of outright collaboration. But placed in the context of occupied Europe in 1942, and against a backdrop of Nazi brutality, this judgment is not so black and white. Many, Gens included, often acted out of the best and most unselfish of intentions.*

Moreover, the majority of Judenrat chairmen maintained a high level of support among ghetto Jews, many of whom had family obligations to children and parents or were simply too weak and terrified to contemplate resistance or escape. Beyond this, physical (and dangerous) resistance of the type advocated by the youth of the ghetto underground was contrary to the religious teachings and traditions of many east European Jews. "In the heritage of Orthodox Jewry," explained historian Philip Friedman, "the concept of heroism was synonymous with spiritual courage, self-sacrifice for the sake of religion — *Kiddush Hashem*. And this was the only possible form of resistance considered by Orthodox Jewry: resistance derived from a deep-rooted heritage summed up in the saying: 'Not with power, and not with force, but with the spirit.' The essence of this creed . . . was reduced to the idea that one must not fight evil in the world or defeat it by physical force, for it is the Divine Protector who will decide the struggle between good and evil."

Added to these pressures were the physical and psychological stresses of daily life in the ghetto or work camp and the constant oppression

---

*Historian Isaiah Trunk discovered, in his 1972 study of 720 Judenrat members, that the majority, 383 people or 53 percent, went to their deaths during the deportations; 182 (25.3 percent) were murdered by the Germans before the deportations to the extermination camps; 21 (2.9 percent) resigned; 9 (1.2 percent) committed suicide; 26 (3.6 percent) died a natural death; and 86 (12 percent) survived the war. (See "Judenrat," *EH* 2: 766.)

waged on the Jews by the Nazis. Some of them were simply too paralyzed to react. Logic also dictated to the Jews that it was impossible to get rid of all of them, so why make things worse by resisting or escaping? Survivor Liza Czapnick has no patience for questions about why Jews did not resist more. She saw thousands of Soviet soldiers who could not do anything against the Nazis, so what could Jews do, she asks? The average ghetto Jew, barely alive in 1942, hoped, like many of the members of the Judenrate who led them, that by following the rules, their lives would be spared. The Soviet army would save them. The Germans would be defeated.

Other, younger Jews knew better.

THE GHETTO OR THE FOREST

Having access to the world outside the ghetto, I might have taken the risk of escaping, but I was afraid my family would be harmed. . . . Should a son or daughter leave elderly parents and endanger their lives? Should a husband forsake his wife and children? Others felt that their responsibility was to remain with their community.

— FAYE SCHULMAN

"EITHER WE ALL STAY ALIVE OR WE ALL PERISH"

In the hundreds of small east European villages and *shtetlach* beyond the large urban centres of Minsk, Bialystok, Kovno, and Vilna, the reactions and attitudes of the Jewish population, including its Judenrat leadership, were markedly different. The class differences so evident among Jews in the cities, differences that divided urban Jews by income, education, and profession, were almost non-existent in the countryside.

Long before the Nazis arrived, these small communities operated in a much more democratic fashion than their urban counterparts. Major decisions affecting a particular Jewish community were made by everyone in the town or village at open meetings held in synagogues. There was a trust and intimacy among neighbours that, due to population numbers alone, was lacking in the cities. Thus these communities tended to act as one when the Nazi onslaught began.

As their numbers dwindled in the carnage perpetrated by the Einsatzgruppen, these largely uneducated tradesmen, cattle buyers, and farmers had no illusions about their fate. Resistance was one option — though, as will be seen, a futile one — and escape to the nearby forest areas another. Unlike many Jews in the cities, these rural residents regarded escape to the woods as a practical and logical alternative. "The East European urban Jew was full of fear of strangers and wild animals and was put off by the difficulties of climate and nature," Holocaust scholar Yisrael Gutman has observed. "The Jews of the villages near the forests and swamps did not share these fears. Moreover, many of these villagers took pride in their physical strength and were full of self-confidence. The secrets of nature and forest were well-known to them. Their spirit of resistance led to collective rebellion."

Because they were spread out over a large area, rural Jews were more able to elude the Nazis once the war started. Or else, like Tuvia Bielski and his two brothers, Zus and Asael, from the small western Belorussian village of Stankiewicze, near Novogrudok, they were on the run from almost the moment the Germans attacked in 1941. Three generations of Bielskis had lived in Stankiewicze. The family farmed a small piece of land and ran a mill. In 1906, when Tuvia was born, the Bielskis were the only Jewish family in the village (in fact, the entire village consisted of less than a dozen families). In all, Tuvia's parents, David and Beila, had twelve children (two daughters and ten sons), although the entire fourteen-member family never lived together in their two-room wooden hut. In 1930, following a two-year stint in the Polish army, Tuvia married a woman named Rifka, from the nearby town of Subotniki, and opened a textile store.

During the summer of 1941, having experienced physical abuse at the hands of the Nazis, Tuvia and two of his brothers decided to avoid them as much as was possible. More than once, they were almost apprehended by the Belorussian police on the lookout for stray Jews, so they went to stay with friends in the country and work as farmhands. But events moved faster than they had anticipated. On December 8, 1941, a major *Aktion* in Novogrudok and the surrounding area took place. That day, 4,000 Jews were murdered, including the Bielskis' parents, who had been taken from their home to the ghetto in Novogrudok; Tuvia's first wife, Rifka (whom he was separated from); and Zus's wife, Cyrl, and their baby daughter. (All had lived in Novogrudok.)

After this, the Bielski brothers decided to take refuge in the forest not far from Novogrudok. They also managed to trade with some Belorussian peasants for a few guns, weapons that had been discarded when the Soviet army retreated. By early March 1942, Asael Bielski had organized a small group of thirteen Jews, which included his younger brother Aharon, his future wife, Chaya, and members of her family. Educated and more refined than Asael, Chaya had resisted both Asael's overtures and his plan to escape to the forest until the December 8 *Aktion*.

Meanwhile, Tuvia Bielski continued to move from one spot to another, keeping one eye on his new love, Sonia — who, with her blonde hair and blue eyes, was hiding with a wealthy Belorussian peasant — and the other on Sonia's family, the Ticktins (including Sonia's sister, Regina; her husband, Alter Ticktin; and young Lilka, Alter's daughter from his first marriage, who would later become Tuvia Bielski's third wife), who were trapped inside the Lida ghetto. Finally, following the May 8 *Aktion* in Lida, Sonia and her family agreed to escape and follow Tuvia to the forest. They soon joined Asael's group and laid the foundations of the Bielski family camp.

The experiences of Harold Werner (born Hershel Zimmerman) were much different, but the end result was the same. Like the Bielskis, Werner was part of that small minority of Jews who managed to stay out of the ghettos. Born in 1918 in Gorzkow, a small Polish village southeast of Lublin, Werner was working in the knitting business in Warsaw when the war broke out in 1939. Single, he lived as a boarder with a family named Freedman who had originally come from a village called Hola in eastern Poland near the Bug River. Having witnessed Nazi brutality, Werner decided to escape from the city with his two brothers, Moishe and Motel; his girlfriend, Manya Freedman; and her brother, Shmuel. Once they were out of Warsaw, Werner's brothers chose to leave the group and travel to the family's home in Gorzkow. He never saw them again. With his girlfriend and her brother, he soon reached the village of Hola, home to a Ukrainian community that spoke a dialect called "Hachlacki," a combination of Russian, Polish, and Ukrainian. The Hachlakis, as the people were called, hated the Poles and were loyal to the Ukrainian nationalist movement. They tolerated the few Jewish families who lived in their midst.

Initially, Werner and his companions contemplated moving farther east, to an area that was by then under the control of the Soviets. But after hearing of the terrible living conditions of Jews east of the Bug River, as well as considering the near absence of Nazi troops and police in the Hola area, Werner convinced them that they might be better off staying where they were. Working as a farm hand, he managed to avoid grave danger until the fall of 1942, more than a year after the Germans occupied the region. Yet by then he had lost contact with his family in Warsaw and Gorzkow, and was uncertain of their fate. He had also been subject to Nazi and Ukrainian brutality as worker on a road gang, from which he managed to escape. He was able to find refuge for a brief period working for a man named Stephan, a Ukrainian farmer, near the village of Lubien.

In the fall of 1942, the Nazis ordered that all of the remaining Jews in the area congregate in the village of Hola for transport to the ghetto in Wlodawa. Jews who refused to report or were caught hiding on local farms were to be killed, along with the farmers and their families who had assisted them.

Werner had no desire to be incarcerated in a ghetto, where he was certain he would die. Stephan, aware of the Einsatzgruppen killings in neighbouring towns and villages, advised Werner to hide in the forest, where he might be able to seek help from Red Army soldiers who had escaped prisoner-of-war camps. In fact, Werner had already encountered Soviet soldiers on the run while working in the fields. They seemed friendly enough, though he knew that living with them might prove more difficult. Manya and her relatives were also sceptical about surviving in the woods for very long. Still, they had no choice. After some heated discussions, a group of fifteen people decided to join Werner and face an uncertain life in the forest rather than the certain hardship of life in the Wlodawa ghetto.

■■

About the same time as Harold Werner and his group ran to the forest, rumours began to circulate among the Jews of the Lachva ghetto that large pits were being dug by local peasants on the outskirts of the village. Lachva was a small town in western Belorussia close to the marshes of the Pripet River and the Grycyn Forest, and its ghetto, established in April 1942, consisted of forty-five wooden houses and was home to more than 2,000 Jews. From the beginning of the German occupation, the head of the local Judenrat, Berl Lopatyn, worked closely with the young Betar leader Yitzhak Rochczyn in arming an underground resistance movement.

On September 2, the ghetto was surrounded by about 350 German and Belorussian policemen. The next morning, Lopatyn was told by the German commander what he already knew: All but thirty of Lachva's Jews were to be shot and the ghetto liquidated. He was to be one of the thirty essential workers whose lives were to be spared. His reply was both courageous and defiant. "Either we all stay alive," he told the German police commander, "or we all perish."

Within moments, the police started their attack, and the Jews of Lachva met them with axes and knives. Before the Nazis and Belorussians could respond, Lopatyn set one house on fire and other Jews followed his lead. With the small ghetto blazing, the Jews attacked and charged the fence. Wielding an axe, Yitzhak Rochczyn split open the head of a German policeman but was then shot. Lopatyn grabbed a machine gun from a Nazi and killed as many of the enemy as was possible.

At least 1,000 Jews died in the battle that day. Though Lopatyn was wounded, he and about 600 other Lachva Jews were able to escape to the forest. The majority were later apprehended and eventually killed, but Lopatyn eluded capture and organized a small Jewish partisan unit of twenty-five men. With only one rifle and one gun in their possession, they were extremely vulnerable, but they were able to join a Soviet partisan brigade. Lopatyn died on February 21, 1944, just a few months before Lachva was liberated, when he stepped on a land mine. Only a few of the town's Jews survived the war.

■ ■

The courage of Berl Lopatyn and the Jews of Lachva was matched by the Jews in the rural Ukrainian town of Tuchin, just east of Rovno. There, in July 1942, the chairman of the Judenrat, Getzel Schwartzman, his two sons, and his deputy, Meir Himmelfarb, were determined to resist. By the middle of September, careful planning and astute bartering had enabled the Tuchin underground to amass five rifles, twenty-five pistols, more than a dozen hand grenades, and enough kerosene to burn the ghetto to the ground. Schwartzman's plan was for the ghetto inmates to set fire to their houses and escape into the forest in the confusion.

The German and Ukrainian police charged the ghetto in the middle of the night on September 24. As in Lachva, that was the signal for the ghetto to go up in flames and the resistance to begin. Approximately 2,000 of Tuchin's Jews, more than 60 percent of the community, succeeded in fleeing north-east to the Postomat Forest. The rest either died in the uprising or, like Schwartzman and Himmelfarb, were caught and executed in the Jewish cemetery. Most of the escapees did not fare any better. Many were later killed in hunts or were informed on by local Ukrainian peasants during the winter, arrested, and then shot. A few joined Soviet partisan units, but only twenty of the original 2,000 who had fled survived to see the end of the war.

"FOR US THE PEOPLE WAS OUR ORIGIN, OUR BEING, AND OUR VERY ESSENCE"

The alternatives facing the Jews in the ghettos of the larger urban centres were more complex. With few weapons at their disposal and limited assistance from local non-Jewish underground movements — whose members were either indifferent or outright anti-Semitic — an uprising seemed destined to fail. By the spring of 1942, rumours were making the rounds that Jews without weapons were not welcome in the forests by Soviet, Lithuanian, or Polish partisans. So when many young Jews took into account the collective responsibility imposed by the Nazis, which meant death and possible torture for their family members, escape to the unknown forests was not an appealing option.

But these young people had strong Jewish identities, a pride in Yiddish culture, and possessed courage and determination beyond their years. They had to do something: resistance was in their blood. Unlike many of the fearful adults in their midst (with, it must be added, responsibilities to spouses and children that teenagers and those in their early twenties did not always understand or appreciate), they were prepared to fight and die for their cause.

For these young Jews, having grown up together and become friends through their participation in a variety of Zionist or Socialist clubs and organizations — Ha-Shomer Hatsair, Betar, Ha-Noar Ha-Tzyyoni, Dror, to list only a few — it was only natural that they gravitated towards those they knew and trusted. For once the underground movement began, there was no turning back. All members placed their lives and the lives of their loved ones in the hands of their comrades. Hence, secrecy was paramount and underground "cells," usually four or five people, purposely kept small.

"Underground life is serious and complicated, with one mistake leading to another if you do not know how to combine caution and daring," asserted Chaika Grosman, a survivor of the resistance in the Bialystok ghetto. That caution, she added, led leaders to hesitate before trusting new people, for "once the Gestapo got hold of you, you never got out."

Their youth worked both for and against them. It provided the single-mindedness, fearlessness, and willingness to risk all. Sixteen-year-old Jewish girls bravely smuggled weapons into the ghetto or, those with blonde hair and blue eyes, disguised themselves as "Aryans" and attempted to make contact with the non-Jewish underground. Some, such as Chaika Grosman, actually travelled throughout the occupied territory on forged papers and snuck in and out of ghettos bringing news and messages from other resistance groups.* But their young years

---

*The important contribution of Irena Adamowicz, a thirty-two-year-old Polish-Catholic woman from Warsaw, should also be noted. Before the war, she was attracted to the Zionist movement, particularly the work of Ha-Shomer Hatsair. She was so popular that the Jewish members affectionately called her the *Chalutzishe Shikse* (the pioneering Gentile girl). In June and July 1942, at great personal risk, she travelled from one ghetto to another, in Warsaw, Vilna, Kovno, and Bialystok, passing important information. To enter the ghettos, she disguised herself as a Jew,

also led them into unnecessary disputes over ideology and strategy. First, the Zionists, who represented every possible position of the political spectrum, had to put their pre-war differences behind them. They not only had to unite in common cause, but also had to embrace their Communist friends, who had much different ideas about Jewish life and resistance strategy. In some of the larger ghettos, like Warsaw, Bialystok, Kovno, and to a lesser extent, Vilna, these ideological differences were not easily bridged.

Admittedly, the tasks confronting the resisters were extremely dangerous — possessing a weapon of any kind in the ghetto meant immediate execution — and the questions impossible to solve: Did they wait until they were completely armed before resisting, or fight as soon as possible before more Jews died? What chance was there of an uprising succeeding if the entire ghetto population did not join in? Should they spend time and energy educating the population on the benefits of such a fight, when the majority were more likely to support the Judenrat's "obey-and-survive" position? And finally, did they have a responsibility to save the ghetto inhabitants, or should they all flee to the forests to continue the fight from there?

Only in hindsight did the answers to these questions become clearer. "If we had foreseen, if we had understood," stated Yitzhak Zukerman, one of the leaders of the Jewish fighters' organization in the Warsaw ghetto. "If I could turn the wheel of history back to 1939, I would say: 'An immediate uprising!' — because then we had much more strength, many more youth; because we had pride, a greater store of human feeling; because we had much more energy . . . many more arms . . . many more soldiers; because then we also had much more hope."

At the time, however, Zionists and Communists approached the serious dilemmas facing them much differently. Young Jewish Communists had heard of Stalin's call to action. For the majority of them, there was no other choice but to flee to the forest, join up with a Soviet partisan

---

complete with a yellow patch on her clothes. Her reports gave the resistance movement impetus and encouragement. After the war, she lived in Poland. On a visit to Israel in 1960, three years before she died, she was declared a "Righteous Gentile" by Yad Vashem for her underground work. (See Tory, *Kovno*, 108, and "Adamowicz, Irena," in *EH* 1: 6.)

unit, and fight the enemy. Life in the ghetto was meaningless and an uprising without outside support as good as a sentence of death. "The Communists had contact with Moscow and knew of partisans. Their end goal was ultimately to join partisans," explains Sara Ginaite, who at sixteen was a member of the Kovno underground before she escaped to the forest. "The Zionists had a different goal. They did not trust the Soviets and did not want contact with them."

Indeed, for many young Zionist fighters, like Mordechai Tenenbaum and Adek Boraks in Bialystok, there was no other choice but to stay and defend the Jews in the ghetto. "Are we to desert the disorganized ghetto, with its old people, women and children and say: we have saved our lives?" asked Boraks at an underground meeting in late 1941. "Where is our movement's vanguard? I see the head of the rebelling masses. The war must be carried out in the ghetto, and we must be in the vanguard together with those others who agree with us. We are being killed as Jews, and it is as Jews that we must fight back; not as individuals but as an organized community."

Chaika Grosman, a friend and comrade of both Tenenbaum and Boraks, put this dilemma into perspective:

The question at issue was the ghetto's priority in determining the underground's combat and ideological programs. The problem was not only theoretical. Its roots were also ideological, but its expression was erratic. Its roots lay in the different attitudes of the Communists and ourselves toward the Jewish people as a nation. For us the people was our origin, our being, and our very essence. We argued that the weapons that had already arrived in the ghetto were sacred for the war there. They were prepared to supply the groups going to the forests with the best of the arms that had been obtained so laboriously and smuggled into the ghetto. We argued that arms for the partisans had to be obtained separately from the weapons in the ghetto stores; they believed the opposite. We decided to divide our manpower, to send good fighters to the forest but to calculate carefully so that the partisan activity did not harm the ghetto's fighting capacity. They sent their best fighters into the forest. What is more, if they had enough weapons they would have sent most of their able bodied people to bear arms without considering the needs of the ghetto.

"There will always be Jews in the ghetto," they argued, "and when the time comes they will fight." We rejected that somewhat mechanistic view of the ghetto revolt. We knew that there would be no armed resistance if it were not led by the most courageous of us. We did not develop any ideology of dying, of the desperate and demonstrative suicide of a small elite group in the ghetto, but of a national war in the streets. Since we were fighting for our national existence in the broadest sense of the term we organized the contact positions outside the ghetto and sent our first emissaries to establish a base for the absorption of thousands of forest fighters.

Other Zionists were not as certain as Grosman and her associates. In Bialystok, members of the right-wing group Betar wavered. One day they decided on the ghetto, the next the forest. In Vilna, a resistance splinter group led by Yechiel Scheinbaum of the Zionist group Dror adopted what became known as "the ideology of the forest." Simply put, it made more sense to them to escape from the ghetto and wage war against the Nazis from the woods.

The result of this debate in both Kovno and Bialystok was a lengthy and crucial period in 1942 and early 1943 when the resistance movements in both ghettos operated without cohesion or an overall plan. Meanwhile, the Jewish populations in the two cities were being gradually deported, starved, or exterminated.

In Kovno, it took until the summer of 1943 for Zionists and Communists to unite as the Yidishe Algemeyne Kamfs Organizatsye, or General Jewish Fighting Organization (JFO). There were about 600 fighters. Direct links with Soviet and Lithuanian partisans were made outside of the ghetto, which enabled the JFO to send groups of partisans to the Augustov Forest, a distance of some 175 kilometres. To get there, however, the Jewish fighters had to travel by foot through open country that was home to a largely anti-Jewish population. They often encountered trouble, and of the one hundred partisans who escaped in September 1943, forty were either killed on the spot or captured and later murdered at the infamous Ninth Fort execution site on the out-skirts of Kovno. During November and December, other groups headed for closer bases in the Rudniki Forest, south of Vilna, where they joined with anti-German Lithuanian partisans. Of the approximately 350 JFO members who departed the ghetto in 1943 and early 1944, about 250 survived. When the Kovno ghetto was liquidated in early July 1944, no uprising occurred. Most Jews were either killed or deported.

To the south-west, in Bialystok, an underground movement had started early in 1942, about six months after the creation of the ghetto. In the summer of 1942, after lengthy negotiations conducted mainly by Grosman and Boraks, members of Ha-Shomer Hatsair, Communists, and representatives of the Jewish Socialist Bund joined together in a group called Bloc No. 1, or Front A. Another segment, Bloc No. 2, was led by Mordechai Tenenbaum of the Dror movement.

A prominent Zionist leader and underground fighter, Tenenbaum, who was born in Warsaw in 1916, travelled from ghetto to ghetto spreading the message of resistance. He was also a prolific writer in the underground press and was in Warsaw in July 1942 when the Jewish Fighting Organization (Zydowska Organizacja Bojowa, or ZOB) was established. In November, he returned to lead the fight in Bialystok, but was nearly killed by a German patrol. After recovering in the Grodno ghetto from a serious leg wound, he reached Bialystok, negotiated with Ephraim Barash, the head of the Judenrat, for help in purchasing weapons, and created a ghetto archives. (It should be noted that while Barash privately gave qualified support to the resistance movement, in public he denounced the fighters as "traitors and provocateurs" and a threat to the ghetto's future existence.)

A staunch Zionist and a passionate and intelligent man, Tenenbaum was committed to defending the ghetto before an attempt was made to escape to the forest. "I don't care about the forest," he'd say. "The main objective is that we succeed in uniting within the ghetto." The slogan that he continually preached was, "After fulfilling our duty in the ghetto, if we remain alive, we must go to the forest to continue with our vengeance."

Blocs 1 and 2 did not unite until July 1943, by which time deporta-tions of Bialystok's large Jewish population (which numbered 50,000 in

August 1941) to Treblinka had commenced. Small armed groups, mainly Communists, had already escaped to the forest to join Soviet partisans. They were joined by other fighters in the spring of 1943. These groups united to form the Forois, or Forward, detachment, under the command of Jonah Suchaczewski, a former printer from Warsaw. Eventually associated with the main Belorussian partisan brigade led by Maj.-Gen. Filip Kapusta, Forois carried out many daring military and sabotage operations until it was disbanded in April 1944 and its members dispersed to other units.

The final battle in the Bialystok ghetto took place on August 16, 1943. The night before, as hundreds of Nazi and Ukrainian soldiers surrounded the ghetto, Barash was informed by the Gestapo that the remaining Jews in the ghetto, about 30,000 people, were to be deported to Lublin and the Majdanek death camp the following day. The underground mobilized its forces.

The next morning, as the ghetto's beaten and downtrodden Jews were obediently moving to the assembly point, the underground, led by Tenenbaum and his deputy, the Communist Daniel Moszkowicz, sprang to action. (Chaika Grosman and a few others managed to escape after the fighting started.) For the next five days, they valiantly battled German troops and police, who outmanned them by a wide margin. Their few guns, rifles, home-made fire bombs (lightbulbs filled with sulfuric acid), and knives fashioned from rusty curtain rods were no match for the Germans' armoured tanks and automatic weapons. At least 300 fighters died the first day and many more after that. One group of seventy-two resisters took refuge in a bunker, only to be found by the Germans on August 19. All but one were executed. Tenenbaum and the group with him lasted for one more day and then most likely committed suicide.

The majority of Bialystok's Jews who did not participate in the resistance were deported to Majdanek, Treblinka, Auschwitz, and other camps, where nearly all of them were killed. Ephraim Barash was kept alive a little longer, along with other members of the Judenrat. The entire group, including Barash and his wife, were then shipped to Majdanek in September 1943, where they were murdered.

.. ∎

In Minsk, the Belorussian capital, where the pre-war Zionist movement was not as strong as Communism among Jews, the history of the underground resistance is more straightforward. For such leaders as Hersh Smolar, a Polish Communist originally from Bialystok, the strategy to be followed was as rudimentary as the underground's slogan: "The ghetto means death. Provide yourself with arms, leave the ghetto and take to the forests!"

Well aware that they required arms to obtain entrance to Soviet partisan units, the Minsk fighters stole, smuggled, and bought what they needed (in a few cases, from Germans themselves). In his memoirs, Smolar related how three of his comrades, Sonya Kaplinski, Shloymke Greenhoyz, and Jaschke Lapidus, with help of former schoolmates Vitke Rudovich and Kolka Pryshtsheptshik, "dug up 540 bullets near the Mohileve highway, along with a machine-gun clip, 12 rifle bolts, two grenades and other gun parts. The first brand-new automatic — every partisan's dream — was brought into the ghetto by . . . Abe Gellman."

In Minsk, unlike other eastern urban ghettos, the underground also had the full support of Elihyahu Mushkin, the first head of the Judenrat (who was hanged in February 1942), and his replacement, Moshe Yaffe. At the end of March 1942, when Smolar had been betrayed by two Russians, Yaffe bravely gave the Gestapo an identity card with Smolar's name on it. The card had been dipped in the blood of a recently murdered Jew. The German police accepted the evidence as proof that Smolar — who was actually hiding in the infectious-disease ward of the ghetto hospital — was dead.

With the determined and unwavering support of the underground, as well as the important assistance offered by friendly Belorussian and Soviet partisans, approximately 10,000 Jews (from a total population that, in August 1941, numbered about 100,000) were able to elude death in the various *Aktionen* and escape from the Minsk ghetto before it was liquidated in October 1943.

In one of the first daring escapes, in December 1941, six Jews fled the ghetto hidden in false-bottomed wooden wagons. Guided by a local peasant, they discovered a cache of thirteen rifles and 4,000 rounds that had been hidden by the retreating Red Army. Led by Boris Khaimovich, a former manager of a textile mill who had spent six years in the Russian army, the group took the weapons, tore the yellow patches from their jackets, and buried them in the hole. They then proceeded to the Bobrovichi Forest, about 24 kilometres south-west of Minsk, where they established a base and made contact with Capt. Sergeyev Bistrov, the Soviet partisan commander in the area.

Escapes from the Minsk ghetto were additionally notable for the brave role several children played as guides to the forest. "In the [Minsk] ghetto," according to Smolar, "a new phrase became a sort of secret password — *Dos Kleynvarg* (the Youngsters). Everyone knew that it was the children who were leading the groups to the forest, but only a very few knew their names."

Twelve-year-old Bunke Hammer, a small, skinny boy, and his friend David "Dovidke" Klonski, thirteen, memorized routes to the Naliboki *puszcza*, about 50 kilometres away. They led more than a hundred Jews to relative safety. Some of these escapees were later killed in Nazi hunts, but many joined such partisan detachments as Kutuzov, Budenny, and Parkhomenko or survived in the family camp established by Shalom Zorin, a Jew from Minsk.

In August 1943, Bunke was caught in a Nazi blockade and discovered by the Germans hiding in a cave with twenty-one men, women, and children of the Parkhomenko unit. After they tied the Jews' hands behind their backs with barbed wire, the Nazis burned the group alive. Jacob Greenstein, a Parkhomenko partisan who later found the grisly sight, remembered Bunke: "His body was half-burned, his eyes open as though petrified. I untied his arms but could not straighten them out. With clenched fists and anguished hearts, we swore to take revenge on their murderers. David stood at [Bunke's] open grave and cried bitterly. The entire detachment cried with him."

Young Sima (Simele) Fiterson, also twelve years old, was a girl with blonde hair and blue eyes. She moved in and out of the ghetto at will, and made contacts with the Belorussian underground on the outside, which in turn put her in touch with partisans in the woods. Carrying a small pistol, which was sewn into a special pocket in her coat, she guided many Minsk Jews to family and partisan camps in the nearby forest.

One day, however, after returning to the ghetto, Sima was followed by a German agent. "That same night," Smolar writes, "the Gestapo broke down her door. Simele managed to get to her hiding place, but her mother and younger brothers were taken away. She became even more taciturn and single-minded as she continued her work — leading Jews out of the ghetto into the forest." She survived the war and was awarded the Order of the Red Star by the Soviets for her bravery as a partisan.

Of course, the Minsk underground's goal of removing all the Jews from the ghetto proved impossible, and many of those who did escape perished in the forest. Still, at least there was consensus between the resistance movement and the Judenrat on the strategy for survival. The same could not be said of the ghetto in Vilna.

"LET US NOT BE LED AS SHEEP TO THE SLAUGHTER"

On New Year's Eve, 1941, 150 young Zionists gathered at a public soup kitchen at 2 Straszuna in the heart of the Vilna ghetto. In attendance were representatives of Ha-Shomer Hatsair, Dror, He-Halutz Hatsair, and Ha-Noar Ha-Tzyyoni. The timing of the meeting was deliberate: the Jewish youth knew that the German and Lithuanian police guarding the ghetto would be occupied with the New Year's festivities.

Before them stood one man. He was short, with a long, distinctive Semitic nose, wavy dark hair, and penetrating eyes. Born in Sevastopol, Russia, in 1918, Abba Kovner was only twenty-three years old when the war broke out, but he had been active in Ha-Shomer Hatsair since he was a boy attending school in Vilna. In June 1941, he had hidden from the Einsatzgruppen at a Dominican convent outside the city, but eventually made his way into the ghetto and learned of the fate of Vilna's Jews at the Ponary. When young ghetto messengers brought him news of similar mass killings throughout the occupied areas, Kovner, more than most Jews, quickly grasped its significance. "One thing is clear to me," he stated at a meeting in December 1941. "Vilna is not Vilna alone,

Ponar is not a unique episode. . . . It is a complete system."

In preparation for the gathering on New Year's Eve, Kovner had written a declaration of resistance. It was an urgent and passionate plea for Vilna's Jews, especially the youth, to rise up against their oppressors. More than fifty years later, Kovner's words remain a symbol of Jewish defiance during the Holocaust:

> Jewish youth!
>
> Do not place your trust in those who deceive you. Of 80,000 Jews in the "Jerusalem of Lithuania," only 20,000 are left. Our parents, brothers, and sisters were torn from us before our eyes. Where are the hundreds of men who were seized for labor?
>
> Where are the naked women and children seized from us on the night of fear? Where were the Jews sent on the Day of Atonement? . . .
>
> All the roads of the Gestapo lead to Ponar. And Ponar means death. Those who waver, put aside all illusion. Your children, your wives and husbands are no more. Ponar is no concentration camp. . . . Hitler conspires to kill all the Jews of Europe. . . . Let us not be led as sheep to the slaughter!
>
> True, we are weak and defenseless. But the only answer to the murderer is: To rise up with arms!
>
> Brethren! Better fall as free fighters than to live at the mercy of murderers. Rise up! Rise up until your last breath.

Three weeks later, following much discussion and negotiation, another significant meeting was convened at the home of Josef Glazman, the twenty-nine-year-old leader of the right-wing Betar movement (and its adult wing, the Revisionists). In November 1941, Glazman had reluctantly accepted Jacob Gens's invitation to join the ghetto police force and become its deputy. His friends had convinced him that it was the only way they could keep an eye on Gens and the activities of the Judenrat.

Besides Glazman and Kovner, the other notable individual present that night was Yitzhak Wittenberg. Born in Vilna in 1907, Wittenberg was a tailor who was very active in the Communist Party. "His willingness to join with Zionists in a united organization — which included the anti-Communist Zionist Revisionists," asserts historian Yisrael Gutman, "is an indication of his personality and his strong ties with the Jewish population."

By the conclusion of the meeting on January 21, it was agreed that Wittenberg, owing to his links with the Communist underground outside the ghetto, would become the leader of a new unified resistance group known as the *Fareynegte Partizaner Organizatsye* (FPO), or United Partisan Organization. Kovner and Glazman were appointed his deputies. The FPO's main objectives, as set out in its charter, were "to establish an armed fighting organization" and to prepare Vilna's Jews for a mass uprising should the Nazis attempt to liquidate the ghetto.

Of those willing to take action against the Germans not everyone supported the FPO's leadership or strategy. It took another month before the members of the Socialist Bund were convinced to join, and a group of fifteen to twenty young Zionists from Dror, led by Yechiel Scheinbaum, remained an independent unit, much to the FPO leadership's dissatisfaction. At the end of 1942, Scheinbaum's group merged with an FPO splinter group led by Leo Bernstein, a Betarist who was unhappy with Glazman. Aware by this time of Soviet partisan activity in the *puszczas* of Belorussia (Soviet and anti-German Lithuanian partisans reached the forest areas near Vilna in the summer of 1943), Scheinbaum and Bernstein argued that escape to the forest was the only hope for resistance and survival. "It soon became apparent that a defense strategy in the conditions of the Vilna ghetto was absurd," Bernstein later explained. "Any resistance, any possibility of retreat, requires space, and after all we had almost none at all. . . . We had no hinterland anywhere." By the spring of 1943, Yechiel's Struggle Group, as it was called, was an organization of about 175 people. Its members began escaping to the nearby Rudniki Forest in September 1943, and linked up with Soviet and Lithuanian partisans already there.

Like all ghetto underground movements, the Vilna resistance groups lacked weapons and acquiring them proved to be next to impossible. The FPO, regarded by the Polish underground as pro-Communist, could not depend on outside help. There was a more supportive non-Jewish

Communist group operating outside of the ghetto, the Zwaizek Walki Czynnej (Union for Active Struggle), but it consisted of just sixty to eighty members and could offer the FPO only limited assistance and few arms.

What weapons the FPO members did obtain were either bought on the black market at exorbitant prices or stolen from munitions factories where Jews happened to be employed. Guns, grenades, rifles, and in the case of Anna Kremer, an FPO courier, a large pair of scissors were smuggled in the false bottoms of tool boxes, inside coat pockets, in coffins, and in garbage trucks. Once the weapons were inside the ghetto, they had to be hidden from not only the Germans and the local police but also inquisitive and fearful family members who usually knew nothing of their children's underground activities. (As Kovner later recalled, one unique hiding spot for light machine gun parts was behind the volumes of Josephus' *Jewish War* in the Jewish Culture Library.) Most would have disapproved had they known, for possessing a weapon meant death for every family member. In the view of many Vilna Jews, this was too great a price to pay for a war of resistance that could never be won. They adhered to Jacob Gens's motto that it was "better to stay alive as a nobody than to die as a hero." Thus the FPO was forced to devise special hiding places in basements and other locales to store the weapons.

As head of the Judenrat, Gens knew of the existence of the FPO and even provided it with money for weapons and supplies. Still, this official support was ambivalent and there were numerous confrontations as the situation in the Vilna ghetto worsened during late 1942 and early 1943. While most members of the FPO were committed to a ghetto uprising — a course of action reaffirmed in the spring of 1943 after reports of the uprising in the Warsaw ghetto reached Vilna — the growth of the Soviet partisan movement in nearby forest areas made escape a more attractive and sensible alternative for many young resisters.

In fact, the Soviet resistance was the talk of the ghetto as early as October 31, 1942. That day, Yitzhok Rudashevski, who was not part of the FPO, recorded in his diary that he had read a Soviet leaflet shown to him by a neighbour. Dated August 11, the leaflet extolled the virtues of the Soviet Union and its fight against "Hitlerism." It also, wrote Rudashevski, told "about the glorious work of the Russian partisans.

The leaflet concludes with an appeal to the male and female partisans to carry on sabotage, to derail German trains! . . . I run with the leaflet to the club to show my friends. I keep it in my bosom. It seems to me that the writing warms me. . . . We stand in the corners of the club and read. Everyone felt for a while so joyous and cheerful."

By the New Year, overtures were made and invitations extended for FPO members to join the battle in the forests. A group of young Jewish fighters from Swieciany, including Yitzhak Arad, visited the Vilna ghetto in April 1943 and suggested to FPO leaders that they unite with them to form a larger and more powerful Jewish *otriad* in the forest. Two months later, Moshe Shutan and Yitzhak Poras, also of Swieciany, brought a message to the FPO urging its fighters to escape to the Narocz Forest (150 kilometres east of Vilna) and join the brigade commanded by Fiodor Markov. On both occasions, the FPO leadership rejected these appeals and continued to believe that their fight with the Germans had to take place inside the ghetto.

Gens was under tremendous pressure. Stubbornly, he stuck to his conviction that the ghetto inhabitants could continue to serve the Nazis and survive. He allowed Moshe Shutan, an outsider with links to the Soviets, to take a group of twenty-five people out of the ghetto in June 1943, but grew terribly concerned about the future ramifications of such escapes. In fact, the ghetto was rampant with rumours and gossip about potential escapes, and the German police had already captured several Jews in possession of weapons. Nazi police officials had warned Gens that the entire ghetto was at risk. Thus less than two weeks later, when ten men from Yechiel's Struggle Group also left for the forest, the confrontation between the FPO and Gens came to a head.

"We are faced with the question of leaving for the forest. . . . Why should I not go? Because the question now arises — 1 or 20,000! The ghetto exists by virtue of 2,500 strong young men," Gens asserted in a speech to his police force. "The rest dance around them. . . . Just imagine if 500 men went out, what would happen then?. . . I put myself in [Obersturmführer Rolf] Neugebauer's place. . . . I would wipe out the entire ghetto, because a man must be an idiot to allow a nest of partisans to develop under his nose. . . . My interest is to preserve a loyal ghetto so long as it maintains itself."

The Judenrat chairman's first target was Josef Glazman, whom he believed was behind the latest departure. Gens and Glazman had had a falling out in November 1942 after Glazman, who was then director of the Housing Department (he had resigned as deputy of the ghetto police following Gens's promotion in July 1942), refused to obey Gens's orders about the reorganization of the nearby Swieciany ghetto. Gens had Glazman arrested and sent to a labour camp 16 kilometres from Vilna. According to Chaim Lazar, an FPO survivor, the Jewish ghetto police had beaten Glazman with a rubber truncheon and dragged him, bound and bleeding, through the alleyways of the ghetto. It took the intervention of the FPO's Yitzhak Wittenberg and Heena Borovska to ensure his return to the ghetto.

At the end of June 1943, Glazman was once again arrested and told that he would be sent to the Reise labour camp. His FPO comrades, however, had other ideas. When they spotted Glazman under Jewish police escort in the middle of the night, they attacked and freed their comrade. Determined to maintain his authority, Gens discussed the situation with the FPO leadership and promised that if Glazman agreed to go to the labour camp, he would be returned to the ghetto within two weeks. After several hours of discussion, Glazman reluctantly agreed. He left for Reise that night and, as Gens had stipulated, was allowed to return to the ghetto fourteen days later.* By freeing Glazman, the FPO had for the first time used force to publicly challenge Gens's authority. Not surprisingly, relations between the two sides remained tense.

Early in July 1943, the Nazi police in Vilna arrested a man named Wladyslaw Kozlowski and accused him of being a member of the Communist underground. Under torture, Kozlowski admitted to his involvement with the resistance and provided the Germans with names

---

* It was during his stay at Reise that Glazman met Hirsh Glik, then nineteen years old, a poet and the composer of the well-known Yiddish "Partisan Hymn." The song, which begins with the words *Zog nit keynmol az du geyst dem letstn veg* ("Never say that you are on your last journey"), is an enduring legacy to the partisan battle. In September 1943, Glik was sent back to the Vilna ghetto and became a member of the FPO. But his group was captured and deported to a labour camp in Estonia. He was later killed while attempting to escape. (See "Glik, Hirsh" *EH* 2: 588; Arad, *Ghetto in Flames*, 387.)

of his associates — among them, Yitzhak Wittenberg.

Gens was ordered by the commander of the Nazi security police, Bruno Kittel, to turn over Wittenberg for questioning. If Gens did not comply, Kittel threatened to destroy the ghetto. By this time, though, Wittenberg was nowhere to be seen. When he learned that his Communist comrades outside the ghetto had been apprehended, he went into hiding.

A week passed before Gens invited the FPO command to his house for a late-night meeting. Unaware of Kittel's ultimatum, Wittenberg (who believed it was safe to attend the gathering), Kovner, and a few other FPO members arrived at Gens's home. At a pre-appointed time, Sala Dessler, the head of the Jewish ghetto police, alerted the Nazi authorities and, within moments, two police officers arrived to place Wittenberg under arrest. A Jewish policeman with ties to the FPO watched these events unfold. He quickly reported what had transpired to FPO headquarters and a group of fighters was mobilized. They attacked the two Lithuanian policemen guarding Wittenberg and set the FPO leader free.

A massive search for Wittenberg ensued, but the Jewish police were unable to find him or his hiding place (a room on Straszuna Street). Threatened with the destruction of the ghetto, Gens attempted to negotiate with the FPO and mobilize public opinion against the resistance movement. That was not difficult. "The consensus among ghetto residents," writes Yitzhak Arad, "was that a ghetto of 20,000 people should not be imperiled for the sake of one man whose activity was connected with Communists outside the ghetto, and that he had jeopardized the ghetto by these activities, which were incompatible with the situation of the Jews within it." After long hours of soul searching, having finally accepted that a majority of Vilna's surviving Jews were not about to join the FPO in a general uprising, Wittenberg was convinced that he had to turn himself in. Abba Kovner later related what took place at the fateful meeting:

We came to Witenberg [sic] after having contacts with Gens, to clarify possibilities other than surrender. We wanted to examine [with Gens] what would happen if we smuggled him out. . . . There was a suggestion that someone else would surrender himself instead of Witenberg [*sic*]. . . . It became evident from the replies that it must be Witenberg [sic]. . . . I then said to him, and Glazman supported me. . . . "Give the order and we'll fight." He did not give the order. . . . Then some of his Communist comrades came to the attic. . . . Witenberg [*sic*] asked every one of us: "What do you say?" Everyone answered: "You must decide." Then he asked [two of his friends]: "What should I do?" And they said: "You must go [to the police]." Witenberg [*sic*] asked if that was the opinion of the [Communist] comrades, and they told him "Yes.". . . Then a moving and dramatic event occurred, that had nothing to do with the underground, between him and his girlfriend. She cried out that we were betraying him and sending him to his death. . . .

That night, while in custody at the Nazi police jail, Yitzhak Wittenberg committed suicide. He had secretly been given a potassium cyanide tablet, possibly by Gens. To his credit, Wittenberg died without giving the Germans any information about the FPO.

It was now clear to Kovner, who was elected head of the FPO following Wittenberg's death, and other members of the movement that their plan to lead a general uprising was unlikely to happen. They began to re-examine their position on the forest and made a more serious effort to forge links with the Soviet partisans. A group led by Glazman was first to leave. They were, as noted, ambushed on their way to the Narocz Forest. More escapes followed and still more were being planned when the Nazis began the final liquidation of the Vilna ghetto on September 1. Six thousand Jews were to be immediately deported to Estonia and Latvia.

It was the moment the FPO had been waiting for, the moment they had endlessly prepared for. As members armed themselves, the leadership posted a declaration for all the residents of the ghetto to join them in the final struggle:

Jews! Defend yourselves with arms! The Germans and Lithuanian hangmen have arrived at the gates of the ghetto. They have come to murder us! Within a short while, they will lead us group after group through the gate. Thus they led out hundreds on the Day of

Atonement! . . . Thus they led our brethren and sisters, our mothers and fathers, our children. Thus were tens of thousands taken out to their death! But we shall not go! We shall not stretch our necks like sheep for the slaughter! Jews! Defend yourselves with arms! . . . There is an organized Jewish force within the walls of the ghetto that will rise up with arms. Lend a hand to the revolt! Do not cower in hideouts and *malines*. Your end will be to die as rats in the grip of the murderers! . . . Jewish masses! Go out into the street! . . . We have nothing to lose! We shall save our lives only if we wipe out our murderers. Long live freedom! Long live armed defense, death to the murderers!

> — *September 1, 1943*
> *The Command of the F.P.O.*

But the call to arms was too late. The support and the will to fight was not there. Years later, Kovner conceded, "As regards the revolt, we cogitated more than anything else over the moral aspect. Were we entitled to do this, and when? Were we entitled to offer people up in flames? Most of them were unarmed — what would happen to all of them?"

That evening, the first armed clash between the FPO and the Nazis occurred. Ironically, one of the first fighters killed in the battle was Yechiel Scheinbaum, whose group had merged with the FPO a short time earlier, and who had from the beginning questioned the logic of a ghetto uprising. Remarkably, Gens was able to appease the Germans by agreeing to deliver the required number of Vilna Jews for deportation to Estonia. Thus, unlike in Warsaw, a large uprising did not break out in the Vilna ghetto.

Lacking the support of the Judenrat and the majority of ghetto inmates, members of the FPO began a series of escapes to the Narocz and Rudniki forests. Many of them were helped by Sonia Madeysker, a Jewish-Communist FPO fighter who had already left the ghetto and made important contacts with the partisans in the forest and the Communist underground in the city.

Other Jews, those not affiliated with the FPO, also escaped at this time. They included Norman Shneidman, then nineteen years old. He and some of his friends were able to leave through the ghetto gate where garbage was transported. It was, he recalls, "difficult, complex and very dangerous." Once outside the ghetto fence, it took them close to a week to travel the 150 kilometres to the Narocz Forest. Eventually, he joined the Jewish partisan group Nekamah (revenge), led by Glazman and Zerakh Ragovski, a Soviet partisan who had parachuted into the region.

Despite the fact that hundreds of people had fled to the forest, the deportations continued throughout the month. On September 14, Gens was ordered to report to Gestapo headquarters. He had been told that the Nazis were intending to kill him, but he refused to flee, fearing that such an action would bring an even quicker destruction of the ghetto. The security police placed Gens under arrest and locked him in a jail cell. He was accused of giving aid to the partisans and of not complying with police orders. At six o'clock in the evening, he was taken from his cell to the yard, blindfolded, and shot. A grave had been dug for his body earlier in the day.

More than five decades later, it is easy to condemn Jacob Gens for the path he chose. Exchanging the lives of some for the deaths of others is an action difficult, if not impossible, to defend or comprehend. But there was nothing normal or comprehensible about life in an eastern European ghetto. Clearly, his efforts to save the Jews of Vilna were futile, yet perhaps no less futile than the belief of the FPO that an uprising would break out with the full support and participation of the ghetto's population. Gens was, above all, a tragic figure. "All that he did during his tenure as Chief of the Ghetto was for his people," former FPO partisan and writer Chaim Lazar has argued. "Everyone knows that Gens had many opportunities to save himself . . . but he renounced his personal safety to devote himself to the ghetto. He believed in his ability, and was convinced to the last moment that he would be able to save the remnants [of the ghetto]."

Within two weeks of Gens's murder, the Nazis ordered that all remaining Jews be deported to labour camps in Estonia. On September 23, led by Kovner, the last eighty to one hundred FPO fighters left the ghetto in a daring escape through the sewer system. The escape began at noon and the full group did not reach the other side of the ghetto walls until seven o'clock. They were guided by Shmuel Kaplinski and A. L. Sapirstein, who knew their way around the sewers, but as Riezel Korczak later remembered, it was a difficult and treacherous journey:

> Darkness prevails in the tunnel. . . . The pale light of a lamp illuminates the way and we advance. My shoulders rub against the narrow pipe, I cannot move my hand. . . . A single thought occupies my mind — not to get my weapon wet and not to fall behind. . . . The pipe which is over 1 meter in diameter ends suddenly, to become a smooth, round tunnel of only 1/2 meter. I crawl. The muddy water covers my garments. . . . The file halts. The report comes back that someone has fainted, he is lying in the middle and blocking the passage. . . . He is put on one side. . . . I lose all sense of time. . . . The order is whispered back: Make ready for exit.

Assisted by the Communist underground, most of the Jews reached a safe hideout. But four fighters were stopped by the German police. In the skirmish, one Nazi was killed and all the Jews captured. The other FPO members waited patiently for two days for partisan guides to show them the way to the Rudniki Forest. On learning that the guides had been killed in an ambush, Kovner decided to lead his group of fifty to the forest on his own. They reached the woods one day later and were joined by another group of about thirty FPO members. There they allied themselves with Soviet and Lithuanian partisans and formed the nucleus of such units as Ha-Nokem, or Avenger, commanded by Kovner, and To Victory, led by Shmuel Kaplinski.

In Vilna, in the dark days that followed, 3,700 men were deported to labour camps in Latvia and Estonia, and 4,000 women, children, and elderly men were sent to the Sobibor concentration camp, where they were gassed. At least 100 children and older Jews were taken to the Ponary and killed immediately. Of the approximately 57,000 Jews in Vilna when the Nazi occupation began in June 1941, only about 2,500 survived.

ESCAPE

If someone tells you that when he went to the partisans he was motivated by a desire to fight and by a desire to take revenge, that is incorrect. All of us left the ghetto in the hope of staying alive. We hoped just for a chance. And if not to survive, at least one wanted to die differently from the way most Jews were dying. Not to be shot in a mass grave and not to go to a concentration camp. I think that these motivations were similar for all who ran away from the ghetto. They did not leave to fight, they left to live.

— ZORACH ARLUK

DECISIONS OF DESPERATION

"Escape from the ghettos was not a problem," asserts Sara Ginaite, who left the Kovno ghetto to join the partisans in 1943. "The ghetto was not a concentration camp. It was possible to escape. The problem was where to go once you were out."

In 1942, the odds of a Jew in the occupied eastern territories surviving on his own were slim indeed. There were police patrols to avoid and collaborators who were more than willing to inform on any escapees found hiding or begging for food. In the region south of Lublin, for instance, it has been estimated that approximately 20,000 Jews escaped to the forest areas during 1942, but that most were later hunted down and killed by German police.

Nazi punishment was swift and harsh. In Grodno, in late 1942, a Jewish woman was discovered outside the ghetto fence. She was arrested along with the woman she happened to be sharing a room with. They were both hanged and their bodies left on the gallows as an example for those contemplating escape. Nazi police units in the *Generalgouvernement* followed the rules established by the *Schiessebefehl*, a shoot-to-kill-order. This, as historian Daniel Goldhagen has noted, "mandated the shooting of all Jews found outside ghettos and camps — on country roads, in woods, hiding in homes or on farms. The *Schiessebefehl* made the Jews, including Jewish children, *vogelfrei*, outlaws facing an automatic death sentence." Needless to say, the order was enforced rigorously.

Still, even before partisan guides reached the ghettos to lead Jews into the forest, many ghetto inmates who were unconnected to underground movements fled for their lives. What choice did they have? Often it was a decision made on the spur of the moment during the chaos of an *Aktion*; a decision of desperation.

In general, both apathy and family responsibilities prevented many Jews from taking concerted action to save themselves. "People found it hard to make decisions," suggests Leni Yahil, "to take initiative, or to launch themselves into the unknown in the forests." In April 1943, Lithuanian friends attempted to convince Avraham Tory, the deputy secretary of the Kovno Judenrat, to escape from the ghetto. What did he have to lose? they asked him. He was torn. "We must flee, but where to? Who should run away? And — the main question — when?" he wrote in his diary. "Is there really any place to run to? Should we, who are so much involved in the Ghetto life with all our heart and conscience, flee too? We are plagued by thousands of questions and we feel the thousands of threads tying us to the place."

For those more willing to contemplate escape, the choice became an impossible dilemma. Peter Silverman recalls that in spring of 1942, his uncle, Meir Smuszkowicz, who was trapped in the Glebokie ghetto, wanted to escape to join his brother-in-law, who had already departed for the forest. But he never did. "To leave the ghetto," states Silverman, "he had to leave behind his wife, Sonia; six-year-old [son], Pesach; and an infant daughter. This he could not do. That does not mean that those who did escape did not care as much for their families. On the contrary, some had even stronger bonds. They saw themselves as pioneers. They searched for hiding places where they could find refuge for their loved ones. Some did succeed in rescuing their families. Others were captured and killed."

In another case, in the town of Orla, not far from Bialystok, a group of young boys fled hoping to join the partisans. But when they learned that the Nazi police were prepared to murder their families unless they returned to the ghetto, they reluctantly did so. They were killed along with the family members whose lives they had slightly prolonged.

For young people, in particular, rumours about partisans awakened feelings of hope and promise. Their parents, however, initially regarded such ideas as dangerous foolishness. Early in 1942, seventeen-year-old Leon Kahn was working as a labourer cutting wood in the vicinity of the Radun ghetto, where his family was living. He would travel to the forest area, sleep at local farmhouses, and work for seven days before returning to the ghetto. It was during his time in the woods that he first heard the stories of the Soviet partisans. And they stirred him. "The realization that there were men somewhere in that very forest, perhaps even close at hand, who had escaped the Germans and had found a way to survive, excited my imagination," he later recalled. "It was the old Tarzan dream again, but this time it was much closer to reality. When I returned to Radun and told my parents, they dismissed it as nonsense."

In 1942, in the ghetto in Novogrudok, Sulia Wolozhinski (later Rubin), then eighteen years of age, read Nazi posters demanding information about "bandits" in the forest. One of the bandits was named Bielski. She had also heard about Soviet soldiers trying to start their own underground army. While Sulia was convinced that there was something to these rumours, her parents were sceptical. "Mama didn't believe in it and said, 'How can a fly fight against an elephant?'" she recalled. "Papa said that they, 'the old,' should sacrifice for the young and remain; we, the young, should escape. How old could they be? My

God, they were young yet! Mama, forty-eight, and Papa, not yet fifty-two! Somehow my parents thought that in the forest, one had to run constantly, and they were afraid they wouldn't be able to keep up and would only be a hindrance and the cause of many deaths."

Sulia, however, was clever. When she and her family were sent to the courthouse that served as a ghetto, Sulia hid each day in a hole during the daily counting of people. She became a non-person and hence not a liability to her parents and sister if and when she escaped. Still, her first attempt nearly ended in disaster. Together with a girlfriend, she tried to walk away from a labour detail. The two girls had made it 3 kilometres down the road before they were caught by the police. Accused of having links to the partisans, they were whipped and sent to the Nazi gendarmerie headquarters to face the wrath of Meister Wolfe.

"Where were you going?" the Nazi policeman demanded.

"To buy potatoes," replied Sulia, standing before him with her back covered in blood. "We were hungry and it makes one desperate."

"You were going to the partisans! Don't lie!" he shouted.

"No, I wasn't," she protested.

The interrogation continued in this vein for several minutes, until Meister Wolfe asked for her parents' names. When Sulia told him that her mother was Anne Wolozhinski, the dentist, the Nazi suddenly became friendlier. As luck would have it, he had been a patient of Sulia's mother's during the First World War, and he was still grateful. He promised to help Sulia and her friend; he also told her that he had a Jewish wife and child who had escaped to England. Within a day, she was back in the courthouse ghetto instead of facing a firing squad at the death pit outside Novogrudok.

Undeterred by her close brush with death, Sulia decided to try one more time three weeks later. There was already snow on the ground. One morning, helped by her older sister, Rita, she was able to leave through the gate. She never saw Rita or her parents again. Wearing only a sweater, she walked quickly. "I didn't know what I would do once I reached the woods," she later remembered. "I didn't dare think." On the way, she encountered a group of three teenage boys and one girl, who were also from the courthouse. She joined them and together they decided to try to make it to a nearby farm, whose owner it was rumoured had connections to the partisans. In time, she was guided by Jewish fighters to the Bielski family camp, where she survived the war.

Motel B. was also in the vicinity of Novogrudok when the Germans attacked and his world collapsed. At twenty-nine, he was young, strong, and able to work. He was working on a road crew when he heard from local peasants that large pits were being dug outside the town. Without thinking, Motel ran into the fields. The next day, December 8, 1941, 4,000 of Novogrudok's Jews, including Motel's family, were massacred. For the next four months, Motel was alone and on the run. Each night, he would sneak into a barn or shed to avoid freezing to death. Once, the police nearly caught him, but thanks to a Belorussian farmer, he was able to avoid capture by hiding in a potato bin. He believed he was the only Jew still alive.

Unable to take it any more, and with no one willing to hide him, he chanced returning to Novogrudok with a work team. There he discovered his fifteen-year-old nephew, who related to him the tragic fate of his family. He worked in the ghetto almost until the next major *Aktion*, on August 7, 1942. Suspecting the worst, he was able to flee into the forest just in time. Another 2,500 Jews from Novogrudok were murdered in that *Aktion*.

In this second flight, Motel had escaped with a friend, but still there was nowhere for them to go. Under the threat of Nazi retaliation, Belorussian farmers refused to assist them or any other Jews on the run. Dejected, Motel soon returned to the ghetto yet again. But he refused to give up hope. Within a couple of weeks, he was planning another escape with a group of seven friends. They had heard about Russian partisans and about the Bielski brothers. One night, they broke through the fence and ran into the forest in search of the partisans. This time, for Motel B., there was no going back.

■ ■

During the bloodshed and massacres of late 1941 and 1942, escape from the ghettos was often unplanned. In the furore of an *Aktion*, the will for self-preservation was great. Sheer luck also played a factor.

The last time Sonia Ostrinsky saw her father alive, she was sixteen years old. It was the middle of the night in the spring of 1942. She was staying in a crowded house in the Sharkovshchina ghetto, across the street from her father and two of her three brothers. (The third brother lived in another town.) At about four o'clock in the morning, she was awakened by a Jewish policeman, who warned her that the *Aktion* was about to begin. She ran to warn her sleeping family. Her brothers managed to flee, but her father was killed.

In the confusion, she was separated from her brothers. She ran towards the river on the outskirts of the village, but the Nazis were waiting. Somehow she was able to squirm through a hole in the fence, but she was shot in the leg and seriously wounded. Dazed and bleeding, she pulled herself up and continued to run. By evening, she had reached the forest and had attached herself to three other Jews and two young children who had also fled the ghetto. Soon the adults deserted her and the children. She headed towards a small village, Novy-Pohost, where she knew there were a few Jewish families, including one man who was a pharmacist.

The first night, she and the children slept in a barn belonging to a friendly peasant. The farmer and his wife gave them warm milk and tended to Sonia's wound, though the infection did not heal for many months. The children remained with the farmer and Sonia left to find the Jewish family she was hunting for. She intended to return for them, yet was unable to and never saw them again.

After a day or two of dangerous wandering, she finally reached Novy-Pohost and contacted the Jewish pharmacist. In his house, she discovered about a dozen scared Jews hiding in a cellar. A short time later, in one of those twists of fate that are more common than not in stories of Holocaust survivors, one of her brothers found her. He had escaped with an uncle, who had been wounded. They came seeking medical aid and iodine from the same Jewish pharmacist that Sonia had run to.

Unwilling to remain in the family's cellar, Sonia's brother took her and together they walked more than 66 kilometres to an isolated town where another brother was living. The Germans had established a small ghetto there, though as Sonia recalls it was not as well guarded as others. Afraid of a major *Aktion* or deportation, Sonia, her two brothers, and about fifty other Jews decided that their only chance for survival was to escape farther into the forest. Late one night, carrying tins of food, warm clothing, and boots, the group set off for the swampy terrain.

■ ■

Not far away, in the town of Zoludek, eighteen-year-old Pessia Lewit (now Bairach) barely survived an *Aktion* on May 9, 1942, that took the lives of her family and hundreds of other Jews. She eluded capture by hiding with two neighbourhood children, whose parents had been shot, in a *maline* that had been built in the attic of a cowshed. All around her, other groups of Jews in hiding were found and executed. Too frightened to react, she remembers hearing the voices of her Polish and Belorussian classmates searching vacant Jewish homes for imagined treasures. Finally, they found something.

"It was our Passover dishes that we kept in the attic," she writes. "The special dishes and glasses aroused, for some reason, their mockery. 'Here are their glasses! And look at their plates!' They would scream in the midst of their excitement. The Gentiles' visits became more and more frequent. They were coming from the villages . . . in search of treasures. With axes and shovels they would hammer the walls."

After more than a week without food and water, Pessia emerged and was immediately apprehended by a Polish policeman she had met earlier. His name was Yanish. She prepared herself to die, but Yanish did not kill her. Instead, he gave her food and water and allowed her to return to her hiding place. He also told her that only eighty Jews, skilled craftsmen and their families, had been allowed to live. Among them was a man named Moshe Bairach, a Jew from a nearby town whom she had been introduced to in the ghetto. Within a few days, Yanish had figured out a way to save Pessia and the two children: She would be listed as Moshe Bairach's wife and the children as part of another family.

Soon after, Bairach was transferred to the Lida ghetto and Pessia was permitted to join him. They had barely known each other in Zoludek, but Bairach was more than happy to care for her. In time, they fell in love and were married. In Lida, Bairach began making contacts with visiting partisans from Tuvia Bielski's group. He and Pessia decided to leave for the forest at the first opportunity. Their escape, together with about thirty other people, including children, finally took place one evening in May 1943.

■ ■

Hours before the beginning of a major *Aktion* in the Slonim ghetto on November 14, 1941, Lisa Nussbaum's mother, Gitel, helped her and her elder sister, Pola, escape under the wire fence. Gitel had arranged for her two daughters to be hidden at the home of Polish neighbours. It was the last time either of the two girls saw their mother alive. She was killed later that day.

With their blonde hair and free of their yellow stars, which they had removed from their jackets, Lisa and Pola safely made it to their hiding place. But the next day, the Polish woman who was helping them became scared. Having heard about the massacre in the ghetto and aware of Nazi regulations forbidding assistance to Jews, the woman ordered Lisa and Pola to leave. "We begged to stay," Lisa remembers. "It was winter and there was snow on the ground. The woman told us to hide in the woods. We had no alternative."

As they walked deeper and deeper into the forest, they suddenly met the local forester, who was armed with a rifle. They told him in Polish that they were out collecting wood, but he did not believe them. "You are Jews and should be shot," he yelled. He ordered them to march in the direction of the road. With the distance between the girls and the forester widening, Pola told Lisa to run. Yet as they attempted to escape, the forester threw his ax at them, catching Pola in the leg. She went down momentarily, but the two girls managed to get away from their attacker.

Although they sought help from various peasants, no one would offer them refuge. The two girls eventually found a hiding place in an unattended barn. Hours later, a woman discovered them there and kindly tended to the wound on Pola's leg. She permitted Lisa and Pola to stay the night, but refused to keep them any longer. With nowhere to go and no one willing to hide them for a long period of time, the girls decided to risk returning to the Slonim ghetto. They were able to join up with a work party and re-enter the ghetto. Their mother had been murdered — she had refused to leave her sister-in-law — but their father and younger brother had escaped the *Aktion* and were in hiding on the outskirts of the town. It was shortly after Lisa came back to Slonim that she met her future husband, Aron Dereczynski (later changed to Derman), then twenty years old and a committed member of Ha-Shomer Hatsair.

During the next major *Aktion*, at the end of June 1942, Pola was killed, but Lisa, disguised as a boy, was able to escape from Slonim and reach the ghetto in Grodno. Aron followed her later. In Grodno, Aron befriended a Pole named Tadek, who was instrumental in engineering their escape to Vilna in March 1943 (on the roof of a military train) as the deportations of Grodno's Jews to Auschwitz were commencing. In Vilna, they were interrogated by Gens and the Jewish police before being given ration cards for food.

Aron knew that they would never survive in the ghetto and, through his Zionist connections, contacted the FPO. In the days after the arrest and suicide of Wittenberg, Aron and Lisa were among a group of twenty-eight FPO fighters who escaped from Vilna and fled to the Narocz Forest. As Lisa recalls, they left one day at six o'clock in the morning. Two young men led the way, but they got lost. Finally they reached the Vileyka River and were nearly captured by a German patrol. When they at last made it into partisan territory, they were greeted by two Jewish resisters, armed and on horseback. "I will never forget this moment," states Lisa. "We had come to the promised land."

■ ■

On Yom Kippur 1942, in a small village east of Vilna, Ralph F. was caught in a round-up of Jews. He was twelve years old going on eighteen. The police locked Ralph and the other 160 people they apprehended in a small building that had once served as a private club. The doors and windows were locked. Most of the people, Ralph recalls, believed that they were going to be transported to a labour camp or another ghetto. The Nazis, however, had other plans.

The next morning, the Jews were taken out of the club and marched in the direction of the Catholic cemetery on the outskirts of the town. "We saw a bunch of SS [men] standing, smoking, and joking," remembers Ralph. "There was some shovels and all the men and boys were commanded to dig a pit." He was scared but determined not to die in this mass grave. "As I was crawling out of the pit, I took dirt and threw it into the face of the first Nazi I saw. I ran in a zigzag. They fired at me and someone was running behind me. I heard a shriek, but I did not turn around. I got away into the forest." He stopped for a moment to catch his breath, then heard the firing of automatic weapons and pistols.

Ralph knew that his father had hid some of their possessions with a local farmer and had built a small hiding place there. He made it to the hut and was later joined by his mother, who had escaped from the ghetto (his father had been sent to a labour camp months earlier). For five long months, Ralph and his mother hid under the floorboards of the farmer's hut. Once a day, they were brought food. Month after month, they just lay there amid the human waste that was pushed to one side. His body grew numb. "I repeated [the Hebrew prayer] Shema Yisrael 10,000 times," he says. "We lived only for the sake of hope."

The Belorussian farmer hiding them eventually became frightened that they would be discovered by the police and that all of them would be killed. Ralph claims that the farmer attempted to kill him and his mother by putting crushed glass in their food. They stopped eating and realized that they would have to leave.

One Sunday, early in the morning, Ralph, barely able to walk after his months in hiding, left his mother and set off in search of another hiding place. He walked about 3 kilometres, until he came to another farm and concealed himself in the barn. He worked out an arrangement with this new farmer, who brought his mother from the other hut. They now hid in a nook behind the oven and only came out late at night for food.

Ralph had heard about the Soviet partisans fighting in the forests and decided that he should attempt to contact them. He went from farmhouse to farmhouse until he found one Polish peasant whose son had joined the partisans. Ralph waited there until the son returned with six of his comrades. They told him he could join their group only if he had a weapon, then took him to a cluster of about thirty-five Jews hiding in a swampy area of the Narocz Forest. Ralph and some other boys from this group learned from a farmer about a Nazi policeman who visited the area regularly to see a young woman. They waited for the officer, then attacked and killed him. In this way, Ralph F. obtained the weapon he required to join the partisans.

MOTHERS AND DAUGHTERS, FATHERS AND SONS

The war destroyed most of the families it touched, Jewish or Christian. In some rare cases, however, Jewish families were able to escape together, either to a hiding place outside the ghetto or to the forest itself. Few families, though, survived intact. In fact, many young Jews only attempted escape when their parents had been murdered, releasing them from familial obligations and responsibilities. As Rochelle Sutin put it, in recounting the death of her family and her departure from the ghetto in Stolpce in September 1942, "There was nothing left for me but escape."

On the evening of December 16, 1941, the Judenrat in the town of Jody, north-east of Vilna, was warned by a friendly Polish police official that death awaited the Jews in the morning. But Alter Silverman, a veteran Russian soldier of the First World War and a grain merchant, was prepared. He had heard the stories of the massacres in other locales and had arranged hiding places on nearby farms for the members of his family. As his son Peter later observed, "I owe my life to the planning and actions of one man, my father, Alter Silverman. Because of his farsightedness, eight members of our family survived the Holocaust."

In the middle of the night, Alter set his escape plan in motion. He awoke Peter, then sixteen years old, and his siblings. "We had all been prepared for the escape," Peter states, "I knew that my hiding place was about one and a half kilometres away, in the village of Vinica, with the family of Antony Pierchorowicz. . . . At 4 a.m. my father rushed us out of the house, reminding us to stay in the fields and to avoid the roads. In half an hour I was knocking at the door of the Pierchorowicz house. They took me right to the barn, where I hid in a stack of hay." After a few days, Peter Silverman joined his father, uncle, and aunt on a more remote farm. Food was scarce, and they were given only one slice of bread and a small amount of water each night.

Once the killing of Jody's Jews had stopped, those in hiding were encouraged by the Nazi and local police to return to their homes with promises that the violence had ended. The Silvermans reluctantly did so. They found that in their absence, their Belorussian neighbours had ripped up the floorboards of their house looking for valuables and money. When he learned more about the massacre and the way it was carried out, Alter Silverman made new hiding arrangements for the eight remaining members of the family. He was also given a handgun by a friendly farmer, who told him, "You will need it."

Two months passed until news came that Jody's Jews were to be deported to another ghetto about 50 kilometres away. The Silvermans and their relatives, the Smuszkowiczes (also spelled Smuschkowitz by some members of the family), feared the worst. They left Jody quickly and hid on two farms. "When I left my home in Jody about [4 a.m.] that March morning in 1942," Peter Silverman writes, "I had no idea that I would be homeless for the next eight years. . . . Little did I know that my next home would be Brooklyn, New York, in August, 1949."

■ ■

Farther to the south-west, in the Radun ghetto, Leon Kahn and his family had survived an *Aktion* during the first week of May 1942 by hiding in a concealed attic. "More than fifty of us lay there in our dark, prison-like sanctuary," recalled Kahn, "without food or water, breathing through the cracks in the concrete blocks." Because they had no means of sanitation, he adds, "We could not deal with our normal bodily functions, and the stench became absolutely unbearable."

Kahn's father, Shael, had hid elsewhere in the house and was discovered by a Polish policeman who was conducting a search. He was ordered to march to the Jewish cemetery with one hundred or so other men to dig the death pit. At a pre-arranged signal, the men started swinging their shovels and picks at the guards. But the fight was over in a matter of minutes. Twenty-eight men died instantly, most were wounded. A few, like Shael Kaganowicz, were able to run to the woods and rejoin their families.

A month later, the remaining Jews of Radun were to be relocated to another ghetto. Young Leon was convinced that such a move would mean death for the entire family and, with help from his brother and sister, succeeded in persuading his father that they must try to escape to the forest. "Even if I lived as the animals lived," Leon explains, "I could die there [in the forest] with the dignity of a man."

Leon's mother, Miriam, however, refused to abandon her own mother. Clearly, the elderly woman could not have endured life on the run. When Leon's grandmother did not give his mother the required permission to leave with her family, she remained behind. As Leon remembered it years later, the final farewell was painful:

> Our parting will remain forever on my mind and my conscience. We hugged and kissed goodbye again and again; then, at the door, I turned to look back, to take one last mental picture of my dear mother. I can still see her, her dark wavy hair now prematurely grey, but her beautiful strong features unchanged. I was torn between my fear of dying and my conviction that I was betraying her, letting her down when she needed me. A hundred times I told myself to stay, a hundred times my terror forced me to leave my adored mother. . . .

That evening, the other members of Leon's family, as well as two neighbours, cautiously made their way out of the Radun ghetto into the countryside.

■ ■

Unlike Leon Kahn, eighteen-year-old Rochelle Sutin found herself orphaned and alone in the Stolpce ghetto at the end of September 1942. Her mother's last words to her were "to take *nekome*, revenge. On a certain abstract level, I could understand. I wanted it myself. But at the same time, it was incomprehensible to me. I was alone, a girl, without weapons or power, surrounded by a world that had shown me nothing but hate."

Still, she was determined that she was not going to be stripped naked and shot in a pit. "I was not going to wait for that," she states. "I decided I would die running!" She found a friend of about the same age, a girl named Tanya whose family had also been murdered. Both women were forced to work at a local sawmill under police supervision. Slowly they planned their escape. They told a young Jewish couple who worked with them what they intended to do and the man, Motel, and his wife decided to join Rochelle and Tanya. For Motel and his wife, however, the decision to escape was painful: they had to leave their five-year-old son behind in the ghetto in the care of an older woman. Such were the terrible choices of life under the Nazis.

The sawmill where Rochelle and her friends worked was situated on the banks of the Niemen River. The forest beckoned on the other side. Still, their plan, to swim across the river and run into the woods, was really no plan at all. "There was no plan beyond that," Rochelle recalls. "We never even talked about what we would do if we reached the woods. We didn't expect to live that long."

One foggy September morning, the four of them made their way to the outhouses at the back of the mill and moved towards the barbed-wire fence. They crawled under the fence and jumped into the river. Rochelle was wearing a skirt, shirt, jacket, and shoes. She remembers what followed like this:

Within a minute we could hear the German police raising a cry. . . . They were fully armed. The machine guns were loud. . . . We heard the bullets hit the water all around us and we thought *that* was what we wanted: to die at any minute. But somehow, I don't know how, we managed to swim all the way across the river to the other side. Then we ran for the woods. The machine guns were still going. You could hear the bullets striking the trees and ripping the leaves that were still left on the branches. Motel and his wife must have run in another direction, because I didn't see them again for a long time. But Tanya and I ran together. Meanwhile, between swimming and running, I had lost my shoes, so I was barefooted. And I had thrown away my jacket just before diving into the river because it would have been hard to swim in it. So I was just in my pleated school skirt and blouse. We ran and ran. But we still heard the machine guns. . . . We ran all day like that. We went deep into the woods and finally had to sit down.

Their wet clothes froze in the cold of the night as they tried to sleep on the ground. They had no food, and no idea where to find any. They hid in the same spot for about two days and tried to figure out what to do next. Tanya had heard rumours of the Soviet partisans and had obtained the name of a friendly Belorussian farmer. This farmer lived in the vicinity of the sawmill, and the girls hoped that he might be in contact with the partisans. Thinking back, Rochelle Sutin remarks that this idea "seemed remote, but what other possibilities did we have?"

Somehow they found the peasant farmer they were searching for. He had little knowledge of the partisans but did give them something to eat and advised them to speak with another Belorussian farmer who lived a few kilometres away. The second farmer gave them something to eat as well and confirmed that there were indeed Russian guerrilla fighters in the area. He told them to wait. Within a few hours, a small group of Soviet resisters arrived at the farm. "They were unshaven, in filthy uniforms," Rochelle writes, "but they were armed to the teeth. . . . We begged them to let us join them. We told them we'd do anything . . . cook, clean wash, whatever was needed for the resistance effort. They felt sorry for us and agreed to take us in."

■ ■

Gershon Seigel, then seventeen years old, lost his family on June 29, 1942, in the Slonim ghetto. It was the beginning of the third *Aktion*. By the time it ended, two weeks later, another 10,000 Jews had been murdered, bringing the total killed in the small eastern Polish town to about 21,500 — nearly the entire pre-war Jewish population.

Seigel survived by hiding in the attic of his house with an older Jewish man who lived with the family. His older brother Michael had also attempted to hide, but he was discovered in a search. The German police, remembers Jerry Seigel (as he is now known), "pulled [Michael] out, yelling at him. [They] hit him three times and asked him if he had any gold, watches, money or other valuables, and if someone else was hiding in the attic with him. I am amazed that Michael . . . didn't lose his nerve then and blurt out about us, but he didn't."

Seigel remained in hiding with the older man throughout the day —

until they smelled smoke. The Nazis had set the ghetto on fire. They stayed where they were, however, and fortunately, the flames did not reach their house. In the middle of the night, they decided to move to a small shed in the yard, where they believed it would be safer. Inside, a *maline* had been previously prepared. There they discovered a woman with two young boys and two teenage girls. In the morning, Jerry and his companion re-entered the house for some food and water and saw that several other Jews had also survived. But the older man had left his shaving kit in the shed and asked Jerry to retrieve it for him.

"It was fate that I agreed," states Seigel, "because I went into the bunker to take out the shaving kit, which was in a Dodge Master cigar box, and just when I opened up the cover of the bunker to come out and return to the house, at that same moment German soldiers arrived at the house and found the occupants. I heard the Germans shouting loudly, ordering them out, and they were all taken away."

He remained in the bunker with the woman and children for another day, then learned, from a Jewish friend who visited his hiding place, that a smaller ghetto was being established in Slonim. He decided that he would try to join a work group as soon as was possible in order to enter the new ghetto. Leaving the two girls in their hiding place (he promised that he would arrange for someone to get them later but was unable to do so), Seigel, the woman, and the two boys left the bunker. They succeeded in making their way into the new ghetto, but arrived without a work permit, which Seigel could not obtain. He knew that without that piece of paper, he would not last long, so he decided to leave Slonim and attempt to reach a cousin in another village, 28 kilometres away.

As he left the ghetto one Sunday afternoon, having removed the Star of David from his jacket, he was immediately stopped by a Polish police-man. He tried to explain that he was going to a new workplace, but since no one worked on Sunday, the policeman told him that he was taking him to the German authorities. The officer then saw that Seigel had a box in his jacket pocket and ordered him to give it to him. It was the shaving kit that had belonged to the old Jewish man. Mistakenly believing that the box contained money or jewellery, the policeman took it from Seigel and told him to return to the ghetto. Seigel did so, but he did not stay long. He walked to the other end of the fence and slipped out of the ghetto once again. The shaving kit had now saved his life on two occasions.

This time, he reached the woods and was able to walk undetected to his cousin's house. Their home and barn now served as the sleeping quarters for a group of Jewish labourers. Two days later, the Gestapo began killing the Jews in the area. Moments before they arrived at his cousin's house, Seigel and several of his relatives ran into the nearby woods. They soon met up with more relatives and these thirteen cousins formed their own partisan group. He was to remain with them for the next two years.

■ ■

For the first six months after the Nazi invasion of Soviet territory, Velvke Yonson, then twenty-one years old, managed to stay one step ahead of Nazi death squads. For a short time, in June 1941, he served in the Red Army. One day, under attack from German troops and artillery, he received orders to run and returned to his family in Novogrudok. He was nearly killed again in a mid-July *Aktion*, but ran away, as he later wrote, "under a hail of bullets." For a month, he hid with relatives in a town a few kilometres away, then made his way back to Novogrudok. Young and strong, he was forced to labour for the Germans and avoided death again in the slaughter of 4,000 of Novogrudok's Jews on December 8, 1941. Most members of his family were not so fortunate. About a month later, his mother, his sister Grunya, her husband, David, and their two young children were among a group of 500 Jews burned alive in a barn in a nearby village.

The next day, a farmer who was able to enter the ghetto brought Yonson the tragic news. "I have turned to stone and cannot cry," he recalled after the war. "Later I began to tremble and I shouted literally like a lion. At night, lying on my hard bench, a fire is lit in my heart, a fire of revenge, and I swear I will not rest until I avenge my dear ones." He soon got his opportunity. Within four days, he and three friends had escaped from the Novogrudok ghetto courthouse. He was nearly apprehended by an Estonian guard, but again eluded capture and a certain death.

It took him two nights to reach the outskirts of Dvorets, where his other sister, Henya, was working in a labour camp. He snuck into the camp and found her for an emotional reunion. But he realized that he endangered the lives of the other Jews in the camp by being there, so he left that same night. His sister begged him to take her, but he didn't know where he was going. He promised he would return for her within a week.

He and his friends walked deep into the woods until they were met by a group of Jewish partisans of the Russian Orlanski *otriad* (most likely Jews who were former Red Army soldiers). The fighters interviewed him, but refused to allow him or his friends to join them. Yonson and his group then decided to move farther south to the Lipiczany Forest. Near the Schara River, not far from Slonim, they met another group of Soviet partisans, this one led by a Russian named Vanushka. "It is worth noting," Yonson writes, "that the Jewish partisans sent us away, but the Gentiles accepted us." After a short training period, Yonson and his friends became members of an *otriad* led by Pavel Bulak, a local Belorussian Communist. In early 1942, the group included about 320 fighters, according to Yonson.

After an attack on the Germans at Derechin, where Yonson states he was able to "take his revenge," he sought permission to rescue his sister from the labour camp at Dvorets, about 120 kilometres away. He arrived one day too late. The Nazis had destroyed the camp and killed its inmates just twenty-four hours earlier. Overcome with sadness and anger, he rejoined his unit ready to do battle.

PARTISANS AND GUIDES

Eighteen-year-old men are not normally described as beautiful, but that is how most women remember Yossel Zelkowicz. Tall, blond, and blue-eyed, Yossel was as intelligent and good-natured as he was handsome. Born in Lodz in 1925, he had attended Polish and Jewish schools and led a normal life before the war.

In the spring of 1942, Yossel, who was able to speak several languages, was working as a translator for the Nazis in the Lida ghetto, where his family — his parents, Lazer and Leska; eleven-year old sister, Gitel; and four-year-old brother, Simon — lived. Yossel's skills and his parents' ability to work saved the family in a *selektion* and *Aktion* on May 8, which took the lives of nearly 6,000 of Lida's Jews.

It was after this killing that Yossel, like many young Jews in Lida, began contemplating escape. With his parents' blessing, he was able to make contact with his friend Ignaz Feldon, a Jewish partisan emissary who had secretly entered the ghetto in search of able-bodied men to join the Soviet-led *otriad* known as Iskra, or the Spark. At the time, Iskra operated in the small forest area between Lida and Novogrudok and consisted of only a half a dozen fighters. Eventually, it grew into an effective fighting force of more than 300 partisans.

Kalman Lichtman, the chairman of the Lida Judenrat, agreed to report that Yossel had come down with typhus so that he could leave the ghetto without arousing German suspicions or endangering the lives of his family. A few days later, he was listed as dead.

Yossel remained with Iskra for about three months and carried out a number of sabotage operations on German trains. But his family's survival was ultimately more important to him than revenge on the Nazis, and his main objective was to bring his family out of the Lida ghetto. There was, however, no place for parents and children in a Russian partisan unit.

At some point during this period, Yossel made contact with Tuvia Bielski and his group, which now included about twenty people and was located in the same woods. They slept in makeshift tents, moved continually, and ate whatever they could find or obtain from local peasants. Potatoes, which were the most plentiful vegetables, were their main staple.

Tuvia and his brothers soon determined that their chances of survival would greatly improve if they enlarged their group with more men and weapons. Messengers were sent into the Novogrudok ghetto and young men began arriving, but few had weapons or ammunition.

This movement of people was greatly assisted by a friendly Belorussian peasant named Konstanty Kozlowski, who acted as a link between the ghetto and the forest. As a young boy, Kozlowski (or Koscik, as he was called) had apprenticed with a Jewish shoemaker and had learned to speak Yiddish. As a result, his hatred for the Nazis was as great as that of any Jew. To help, he turned his isolated peasant farmhouse, or *hutor*, which was about 11 kilometres from Novogrudok, into a transition point for escaped Jews who wanted to contact the Bielskis. On a number of occasions, he also slipped into different ghettos and led Jews to the forest.

In the summer of 1942, to give it more credibility, the Bielskis' expanded group was reorganized into an official Soviet-style *otriad*, known as the Zhukov *otriad* after Marshal Grigori Zhukov, the Red Army commander of the Western Front. Tuvia was formally made the head of the detachment, and took responsibility for the group's policies and security. Asael Bielski became deputy commander and their brother Zus was made head of intelligence. It was his task to scout the region, make contacts with peasants, and watch for signs of danger.

In the fall of 1942, Yossel Zelkowicz obtained permission from his Russian leader to transfer from Iskra to the Bielski *otriad*. It was the only way he could arrange for his family to leave the Lida ghetto. By then, Tuvia had decided to accept any Jewish fugitive — man, woman, or child — who came to him. "Would that there were thousands of Jews who could reach our camp," Tuvia was reported to have said. "We would take all of them in." Such a policy was not popular with everyone. Even Zus Bielski questioned the practicality of accepting so many defenceless people who needed to be looked after. But Tuvia stubbornly insisted and others soon followed.

The escape from Lida took place one dark evening. Approximately sixty Jews, including the four members of the Zelkowicz family, departed for the forests and the Bielski camp. Young Simon was carried on his father's shoulders, and the escape remains one of his earliest and most vivid childhood memories. He recalls walking and running through water. "After a time, we were allowed to rest by a fire," he says. "I took off my boots to dry them and they shriveled up. After that, I did not have shoes for a long while." Gitel adds that all they had were berries to eat and muddy water to drink. Her father would dip his handkerchief in the water and wring drops of it into his children's mouths.

After several days, the Zelkowiczes reached the Bielski camp, where they lived out the war. Unfortunately, Yossel was not as lucky. On a reconnaissance mission in March 1943, he was caught in a Nazi ambush and shot in the back. His body was never found.

■ ■

As the movement continued to grow in late 1942 and early 1943, more and more Jews like the Zelkowiczes were rescued by partisan guides. Young resisters from the ghettos of Minsk, Kovno, and Vilna were brought to join fighting *otriady*, but families, older men and women, and orphaned children were saved as well — at least temporarily. Historian Dov Levin estimates, for instance, that in Lithuania, of the 40,000 Jews still alive at the beginning of 1943, 1,800 were able to escape to the forests from the ghettos, though many died en route or later in the Nazi hunts that followed.

The Bielski *otriad*, in particular, became a magnet for a wide range of people. Jacob Druk, his wife, Faye, and their baby son, Joey, were friends of Tuvia's. Though the idea of bringing these people out of the Lida ghetto with an infant was disapproved of by almost everyone, Tuvia insisted that the Druks be given assistance. Led by Zus Bielski on horseback, they reached the Bielski camp in September 1942. Jacob Druk soon became a scout and guided other Jews still trapped in ghettos or lost in the forest. On one such journey, he found a young woman named Hana Berkowitz wandering in the woods. She had been forced out of her hiding place on a peasant's farm and was searching for partisans to help her. Druk took her to the Bielskis, who accepted her into their camp.

Tuvia rescued other friends and acquaintances in Lida, including Chaim Dworecki, his wife, and their two daughters. In the letter inviting Chaim to join him, Tuvia wrote, "It does not interest me if you have a gun or not, you are coming with your wife and children. Nothing is important. Just come." The family accepted Tuvia's offer and survived. The mother and brothers of Leah Bedzow (who later married Velvke Yonson) were brought out of Lida in much the same way, and were delivered to the Bielskis in February 1943 by the peasant Kozlowski.

Jews from the nearby town of Mir, south-east of Novogrudok, reached the Bielski *otriad* under more unique circumstances, however. Their escape is an integral part of the remarkable story of Samuel Rufeisen.

OSWALD

Above anything else, Samuel Rufeisen was a superb actor. During the war, Jews who attempted to pass themselves off as Poles or Ukrainians all too frequently gave themselves away by "fear, uncertainty [and] hesitation." But not Rufeisen. Not only did the twenty-year-old Polish Jew succeed in posing as a Christian, his ruse was so clever that he was employed by the Nazi police for nearly a year.

It was not that Rufeisen did not look Jewish; on the contrary, his dark hair, long nose, and large brown eyes should (and almost did) have betrayed his secret. Yet he could speak both German and Polish fluently and possessed "impeccable Christian manners." Having taken riding lessons as a student, Rufeisen was also superb with horses, an uncommon talent among most east European Jews, the majority of whom resided in urban centres. Hence those who suspected Rufeisen of hiding his true identity immediately changed their minds when they saw him sitting tall in the saddle. As one of his suspicious Polish friends remarked, "No Jew could ride like that."

Born in 1922 in the small Polish village of Zadziele, near Cracow, Rufeisen was active in the Akiva youth movement. When the war broke out in 1939, Rufeisen and his brother, Arye, escaped Nazi rule by fleeing to Vilna. Arye left Europe for Palestine before the Germans attacked in June 1941. But Samuel was arrested.

In the fall of 1941, having escaped imprisonment and death in Vilna, Samuel altered his identity to become Josef Oswald, a *Volksdeutsche* (a Pole with a German father or mother), and found work as an interpreter in the Belorussian town of Turocz. His employer was the local regional police chief and collaborator, Siemion Serafimowicz. When Serafimowicz was transferred to the nearby village of Mir, Rufeisen accompanied him. There he was befriended by Nazi police official Reinhold Hein, head of the gendarmerie units in the area. Hein was a Nazi with a conscience: he abhorred violence and senseless killing, but nonetheless ordered the mass murder of Mir's Jews.

The first *Aktion* had taken place in Mir in November 1941, when approximately 1,500 of the town's 2,350 Jews were killed. Before the war, Mir had been home to several well-known rabbinical scholars who taught at the town's famous *yeshivah*, which attracted students from all over the world. When the war broke out in 1939, most of the teachers and students escaped to Vilna and then to Shanghai, China, where they survived the Holocaust.

In May 1942, the remaining 850 Jews of Mir were relocated into the Mirski Castle or, in Polish, the Mir *zamek*. Once home to the local nobility, the eighteenth-century castle was, by 1941, a dilapidated and damp prison with limited water and sanitary facilities. Conditions behind the barbed wire the Nazis had placed on top of the walls were abysmal. "The *zamek* had an eerie atmosphere, there were old dungeons in the basement with rusted iron bars," recalls Jack Sutin, who was imprisoned there as a teenager. "Its thick outer stone wall had a single gate, as well as a number of small window-like openings that were high above the ground. . . . What few bathroom facilities there were in the *zamek* were totally inadequate for the 800 some Jews crammed within it."

For nine months, Oswald worked as the secretary of the regional police and acted as an interpreter for Polizei Meister Hein, a job that often put him in an impossible position. Morally, he felt compelled to save Jews if he could and to warn them of any impending assaults. But his instinct for self-preservation was equally great. Though he did witness countless executions, he also managed to save a few victims. Once, for example, he convinced Hein that an apprehended Jewish woman and her child were only Russians and not worth bothering with. Hein released them.

Alone in his office one day, Oswald finally took an enormous risk and made contact with Dov Resnik, a Jewish electrician he had casually known in Vilna. He promised to provide Resnik with information on the Nazis' plans for the ghetto.

Meanwhile, inside the Mirski Castle and against the better judgment of the Judenrat, a group of young Zionists, Jack Sutin among them, were determined to resist the Nazis and were prepared to die fighting. Their expectations for survival were nearly non-existent. "We had no weapons except for rocks, bottles, a few knives," Sutin remembers. "We were completely outnumbered and surrounded by a trained German military force supported by the local population."

Early in August 1942, Oswald overheard Hein on the telephone confirming that the date for the liquidation of the Mir ghetto was set for August 13. By this time, Oswald was smuggling weapons and ammunition to Resnik and his friends. (The arms had been confiscated by the gendarmerie from locals and escaped Russian soldiers, and Oswald had access to them.) He also attempted to convince them that their only hope for salvation was to escape to the forest rather than fight. Eventually, they agreed with him.

The escape was set for Sunday night, August 9. Oswald planned to fabricate a report about a partisan sighting in a town several miles away, and thereby send the bulk of the police on a wild-goose chase. But as the moment for the departure neared, emotions ran high in the ghetto. Despite Oswald's best efforts, there were enough arms for only fifty people. Those who still had young children worried that they would be shot the second they left the castle.

Adding to the tension were the reports of a recent arrival named Goldberg and his teenage son, two Jews who had escaped an *Aktion* in the town of Nieswiez. They had been on the run for a week, searching for partisan groups to take them. Not only were they unable to locate any partisans in the nearby forest area, but their attempt to find food and shelter was a total disaster. They came into the Mirski Castle with only rags for clothes and "warned that anyone leaving a ghetto can expect either a quick death from a bullet or a slow one caused by total rejection and starvation." Many residents of Mir, once intent on escaping on August 9, began to question their decision.

Most members of the Judenrat were opposed to the escape. Resnik had refused to reveal Oswald's true identity to them, and they were naturally suspicious of any information he brought. Some of the ghetto leaders believed that Oswald was laying a trap for them; others refused to accept that their fate was sealed. When arguments and disagreements threatened the entire operation, Dov Resnik finally revealed Oswald's Jewish background to several key Judenrat officials, many of whom were now prepared to flee themselves. But at a meeting held on August 7, the majority of Mir's 850 residents decided that they were going to stay and accept whatever God had in store for them. It was agreed, however, that no one would stand in the way of those opting to leave.

Cila Kapelowicz, then a young teenager, was not fully informed about the escape plans and was unsure what to do. "On Saturday, I went into the courtyard and saw that people were getting ready for departure. I did not know a thing. No one told me. . . . Even as some were getting ready to leave, there were those who doubted that there will be an *Aktion*. . . . No one explained to us a thing. Nothing was clear. But I sensed that there will be an end. I knew it in my bones. . . . All over it was 'Judenrein' and we knew that we had to leave if we wanted to avoid death. I did not know that Oswald arranged it, only that around us people were being executed and that our end was coming." Cila decided she was going to run.

Sunday night. For those not in the small and relatively well-organized resistance group, the escape proceeded spontaneously but in an atmosphere of desperation. Last minute life-and-death decisions still had to be made. Could a father desert his children, a child her elderly parent?

When it was his turn to run, Jack Sutin remembers how fast his legs carried him. "When I had played soccer, I was pretty good at getting up and down the field at full speed. But running in pure terror was new to me. My head was spinning. I was so afraid, so excited, that I wasn't myself at all. I felt like someone watching myself from above, racing for my life."

■ ■

About 300 people escaped from the Mir ghetto that night in August, leaving more than 500 to die at the hands of the Nazis and the Belorussian policemen four days later. As many had feared, the long-term survival rate of those on the run was not good. Within days, one group was shot by Soviet partisans who wanted their valuables; others died later in Nazi attacks on the forest. Jack Sutin and Cila Kapelowicz made their way to the great Naliboki Forest in western Belorussia on the banks of the Niemen River, where they linked up with the Zorin and Bielski family camps and survived the war.

Furious about the escape, Meister Hein launched an investigation. He learned from a Jew named Stanislawski, who worked in the gendarmerie's stables, that Oswald had told the residents of the ghetto about the impending *Aktion*. (For his help, Stanislawski was shot to death on August 14, one day after the main massacre.) When confronted by Hein, Oswald admitted to warning the Jews out of pity. Questioned further, he also admitted to giving the Jews weapons. Eventually, following more heated discussions, Oswald confessed the entire story, including his Jewish identity. Hein was astonished, and had Oswald arrested and imprisoned. One day later, Oswald was brought to see Hein, but in a moment of confusion, he managed to flee.

Despite having a price of 100,000 marks on his head, he found sanctuary in a nearby convent and in time, converted to Christianity. It was his way of finding further salvation. Later he was forced to take refuge in the forest and joined up with the Ponomarenko partisan group. Yet owing to his brief connections with the Nazis, some Jewish fugitives and fighters in the detachment regarded Oswald with great suspicion.

After the war, Oswald's amazing transformation continued when he took his vows as a monk in Cracow, changed his name to Father Daniel, and was accepted as a Carmelite monk in the Stella Maris monastery near Haifa, where he lives to this day. In 1962, Father Daniel made headlines in Israel when he challenged the Israeli Law of Return, which refused him status as a "Catholic Jew." But the Israeli Supreme Court voted against his appeal. Nevertheless, his actions in August 1942 are legendary, and Samuel Rufeisen will always be a genuine hero and a saint to the survivors of the Mir ghetto.

PART TWO

■

THE FOREST
AND
RESISTANCE

INTO THE FOREST

*On Saturday, January 23, 1943, the Germans found several Jews in a
nearby forest. They were shot on the spot.*

*Next day, January 24, 1943, we observed through an interstice in
our hiding place, how the Germans were escorting Berl Natan Zajd
from Pinczow with his wife and their two children. They had been
captured by peasants whom they approached for shelter. . . .*

*On February 16, the Germans together with the Poles were
assiduously searching the entire vicinity. Eighteen Jews were found;
all were shot on the spot. . . .*

— FROM THE DIARY OF SZLOMO SCHEINER

ON THE RUN

By the time he caught up with the ragged-looking woman at the edge of
the Skrzynice Forest, not far from Lublin, he was out of breath. Only
one word came out of his mouth. *"Amcha?"* he asked her in Hebrew.
Frightened but clearly relieved, she nodded her head. Yes, she too was
Jewish and a member of the "people."

For Jewish fugitives, faced with terror and death at every turn and
uncertain whom to approach for assistance, *amcha* (the nation or
people) quickly became a code word, a signal that strangers could be

trusted and food and shelter shared. This bit of Hebrew was the watchword of the forest.

Identified in a testimony given in New York City in 1955 only by his initials, A. G., this particular thirty-year-old Jewish fugitive from the Lublin ghetto had eluded Polish police patrols and wild dogs for more than twelve hours until he reached the woods. But as he was about to learn, life on the run for a Jew in occupied Poland in the fall of 1942 was no life at all. The young woman he encountered led him deeper into the forest to her makeshift camp, where eleven other people, all women and children, lay hidden among the trees. They too were escapees from the Lublin ghetto.

It was a "horrible sight," he later recalled. "The women and children lay stretched out on the ground, bundled up in rags. The small children cried terribly and a fire had started in the underbrush and was spreading all around them." A. G. helped put out the fire and learned that this group had survived as a result of the aid given to them by a Jew named Yulek Rozenshtayn. Originally from Lodz, Rozenshtayn had successfully posed as a Christian Pole for more than two years. Having discovered these women and children hiding in the forest, he brought them food whenever it was possible. But it was dangerous, since peasants in the area were on the watch for Jewish fugitives, whom they robbed and usually killed.

That evening, Rozenshtayn visited the camp and A. G. accompanied him to his own hiding place in the cellar of a nearby farmhouse. The following day, A. G. returned to the forest campsite with a pot of soup. Suddenly, the group was attacked by a Pole and Russian, both armed with rifles. Although they robbed A. G. of his boots, they did not harm the women and children. On this occasion, they were lucky, but too many people in the area knew of their existence. Indeed, two days later, as A. G. related, "a mob of peasants stormed into the woods, dragged the Jewish women and children from [their bunker], and took them to the Germans. The women were forced to go on foot, and the children were dumped into a wagon." They were taken to the Gestapo in Glusk and murdered.

■ ■

A. G. eventually met up with a small group of armed Jewish partisans and managed to survive the war by constantly moving from one spot to the other. Yet the possibility of the local peasants collaborating with the Nazis always posed a tremendous threat.

No guerrilla operation — let alone a band of helpless fugitives — can survive very long without some support from the local population, who provide intelligence information, food, shelter, and often ammunition and weapons. For a variety of reasons — including anti-Semitism, fear, and apathy — such support was rarely available or offered to Jewish escapees from the ghettos. They were, like the women and children A. G. encountered, entirely on their own, living a precarious and lonely existence. Consequently, the survival rate for the estimated 100,000 Jews on the run during 1942 and 1943 was low. This was particularly true for those who were unable to link up with Soviet partisans or established Jewish family camps like the one organized by Tuvia Bielski. In the Volhynia district alone, of the approximately 40,000 Jews hiding in the forest and on farms in the summer of 1942, more than 37,000 had been killed or were dead from hunger by the end of 1943.

It was the attitude and actions of Polish, Lithuanian, Ukrainian, and Belorussian peasants that determined the immediate fate of countless Jewish fugitives when they first arrived in the forest areas. It was clearly dangerous to either hide or give aid to a Jew. Offering protection or food put the peasant, his family, and the entire village at risk. German authorities even instituted a quota system for food and produce deliveries, and farmers who could not account for missing cows or an insufficient number of eggs were accused of helping partisans and Jews. The punishment was death.

Still, it is impossible to generalize about the behaviour of east European peasants towards Jewish fugitives. "There was no uniformity," historian Richard Lukas has argued. Some did indeed risk everything. They permitted escaped Jews to hide in their cellars and barns, made weekly trips into the forest with food and supplies to sustain family groups, and acted as liaisons for partisan detachments.

Some, like the Lithuanian peasant woman who hid Aba Gefen and his fourteen-year-old brother, Joseph, on a farm near Kovno, were motivated purely by profit and promises of Jewish gold. Day after day, with veiled threats about turning them over to the Germans, she demanded Gefen provide her with money and fur coats.

Others acted out of genuine kindness. For several months, before circumstances forced them into the forest, Peter Silverman and his cousins from the town of Jody were able to take refuge in a variety of barns and attics. On the farms, the accommodations were cramped and the food minimal, but the generosity of a handful of Polish farmers had saved them. "Most of the hundred Jews [from Jody] still alive on New Year's Day, 1942," Silverman asserts, "owed their lives to righteous Gentiles who risked their property, their lives, and the lives of their families to help Jews survive. Every Jew from Jody alive today owes his life to at least one, if not many, Gentile families. Every Jew from Jody that survived the Holocaust in the forest and with the partisans was at one time or another hidden in the attic or barn, bunker or basement of some courageous Gentile."

More often than not, however, fear of German brutality, poverty, and a lack of food supplies persuaded many good-hearted people to protect their own families first. "Passive humanitarians" is what Holocaust scholar Philip Friedman called them. They truly wanted to help their Jewish friends, but could not bring themselves to do it. Still others were resentful. "Before the war, they called me *goy, goy!*" declared one former member of the Polish underground. "Now they wanted my help. . . . Do you realize how difficult it was to save a person who obviously looked Semitic? They had to be hidden all the time, because if they dared to venture out the Germans would pounce on them."

Not surprisingly, Jews remember the situation quite differently. On the run after their escape from the Radun ghetto, Leon Kahn and his group went from farmhouse to farmhouse, but few of the peasants would allow them to stay for very long. "The ironic thing was that my father chose these farmers because they were old friends," states Kahn. "Most of them had been quite happy to sleep at our house the night before market day in Eisiskes . . . and that was only [the previous] year."

Eventually, Kahn and his family did find a friendly Polish farmer who was willing to hide them. Two weeks after they arrived, however, this peasant, concerned about the safety of his family, begged the Jews to leave. They had no choice but to comply. Before they departed, the Pole did supply them with a stock of food, money to buy weapons, and directions to the home of another farmer who could guide them into the Nacha Forest. Four days later, with two rifles they had bought from another peasant they knew, they came to the small farmhouse where their guide lived. Once night had fallen, he took them deep into the forest, through swamps and thick woods, where a camp of other Jewish escapees from nearby towns were hiding.

"Just after dawn, we arrived at the camp," recalls Kahn. "It was an incredible sight. Almost 300 were living openly and apparently without fear in the middle of the forest. They laughed and called to one another, and the children played noisily. Women prepared breakfast over open fires and cows grazed nearby. We were terrified! We had an awful compulsion to tell them to be quiet, to take cover before they were killed! What on earth were these Jews doing, taking such risks? Where were the sentries? What if we had been Germans or Lithuanians sneaking up on them?"

JEW HUNTS

Kahn's concerns were well founded, for many peasants regarded the fugitives with an anti-Semitic disdain. The Jews were Communists and pests, they declared, who endangered their lives and pilfered their crops. Fed with anti-Jewish German propaganda — which portrayed Jews and Russians as murderers, plunderers, and mortal enemies of the Christian world — and promised rewards of salt, sugar, and money, the peasants formed mobs and so-called Jew hunts became a daily occurrence.

This was what happened in 1942 in the town of Korets in the Volhynia district, when the Nazi police promised a few pounds of precious salt to Ukrainian peasants who delivered Jewish fugitives to them. "The Ukrainian murderers fanned out through the forest to hunt Jews," remembered Dr. Jacob Wallah, a Korets survivor. "They murdered them, cut off their heads, and brought them to the commandant. It was terrible to see the murderers walking the streets of the town clasping the severed heads of Jews."

In some cases, these hunts were organized by the Nazi police; peasants and government-employed forest wardens only guided the Germans to the right locales. "A large number of Jews continue to stay in hiding, either in the forests or in towns and villages in the midst of the Aryan population," stated a 1943 report to the Polish government-in-exile. "The Germans chase them relentlessly, organizing raids to capture them. In villages and forests the raids have become virtual manhunts. The Jews who are captured are most often murdered on the spot. . . . In the vicinity of Otwock the Germans have encouraged the local toughs to track down the Jews and deliver them to German gendarmerie stations. A Pole who turns up with a captured Jew is first ordered to dig a grave for him. Immediately after his luckless victim is executed, he receives a reward of 200 zlotys plus the clothes and the shoes of the deceased."

There are also many stories of local leaders taking independent action to rid their area of Jewish fugitives. On November 5, 1942, for example, a Polish teacher from Lukow by the name of Zieminski stopped into a store in the village of Siedlce, east of Warsaw. "The peasants were buying scythes," he recorded in his diary. "I heard the saleswoman say: 'They will be helpful during the raid today.' I asked about the nature of the raid. 'Against the Jews.' I then asked: 'And how much do you get for a captured Jew?' No one answered. I therefore went on: 'For Christ they paid thirty pieces of silver; so make sure that you are paid no less.' Again no one replied. But the answer came a little later. While crossing the forest, I heard salvos of machine gun fire. The raid was in progress."

Farther south, near Lublin, similar events were unfolding. Krystyna Modrzewska, a Jewish woman who survived by posing as a Pole, told of how Jewish fugitives were treated:

The German gendarmerie and the Polish police were on the alert. Groups of Jews who had fled towns and townlets were roaming the countryside. . . . Peasant farms were raided at night by groups of miserable, starving people who robbed them of bread, flour, pigs and clothes. Single Jews — mostly women, old people and children — took their lives in their hands and at night came to beg for food from cottages standing close to the woods. . . . Sometimes they were given a bowl of soup or a piece of bread. . . . Not infrequently, Jews were detained and dragged to the nearest [Polish] police station where they were either finished off on the spot or — and this was quite common — dragged to the nearest [gendarmerie] post by policemen who wanted to prove their zeal to their German superiors. For delivering a Jew a Polish policeman could earn both praise and an award. To help track down the Jews, volunteer village guards were organized in each village of our rural district and in all the rural districts of Lublin region. There were many lads who joined the guard willingly. They were not issued with arms, but was not a solid club sufficient to deal with that kind of Jew?

The farmers of Hola had also taken matters into their own hands in the fall of 1942. By this time, Harold Werner and his group of fifteen, who had chosen the relative safety of the forest over internment in the Wlodawa ghetto, were in trouble. They had hoped to make contact with Soviet partisans, but after several weeks the Soviets were nowhere to be found. And their small supply of food was dwindling. Harold and two friends decided to risk returning to the home of Stephan, the farmer who had first helped them. Yet with German patrols on the lookout for Jews, Stephan was less than pleased to see Harold standing in his doorway. Pointing a rifle at him, he gave him and his companions some bread and pork and warned them never to return again. "He told me in a firm tone," Werner recalled in his memoirs, "that if I came to him again he would kill me, and motioned threateningly toward me with his rifle. He said he had nothing against me, but his life was dearer to him than mine."

Meanwhile, the village elders had decided to solve their Jewish "problem" by themselves. Armed with clubs and pitchforks, a mob of about fifty peasants ventured into the forest and captured the dozen remaining members of Werner's group. Then they marched them to the Nazi police, who immediately murdered all of them. "The men who participated in the raid were all local villagers who had lived together all their lives with many of the Jews of our group," Werner pointed out.

"They knew in advance what the Germans would do to the Jews they rounded up."

After the murder of their friends and family, Werner, his girlfriend, Manya, and their companion, Moniek, travelled into the forest area near Zamolodycze, a small village close to Hola. There they stumbled across a group of eighteen escaped Jews hiding in a dugout. The bunker, really just a large hole in the ground covered with branches, was too small for so many people, but Werner, Manya, and Moniek stayed for a few days. It was one day too many.

Just before dawn one morning, the dugout was surrounded by a mob of seventy Ukrainians from Zamolodycze who had learned of the Jews' hiding place. Armed with sticks and pitchforks, they ordered Werner and the other Jews to come out of the bunker. "I looked around at our captors," Werner recalled, "and did not see any Germans — just a mob of villagers. I asked one of them whether there were any Germans accompanying them, and I was told no." The peasants ordered the Jews to march towards Zamolodycze. On the road back to the village, Werner suddenly yelled in Yiddish for the group to run in all directions. In the chaos, Werner and Manya were able to escape, but many of the Jews were caught. They were locked in a house and turned over to the Nazi police, who murdered them one by one. "The villagers of Zamolodycze watched in a crowd as the killings took place," Werner wrote. "They knew all these Jews. They had grown up together and done business together. . . . Zelik [one of the Jews caught] was the village shoemaker, who made the shoes for most of the villagers and their families. His son, Mendel, had tried to escape . . . but the villagers caught him and the Germans shot him also."

If they were not participating in actual raids, many local peasants either took the time to beat and rob any Jews they found or willingly informed the Germans of their whereabouts. In fact, historians Yisrael Gutman and Shmuel Krakowski, who have catalogued thousands of wartime incidents between Jews and Poles, regard informing as the "most common and probably the most lethal" crime committed against Jews. "It assumed," they suggest, "epidemic proportions." A 1961 Polish study by Tatiana Berenstein and Adam Rukowski arrived at a similar conclusion: "In no other country in Europe did such police informing and unsolicited cooperation with the SS assume the massive proportions they took on in Poland."

These incidents are just a few of the numerous examples listed by Gutman and Krakowski:

Ten Jews were hiding on farmland adjacent to the forest near Okrzeja, Lukow county. In the summer of 1943, they were betrayed by the farm owner's son. The Germans murdered them all. . . .

In the locality of Januszkowice near Jaslo over a dozen Jews were hiding for pay in a cellar of a local farmer's house. The farmer's neighbour happened to be arrested for unlawful hog slaughter. In order to avoid prosecution, he revealed the location of the cellar to the gendarmes. All Jews were shot, along with the farmer who sheltered them. . . .

In the vicinity of the village of Wisnicz Nowy near Bochnia a forester tracked down and notified the Germans about a bunker occupied by some ten Jews. The Germans shot them all. . . .

A Pole by the name of Wojek from the village of Krolowka near Wlodawa supplied two Jewish fugitives from Sobibor [concentration camp] with bread in exchange for gold. Once he realized that the two had exhausted their supply of gold, he revealed the location of their hiding place in the forest to the Germans. . . .

■ ■

In time, as Jews acquired weapons, organized their own partisan units, or joined Soviet *otriady*, such actions by the local population were avenged in kind. Partisans were particularly angered on those many occasions when they discovered peasants in possession of Jewish ornaments, or in one case, wearing a blouse made from a prayer shawl. In some instances, entire villages were burned to the ground and peasants executed for their acts of betrayal and looting. Harold Werner and several of his friends, for example, finally had their revenge on the villagers of Zamolodycze, although it took nearly a year. Having acquired a rifle, they shot several of the Ukrainian peasants who had attacked them in their forest bunker, including one farmer who was still wearing the boots belonging to Zelik, the town's shoemaker.

Leib Reiser, a Jew who had escaped from the Minsk ghetto in late 1941, eventually became a member of the Leninski Komsomol, a Soviet partisan unit operating in the Nacha Forest, south of Vilna. In early 1943, Reiser and his group discovered the few remaining survivors of a small Jewish family camp. The rest of the camp — seventeen men, women, and children — had been slaughtered by a local gang of Poles led by a peasant named Temoshka and his sons. "The Leninski Komsomol," Reiser notes, "took revenge on the Temoshka family. They shot the entire family and burned their house. Both Jews and Gentiles participated in this expedition. . . . After this, things quieted down in our area."

Eugene Katz had escaped from the ghetto in Dzisna in June 1942, on the day that 4,000 Jews were slaughtered. Together with his brother, he hid out in the nearby swamps for several weeks until he was able to join a group of Belorussian partisans. Katz regularly visited a farmer whom he had known for many years and who, in fact, had agreed several months earlier to hide the Katz family's belongings.

On a visit in early January 1943, Katz and his brother entered the peasant's hut only to find the German police waiting for them. Hoping to keep the Katz family's suits, linens, and sewing machine, one of the farmer's sons had informed the Nazis about them. As the police were leading Katz and his brother to their wagon, the two men fled. Katz managed to elude his captors, but his brother was shot in the back.

Weeks passed, and then Katz sought his revenge. He returned to the village, found the Belorussian who had betrayed him, and killed him. He left the man's wife and child alive to warn other peasants about the consequences of informing on Jews.

Tuvia Bielski also did not let such acts go unpunished. In late 1942, Bielski and some of his men paid a visit to the farm of a Belorussian named Albelkiewicz, who was suspected of informing on Jews. Pretending to be a group of anti-Semitic Polish partisans, Bielski and his comrades eventually got Albelkiewicz to brag about all the Jews he had turned over to the Gestapo. Within moments, the peasant and his family were dead. Before they left, the Jews posted a Russian sign on the farmhouse door, which read: "This family was wiped out for collaboration with the Germans and for turning Jews over to them . . . signed . . . The [Bielski] Company."

Some months after this incident, a group of ten fighters from the Bielski camp out on a food-gathering expedition were betrayed by another Belorussian peasant. As they slept in a barn not far from Novogrudok, the fighters were surrounded by the police, who had been notified of their visit by the peasant's son. Before they could react, the partisans were shot to death. Once Tuvia had determined the facts, the family was interrogated and then punished. They were killed and their house burned. A note was left there too, proclaiming the circumstances of the case and the reason for the death sentence.

Whether such acts of retribution made a difference is debatable. In some instances, it merely reinforced anti-Semitic feelings and promoted the view that the Jewish partisans were as bad as the Germans and Russians. In other cases, argues Peter Silverman, these actions "brought the open season against Jews to an end, as news of Jewish retribution travelled from peasant to peasant. Now, the [local inhabitants] feared armed Jews." The Jews had made their point. No longer could they be regarded as compliant victims. Peasants soon learned that those who collaborated with the Nazis did so at their peril.

GUNS

For Jews on the run or in hiding, making the transition from fugitive to partisan was not easy. Age, physical endurance, and military experience all played factors. In the early stages of the Soviet partisan movement, in particular, many former Red Army soldiers showed little or no desire to protect defenceless Jewish men, women, and children, whom they regarded as both an unnecessary competitor for the scarce food resources and a magnet that would draw the German and local police into the forest.

Until the summer and fall of 1942, when centralized control of the Russian partisans was instituted and more discipline among the rank and file was enforced, it was not uncommon for the Soviets to attack Jewish family groups, rob them, rape the women, and often kill them. In the fall of 1942, in the forests near the town of Parczew, north-east of Lublin, for example, Soviet partisans beat and tortured an elderly Jewish woman for hiding her daughter from them. They wanted to rape her. Several months later, not far away, Harold Werner and his friends stood by helplessly as a group of forty Soviet fighters abused and raped the few women with them. "Although we protested," he writes, "they were armed and we were not, so there was little we could do to stop them."

Without weapons, it was impossible for Jews to defend themselves or take revenge. Possessing a gun or rifle was also, ironically, usually a requirement for a Jew to join a Soviet *otriad*. And even this was no guarantee of acceptance. Russians, Poles, Belorussians, and Ukrainians often took what they needed without asking. This led to many deadly altercations.

Alter Dworzecki, for instance, escaped in late April 1942 from the ghetto in Zdzieciol, south of Slonim, where he had served as head of the local Judenrat. He and the small group of resisters he led into the nearby forest possessed a few handguns. Their intention was to organize an effective guerrilla unit and attack the Nazi police guarding the Zdzieciol ghetto. But due to their lack of weapons, their plan, as well as their survival, was dependent on their linking up with Soviet fighters who were better armed — or so they thought.

In the forest, Dworzecki found the Russian fighters he was searching for, though they rejected his plan to attack the German troops in Zdzieciol. The partisans were outnumbered, and dying in a lost cause rescuing Jews was undoubtedly the last thing they wanted to do. Two days later, Dworzecki and another member of his group became embroiled in a dispute with the Russians when Dworzecki refused to give them his pistol. The Soviets murdered both of them.

Hershel Posesorki, a daring young partisan who led numerous Jewish groups out of labour camps and ghettos in the Minsk region, was also killed in the spring of 1943 by his Ukrainian unit commander when he would not relinquish his machine gun. Posesorki's Jewish comrades protested to the Soviet brigade commander, but he refused to take any action against the Ukrainian, or permit the Jews to form their own detachment as they had requested. For the duration of the war, such incidents were all too frequent.

Apart from these skirmishes, the search for weapons occupied a great deal of the Jews' time. Before the war, Jews and guns rarely went together. In both Poland and the Soviet Union, a police permit was required to own a weapon and few Jews qualified. Local peasants, too, had a difficult time obtaining permission for arms, but during the First World War and the Russian-Polish War of 1919–20 many farmers had stockpiled abandoned rifles. They cut off the barrels and hid these sawed-off shotguns in their barns and cellars. When the Germans began to occupy the east in June 1941, still more arms were collected by the peasants as the Soviets hastily retreated. Given their general antagonism towards Jews, however, few farmers were willing to part with their prized possessions and usually not without a steep price attached.

Other than dealing with the local population, however, Jews had few options available to them. They could attack the German police and confiscate the arms and ammunition they needed, but without possessing some weapons first, this was akin to suicide. In a few cases, they were able to tap into the Polish and Russian underground network, but this too proved unreliable. They could make their own bombs and pistols, as Jewish fighters did in the ghettos in Warsaw and Bialystok, although this was obviously inadequate for the type of guerrilla warfare they wanted to engage in.

The Jews were desperate for guns, and if it meant beating a peasant who refused to either give or sell them a weapon for a reasonable price, they did so. They also took enormous risks to retrieve any gun or pistol — no matter what poor shape it might have been in. One day in early 1942, a Polish farmer had presented Peter Silverman's father with a Belgian Browning pistol and a grand total of three bullets. Later, Silverman and his group were able to purchase an Austro-Hungarian army rifle that had been used during the First World War, but this was still not sufficient. Peter and his cousin Dave Smuschkowitz, both only teenagers, learned that one of their relatives had buried an automatic handgun in his barn back in Jody. They decided to return to the ghetto to find it.

"I shiver just thinking about what we did as seventeen-year-olds in those dangerous times," Silverman states. The two boys successfully snuck into Jody, eluding the armed police guards, and dug up the weapon. "It took about ten or fifteen minutes, but at the time it seemed like an eternity," recalls Silverman. "It was a dark evening, but I could see some people moving around. As soon as we could, we left with the pistol. It was wrapped in oil-soaked rags." They added the gun to their growing arsenal.

Even with the newly acquired weapons, Silverman and his cousins remained lone Jewish fugitives one step ahead of the police. The closest they came to being caught and killed occurred one day in April 1942, when they were stopped by a local police patrol while out searching for potatoes. Only some quick thinking and a bit of daring saved them. They were able to kill one of the officers guarding them and flee in the melee that followed. "This was," Silverman notes, "the first time that Jewish armed resistance occurred in our area; the first message to the Germans and their collaborators that not all Jews were going passively to their deaths."

■ ■

Samuel Gruber's experiences were slightly different than Peter Silverman's, but typical of how Jews obtained weapons and became active partisans. A former Jewish officer in the Polish army, Gruber had been interned in a dreaded SS-governed POW camp at Lipowa Street in Lublin, where beatings and torture were routine. He was also one of many Jews forced by the Germans to work on the construction of the Majdanek concentration camp. In late October 1942, Gruber and another POW by the name of Kaganowicz led a group of thirty-five men into the Kozlow woods north of the city. They were guided by two Poles working with the Gwardia Ludowa, the underground movement of the Polish Workers' Party.

Between them, the prospective Jewish partisans had one pistol, no supplies, and no warm clothing — and winter was coming fast. After two difficult weeks on the run, it was decided to send the Poles back to Lublin for weapons, food, and supplies. They were given all the money, watches, and any other valuables the men had. "We saw no reason not to trust the two underground fighters," remembers Gruber, who became known by the Polish pseudonym Mietek. "They left us at twelve that night, laden with our last possessions, and that was the last we ever saw or heard of them."

Now defenceless and without money, Gruber wandered the Kozlow Forest until he discovered dozens of Jewish refugees who had fled from the nearby town of Markuszow. These Jews in turn introduced Gruber to two Soviet soldiers named Tolka and Mikoi who had escaped from a Nazi POW camp in Lubartow. They proved to be important contacts.

It had been Tolka's intention to form a fighting unit, though training the Jewish refugees from Markuszow for combat was next to impossible. Gruber and his men were another matter. Tolka arranged a meeting for Gruber with a fighter named Genek, the Polish-Communist partisan leader in the region. Genek was more than willing to admit Gruber and his group into his detachment, but on the condition that they first obtain weapons. He provided them with the names of local peasants who were known to be hiding arms.

Gruber soon visited these farmers, who were indeed in possession of guns and ammunition. They, however, detested Communists and Jews as much as they did Nazis, and did not want to part with their precious stash of rifles. "The result was that we had to administer a few good beatings to those peasants before we could get any weapons at all," Gruber explains. "But in some instances my one pistol, brandished with the proper gestures into a slow-witted peasant's face, was sufficient." In this way, the group acquired ten Russian rifles and a dozen rounds of ammunition.

Still feeling that they were not adequately armed, Gruber and Kaganowicz sent one Jewish fighter, Stefan Finkel, to steal weapons from the German military hospital in Lublin. It was clearly a dangerous mission, though Finkel was resourceful. With the aid of two Jews who worked in the hospital, Finkel was able to collect a sufficient quantity of guns, uniforms, and blankets. Then, with about sixteen other POWs who wanted to escape, he commandeered a German army truck and delivered his cargo right into the forest. Now Gruber had a new

German rifle and an overcoat, which he wore until the end of the war.

The fighting now began in earnest, but unfortunately for Gruber, it started on a sad note: While waiting for Finkel to return, Kaganowicz, who was hiding out with some of the men near the village of Kawki, had been ambushed by a German patrol. Days later, their bodies were discovered in the woods. Gruber buried his comrades and took his men farther east, towards the Garbow Forest.

While both Gruber and Silverman had entered the partisan movement mainly through their links with Russians and Poles — a typical wartime experience — there were other Jews who took matters into their own hands almost from the start.

DR. ATLAS

When Yeheskel Atlas asked a potential candidate for his partisan unit the question, What do you want? he expected only one answer: "I want to die fighting the enemy." Any other response was not acceptable.

Atlas, a distinguished man with dark blue eyes and wavy brown hair, was the most unlikely of heroes. A trained medical doctor who was driven to the forest after his family was slaughtered, he became the embodiment of the Jewish resistance fighter: brave, fair-minded, and ready to die. And he looked the part. In the forest, according to one of the partisans who served under him, "he wore a tattered army uniform with oversized boots and was armed with hand grenades which protruded from his pockets." An intellectual by temperament, he treated his men as equals, and they held their commander in high esteem.

It was not only his leadership abilities, however, that made Atlas special. He was a man of high principle. In spite of the terrible circumstances that had destroyed his family, he never lost his sense of community. Atlas had vowed to say *kaddish*, the prayer for the dead, over the graves of any parents and sisters murdered by the Einsatzgruppen. One night, together with another partisan named Berik who had also lost his family, Atlas snuck away from the camp to the mass grave near Kozlovshchina. There, with the German enemy not far away, the two men performed their religious duty.

Yeheskel Atlas was born in 1913 in Rawa Mazowiecka, a *shtetl* near Lodz in Poland. His father made a living as a merchant. Young Yeheskel was an excellent student with an interest in pursuing a career in medicine. But owing to the quota restrictions then in place in Poland (*numerus clausus*), which prevented Jews from entering Polish medical schools, he was forced to leave the country. Atlas studied medicine in France and Italy, and received his medical degree from the University of Bologna in 1939. He returned to Poland only a few months before the war broke out.

For two years, he lived under Soviet rule in Kozlovshchina, near Slonim (in the Baranowicze region), with his parents and his seventeen-year-old sister, Cila, a dental student. In June 1941, the Nazis invaded the town, but Yeheskel was still able to practise medicine. The assault on Kozlovshchina the following May was led by a Gestapo officer named Heyk who, with a band of Lithuanians, killed most of the town's Jews. This included the members of Atlas's family. A sadist, Heyk forced Kozlovshchina's rabbi to pull a cart as if he were a horse and then buried him alive.

Atlas's life was spared because he was a physician. He was sent to the village of Wielka Wola, close to the Schara River and the Lipiczany Forest, where his skills could serve the German war interests. There he began to hear stories about Soviet partisans attacking Nazi soldiers. At some point, several of his Belorussian peasant patients put him in touch with the former Red Army fighters hiding out in the thick and swampy territory of the Lipiczany Forest, and he agreed to secretly provide them with medical treatment. The Soviet partisan commanders in this region were Boris Bulat and Pavel Bulak, though in the summer of 1942 their brigade was not yet a cohesive unit.

On July 24, the Nazis liquidated the ghetto in Derechin, a town about 30 kilometres from Wielka Wola. More than 2,700 of Derechin's 3,000 Jews were slaughtered. Some of the survivors managed to escape and made contact with Atlas. The doctor, in turn, introduced the fugitives to Captain Bulat, and began smuggling them supplies and the few weapons he could find so they could fight side by side with the Russians.

In the back of Atlas's mind was the idea that he could transform bakers, shoemakers, and peddlers into an effective partisan force. Indeed, by early August, Atlas had escaped from Wielka Wola, selected fifty of the best men from among the refugees, and formed his own partisan band. "Every additional day of your life is not yours," he told his men, "but belongs to your murdered families. You must avenge them."

Atlas convinced Bulat to help the Jews in their first major operation: a full-scale assault on the garrison at Derechin. Reluctantly, the Soviet commander agreed, and on August 24, about 300 partisans moved against the Germans and Lithuanians at Derechin. The force included Atlas's unit, which had doubled, and another Jewish group that had been formed by Ha-Shomer Hatsair leader Hirsh Kaplinski and other survivors from the August 6 mass murder at the nearby town of Zdzieciol. When the battle ended, forty-four Lithuanian policemen who had participated in the liquidation of the Derechin ghetto were taken to the same pits where they had slaughtered their Jewish victims and were executed.

The complete success of this operation convinced the sceptical Soviets that Jews could fight. The Soviets had initially planned for Atlas to serve as a field surgeon — given the shortage of qualified physicians in the forest — but now they allowed him to maintain his own military command. Less than a week after the Derechin attack, the Atlas group travelled 20 kilometres to the town of Bielce, where they blew up a bridge over the Niemen River and blocked German military shipments heading east.

More significantly, Atlas and his men sabotaged a train on the Lida-Grodno line by converting two artillery shells into mines. This marked the beginning of the effective "railway war" carried on by Soviet and Jewish partisans, which played havoc with Nazi transports. Former Atlas partisan Samuel Bornstein remembered it like this: "A violent explosion ripped through the air. The engine and several cars left the rails and plunged down the embankment. The scene was bedlam. The injured and confused Germans were shouting and screaming. Their noise was soon silenced by the sound of heavy firing from our positions. When the job was completed we melted into the darkness. Again the forest was silent."

The more celebrated the feats of Atlas and his men, the angrier the Germans became. In mid-September, a combined Nazi, Ukrainian, and Lithuanian force of 1,100 men attempted to destroy the Soviet and Jewish partisans haranguing them. In a battle on September 15 in the woods near the Schara River, the Nazi soldiers attempted to cross the water on boats but were fired on by Atlas and his group. Most of the Germans drowned, but two Ukrainians escaped. Moving quickly, Atlas and his second-in-command, Eliyahu Kowienski (who was said to be so strong that "he could bend an iron bar with his bare hands or lift a cart unaided"), jumped into the river and killed the two enemy soldiers. Then, under a hail of bullets, they swam back to shore with the Ukrainians' weapons held high over their heads. Similar battles in October at Ruda and Huta Jaworska resulted in the death of more Germans and collaborators, as well as the further acquisition of enemy arms. In these engagements, however, some Jewish partisans were killed.

Unlike his Soviet allies, who did not have to worry about saving civilians, Atlas also took some responsibility for the large number of Jews who sought refuge in the forest by offering protection and supplies. One family camp of the survivors from Derechin "lacked the appearance of a military center," recalled Samuel Bornstein. "The wooden huts which served as living quarters were scattered and the populace itself was divided into several units, each containing some thirty or forty people. These units did their own cooking and their rations were very limited and not like those of the partisans."

Still, Atlas was not prepared to make the survival of the family camps his major goal, as Tuvia Bielski did. Consequently, many of the refugees starved, died of disease, or were beaten and robbed by roving bands of partisans beyond the control of Bulat and the Soviet command. Right or wrong, there was only vengeance in the doctor's heart and mass murder to answer for.

■ ■

Unwilling to surrender the region to the partisans, the Germans launched an even larger offensive near the end of November 1942. Planes of the Luftwaffe were employed to report on partisan ground positions. At a fierce battle on December 5 at the village of Wielka Wola, Yeheskel Atlas was seriously wounded while leading his men into action. He died minutes later in the arms of Eliyahu Kowienski. (In the same battle, Hirsh Kaplinski was also wounded. He took refuge in a nearby barn, but was murdered by non-Jewish partisans who wanted his machine gun.)

"Our platoon attempted to move into a better position and Dr. Atlas led us in our slow advance," wrote Bornstein in his memoirs. "Shells were bursting all around and the air was virtually saturated with bullets. We ran a few feet and then fell down to the ground for cover from the delayed flying metal aimed at us. Our only chance to move came when the Germans briefly concentrated their fire in another direction. Atlas held the charge and, as fire again was directed against us, hit the dirt. We followed his action, thinking that this was a signal to take cover, but suddenly somebody shouted: 'Atlas is wounded!' . . . Blood poured from his side."

When the men heard the nurse shout that the doctor was dead, many of them "wept openly and for a moment all seemed lost. The spirit to fight died with our leader." But Kowienski immediately took command until the fight that day was finished.

Did Yeheskel Atlas die in vain? In retrospect, historian Nechama Tec, among others, questions Atlas's choices. She maintains that Atlas could have better used his talents and energies for saving Jewish lives than taking revenge. Maybe so. But given the horrific and unique circumstances that Atlas and other Jewish survivors found themselves in, as well as the military attitude of the Soviet partisans among whom they lived, the doctor's need to avenge the deaths of his family and other Jews slaughtered by the Einsatzgruppen is understandable. In 1942, Dr. Yeheskel Atlas made the only choice he could. He was posthumously awarded a Hero's medal by the Soviet Union after the war.

DIADIA MISHA

The gathering that evening at the synagogue was naturally filled with despair and sorrow. Earlier that day, the Einsatzgruppen had brutally slaughtered more than 2,000 Jews, all inhabitants of Korets, a small town 175 kilometres west of Kiev in the Volhynia district. Typically, the Nazis had chosen May 21, 1942, the eve of Shavuot, the Feast of Weeks, as the day for the mass murder. The killing started at 4 a.m. and lasted for the next twelve hours.

The husbands and sons of Korets, whose lives had been spared for the time being because they possessed skills the Nazis found useful, were in shock. They had come to the town's synagogue to recite Kaddish. In the congregation was a tall, forty-four-year-old civil engineer named Misha Gildenman whose wife and thirteen-year-old daughter, Manya, had been murdered. Unlike the other men, however, Gildenman's heart was not filled with fear or terror, but anger and revenge.

When the prayers were finished, he stood on the dais at the front of the sanctuary and addressed his friends: "Listen to me, you unfortunate, doomed Jews! When I saw the unflinching face of the Gestapo commander, I wondered whether he was human. If he was human, then I am ashamed to belong to the human race. When I see your reactions to the terrible atrocity committed against us by the Germans and Ukrainians, I begin to wonder whether we are the descendants of the Maccabeans and I am ashamed. Know that we are all doomed to die sooner or later. I shall not stretch out my neck to the slaughterers. Before I die I must take revenge on the Germans and only then will I die with a clear conscience."

Until the war started, the mild-mannered Gildenman, who was born in Korets and had spent his entire life there, ran his cement business, participated in the life of the community, and cherished his family. "They lived in a beautiful house in a nice part of the city," remembers Rachel Goldstein, who went to school with Manya Gildenman. After the massacre, against great odds, Misha Gildenman and his teenage son, Simcha, attempted to organize a local resistance underground. Simcha, who had worked in the forest north-east of the town, was already aware of a small number of escaped Soviet POWs trying to establish a partisan unit. He hoped a group from Korets might join them in the near future.

Misha Gildenman was a persuasive man who did not take no for an answer. Yet for months, he and his son continually confronted apathy mixed with fear. As in other towns and villages throughout the occupied territories, Jews still alive in Korets were either too scared to join a resistance group or believed that compliance was the best policy. "If [Hitler] exterminates us, he will have to replace us by Germans he needs in the front line. And Hitler is not stupid enough to do that," rationalized one of Gildenman's friends, who refused to join him.

Gildenman waited until the last possible moment to flee from Korets. On September 23, 1942, German and Ukrainian police surrounded the ghetto in preparation for its liquidation. At that point, Gildenman, his son, and about sixteen other men and women, aged eighteen to twenty, escaped the ghetto in groups of threes. They were armed with one pistol, five bullets, and a butcher knife — hardly enough to defend themselves, let alone carry out a military action.

For two weeks, Gildenman led his group north through the heavily wooded western Ukraine. At one point in their long journey, they encountered a detachment of Soviet partisans from the brigade commanded by Col. Dimitry Medvedev, who had brought his men from the east to fight the Germans. The Soviets, however, were not interested in accepting a group of largely unarmed Jews, though they did inform Gildenman about a small contingent of Jewish survivors from the Klesov area who were travelling farther north and did have weapons. Gildenman decided to follow their trail.

Within a few days, Gildenman and his group caught up with the Klesov survivors, but they too were poorly armed. Nevertheless, the two groups united. Gildenman remained in command, while Alexander Kutz, the leader of the Klesov Jews, was made his chief of staff.

That October night, Gildenman recorded in his diary, he could not sleep. He awoke in the morning determined to find more weapons. He had been told about a Polish forester in the vicinity who was supposed to have a double-barrelled rifle in his possession. Armed with their lone gun and some imitation pistols sewn together from bark, Gildenman and a few of his men went to visit the forest warden.

They arrived at the forester's house on the evening of October 6, but the Pole was nowhere to be found. His frightened wife claimed that her husband, hearing that there were partisans in the area, had given all of his weapons to the Nazis. Instinct told Gildenman that the woman was lying. He ordered her to take a shovel and begin digging her grave. At that moment, she fell on the ground and yelled for her husband. Slowly, a door in the hut opened and out stepped the forester. He too fell on his knees and begged for mercy.

Gildenman demanded that the man show him his weapons. The forester took him to a back room and pushed a cabinet to the side. Under a loose floorboard, Gildenman found the double-barrelled rifle with twelve rounds of ammunition and another rifle with forty rounds. He told the forester that he was not going to kill him. Instead, he locked the couple in a room and ordered them not to step out of the house until morning or they would be shot.

Before Gildenman left, the forester pleaded with him to leave a note explaining that he had taken the man's guns. That way, the Nazis would not consider him a partisan supporter. Gildenman obliged him. "These weapons," he wrote on a crumpled piece of paper, "are going to be used to avenge the blood which was spilled by the Germans." He hesitated for a moment, not certain how to sign it. His nephew Sioma, he recalled, always called him Diadia Misha, or Uncle Misha, and that was the name he left on the note. From that day on, Misha Gildenman, civil engineer and family man, became Diadia Misha, partisan and saboteur.

■ ■

Gildenman set up a new base in the swampy and sometimes treacherous forest area north of Sarny in the Polesie region. Not only did he and his men (including Kutz's Klesov group) have to contend with German patrols, but they also had to be on guard against roving bands of Ukrainian fascists known as the Bandera or Banderovtsy, named after the Ukrainian nationalist leader Stefan Bandera. At the outset of the Nazi invasion of Soviet-occupied territory, Bandera and other Ukrainian leaders had welcomed the Germans as saviours from the Communist menace. But Bandera and his faction regarded the Jews with disdain. At a congress held in April 1941, a resolution was adopted that declared that "the Jews in the U.S.S.R constitute the most faithful support of the ruling Bolshevik regime and the vanguard of Muscovite imperialism in the Ukraine."

Bandera's subsequent campaign for an independent Ukraine led to his arrest by the Gestapo in September 1942 and his imprisonment in a concentration camp near Berlin. His many followers, however, carried on and established the Ukrainian Insurgent Army (Ukrainska Povstanska Armyia). Based in the forests of Polesie, Volhynia, and eastern Galicia, the Bandera declared war on everyone: Germans, Soviet partisans, Poles, Ukrainians with different political or religious affiliations, and Jews. Indeed, when it came to the Bandera, no Jewish fugitive or partisan was safe.* In the spring of 1943, their numbers swelled when they were joined by about 4,000 Ukrainian policemen who chose to fight for a free Ukraine instead of serving their German masters. The Nazis were more than happy to allow their former allies to continue the battle against the Soviet and Jewish partisans then making life difficult for them.

Nonetheless, in quick order Diadia Misha and his men established their fierce reputations by ambushing and killing a small group of Nazi and Ukrainian police and later raiding a German police station. In both operations, they were able to add to their ever-increasing arsenal.

On New Year's Eve, 1942, in a snowstorm with the temperature hovering around -25°C, they staged a daring attack on the town of Rozvazhev, a village north of Rovno that had a garrison of approximately 200 German soldiers and policemen. Divided into five groups, the Jewish partisans commenced their attack at one o'clock in the morning. With little trouble, they seized control of the telegraph office, the police headquarters, the soldiers' barracks, and the supply depot, where they found a treasure trove of supplies, food, and arms.

Gildenman then led the assault on the house of the regional commander. He quickly disposed of the guards and moved towards the front door and windows. "When I peered into the house through frosted windowpanes," Gildenman later recollected, "I saw seated around the

---

*In his book *People without a Clean Conscience* (Moscow, 1955), Pyotr Vershigora, a Ukrainian partisan who fought in a Soviet brigade commanded by Maj.-Gen. Sidor Kovpak, tells of a meeting he had in 1943 with a Ukrainian Bandera who was ordered "to kill his Polish wife to prove to his . . . comrades that he was a good Ukrainian. After he had killed his wife, his [Bandera] commander ordered him to slay his twelve-year-old girl and five-year-old boy because they were of 'impure blood' and when he refused, the [Bandera] men cut them down with axes before his eyes." (See Ainsztein, *Jewish Resistance*, 254.)

table nine officers, their uniforms buttoned up, their faces flushed. The table was laden with food and drinks; the room was filled with cigar smoke. The eyes of the drunken officers were on a beautiful woman [who] stood in the middle of the room, singing a Russian love song and accompanying herself on a guitar. We pushed the door open, stormed into the room, and began shooting at the officers. The attack was so swift and unexpected that only one officer managed to whip out his pistol and shoot in our direction, wounding one of my partisans. But he soon fell on the floor with a bullet in his head. Within a matter of minutes all the officers were dead."

Next, Gildenman freed forty Jews who were working in a sawmill near the town of Vlednik, and then successfully sabotaged a train carrying several hundred German pilots on the Shepetovka-Chernigov line. All the Nazi air force men were killed and twenty-two rail cars dislodged or blown up.

Of the many stories about Uncle Misha's partisans, none is more famous than the daring tale of twelve-year-old Mordechai "Motele" Shlayan. The only member of his family to survive an attack in the Ukrainian village of Krasnuvka, the young boy had been found by Gildenman wandering in the forest during the winter of 1943. Some months later, Motele, whose blond hair and fair appearance made it easy for him to pass as a Pole or Russian, was sent by Gildenman on a reconnaissance mission into the town of Ovruch. Motele was an accomplished violin player, and while playing outside the church in Ovruch, he caught the attention of a Nazi officer. So impressed was the German with the boy's talents that he offered him a job playing at the Soldiers' Home, a fine restaurant commandeered by the German army and police.

For two weeks, Motele entertained the Nazi troops. All the while, he smuggled explosives in his violin case and hid them in the basement of the restaurant. The plan, conceived by the boy and approved by Gildenman, was for Motele to amass a sufficient amount of explosives to blow up the Soldiers' Home. Finally, after weeks of preparation, Motele was ready. After he finished playing late one evening, he went to the basement to eat his dinner as he always did. There he quietly placed the explosives into a crack in the basement wall and lit the fuse.

Charging up the stairs, he ran directly into a German officer.

"Heil Hitler," he yelled out.

"Ach, you little Ukrainian swine," the Nazi said, laughing.

Motele quickly excused himself and ran down the road. Minutes later, the night erupted in a violent explosion. Shaken, Motele made it to the river and swam across. There, waiting for him, were five of Gildenman's men. "Ten hands reached out to hoist the boy into the wagon," wrote Gildenman. "With lightning speed the horses . . . galloped away and disappeared into the nearest woods. For the first few moments, Motele was speechless. Gradually, he calmed down and, raising his clenched fist to the red sky, said in a trembling voice, 'This is for my parents and little Bashiale, my sister.'"

By this time, Gildenman had linked his group with the Soviet partisan brigade led by Gen. Aleksander Saburov. A minor NKVD official in Kiev, Saburov had escaped into the woods with a small group of men prior to the capitulation of the city in mid-September 1941. First, he headed east to the Bryansk Forest and the front line. Then he altered his plans, deciding instead to remain behind enemy lines and establish a partisan unit. By May 1942, his original group of fifteen had grown to several *otriady* of 2,800 men, mainly armed with captured Nazi weapons. Airdrops later supplemented his arsenal. In the fall, Saburov joined forces with the 1,500 partisans under the command of Maj.-Gen. Sidor Kovpak. Together, the two Soviet leaders and their men initiated a successful guerrilla operation that eventually led to Soviet control of the western and northern parts of the Ukraine.

It was while Saburov was in the area near Zhitomir that he met Misha Gildenman and his partisans. Initially, Gildenman was allowed to maintain a separate Jewish unit — not something the Soviets favoured — but over time, Russians were added and the Jews became a minority. Still, Gildenman retained his command and his son, Simcha, served as chief of intelligence. Gildenman's unit was now fully stocked with weapons and supplies, courtesy of the numerous airdrops arranged by the Soviet partisan leadership in Moscow.

In October 1943, Gildenman's unit played an important role in the rescue of a Red Army detachment surrounded by German forces in north-western Ukraine. By this time, the war in that region was nearly over. Once the Soviets had assumed control, Gildenman was flown to Moscow, where he was decorated with the Order of the Red Star. Still, determined not to stop fighting until the Nazis surrendered, he became a captain in an engineer corps and was in Berlin when Hitler committed suicide in May 1945. He emigrated to Israel in the early 1950s with his son, Simcha, and settled in the town of Rehovot. Diadia Misha died there in 1958.

RUSSIANS AND JEWS

We learned early in the game that in order to be equal, we had to be superior, and in order to be better, we had to be excellent. When we showed bravery, then they learned that all the jokes about Jews being scared and not being able to fight were not true. When they slept with us in the same bunker, when we shared with them bread that we had obtained, and shared with them bullets — then they realized that the Jews are not the ones described in the jokes.

— PETER SILVERMAN

"REVENGE WAS IN OUR BLOOD"

The killing of a local policeman on a road outside Jody in early April 1942 marked Peter Silverman and his cousin David Smuschkowitz as dangerous enemies of the Nazi state. Authorities now wanted them apprehended, dead or alive. Yet with this brave act of defiance, the two Jewish teenagers had taken their first significant steps towards becoming full-fledged partisans. In the following months, they amassed more arms, while still remaining hidden on a peasant farm. Although they had heard stories about Soviet POWs roaming the Koziany Forest, they had also heard that these bands were not interested in teaming up with or assisting Jewish fugitives.

"They killed Jews and raped Jewish girls," Silverman asserts. "There was no discipline. These were gangs of men who lived off farms [and] who stole what they needed."

At the beginning of the summer, the situation changed for the better with the arrival of a sixty-person Soviet partisan detachment from the east. These disciplined fighters and their commander introduced a sense of order and a plan of action into the forest. Young Jews with weapons were now invited to join the battle of the Spartak Brigade, as the unit called itself. The presence of so many well-armed Soviet soldiers also had an impact on the local peasants. Fearing retribution and punishment, farmers were quicker to provide Soviets and Jews with food and shelter.

As Silverman and Smuschkowitz were deciding whether to relocate to the forest and join Spartak, the Nazis unleashed a new wave of terror that further destroyed the dwindling Jewish population in the region's remaining ghettos. By the end of August, another 20,000 Jews had been slaughtered. Then, a few months later, the Germans massed a large force — comprising soldiers, police, and local collaborators — to deal with the partisans and fugitives in the forest. Their objective, says Silverman, was to kill them all.

Though the Soviet partisans were caught off guard by the Nazi blockade that surrounded the forest area, the majority were able to break through the line and retreat 150 kilometres east. Many of the Jewish men, women, and children taking refuge in the woods were not so lucky. Hundreds were murdered. Silverman's group managed to survive the attack by hiding in a barn about 25 kilometres from the forest. Three weeks later, the assault abruptly stopped. German reinforcements were required on the eastern front, and the troops near Jody were dispatched to Stalingrad. Before they departed, however, they made a special effort to cut off the partisans' supply lines. Thousands of local villagers were killed and their farms and towns set on fire. A band of Ukrainian collaborators who had been transferred into the region remained in the area to finish the job in the forest.

The winter of 1942–43 was long and cold. Without the Soviet partisans around to scare them, those peasants who had not been harmed by the Nazis grew even more hostile towards the Jewish fugitives who came to their doorsteps begging for food. Silverman and Smuschkowitz lived one day to the next during these harsh months, always on the move and constantly on guard.

Only once during this period were they nearly captured, when the farm they were hiding at was visited by a Nazi and Belorussian police detachment. Concealed in the attic, they held their breath, readied their guns and grenades, and waited. "We knew we were about to die," recalls Silverman. Yet miraculously, they were not detected. "Many times I have relived that episode in my mind," Silverman writes, "trying to analyze what happened. I think that the Belorussian police were angry with the Germans for sending them to face certain death against the partisans. They were afraid of us, afraid to look into that attic. Perhaps that is what saved us."

When the snow melted in the spring, the Soviet partisans of the Spartak Brigade returned to the Koziany Forest. This time, Silverman and Smuschkowitz did not waste a moment. They immediately made contact with the group and were introduced to the commander. As they ate lunch with him, the Soviet leader explained his views on a number of things, including Jews, which he classified into two categories, Yevrei (or Yewrei) and the derogatory, Zhydy.

"He openly told us at that first meeting," remembered Silverman, "that he liked Yewreis [sic] but hated Zyds [sic]. According to his definitions, a Yewrei was a Jew who was not afraid of anything, who would integrate himself with the Russians in every respect, set an example in heroism and devotion to his commanders, share his last piece of bread and his last bullet with his comrades, never abandon a sick or wounded comrade, and always volunteer whenever volunteers were called for. On the other hand, a Zyd [sic] was the opposite of everything he had described."

The commander believed that Silverman and Smuschkowitz were Yevrei, not Zhydy, and admitted them into the brigade. Although neither man had appreciated the commander's critical comments about

Jews, they had few alternatives. "We needed them," says Silverman. "We were nothing but a bunch of kids. We knew nothing about weapons." By then, Spartak consisted of approximately 300 fighters and had a fair selection of weapons, including machine guns and mortar. Ammunition, though, was always in short supply.

In time, the Russians trained the two Jewish teens, as well as many others, in the art of sabotage and guerrilla warfare. They taught them physical and mental endurance: how to cope with little sleep and food for days on end, how to ride a horse and shoot a rifle, how to trek long distances in thick bush during the dark night, and how to inflict the maximum amount of damage with the least amount of casualties.

In turn, the Jewish youths provided the Soviets with important information about the region, its geography, and its people. They helped them identify which peasants could be trusted and which could not. "It was," explains Silverman, "a symbiotic relationship. They needed us as much as we needed them." Jews like Silverman and his cousin also brought to the Soviet unit a desire for revenge and, more important, a greater sense of purpose.

"On the day any Jewish boy or girl, man or woman, joined the partisans," adds Silverman, "our mission was accomplished. We joined, not to survive the war, but to die fighting rather than be slaughtered like cattle. By being a member of the organized resistance our mission was accomplished, and if by any chance some of us survived the war, that was a bonus. We all were resigned to die in battle but tried to live a little longer so that we could kill as many more Nazis and collaborators as possible."

Partisan warfare in the Koziany Forest and throughout eastern Europe was a hit-and-run operation. Outnumbered in both manpower and weapons, partisan units had to rely on speed, cunning, and as far as was possible, a minimum of direct confrontation with the enemy. When such confrontation was necessary or could not be avoided, it was done with caution and surprise. "Hunting a German is similar to hunting partridges," partisan recruits were taught. "One creeps up to a partridge whilst it is singing, and one sits in hiding when it looks around. The same method applies to a German sentry. Armed with a hatchet, one creeps up to him in the dark. If he is walking to and fro or looking around, stand still. If he stands deep in thought, one slinks near him step by step. When you are close enough to grasp him, you suddenly give him a blow on his skull with the hatchet with all your strength. Do it so swiftly that he has no time to cry out."

Staying alive to kill again was, of course, the name of the game. "I do not need and I do not ask you to be dead heroes," the Spartak commander would tell his men. "I would rather see you alive and just plain brave; a dead hero cannot kill Germans and is unable to take revenge." The Jewish fighters hardly needed convincing. "We were like reinforcing steel rods," states Peter Silverman, "because revenge was in our blood. No one could hate the Nazis as we did."

Indeed, the Russians may have provided the young Jews from Jody with training, weapons and discipline, but courage and a willingness to die for a righteous cause were not things that could be taught around a campfire. These qualities had to come from within.

Such was the case with a "frail" eighteen-year-old Jewish teen named Isaac Firt, from Czartorysk, a village in northern Volhynia. In early 1943, Firt fled to the forest with hundreds of other Jews trying to escape incarceration in the ghetto. He hoped to join the Soviet partisans and continue the fight against the Nazis from the woods.

The Soviet fighters in northern Volhynia were part of the Za Rodinu (For the Homeland) Brigade and were under the command of Maj.-Gen. Aleksei Fyodorov. One of its detachments was led by a Captain Koncha, who, like many Russians, was sceptical about the fighting abilities of Jewish fugitives like Firt. When Koncha first laid eyes on the teen, he was not impressed by his physical stature or the fact that Firt did not have his own weapon. Nevertheless, Koncha agreed to give Firt a chance to prove himself.

The Jewish youth was given a few grenades and sent on a mission into Rafalowka, where a large Nazi and Ukrainian garrison was stationed. Without a moment's hesitation, he blew up the town's grain stores and panicked the enemy soldiers. When Firt returned, Koncha admitted him into his *otriad*. The eighteen-year-old was later appointed the leader of the Jewish platoon and led other sabotage missions against German rail transports. At the end of the war, Isaac Firt was awarded numerous Soviet medals for his heroism.

■ ■

Like Peter Silverman, Dave Smuschkowitz, and Isaac Firt — just three among thousands — the majority of young Jewish men and women who escaped the ghettos to fight in the forests were inexperienced, unprepared, and unarmed. Consequently, they were easy targets for Nazi patrols, undisciplined bands of Soviet partisans, and local collaborators. Many were killed within weeks. In fact, few of the Jews who sought out the partisans were fit for combat or ready for rugged life in the wilderness. Their skills as shoemakers, carpenters, tailors, and locksmiths were not initially useful or generally appreciated by the Russians whom they encountered. Only time proved the Soviets wrong. Soon they were grateful for the Jewish shoemaker who could repair a hole in a boot or a locksmith who was able to fix a rusted rifle.

And for Jews, the physical and mental pressures were enormous. Even those rural Jews who were more comfortable in the woods often found the transition difficult. Many had been starved or worn out by the harsh life in the ghettos. Nearly all had already lost some, if not all, members of their immediate families; still others had left parents and younger siblings behind the barbed wire.

There was a small minority of Jews who had served in the Polish and Soviet armies and were familiar with the order and discipline that guerrilla warfare demanded. They generally adapted more easily to life in the woods, although even these experienced fighters faced adversity that they had never before confronted.

"The non-Jew went off [to the forest] to fulfill his national obligation," Yisrael Gutman writes, "knowing that he had the support of the allies, a great power, or a government-in-exile in whose name he acted. . . . The Jew was foreign, persecuted, abandoned."

Submission and capitulation, however, were not options, no matter how daunting the obstacles. Men like Shalom Radziecki, a school teacher from the small town of Zhetel near Slonim, fled to the Lipiczany Forest in 1941, well before there was a Soviet presence. He established

Yossel Zelkowicz and a friend, in Kovno in 1939. Yossel, who became a partisan fighter in the Naliboki forest, was killed in March 1943 while on a reconnaissance mission.
— *Courtesy of Gitel Morrison*

The Zelkowicz family, Lodz, Poland, 1931. Left to right: Leska, Gitel (at 9 months old), Lazer, Yossel (6 years old), and Sora (Leska's mother). This photo was discovered in the ruins of the family's house in Lida, Poland, after the war. — *Courtesy of Gitel Morrison*

Misha Gildenman. Uncle Misha, the great partisan fighter, led a successful guerrilla unit in the Volhynian forests. — *Yad Vashem*

A partisan camp. — *Ghetto Fighters' House*

Dr. Yeheskel Atlas. Dr. Atlas organized 120 Jews into a partisan unit in the Lipiczany forest. Famous for his daring exploits, he was killed in combat in 1942. — *Yad Vashem*

Jacob Gens, head of the Vilna ghetto Judenrat. — *Yad Vashem*

Partisans at the family camp established by Tuvia Bielski in the Naliboki forest in May 1944. — *Yad Vashem*

Jewish partisans from Chil Grynszpan's group in the Parczew forest. — *Yad Vashem*

A *zemlianka* in the Naliboki forest, which housed partisans between 1943 and 1944. — *Ghetto Fighters' House*

Shalom Zorin, leader of a family camp in the Naliboki forest. Zorin was responsible for saving the lives of 800 fighters and civilians. — *Yad Vashem*

Joseph Glazman. One of the leaders of the Vilna ghetto underground, the FPO, Glazman was killed in a German ambush after he had escaped into the forest in 1943. — *Yad Vashem*

The death pits at the Ponary near Vilna. Between 1941 and 1944, approximately 70,000 to 100,000 people, mostly Jews, were murdered at the Ponary by the Einsatzgruppen, the Nazi death squads. — *Yad Vashem*

Tuvia Bielski and his brothers organized the largest family camp in eastern Europe.
— *Yad Vashem*

Partisans from Chil Grynszpan's unit. Foreground from left: Shienka from Wlodawa, Abram the Patzan, and Chanina Barbanel. Back, from left: Harold Werner, Symcha Barbanel, Dora Grynszpan, Abram Grynszpan, and Velvale the Patzan. — *Yad Vashem*

Partisan sabotage. — *Ghetto Fighters' House*

Vilna partisans, July 1944. Rozka Korczak is third from the left (back), and to her right are Abba Kovner and Vitka Kempner. — *Yad Vashem*

Peter Silverman, Dave Smuschkowitz, and Tania Silverman (Peter's sister) at liberation in July 1944. — *Courtesy of Peter Silverman*

Leon Kahn in Lodz, Poland, August 1945. — *Courtesy of Leon Kahn*

one of the first partisan groups in the area.

Yitzhak Einbinder from Kurzeniec, a village north of Vilna, also reached the dense woods of the Lipiczany, along with his friends Ida Golferstein and Jacob Alperowitch. In time, they joined the Borba, or struggle, group, the *otriad* organized by Hirsh Kaplinski. The Soviets were so impressed with Einbinder's skills that they sent him back to Moscow, where he attended one of their schools for guerrilla warfare. Once he graduated, he returned to the *puszcza* with a band of 300 men and earned the nickname the Fearless for his courageous and daring fighting abilities. About a year later, Einbinder was killed in a German ambush.

DEFENDERS OF THE GREAT LAND

From the perspective of Soviet officials back in Moscow, Jews like Yitzhak Einbinder were perfect candidates for the partisan movement. They demanded loyal, obedient, and disciplined fighters who were willing to place the interests of the Communist state — the Great Land, as the Russians respectfully referred to it — above their own. Death and suffering were considered unfortunate but sometimes necessary consequences of defeating the Nazi menace. As historian John Armstrong has observed, "no human costs, in individual or social terms, were regarded as too high, so long as the partisan activity contributed to the overriding goal of preserving the Soviet system." Saving the lives of Jews, particularly those incapable of fighting, was thus a low priority.

In theory, the Soviet partisans were to act as a powerful rear army, harassing German supply lines, sabotaging trains, and disrupting their progress eastward. And while the 150,000 or so fighters roaming the forests of Belorussia, Volhynia, and other eastern areas had had some success by the summer of 1942, Stalin and his top-ranking generals were far from satisfied. In the south, Soviet partisans, despite their considerable numbers, had had little effect on Nazi military movements.

For the most part, the fighters were not anxious to engage the Germans in battle. The Nazis' sheer numerical strength and overwhelming firepower were enough of a deterrent. In the Spadshchansky Forest in the eastern Ukraine, for example, Sidor Kovpak's detachment in November 1941 consisted of only seventy-three men. They faced a German enemy of police and troops that exceeded 3,000. After a brief battle in which the Soviets fared well, Kovpak decided that he still had no choice but to relocate farther north to the Bryansk Forest, which offered better protection. Less capable Soviet fighters, meanwhile, were content to sit back and wait for the war to pass them by. Local peasants who had fled to the forest to join partisan units became particularly worried that any action on their part could lead to retaliation against their families back home.

The high command hardly cared about such personal concerns. "Procrastination and inactivity, still to be found in some partisan groups, must by all means cease," proclaimed Pateleymon Ponomarenko, the head of the Central Staff, in a top secret order that was widely distributed to partisan commanders at the beginning of August 1942. "It is necessary to attack the enemy with the greatest possible energy."

Soviet propaganda continued to bombard peasants with a similar message, urging them to join the battle against Hitler — "the bandit, bloodsucker and cannibal" — and "fight for the honor, freedom, and independence of the fatherland." Even collaborators were offered amnesty if they switched sides. In a 1942 leaflet addressed to Russians, Ukrainians, and Belorussians who were cooperating with the Nazis, the Soviets asked, "Do you really want to shed your blood and sacrifice yourselves as mercenaries of fascism in [the] fight against the Soviet people, who are bravely defending the honor, freedom, and independence of their native country, their families, and their soil? . . . In the end you will be unhappy if you tie yourselves irrevocably to the Hitlerites. . . . Fascism is slavery, corruption, poverty, hunger, and death. Everything for the fight against fascism!" Despite such pleas, the situation remained unchanged during the summer.

At the end of the August, Stalin convened a special three-day meeting of partisan leaders at the Kremlin. Brigade commanders behind enemy lines were flown back to Moscow for the gathering. This included two of the most important partisan generals, Sidor Kovpak and Aleksander Saburov, who departed from their respective bases in the Bryansk Forest. In recognition of their military exploits, the two partisan commanders, along with Aleksei Fyodorov, had already been awarded one of their nation's highest distinctions, the Hero of the Soviet Union. Fyodorov, operating farther east in the Orel region, had been invited to Moscow as well, but problems with his radio communication meant he did not learn of the meeting until it was too late to attend. Moreover, his detachment was under constant attack by the Germans and landing a plane in the area would have been difficult. Fyodorov would have to wait until November to fly to Moscow and deliver a report to Soviet officials.

When the plane carrying Kovpak and Saburov flew over the front line at night, at a height of 10,000 feet, the Nazis fired at it from the ground, but to no avail. Once they were in Moscow, the commanders were taken first to the Moskva Hotel for a brief rest, and then to Stalin's office in the Kremlin. This was the first time that Kovpak had met the Soviet leader, and the fifty-six-year-old partisan commander was both honoured and excited. "Before coming to Stalin's office," he recalled several years later, "we passed through several rooms. I was thinking: 'Now I shall see him.' All the time Stalin stood before my eyes just as I knew him from his portraits. And that is exactly how I saw Comrade Stalin when the door of his office opened. Why, it was just as if I had met him many times before, and knew him personally."

Kovpak had anticipated that the meeting would be "all business," but before the formal discussions got under way, Stalin inquired about the partisan leaders' families, about life in the woods, and about relations with the local population. When the meeting was finished, Stalin's orders were clear: More partisan fighters had to be recruited and the movement had to become much more offensive. In particular, he insisted that German supply and communication lines be destroyed. The decision was made as well to introduce further discipline into the ranks and to severely punish those who were not up to the task. In the forest, indolence was unacceptable and cowardliness a crime deserving of the death penalty.

In the ensuing months, training schools turned out more partisan graduates, who were dispatched to the forests in an attempt to co-ordinate guerrilla operations. Time and again, the Soviet leader's declaration of May 1, 1942, was reiterated in the field:

Fulfill your Partisan oath
Carry iron discipline
Guard your Partisan secrecy
Have your weapons ever at the ready
Recruit for the Partisan cause

It was left to experienced commanders like Kovpak to put Stalin's orders into action. With some prodding from the Soviet leader, Kovpak agreed to move his men farther west from the Bryansk Forest to the right side of the Dnieper River — where there was still no official Soviet partisan operation — providing he was allocated more weapons and supplies. Before Kovpak had left the Kremlin and flown back to his Bryansk base, Stalin had arranged for everything the partisan commander had requested.

Born in 1887 in the village of Kotelva, in the Poltava district southeast of Kiev, Sidor Artemovich Kovpak was a "simple, fatherly man," according to American historian John Armstrong. His character probably explains his relative success and popularity as a partisan leader among men who were considerably younger than he was. As a loyal Ukrainian Bolshevik, Kovpak served in the Red Army during the Russian Civil War and was employed by the Party after the hostilities had ceased. When war broke out in Russia in 1941, he was a high-ranking civic official in the Putivl municipality in the Sumy district, not far from the village where he had been born.

Before the Nazis arrived in mid-September, Kovpak and Semyon Vaislyevich Rudnyev, a local Party official, escaped to the nearby Spadshchansky Forest with a small group of men. A base was established around a forester's hut, and a series of outposts linked to the main headquarters by a telephone wire guarded against German advancement. The base consisted of a number of bunkers for sleeping, and a storehouse and kitchen where potatoes and cabbages were kept. A nearby stream provided water.

From the beginning, Kovpak's objectives were clear. "We had by no means come to the wood to hide from the Germans," he wrote in his memoirs. "Our aim was to destroy Germans, not to give the enemy a minute's peace, not to permit him to make himself master in our district. We were masters here and masters we would remain."

In fact, until the meeting with Stalin took place in August 1942, Kovpak's unit remained small and his military and sabotage operations limited (though he and his men did manage to capture two German tanks after a short battle in October 1941). By early October 1942, having received the airdrops of supplies, weapons, and men that Stalin had promised, Kovpak and Rudnyev, his political commissar, had amassed a partisan brigade of approximately 1,500 fighters. Defiantly, they marched west towards Pinsk, fighting Germans all the way. It took them nearly three weeks to reach the banks of the Dnieper and three nights to get all of the partisans and supplies across the river.

During the winter of 1942–43, Kovpak and his men sabotaged at least nine major railway bridges and attacked several Nazi police stations and garrisons throughout northern Volhynia and southern Polesie. In the early spring, he took his men farther south, to the area near Rovno. Soon after, Kovpak was made a major-general and appointed the supreme partisan commander in the Ukraine region west of the Dnieper River. In the aftermath of the German defeat at Stalingrad in February 1943, Kovpak's roaming bands continued to harass the enemy whenever possible and pass on intelligence about Nazi movements to Soviet authorities at the front lines, but their military effectiveness was admittedly limited. "It was not until the Red Army was close enough to give them active support [nearly a year later]," historian Matthew Cooper has argued, "that [partisans in the western Ukraine, including Kovpak and Saburov] became anything more than a passing nuisance to the Germans."

Much of Kovpak's time, in fact, was spent recruiting local peasants to join the Soviet side. His men were specifically ordered to treat the Poles they encountered in a friendly manner. "One should not shoot at those inhabitants who flee," Kovpak told them. Looting, especially, was forbidden and regarded as a serious violation of partisan and military law. Such acts, declared the official Soviet line, merely helped "the enemy to conduct his propaganda against us . . . and besmirch the honorable calling of the avengers of the people." Nevertheless, it occurred more often than commanders like Kovpak would have readily admitted.

In one incident in early July 1943, two young Russian fighters of the Kovpak brigade, both considered to be loyal Communists and brave soldiers, were caught stealing. According to the charge, the men took "a bucket of lard, a bucket of honey, clothing, shoes, and other things from the home of a peaceful inhabitant in the village of Shladava." No excuses were accepted. As punishment for their crime, the two partisans were shot by a firing squad while the members of their company looked on.

Kovpak was by no means the only commander to have trouble instituting discipline among the rank and file. More than 50 percent of the fighters had little or no prior military experience; many were conscripted against their will or had joined the guerrillas once the war had turned against the Germans. In his memoirs, as partisan leader Aleksei Fyodorov wrote about escaped Russian POWs, or hubbies, as he called them, fighters who had married local peasant women. "Among the 'hubbies' there were specimens who would have been glad to sit out the war behind a woman's skirt, but the Hitlerites would either drive them off to work in Germany or else made them join the police. After turning this over in his mind, such a man would come to the conclusion that, after all, joining the partisans was more advantageous." (German police saw the situation slightly differently. In a brief memorandum about Red Army deserters prepared by Nazi police in Riga in June 1942, it was pointed out that the Russian soldiers "would much prefer simply to be sheltered by a farmer and would have little interest in fighting again were they not compelled to do so through terror.")

In the forest, concerted efforts were made to instil pride and a sense of responsibility in the troops. Units were given names like Stalin, Lenin, and the Red Banner, which were supposed to stir patriotic passions among the fighters, and acts of bravery were widely publicized. Beginning in 1942, partisans were often referred to in official declarations as "soldiers of the Red Army in the rear of the enemy." Regular lectures around the campfire were also delivered by political commissars that stressed duty to "Mother Russia" and the "Great Land."

Yet many of these endeavours (which also included strict supervision and spying by Party members in some units) had little or no effect.

Partisan commanders routinely complained about everything from drunkenness, fraternizing with local women, and excessive cursing — which they argued were bad for a unit's morale — to more serious offences like desertion, looting, and cowardice.

"My persistent requests to maintain order and discipline are disregarded again and again," reported Cmdr. S. V. Grishin in May 1943, from his base east of Minsk. "Lack of restraint in relations with women have been noted at different times. In seven cases this has resulted in pregnancy."

Such behaviour was tolerated, if barely, but desertion and falling asleep on guard duty quickly led to death. Earlier in 1943, for instance, Grishin had executed a female scout named Andrenkova "for failure to execute reconnaissance assignments, for violating security regulations, and for theft." In September of that year, Grishin ordered that a squad leader named Bacharov be shot "for leaving his post without orders, for cowardice, for being panicky, and for nonfulfillment of orders." Partisans who deserted and were then caught — and there were many — received even worse treatment: They were tortured first and then shot in the neck.

YEVREI AND ZHYDY

Soviet partisan propaganda deliberately did not mention Jews or the atrocities that had been perpetrated on them. (Neither, for that matter, do the memoirs of a partisan leader like Kovpak.*) In the interests of the collective spirit of resistance that the Soviets were attempting to engender, it was felt that nothing positive could come from singling out one group of people. Certainly, anti-Semitism was a factor in the decision.

---

*In Kovpak's memoirs, the only reference to Jews is this observation about one of his men, a tank-gunner named Abram (undoubtedly Jewish, though not identified as such), during a battle when he was still in the Spadshchansky Forest: "The Germans came up so near to [one of the tanks they had captured] . . . that the faces of the soldiers could be seen. The tank met the Germans with fire, they scattered, ran away, reassembled, again went into the attack and once more retreated, leaving the dead whom our tank-gunner, thrusting his head out of the hatch after the firing, counted one by one with his fingers. I cannot remember his name — it was one that nobody could pronounce. Everyone called him by his first name, Abram, or simply Gunner." (Kovpak, *Our Partisan Course*, 35). On the other hand, in his memoirs, partisan leader Aleksei Fyodorov included information about the experiences of a Jewish comrade, Yakov Zusserman. (See Fyodorov, *The Underground Committee Carries On*, 67, 194–95.)

Although it was not endemic among Soviet and Polish partisans, it existed nonetheless. Sometimes it was as subtle as the distinction between Yevrei and Zhydy that was made by Peter Silverman's Soviet commander; on other occasions, it was as blatant and as physical as almost anything Jews had experienced from the Nazis.

According to the testimonies of many survivors, the brigade commander made all the difference. Far from the officials in Moscow, partisan leaders had a certain amount of independence and discretionary power when it came to interpreting orders, enforcing rules, meting out punishment, and dealing with Jewish fugitives. In some units, the commander, with his Nagan pistol at his side and a woman (often Jewish) close by, set the tone of the fighters' day-to-day life. His attitude towards and treatment of the Jews, both within and outside the unit, greatly influenced forest relationships.

Even though it was official Soviet policy throughout the war not to allow the plight of the Jews to detract from the overall goal of defeating the Nazis, many Soviet partisan leaders did risk their lives helping Jews to safety. Aleksei Fyodorov, for example, who by 1943 commanded a brigade of 1,700 fighters in the forests of Volhynia, was credited with rescuing hundreds of Jewish children and offering them protection in a family camp. In the same region, Col. Dimitry Medvedev accepted Jews from Rovno and Korets into his detachment (although he did turn away Misha Gildenman's group), and provided food, supplies, and weapons to an adjacent family camp of 150 Jews. And as we will see, Tuvia Bielski's large family camp in the Naliboki Forest owed its survival to the support it received from Belorussian commander Vasily Yehimovich Chernyshev, or General Platon, as he was known in the *puszcza*.

Still, Kovpak's attitude was more typical. Jews who were ready to fight the enemy were more than welcome in his brigade, but civilians would have to fend for themselves. As early as December 1942, Kovpak courted armed Jews from villages in the vicinity of Sarny in the southern Polesie. Later, he collaborated with Misha Gildenman's unit in a joint sabotage operation. But when he encountered Jewish fugitives from Korets, only those younger than forty and fit for combat were permitted to stay with him.

In June 1943, Kovpak led his brigade south-west into eastern Galicia, to the oilfields near Drohobycz, which he intended to destroy. These installations provided the Germans with fuel for their eastern front operations. Along the way, one of his battalions attacked the town of Skalat and discovered a labour camp of 300 half-starved Jews. The Soviets freed all of them and carried the weakest ones to the forest on wagons. But it was clear to Kovpak that keeping women, children, and anyone incapable of combat would jeopardize his operation. Two days later, he gave the Skalat Jews a choice. Those who could endure a "military life," as he put it, "who can bear arms" and "hate fascists," were urged to join his detachments. Many of the younger Jews accepted his offer. Those not up to the challenge found refuge in the homes of Polish peasants.

Consistent behaviour, however, was one of the casualties of the war. Forest relationships were rarely straightforward, especially those between Russians and Jews. Each side had different objectives and goals — the Soviets viewed the world from a military perspective, while the Jews despaired of the survival of their people — and past experiences and long-held beliefs coloured an already tense situation. Naturally, Soviet partisans were reluctant to trust anyone they did not know. The Nazis regularly sent their agents into the forest disguised as peasants to infiltrate the partisan ranks. A cautious attitude towards new recruits was thus essential, and in many detachments, an extensive screening process took place before admission was granted.

Some Jews — like Jacob and Bela Greenstein, who wanted to remain together — had difficulty joining a Russian detachment. The Soviets did not look favourably on the admission of married couples. Yet shortly after their escape from the Minsk ghetto in May 1942, the Greensteins were invited into the Parkhomenko combat brigade. The commander of their *otriad* was Vasil Ivanovitch, a Ukrainian lieutenant in the Red Army. "He was a good man," recalls Jacob, "and a very good commander." But Ivanovitch was an exception. In other regions, anxious fighters were ordered to shoot on sight any strangers they might encounter. Many were Jewish fugitives seeking refuge.

Of course, acceptance into a brigade was merely a first step. The notion persisted among the Soviets — from Stalin down to the lowliest private — that Jews were and always would be poor partisans, or "poor warriors," as the Soviet leader put it at a meeting in early December 1941. In fact, many Soviets believed that the Jews were cowards who had only fled to the forest "to save their skins." One Soviet commander was reported to have yelled at a group of Jewish fugitives from Kamen Kashirski in northern Volhynia who wanted to join his detachment. "You call yourselves partisans?" he shouted. "You are wretches and not partisans. Why have you turned over all your gold to the Germans? Get out of here and don't let me see your faces again." Family camps of Jewish civilians, in particular, were regarded by the Soviets with suspicion and, more often, contempt. In the opinion of many Russian partisans, these Jews attracted German patrols, antagonized the local population, and competed for the limited food supply.

When Irving F. from Baranowicze reached the forest in December 1942, he had a gun but no bullets for it. The Soviet partisan commander he encountered was not friendly and did not believe Irving, who was twenty-seven years old, had what it took to become a guerrilla. He seized Irving's gun and his boots and sent him to a nearby family camp. "The Russians thought we were parasites," Irving claims. "They believed Jews could not fight."

In the Naliboki Forest, some Soviet fighters even believed the rumours circulating in the nearby villages that Jews had been sent by the Germans to murder them. There was also talk that the Nazis had infected Jewish women with venereal disease. (In fact, Faye Schulman alleges that in Pinsk, it was local peasant girls who were more likely to be infected, since the Nazis knew that Soviet partisans regularly emerged from the forest looking for the company of women.) In one case, three Jewish women who had attempted to swim across the Niemen River were killed by the Soviets the moment they reached the banks on the other side. Having seen the bodies for himself, Hersh Smolar respectfully asked his Belorussian commander why the women had been shot. "Avoiding my eyes, and speaking so softly I could barely hear him," Smolar recalled, "[the partisan leader] explained: 'We were warned by reliable sources that the Gestapo had sent out a group of women to put poison in our food kettles — we're in a war [and] can't do anything about it now. . . ." There was little that Smolar could say.

Even when they proved to be false, negative attitudes and rumours about Jews continued to linger. According to many survivors, double standards existed in Soviet units and Jews constantly had to prove themselves. Often, one poor experience with a Jewish fugitive convinced Russian partisans that no Jews were to be trusted. "We took a Jew into our *otriad*, we trusted him and treated him well," a Soviet fighter told young Jashke Mazowi, an escapee from the Lida ghetto who wanted to join their unit. "He ran away on the sly, without telling us. Because of what he did we shoot all Jews we meet." In fact, the Russians decided to take a chance with Mazowi, who proved to be a brave and effective partisan. Still, when they were among their Soviet comrades, Jews had to be cautious.

"Jewish partisans found themselves under constant scrutiny and in a constant struggle to justify their right to fight," states Faye Schulman, who served in a Soviet brigade in the forests near Pinsk. "If a Jew was brave and walked at the head of the line to be first to attack, the anti-Semites would say, 'Hey! Why are you in front of us? Are you better than we are? You are running ahead of us!' If the Jewish fighter kept in the rear, they said, 'Hey! Why are you lagging behind? You must be a coward!' There was nothing worse among the partisans than to be labelled a coward."

For Jews, the fight for respect and equal treatment was an uphill battle. In most but certainly not all cases, for instance, Jews had to possess a weapon before they were allowed to become full-fledged members of a detachment. In Silverman's Spartak Brigade, even after there was a surplus of guns and rifles from airdrops in the summer of 1943, the rule about Jews having a weapon continued to be enforced.

No Jew could refuse to go on a mission, no matter how risky or dangerous, and none could return without having fulfilled his duty. "You were not allowed to complain," says Rubin Pinsky, who escaped from the ghetto in Zdzieciol when he was eighteen years old and fought in a Russian and Jewish *otriad* in the Lipiczany Forest. He believes that Jews were more often ordered to go on dangerous missions than Russians. Most were willing, but many did not return.

In May 1943, young Yitzhak Arad and his friends in the Koziany Forest were given one rifle and one sawed-off shotgun and were ordered by their Soviet commander in the Chapayev *otriad* (part of Markov's Voroshilov Brigade) to procure more weapons from unfriendly local peasants.

"We were stunned," Arad recalled in his memoirs. "We had expected to be sent with other partisans, armed with the best weapons the unit possessed. It had never occurred to us that the mission would be entrusted to our members alone; they lacked partisan experience, and inadequate knowledge of the surrounding area, and had been deprived of several of their weapons. Yet there was no choice but to obey. Opposition, refusal to fulfill a command of the leader of the unit in the organized Soviet partisan movement, meant death."

Jewish partisans, moreover, rarely received the benefit of the doubt, and according to Hersh Smolar and other Jewish fighters, there were numerous cases of Jews "being sentenced to death for negligence when the circumstances did not warrant such punishment." Consider the tragedy that befell a group of young boys from Kovel in north-west Volhynia, an all-too-typical example of Russian-Jewish relations in the forest.

Sometime in late 1942, about seven Jewish teenagers, having obtained several guns with ammunition, escaped to the woods. There they met up with Soviet partisans led by a Lieutenant Nasyekin, who were supposedly connected with Cmdr. Grigorii Linkov's large brigade. The Jewish youth were ordered to hand over their weapons and return to the ghetto to acquire more arms. When they resisted, the Soviets killed all of them but one, who managed to escape unharmed. It must be noted, too, that several months later, Nasyekin was involved in a plot to murder more Jewish partisans. He was arrested and executed on the orders of Col. Anton Brinsky, a Soviet partisan commander sent by Linkov to institute discipline in Volhynia.

The anti-Semitism Jews felt from many of their Russian, Lithuanian, Ukrainian, and Polish comrades was both subtle and blatant. One popular joke among the Soviets went as follows: "What have the various nationalities invented? The Russians — vodka; the French —

champagne; the Jews — pause — the Jews invented the *kolkhoz* [collective farm]." One prominent Ukrainian partisan commander, Timofei Strokach, who led more than 6,000 men in the forests near Kiev, was known to "rail" against Jews after he had had a bit too much vodka. Such disrespect was common. "The [Soviets] tried to minimize our devotion, dedication and heroism in battle," asserted Yitzhak Lichtenberg, an escapee from the Lachva ghetto who joined a Soviet group in the Pripet Marshes.

The situation in Sara Ginaite's unit in the Rudniki Forest was so bad that the sixteen-year-old actually returned to the Kovno ghetto in early 1944 for a brief stay. "There was a Russian commissar who was so anti-Semitic," Ginaite remembers, "that one day I threatened to kill him." Peter Silverman and his friends in the Koziany Forest suspected that many Jewish fighters were murdered by Soviet partisans while on reconnaissance missions and food expeditions, though such charges were difficult to prove. Other Jews in the woods felt the same way.

Velvke Yonson's experiences reflect the complex and often strained relations that existed between Russians and Jews. Until a massive German attack in late 1942 made life unbearable in the forest area near Slonim, Yonson and other Jews had got along fairly well with their Soviet comrades. Yet in the aftermath of the Nazi assault, the Russian fighters, who were outnumbered and overwhelmed, blamed the Jews for their desperate situation.

In the confusion, Yonson and another Jewish partisan, Ichik Levin, were separated from their unit and found refuge in a small Jewish family camp deep in the marshland. Wet and tired, Yonson soon became ill with typhus — a common ailment among partisans — and was forced to spend three weeks hiding in a bunker where, thanks to the care provided by the Jewish families, he recuperated. One day, a group of Soviet partisans arrived at the camp and accused Yonson and Levin of being deserters. After a few tense moments, during which the two Jews were threatened, the Russians accepted their explanation that they were planning to return to their unit once Yonson's health had improved.

Still weak, Yonson and Levin rejoined a Russian unit, but now as Yonson recalled, "anti-Semitism raged" in the forest. Wherever Yonson went, he found bodies of Jewish men, women, and children whom he was certain had been slain by the Soviets. When several Jewish fighters guarding the few tanks kept by the *otriad* were accidentally blown up, Yonson and his friends decided they had had enough.

With fifty fellow Jewish partisans, they did what many Jews trapped in the forests of eastern Europe did: They met their Russian commander and asked that they be allowed to form a separate unit. Only in this way, they believed, would they know for certain whom they could trust. Such independence would have also permitted them to offer assistance to Jewish family camps in the area without Russian interference. They had sufficient arms to last them a few months and were confident they could procure enough supplies and food from local peasants. But there were other considerations.

■ ■

By early 1943, it was an established Soviet policy that partisan groups be created on a "national-territorial basis." While Lithuanians, Belorussians, and Ukrainians were permitted to have their own brigades, Jews, without territory they could call their own, were not. Some Jewish partisans initially wanted to defy the Soviet authorities (and the odds) and organize their own groups. In particular, many of the young Zionists who escaped from ghettos in Vilna, Kovno, and Bialystok regarded separate units "as an expression of their national aspirations," as Yitzhak Arad has noted. They had started the fight in the ghetto; they wanted to finish it in the forest. (Jewish Communists, on the other hand, opposed separate Jewish units on principle and policy.)

Their situation, however, was extremely precarious. Misha Gildenman and Chil Grynszpan, among many others, operated independently for a short time, yet survived only because they eventually linked up with Russian and Polish groups. It was the same story with the ghetto fighters around Vilna. They had no choice but to accept the authority of the Soviet and Lithuanian partisan command if they intended to continue their resistance. From any perspective, it made sense to put up with the anti-Semitism — providing it was not fatal — and benefit from the arms, supplies, and resources that the Soviets and Poles had at their disposal.

Often, in fact, the Soviets did not give the Jews a choice. Peter Silverman's cousin Peter Smuszkowicz and his friend David Pincov, for example, initially attempted to organize their own unit in the forest near Jody, but the Soviet commander in the area would not allow it. "They were given an ultimatum," writes Silverman. "Join the Soviet partisans or be disarmed and shot."

Jewish escapees from Slonim were fortunate enough to be assigned to Group 51 of the Shchors detachment, which was under the command of a Russian Jew, Lt. Yakov Fyodorovich. Born in Gomel, a town south-east of Minsk, Fyodorovich was a hero of the Soviet Union for his bravery during the Finnish campaign of 1940. He had reached the forest south of Slonim after he escaped from a POW camp near Bialystok. Fyodorovich was a superb military tactician and immediately commanded the respect and loyalty of his men. He not only spoke Yiddish to the Jews who joined him, but he taught them how to be soldiers and guerrilla fighters as well. They learned, observed Nachum Albert in his history of Slonim's Jews, "to understand the power of the forest and its secret language: how to interpret various sounds among the rustling of the leaves, how to differentiate between a real echo and a simulated one, how to tell the direction a shot came from, how to 'read' footsteps — was it a stray cow or a human being out there in the darkness? And above all, to be bold and daring and to abhor cowardice."

In early August 1942, Group 51 participated in a successful raid on the town of Kosow, north-east of Pinsk, in which 150 Nazi soldiers and Belorussian policemen were killed and 300 of the town's 500 surviving Jews were rescued. Several months later, in a battle with Nazi and Latvian troops, Fyodorovich was fatally wounded and his own men had to put him out of his misery lest he fall into the enemy's hands. With Fyodorovich's death, Group 51 quickly lost its Jewish identity and eventually split up.

Similarly, a large group of Jews from Maniewicze, Rafalowka, Kamen Kashirski, and other towns in northern Volhynia were able to remain together because of the enlightened attitudes of two Soviet partisan commanders, Nikolai Konishchuk, known in the forest as Kruk, and Josef Sobiesiak, or Max. Konishchuk, a Ukrainian-Communist peasant, had fled to the forest in 1941 from the village of Griva (near Kamen Kashirski), where he had served as mayor. He soon linked up with Sobiesiak, a Polish Communist official from the Lublin region who had escaped east to nearby Kovel when the war began. Sobiesiak eventually also fled to the forests of northern Volhynia and organized a small Ukrainian and Soviet partisan group. Initially, Konishchuk served as Sobiesiak's commissar, but eventually he was appointed commander of his own detachment. Both leaders demonstrated an uncompromising and singular compassion when it came to helping Jewish fugitives.

At first, only a small contingent of Jews, including Dov Lorber and Joseph Zweible from Maniewicze, reached Konishchuk's camp. (At the time, Sobiesiak was with a group of partisans in another area.) But soon they were joined by hundreds more — men, women, and children. Konishchuk did not turn any of them away, and Sobiesiak supported his position when he returned. Both believed, more than most non-Jewish partisans, that "to save human lives is to fight the enemy."

But Dov Lorber takes a more cynical view of the motives of Konishchuk, in particular. "The reason that Kruk kept close to the Jews was well understood," he has written. "With us, he was commander of a unit where everyone respected him. Without us, he would have been an ordinary partisan, and would have gotten no credit for his initiative to organize a unit which had such a just cause to fight against the Nazis."

Whatever his reasons, Konishchuk (with Sobiesiak's approval) organized several family camps that also functioned as supply and repair depots for sceptical Soviet partisans. Jews who could not fight instead used their skills as shoemakers and tailors in a productive way. For his efforts, Konishchuk was referred to behind his back by other Russian and Ukrainian fighters as the Jewish Messiah. Though he was easily angered — he once took a shot at Lorber because he mistakenly thought Lorber had stolen a potato — Konishchuk did not tolerate anti-Semitism and defended the many Jews in his unit against unwarranted charges and accusations. He approved, as well, of taking retribution against known collaborators who had taken part in the liquidation of the Maniewicze ghetto. In late 1942, Kruk's detachment became part of a brigade organized by Col. Anton Brinsky and participated in numerous successful sabotage missions, destroying Nazi transports and communication systems.

■ ■

Perhaps wanting to ease the tension in the unit, Velvke Yonson's Soviet commander gave him and other Jewish partisans permission to go off on their own. They were grateful, but determined to avenge the deaths of their fallen comrades. "We do to the Russian partisans what they did to our Jews," remembered Yonson. "We kill everyone that comes near us." Soon members of the group, which was led by Senke Brosh, a Jew from Minsk, were regarded as nothing but "Jewish bandits" by both Russians and Germans in the area.

The unit survived intact for about three months, always moving and being particularly vigilant. One night, the men were resting comfortably in two farmhouses, but the guard they posted had fallen asleep. Without warning, the Jewish fighters were surrounded by a larger contingent of unfriendly Russians. The Soviets entered one of the huts and quickly murdered eighteen Jews. As soon as they entered the other house, where Yonson and Brosh were, a battle ensued.

"In the blink of an eye, the Russians are in the house, pointing guns at us," Yonson recalled. "They knew that they would never take us alive. Senke throws me my machine gun and grabs his own. He manages to yell "strellai," shoot, and in that moment he takes a bullet to the forehead and falls on me. This causes a spate of firing."

When the smoke cleared, only sixteen Jews remained alive. They were arrested by the Russians and brought before the *otriad*'s commissar, who condemned them to death for crimes against the state. After a brief discussion, it was decided that only Yonson, as the second-in-command, would be shot. The others were ordered to leave the region.

As Yonson was led into the forest to be executed, "a miracle occurred," as he puts it. The partisan who was ordered to shoot him slapped him instead. Instinctively, Yonson fought back and started to choke his opponent. But the man cried out that he was also a Jew, though his Russian comrades did not know his true identity. The fighter led Yonson farther into the woods, shot his rifle into the air several times, then kissed Yonson's cheek and told him to flee. Yonson rejoined his men and headed south for the Lipiczany Forest. There, despite his various problems with Russian partisans, he joined another *otriad*. As a Jewish fugitive with vengeance in his heart, it was the only choice he could have made.

"ONE OF THE HUNTERS INSTEAD OF ONE OF THE HUNTED"

In large part, the Soviets were wrong about the fighting abilities of many Jews. They were, in fact, the most unlikely of heroes. A Jewish bookkeeper named Minich from Rafalowka was transformed into a demolitions expert. Fighting with a Belorussian and Jewish *otriad* in the district of Vitebsk, he participated in the destruction of nine German trains and two bridges. Not far away, young Simon Kagan, only twelve years old when he ran from the ghetto in Mir, was converted into a saboteur by the Russian soldiers he joined in the Naliboki puszcza. From his base in the Nacha Forest, young Leon Kahn learned the ways of the resistance from his Russian comrades. Becoming a partisan allowed him, he later wrote, to be "one of the hunters instead of one of the hunted."

Within a week of joining an otriad of Russians and Jews, Kahn went on his first mission, successfully blowing up a German train. The group did not have any explosives, so they improvised. A large artillery shell was carefully positioned between two railway ties. A few feet away, a rifle was set up so that it was directly aimed at the shell's firing pin. And a cord of rope that was tied to the rifle's trigger led into the forest, where the men were hidden.

Nervously, Kahn and his comrades waited in silence for the train to arrive. They had no idea if their crude bomb would detonate. "If the gun went off but missed the firing pin of the shell," Kahn remembered, "the German guards on the train would immediately start a search for the person who had fired the shot. Even if the shell exploded but didn't damage the engine, we were still likely to get caught."

In fact, the device worked as planned, setting off a large and powerful explosion that threw even the partisans to the ground. "The shell had exploded under the engine," continues Kahn, "stopping it instantly, and the cars had toppled and folded like a broken-down accordion behind it. It was a marvelous, chaotic scene and we were tremendously pleased with ourselves! What a sense of accomplishment! I've never again felt such a surge of wild excitement as I felt that night." Leon Kahn's initiation as a guerrilla fighter was now complete, but his war with the Nazi enemy was just beginning.

■ ■

Faye Schulman's entry into the world of the partisans was more unusual. Among the Soviet brigades, there was, not surprisingly, a great demand for medical personnel of any type. In fact, the Russians were desperate for both medical expertise and supplies. Before the war, the doctors in some eastern European towns were Jewish. Though quota systems were instituted at Polish medical schools, some Jews managed to slip through the barriers or attended universities and colleges in other countries. But many Jewish physicians were among the multitude murdered during the first days of the war in the east, which meant there was a severe shortage by the time the Soviet partisan movement was more organized in the summer and fall of 1942. Those who did survive and managed to reach the forest were in great demand.*

The 12,000 people (half of whom were Jews) of Lenin, a town in eastern Poland, were served by one Jewish doctor. On the eve of the war, he was joined in the town's hospital by Meyer Feldman, a young physician from Pinsk who attracted the attention of Faye Schulman's older sister Esther. The couple was married soon after. The fact that Faye's brother-in-law was a physician later saved her life.

Nearly all the members of Schulman's large family, including Esther and Meyer, were murdered during a mass *Aktion* on August 14, 1942,

---

*One of the few Jewish partisan doctors to survive the war was Michael Temchin. Born in Pinsk in 1909, Temchin graduated from a Warsaw medical school in 1937. When the war broke out two years later, he was mobilized into the Polish army and fought near Brest-Litovsk. Captured, he was forced to serve as a physician in a front-line German medical unit and was then transferred to a POW camp. In 1942, Temchin jumped from a train bound for the Sobibor death camp and was able to join a Polish-Communist partisan detachment. His superb medical skills and his bravery as a fighter earned him the name *Znachor*, or Witch Doctor. Before the war ended, Temchin had been appointed the Armia Ludowa's chief medical officer. (See Temchin, *The Witch Doctor*, and Spector, *Volhynian Jews*, 326.)

that took the lives of nearly two thousand of Lenin's Jewish citizens. As a doctor, Meyer Feldman could have saved himself by agreeing to work for the Nazis, but he refused to abandon his wife. Twenty-six people did elude death that day, and nineteen-year-old Faye was one of them.

Several years earlier, Faye Schulman had apprenticed as a photographer with her older brother Moishe, who lived in a nearby village. The Nazis, obsessed with documenting their conquest of the east, valued Faye's photographic skills and separated her from the other members of her family. She remained alive, while her parents and siblings were slaughtered in a pit outside the town.

Life in Lenin quickly returned to normal — as if the killings had not occurred. The Germans returned Faye's camera which they had confiscated, and allowed her to use her studio. They also ordered her to teach a young Ukrainian girl named Marisha everything there was to know about photography. Schulman was naturally troubled. "It was obvious," she writes in her memoirs, "that she was going to replace me and that I would soon become redundant to them." She came to the conclusion that if she was to survive she would have to escape from the ghetto.

Schulman was not certain when or where to run, but once again fate intervened. One day, a Jewish teenager from Lenin who had escaped and joined a Russian partisan unit returned to rescue the town's surviving Jews. He warned them that they would all be shot the next day. Without a moment's hesitation, Schulman and the other survivors followed the partisan out of the ghetto and into the countryside. Once they were near the forest, they met up with a group of fighters who had been waiting for them. Schulman told them she wanted to join their detachment, but they were sceptical of the usefulness of an unarmed woman. When she told them her name, the Jewish partisan who had first helped her informed his comrades that she was the sister-in-law of Dr. Meyer Feldman. That was good enough for them. Their brigade did not require a photographer, but they were in dire need of anyone with medical knowledge — no matter how scant.

Hours later, after hiking through the thick forest and muddy trails north of Pinsk, Schulman arrived at one of the camps of the Molotava Brigade. It was sparse, with no huts or tents. The fighters, mainly former

Red Army soldiers, slept on the ground. Schulman found a spot to rest. "I lay down under a tall, old tree," she recalled. "Its protruding roots pressed against the bones of my forty kilogram body. I could not fall asleep. I realized that from now on my bed would be the grass, my roof the sky and my walls the trees."

Led by Misha Gerasimov, the Molotava Brigade, with its nine detachments of 2,000 fighters, was one of five brigades under the command of the Red Army's Maj.-Gen. Vasily Zakharovich Komarov. Born in a village near Pinsk, Komarov had fought in the Russian Civil War. He moved into the Polesie forests in mid-1942 and, with his political commissar, Alexei Yefimovich Kleschov, first secretary of the Communist Party in Pinsk, united the various POW factions into an effective fighting force.

Schulman's association with her departed brother-in-law now took on a new significance. She was invited to join the brigade as a nurse. It was, she states, a difficult challenge for her just to "overcome my fear and squeamishness about blood and open wounds." With the assistance, however, of another female nurse and the brigade's doctor, Ivan Vasilievich — who was, in fact, a veterinarian by training — Schulman became a first-rate field nurse and partisan fighter. (She was also able to retrieve her photographic equipment from Lenin and became the brigade's official photographer.)

"I soon found myself able to care for partisans wounded in every part of the body, by every type of bullet, shrapnel and shell," she writes. "A wound caused by a bullet that passed cleanly through the body and out again was not too bad. But when the bullet lodged in the body, the situation was much more serious and we would have to operate. The most difficult circumstance was when an exploding bullet hit the body, tearing out parts of the flesh. Medication was very limited in the woods. Salt water was the only available disinfectant for the wounded. We therefore could never spare salt for cooking. Vodka was the main anesthetic."

Schulman also learned to shoot a rifle and occasionally was permitted to accompany her male comrades on food collection and reconnaissance missions. When she went on food or supply missions, like all partisans, she kept a grenade on her belt in case she had to kill herself. No Jewish fighter wanted to be taken alive by the Nazis, and incidents of suicide were common. (In fact, a directive from Berlin in January 1943 noted that too many captured partisans were poisoning themselves with cyanide pills before they could be questioned. The directive stipulated that all prisoners were to be shackled and gagged to prevent suicide.) Those unlucky few who were captured suffered unimaginable tortures before they were executed. Schulman recalls hearing of one Jewish partisan who was captured and skinned alive. In the forests near Vilna, two Jewish paratroopers, out without weapons or grenades, were apprehended by the German police. Their eyes were burnt out and they were forced to march through the town "until they died in terrible agony."

In their efforts to inflict the maximum amount of pain and suffering, the Germans did not discriminate. Captured Soviet partisans suffered similar fates. In the area near Dedovichi, one Soviet partisan leader by the name of Porudzenko reported in July 1942 that "the spy Ivanova was bestially tortured by the Germans. When her corpse was found she was unrecognizable. Hands and feet were broken, the skin [was] torn off, a part of it hung down in shreds, and on her back alone were seventeen knife wounds." He also added that "Comrade Osipov, Party candidate, was captured and bestially tortured. His eyes were cut out, a hot wire pulled through his nose — but being a proud Russian, an honest son of the Party, he did not reveal anything to the German beasts."

Faye Schulman remained with the Molotava Brigade as a nurse, photographer, and occasional fighter and saboteur for nearly two years. She participated in many dangerous missions in which trains were blown up and Nazi collaborators attacked and killed. She was generally treated respectfully by her Russian comrades — "so young, so pretty, so nice, so beautiful," they would compliment her — but falling in love with a fighter was out of the question. "My family was killed, having been tortured and brutalized," she writes. "I could not allow myself to have fun or be happy. . . . Fighting and helping the wounded — that was my destiny. It was my duty to mourn as long as I lived."

PARTISANS

The backbone of the resistance was not those educated Jews but the "salt of the earth," the plain people of city and country. They didn't philosophize about how to save oneself or how long the war would last. They didn't waste time on empty debates, but went about the business of outwitting the enemy.

— SULIA RUBIN

CHIL'S DETACHMENT

The plan to rid Parczew and the small collection of neighbouring Polish towns north-east of Lublin of Jews was implemented with typical Nazi precision. Beginning in mid-August 1942, thousands were rounded up and crammed into cattle cars bound for the Treblinka death camp. The sick and elderly who were not able to march the two or three kilometres to the railway station were shot on the spot. But as in all such *Aktionen*, many Jews refused to willingly accept their hopeless fate. So they hid or fled into the forest, a vast expanse of thick woods and swampy marshland that starts south of Parczew and stretches in all directions, from the Wieprz River in the west to the Bug River in the east.

Hundreds later died from the cold and lack of food, or in the massive hunts for fugitives conducted by German police and troops during the late fall. Weaponless, the terrified Jews, one survivor recalled, "ran like a herd of rabbits from a hunter straight into the hands of the Germans. They died easily, and lost one another; afterwards children without parents, husband without wives, and vice versa wandered about the forest." In one *Judenjagd*, or Jew hunt, as the Nazi policemen referred to such operations, a group of fifty Parczew Jews was discovered hiding in a few underground forest bunkers. "They were hauled out, with resistance in only one bunker," one policeman later testified. "Some of the comrades climbed down into this bunker and hauled the Jews out. The Jews were then shot on the spot. . . . The Jews had to lie face down on the ground and were killed by a neck shot." In the month of October alone, approximately 500 Jews met a similar fate in the woods near Parczew.

One of those not captured or killed was a twenty-four-year-old Jew from the village of Sosnowica. He was of medium height and was broad-shouldered, a mild-mannered and simple man whose family bought and sold horses and cattle for a living. Before the war, he had served as a platoon leader in the Polish army. His name was Yechiel Grynszpan, but his friends called him Chil.

The youngest son in a family of six children, Chil had escaped to the woods with his brother Avram. The two left behind their parents, Mozko and Sura Grynszpan; their oldest sister, Mindel, who was married and had two children; and their seventeen-year-old sister, Hindel. None was prepared to join the two boys for an unknown life as a fugitive, nor were Mindel and her husband willing to abandon their young children. All of them eventually perished. Several years earlier, their older brother, Aizik, had emigrated to Brazil and was joined there by his sister Heni, who managed to leave Europe on one of the last passenger ships bound for South America as the war was beginning in 1939.

From the fall of 1942 until the end of the war, Chil Grynszpan led one of the most effective all-Jewish partisan detachments in eastern Europe. His courage, resourcefulness, and ability to command hundreds of fighters, both male and female, earned him the respect of Russians, Poles, and Jews alike. "It was not only his military training that made him well equipped to be the leader of his partisan unit," writes Harold

Werner, who became one of Grynszpan's partisans in the spring of 1943. "He also possessed good judgments about situations and about people, and he was able to instill confidence among the group that his decisions were usually the best course of action."

Grynszpan was not driven by ambition or a quest for glory. Rather, his chief objectives were survival, revenge, and the protection of the nearly one thousand Jewish men, women, and children who had sought refuge at two large family camps deep in the Parczew Forest. How did a man, even one as resourceful as Grynszpan, transform a group of shoemakers, tradesmen, and cattle and horse buyers with limited military experience and few weapons into a potent fighting force?

Grynszpan wasted no time. As a horse trader, he was more familiar with the land and the local peasants than most Jews. And the farmers around Parczew, unlike in other areas of Poland, were willing to supply Grynszpan and his men with whatever weapons they had found and hidden after the Polish army retreated. By January 1943, through his contacts with peasants and several daring raids on police stations, Grynszpan's arsenal had grown from two rifles and a pistol to enough weapons to properly arm a partisan detachment of fifty fighters.

As his cache of rifles and grenades increased, so too did his manpower. Grynszpan recruited and trained young men and women from the two main family camps in the forest, Altana and Tabor. Jews who escaped from the Wlodawa ghetto joined his detachment in the spring of 1943 as well. Many of them had been brought out by another group of Jewish partisans, led by a Wlodawa Jew named Moshe Lichtenberg. He had rescued more than a dozen Jews on the first night of Passover. One of the fighters in Lichtenberg's group was Harold Werner, whose own band had linked up with Lichtenberg's only weeks earlier.

During a scouting trip to the southern part of the Parczew Forest and the adjacent Skorodinica Forest, Werner was guided to Grynszpan by a group of Polish and Soviet partisans. At that time, Grynszpan's unit was in disarray. The Nazis had recently carried out one of their large, periodic sweeps of the forest region. On Easter Sunday, a force of more than 1,600 well-armed German police and soldiers had stormed the woods, killing hundreds of Jews at the Altana family camp, some of whom had been tortured to death. Grynszpan, Werner, and others reasoned that a stronger and more powerful Jewish company stood a better chance of surviving the next time the Nazis attacked. It only made sense for the two Jewish units, about 200 fighters in all, to unite. But Lichtenberg was reluctant to agree.

In the aftermath of the German operation, the Polish Communist underground army, the Gwardia Ludowa (GL), or People's Guard, arrived in the Parczew Forest. They were led by Jan Holod, a local member of the Polish Workers' Party whose partisan codename was Vanka Kirpiczny. Fully prepared to work with Jews to combat the enemy, Holod proposed that Grynszpan and his unit officially align themselves with the GL. After some discussions, Grynszpan agreed, providing the Jewish company could remain intact. Holod accepted the terms, and the Jewish partisans became known as People's Guard Unit–Chil.

From a military perspective, this was, without question, the most astute decision Grynszpan could have made. In joining forces with the GL — who, in turn, were allied with the Soviets — the Jewish fighters became part of the larger and better armed Polish-Russian Communist partisan network. The alliance meant more weapons for the Jews, better treatment from the local peasants, and more food and protection for the family camps. Grynszpan's stature as a GL commander also proved important in later confrontations with the anti-Communist Armia Krajowa (AK), or Home Army, who were generally not friendly or sympathetic to Jewish partisans and fugitives.

With no other political or military faction willing to help them, Jews naturally allied themselves with the Polish Communists of the GL and willingly accepted invitations to join their units. (It should be stressed that the GL was the smallest of all Polish resistance groups. At the end of 1943, there were only sixty-four GL detachments and a total of about 1,500 partisans — many of whom were Jews and Russians — compared with 70,000 members of the fascist and openly anti-Semitic Polish underground Narodowe Siły Zbrojne (NSZ), or National Armed Forces, who were registered to fight with the AK.) This was a pattern followed throughout the forest regions of the *Generalgouvernement*, wherever Jewish partisans fought.

In the Radom district, for instance, Yechiel Brawerman, a Jewish escapee from the ghetto in Opatow who was known in the forest as Baca, was second-in-command in a 120-man Jewish GL unit led by a Pole named Stanislaw Olczyk. Until he died in battle during the summer of 1943, Brawerman distinguished himself as an exceptional partisan. In the same area, the Land of Kielce detachment, which was led for a time by the Jewish GL commander Igancy Rosenfarb, carried out many successful operations. One mission in December 1942 destroyed an important mine used by the Germans in Rudki. The unit fell apart only when Rosenfarb was reassigned by GL headquarters in the spring of 1943. All of the Jews who remained behind were killed a month later in a bloody confrontation with Nazi police.

Grynszpan's decision about the GL was thus the same one made by hundreds of Jews who reached the forests. Moshe Lichtenberg, however, was not convinced of the GL's sincerity and refused to remain with Grynszpan. (Grynszpan today claims that he too "never completely trusted the GL," but it made more sense to join them than to remain independent.) Still, Lichtenberg's view that members of the GL were as anti-Semitic as he believed all Poles to be was not entirely correct. True, there were many incidents in which Jews were betrayed and killed by GL fighters in altercations over weapons, military strategy, and discipline. In one such episode in June 1943, a GL representative named Krzaczek robbed and murdered Yitzhak Winderman, a Jewish partisan with links to the underground movement in Czestochowa, south of Warsaw. On another occasion, three months later in the woods near Janow, south of Lublin, nineteen Jewish fighters died as a result of a plot against them engineered by a GL commander whom the Jews trusted.

But of all the various partisan groups Jews encountered during the war, the GL was still the most tolerant and supportive. In the forest area north of Lublin, for example, GL contacts among the peasants in the nearby villages willingly assisted Jewish partisans with food and supplies, and GL guerrillas generally welcomed Jewish fugitives to their ranks. In May 1943, during the Warsaw ghetto uprising, GL partisans helped fifty Jewish resisters escape to the forest.

GL newsletters and reports condemned Nazi brutality and appealed to Poles to assist Jewish fugitives. "The day has come to say loudly and clearly that the murder of the Jewish population has meant the destruction of a part of the Polish people and its weakening not merely in numerical terms," a Polish Workers' Party journal argued in October 1942. "Each Pole who has not been infected by the Nazi poison understands without difficulty that the Germans have murdered not just a few thousand factory-owners, landlords, stockbrokers and other social parasites, but mostly tens of thousands of working people [and] artisans skilled in many trades. . . ."

Another socialist newsletter, published in Cracow in February 1943, was more concise. "Give shelter to fleeing Jews who turn to you for help! Help Jews to escape from the hands of the fascist thugs if that is possible and warn them of impending dangers. Save Jewish children wandering in the forests and through the countryside from a hunger-death. Brand as traitors and allies of Hitler those Poles with whom our nation will settle accounts in the future. . . . Let us remember and proclaim aloud that an anti-Semite is the ally of Hitler and that a Jew is our ally in the struggle against him!"

Harold Werner attributed Lichtenberg's negative attitude to the fact that he was "power hungry" and was not prepared to relinquish his command to Grynszpan. Whatever his reasons, Lichtenberg, and the men who remained with him, decided to head east across the Bug River with a small group of Soviet POWs. Along the way, the Soviets deserted the Jews, but not before they tricked Lichtenberg's group into giving them their best weapons. When the Jewish partisans went to find the Soviets and their arms, a fight ensued and Lichtenberg and several of his men were killed.

Meanwhile, Werner returned to Grynszpan's home base in the Ochoza Marsh, in the western section of the Parczew Forest. He remembered the unique journey like this: "In order to get there we had to go through swamps. In some places we could only proceed by swinging from one tree branch to another, like monkeys, in order to avoid sinking into the mud. The woods in that area were full of swamps, in the middle of which were small islands with clumps of trees growing on them. In order to reach the island where the partisans were camped, we had to be careful not to fall into the surrounding swamp."

Until the summer of 1943, Grynszpan's company had had little time for any type of offensive or sabotage activity. Though they did rescue forty Jews from a slave labour camp at Adampol, they spent much of their time searching for food for the Jews in the family camps and fending off attacks from both Nazis and Polish partisans of the AK. The GL commander in the Lublin district, Mieczyslaw Moczar, explained their situation in a June 1943 report:

> The Germans are moving about the area in so many groups that one cannot dream of defeating them. The same goes for their arms storehouses and other military installations, near which are garrisoned forces which dispose such great fire power that we without ammunition supply cannot contest them. . . . Our units are now forced to fight on two fronts. [The AK command] is organizing units whose role it is to wipe out the "communist gangs, prisoners of war, and the Jews." They openly admit to having this role, which is the basis of their orders. They are fully armed and walk about mostly overtly. The Germans do not touch them, and they also do not attack the Germans.

Because the AK, as the military arm of the Polish government-in-exile, fought for an independent Poland and played a key role in the struggle against the forces of Nazism, its less than positive attitude towards Jewish partisans and non-combatants has become a matter of great historical debate. A Polish apologist like American historian Richard Lukas, for instance, justifies AK ambivalence and even violence towards Jews on the grounds that the Jews were either Communists or Communist sympathizers, or were aligned with Communist factions like the GL and the Soviets. He also makes a distinction between the AK command and the less disciplined rank and file. "To be sure, there were incidents of AK units attacking Jewish partisans," concludes Lukas, "but most of these seem to have been motivated primarily by political rather than anti-Semitic reasons." That the AK, beginning in the summer of 1943, was also affiliated with the fascist and openly anti-Semitic Polish underground NSZ (whose members, it should be pointed out, did not always accept AK command), is either not significant or easily explained away. Lukas, in fact, maintains that NSZ fighters were probably responsible for many of the atrocities on Jews blamed on the AK. In some cases, this was undoubtedly true.

In the Polish version of the Holocaust, Jews are conveniently blamed for much of the hostility and tragedy that befell them. The fault for their various hardships was (and still is, in some quarters) laid squarely on their shoulders. This AK report to the Polish government-in-exile in London on December 20, 1942, was typical: "Bands of Jews and mixed bands of Jews and peasants are operating parallel of the regular partisan units. . . . These bands are committing acts of robbery and murder, attacking farms and murdering the owners. Jews who escaped from ghettos constitute approximately 60% of these bands. . . . The Jewish bands are particularly cruel."

This was followed in early January by a report from the occupied territory, in which it was added:

It is most typical that the stories of people from the counties of Lukow, Radzyn, Sokolow, and other places contain insistent information on the participation of Jews in assaults, whose objective is the confiscation of supplies. . . . The gangs, which take money and clothing . . . and food, undoubtedly, as the testimonies verify, include Russian speaking people and also Jews. This testifies to the fact that — as was foreseen — the persecution of the Jewish population really pushed some of the survivors of the terror to search for a refuge by relying on Bolshevik terrorists, or simply on bands of robbers, who wander around the field towns between the Vistula and Bug rivers.

Yet another dispatch to London several months later similarly maintained that "apart from the guerrilla regulars, the murders of Poles and the wreckage of their property are perpetrated by joint gangs of Jews and POWs. . . . The gangs which are exclusively Jewish are notable for their atrocities."

This was a selective and distorted view of Jewish actions and behaviour during the Nazi occupation, but one that was deeply ingrained and reinforced by the chief commander of the AK, Tadeusz Bor-Komorowski. Appointed head of the Home Army in the summer of 1943, Bor-Komorowski had been a supporter of the right-wing National Democratic Party (the Endecja) before the war. One of his first acts as commander was an attempt to incorporate the NSZ into the AK. It met with limited success. More significantly, he ordered his men to halt the "pillaging" and "banditry" being perpetrated on the Polish peasant population by "gangs" of Jews and Soviet partisans.

In the eyes of many AK soldiers, then, Jews were regarded as Communists, criminals, and an enemy who was to be dealt with harshly. Stephan Balinski, a veteran of the Home Army now living in Winnipeg, Canada, denies that his comrades were anti-Semitic and blames any conflict between the AK and Jews on the fact that most of them were "Communist spies sent by the Russians."

Not surprisingly, AK partisans rarely asked questions or offered help to any Jews that they encountered. In fact, a meeting in the forest between an AK unit and a group of Jewish fugitives often ended in violence and death. In *Unequal Victims*, Gutman and Krakowski showed that examples of AK anti-Semitism, brutality, and murder abounded in Jewish and Polish testimonies and reports. In his diary for September 10 and 11, 1943, one AK fighter recorded what happened when his unit discovered a group of five Jewish and two Polish partisans (most likely GL members) near the village of Starzyna, in western Poland. Believing that the Jews "came to plunder" because they had already killed a bull, the AK partisans shot them immediately. The two captured Poles were taken back to the AK company's base, where the next morning they were beaten until they revealed the whereabouts of the Jews' bunker. Then they, too, were murdered.

At first, recalled Jacob Greenstein, AK partisans in the Naliboki Forest were willing to work side by side with Jewish and Soviet fighters. Then, in December 1943, the Poles received an order from London "to get rid of the Red partisans, especially the Jews." "Within a short time," says Greenstein, "they shot two groups of Jews — fifteen men — of the family camp who were gathering food supplies for the *otriad*. These actions revealed the Poles were at cross purposes with us."

AK soldiers in the Rudniki Forest near Vilna were also on the lookout for Jewish fugitives. "For a day we stopped in old Jewish bunkers," recalled Tadeusz Konwicki about his wartime experiences in 1944. "About one thousand Jews had survived German raids there. The bunkers were shoddy. But the Jews had apparently been helped by the Soviet partisans, because from us they could expect one thing only, a bullet in the neck." (On the other hand, one former member of the Home Army, Stanislaw Burza-Karlinksi, now living in Toronto, relates how he sheltered and fed hidden Jews. There were undoubtedly many others like him.)

■ ■

For good reason, therefore, Grynszpan and his partisans in the Parczew Forest took the possibility of an AK attack very seriously. "The [Home Army] hated us because we were Jews, no matter how useful we could be to them in the battle against the Germans," claimed Harold Werner. "They were deadly anti-Semitic and seemed just as intent upon killing Jews as they were in fighting Germans. We regarded them as just as great a threat to our survival as was the German army. It had nothing to do with political ideology. Few, if any, of our fighters were communists or leftists."

But according to another Grynszpan fighter, Eliahu Liberman, the AK were cautious about attacking the Jewish company, even if they did find them confiscating food. "They were afraid to provoke us," he says. "They knew that any time they tried to take away our weapons, we could fire. Yet more than one of our Jewish partisans was killed at the hands of the AK." In one particular episode, Liberman recalled, three Jewish partisans went out on patrol but did not return. Several days later, a search party discovered their bodies behind a peasant's barn near the village of Glebokie. Grynszpan's men learned from the local farmers that their comrades had been captured and then shot by the AK. Other confrontations followed in the fall of 1943 and the spring of 1944, leaving both Polish and Jewish fighters dead. They included an assault on the Jewish family camp, Altana, in June 1944, when AK men robbed the Jews of horses, clothes, and weapons.

Despite the long and tense relationship between Jews and Poles, this needless violence left Harold Werner, for one, perplexed. "Even though we fought the same common enemy," he observed, "the [AK] took every opportunity to kill Jews. It even sometimes seemed that they were more interested in killing Jews than in fighting the Germans."

■ ■

The continuing hostility of the Home Army naturally reinforced the Jewish partisans' alliance with the GL, and encouraged them to seek support from the Soviets. Grynszpan first dispatched reconnaissance teams eastward across the Bug River during the summer of 1943. Their contact with Soviet partisan leader Zachar Poplavski resulted in shipments of weapons and explosives back west and lessons on sabotage for several of Grynszpan's men. On their return, they put their new knowledge into action. A long list of sabotage operations was carried out, including the destruction of a tar factory in Wlodawa and of bridges and rail lines throughout the Parczew region, which upset German transports and left Nazi soldiers dead.

Harold Werner participated in many such sabotage missions, including the bombing of a bridge and train along the Wlodawa-Chelm rail line. Late one night in August 1943, seventy-five Jewish fighters led by Grynszpan trekked the 40 kilometres to the bridge, set the explosive charge — a heavy shell four feet long that had to be carted by a horse-pulled wagon — in place, and anxiously waited for the train to arrive.

"I strained my eyes peering into the darkness. . . . Finally I saw a very small light, which quickly grew larger and larger. . . ." Werner remembered. "The train was rushing towards us at a tremendous speed. We held our breath when the locomotive reached the bridge. Chil triggered the fuse, and a tremendous explosion obliterated the bridge just ahead of the locomotive. The ground where we stood shook, and our ears hurt from the blast. The locomotive hurtled into the river forty feet below, pulling the rest of the train with it." By chance, the train was transporting a large company of German soldiers, many of whom were killed or wounded in the explosion and resulting wreck. That night, Werner and his comrades felt that they had taken a small degree of vengeance for the treacherous murders of their families.

As the war turned against the Germans during late 1943 and 1944, the Polish and Jewish partisan units grew stronger and braver. The reorganization of the GL in early 1944 into the Armia Ludowa (AL), or People's Army, brought Capt. Aleksander Skotnicki to the Parczew Forest. Known by his codename, Zemsta (revenge), Skotniki, a Jew, had been an officer in the Polish army and a lecturer in the faculty of veterinary medicine at the University of Lvov. He was by all accounts an ambitious, talented, and energetic partisan commander who welcomed Grynszpan's company into his battalion.

By this time, there was no stopping the more than 400 Polish and Jewish partisans controlling the large area around Parczew. Grynszpan and his unit carried out a succession of daring assaults in February 1944, which included the capture and destruction of the police station in the village of Kaplonosy.

A month later, more Soviets and Jews came from both east of the Bug River and west of the Wieprz River to join the battle in eastern Poland. Among the new arrivals were thirty partisans from north-west of Lublin led by Sam "Mietek" Gruber, who had fled to the Kozlow Forest from a Nazi labour camp. Gruber was "amazed" at the size, arsenal, and daring of Grynszpan and his company. "[Chil] was extremely popular. . . . Like some gallant hero of a ballad, he freely roamed the woods and did not hide in bunkers," Gruber states. "Far from hindering him as an interloper and Jew, the local population lent him their assistance so that unlike my men, Chil's group was well-equipped with horses and with weapons supplied by the peasants."

The two leaders decided to join forces, though Grynszpan's unit still remained autonomous. Then, replenished with another airdrop of Soviet arms and grenades, the Jewish partisans continued their assault on German positions. Desperate, the Nazi Order Police mounted yet another offensive on the partisans during most of April 1944. It did not work. On April 16, Grynszpan's company were part of a large contingent of partisans who attacked the town of Parczew and destroyed both the town hall and the police headquarters. "This was," historian Shmuel Krakowski points out, "the first time that partisans entered a country town in the *General-Gouvernement*."

By the end of the month, Soviet reinforcements had arrived from east of the Bug, so there were close to 2,000 partisans roaming the nearby forests. The AL decided to move farther west, towards Lublin. In conjunction with this relocation, Gen. Michael Rola-Zymierski, the supreme AL commander, visited the Parczew region. At an official ceremony held in the woods, Grynszpan and Gruber, among others, were promoted to the rank of lieutenant.

The Jewish leaders were delighted with this recognition, but troubled about the move out of the area. First, they were concerned about the attitudes of Poles west of Vistula River, which, according to Gruber, were not good. More important, they did not want to abandon the Jews still surviving at the family camps. They made their case to Zymierski, and the AL commander agreed to allow the Jewish partisans to remain. They were immediately faced with assaults on two fronts: from the AK, which attempted to gain control of the Parczew Forest as the AL vacated, and from a massive Nazi assault of police, SS, and land and air forces determined to defeat the elusive partisans. Both attacks forced the Jewish fighters to split up and seek refuge in other areas of the woods. Later they were able to regroup and return to their Parczew base.

By this time, in mid-May 1944, some of the AL partisans under Zemsta's command had also come back to Parczew Forest. One morning, Zemsta and several of his men — who had spent the previous night at a farmhouse near Volka Zawieprzanska — awoke to find themselves surrounded by Germans. "Zemsta was shaving when he heard the rumble of approaching tanks and the rat-tat-tat of machine-gun fire," Gruber relates. In the ensuing battle, the AL commander was hit by a shell and killed.

Zemsta was replaced by a Ukrainian AL partisan named Mikolaj Meluch, known in the forest as Kolka. Among the Jewish fighters, he had a well-deserved reputation for being a rabid anti-Semite, angering them by continually using the term "Jew" (in a pejorative sense) instead of the more respectful "comrade." Once, Gruber became so infuriated with

Kolka that he dragged him off his horse and a brief scuffle took place. Now that Kolka was in command, he made no secret of his desire to rid the area of the women and children at the family camps. The tension became so great that Grynszpan felt he had no choice but to declare his independence from the AL.

For a short time, Grynszpan linked his unit with a group of Soviet fighters in the district. But General Zymierski, disturbed by these events, decided to remove Kolka from his position and replace him with Zbigniew Stempka, an AL partisan who commanded greater respect. Under these circumstances, the Jewish partisans agreed to rejoin the AL.

The Germans made one last assault on the forest during July 1944, attempting to clear a path for their retreating troops. With Nazi soldiers swarming the area, the Jews in the family camps were at greater risk than usual. After engaging in a brief but heated battle with the Germans at Ostrow Lubelski in the southern part of the forest, Grynszpan and Gruber led the fugitives out of the woods. For two long days, as waves of German troops passed by, the Jews were forced to take cover in cornfields. With no food or water, it was a desperate situation. "We were lying flat in the middle of the field watching German troops searching the edge of the woods to our left from where we had come," explains Gruber. "I was afraid that the Germans might find the horses we had abandoned, and track us down after all. . . . We spent the entire night of July 20 in the cornfield. . . . It was a night of torrential rain, such as none of us could remember ever having experienced before. . . . By the morning of July 21 the rain had stopped, but the ground had turned into mud and we were still soaked to the skin." And then, just when it seemed as if they could not go on any longer, the Nazis vanished and the Soviet Red Army arrived.

"I was sick and weak," remembered Avraham Lewenbaum, a former partisan, about that day at the end of July 1944. "I fell asleep exhausted under a tree. Someone from our group, Yankel Holender, woke me up saying that the Russians were already there. Soon Russian soldiers and artillery began streaming in non-stop, day and night. One major, a Jew, burst out crying when he met us. He said that he had been marching from Kiev and we were the first Jews he had met."

In the days leading up to the liberation, Gruber and his men captured three Nazi soldiers whose truck had broken down. They were interrogated and then he and Grynszpan, without notifying the AL command, decided to execute them. "I suppose I am sorry about it now," admits Gruber, more than five decades later. "The AL commander was not happy about us shooting POWs, but they were Nazis and that was it."

In total, Chil Grynszpan, Sam Gruber, and their 150 fighters had saved about 200 of the nearly 4,000 Jewish fugitives who had fled to the Parczew Forest from the ghettos of eastern Poland. For a short time after the war, both partisan leaders served as police chiefs — Grynszpan in the Lublin district and Gruber in Breslau. But like most Polish-Jewish survivors, both had left the country for good within a few years. Gruber found his sister in New York, while Grynszpan joined the only surviving members of his immediate family in Brazil.

GHETTO FIGHTERS IN THE FOREST

By the time Josef Glazman had escaped from the Vilna ghetto and arrived in the Narocz Forest in late July 1943, the partisan operations in the *puszcza* were under the command of the Soviet leader, Fiodor Markov. A Belorussian and a loyal Communist, Markov had been a teacher in the town of Swieciany and had married a local Jewish woman named Etel Desyatnik. This may have accounted for his initial positive attitude towards the Jewish fighters.

Markov had fled to the forest in the spring of 1942, and had immediately begun to bring together escaped Soviet POWs, Red Army stragglers, and local peasants who wanted to fight. Within a year, Markov's small group had grown into the Voroshilov Brigade — named after Marshal Klimentii Voroshilov, one of the supreme commanders of the Soviet partisan movement — and consisted of four detachments of more than 300 men. Night airdrops, guided by large bonfires, provided the brigade with more weapons, explosives, short-wave radios, and clothing.

Markov also welcomed young Jews willing to fight and later sent emissaries to the Vilna ghetto to invite members of the underground to join him. Few at first took up his offer, however, maintaining that their battle with the Nazis had to take place within the ghetto. Meanwhile, hundreds of other Jews from surrounding villages and towns — many of them women, children, and men too old to become partisans — also found their way to the vast wooded and marshland area around Lake Narocz during 1942 and 1943. Yet, given the general Soviet antagonism to Jews who were unable to fight, many were killed by Nazi patrols, unfriendly peasants, and undisciplined partisans.

Glazman and his group found Markov accommodating but curt and sharp. He was dressed, recalled Bernard Drushkin, "like a general — epaulets, two [weapons] — one a German Luger and the other a Russian *pepesha* [a submachine gun]. He had no faith in either and therefore wore them both. His face was red and bulging. . . . He added a long harangue, the gist of which was: 'Now you are in the forest. Now that we have taken care of the Germans, you come along and want a hiding place. That's it.'"

Still, Markov approved the Jewish fighters' request that they be allowed to establish their own unit. The Russians called it Mest, while the Jews preferred the Hebrew Nekamah. In whatever language, the name symbolized the group's identity and its goal: revenge. In the beginning, Nekamah numbered seventy partisans. Owing to Glazman's anti-Communist political views, command of the Jewish detachment was given to Zerakh Ragovski, a Jewish partisan from Kovno with Communist leanings who was known in the woods by the codename Butenas. Glazman was made his chief of staff.

A few days after Nekamah's establishment, Markov stood before the fighters and delivered what Chaim Lazar remembered as a "stirring speech" about the atrocities committed against Jews. "Who, more than you, must fight against the Nazi enemy and avenge the spilt blood of your brothers and sisters?" the Soviet commander asked them. "Try to be good, brave, and loyal fighters. We shall help you with all the means at our disposal; guides, arms, instructions."

The Jewish fighters hardly needed such encouragement to avenge the mass murders of their families. They were willing and able to go on dangerous missions. When a major attack on a German garrison in the town of Miadziol was carried out, Glazman and a contingent of his fighters gladly participated even though most of them were armed with only the handguns they had brought with them from the ghetto.

But their initial exuberance soon faded. The weapons Markov had promised them were not forthcoming and the food supply was limited. Worse, there were, according to Chaim Lazar, incidents of robbery and murder. "One of our boys returned to the camp barefooted," Lazar recalled. "He said that he met up with Russian partisans in the woods and they ordered him to take off his boots. While one took his gun, another removed his watch." Protestations to Markov about such incidents accomplished nothing.

Dejected but not yet defeated, Glazman sent word back to his friends in the Vilna ghetto underground that more Jews should join him in the forest. Within a few weeks, Nekamah had grown to more than 250 men and women. For would-be resisters like Aron Derman and Lisa Nussbaum, who escaped from the ghetto in early September 1943, possession of a weapon was no longer a prerequisite for admittance into a partisan unit. "We were welcomed by Glazman, who accepted us with warm arms," remembers Nussbaum.

The Narocz Forest was also a base for anti-German, pro-Communist Lithuanian partisans. One of their leaders, who had been flown into northern Lithuania in June 1943 and had made his way to the Narocz area, was Henrik Ziman (or Genrikas Zimanas). Known in the forest as Yurgis, Ziman was a thirty-three-year-old Lithuanian Jew who was educated at Kovno University and dedicated to Communist doctrine. He had played a key role in stamping out Zionism during the Soviet Union's brief rule in Lithuania prior to the German attack. Ziman had eluded capture by the Nazis by escaping into Russia once the war had started. He was appointed deputy chief of staff of the Lithuanian partisan movement in November 1942.

The work was difficult. His Lithuanian brethren, most of whom hated the Soviets more than the Germans, were not anxious to join him. Ziman allied his group with the partisans of the Voroshilov Brigade, and reluctantly turned to the one group of Lithuanians he knew would not reject his offer: the young Jewish Zionists and Communists from Vilna.

Ziman's plan was to travel back west to the Rudniki Forest and establish a stronger partisan presence there. With Markov's permission, Glazman and twenty of his fighters decided to leave Nekamah and join Ziman's Lithuanian Brigade.

As a first step towards infiltrating the Rudniki woods, Ziman dispatched a reconnaissance team that included five Jewish fighters. Their task was to establish a base from which partisan operations could be carried out. Among the members of the small group was Chaim Lazar. Glazman and Lazar had been friends for many years, first as young supporters of the right-wing Betar Zionist movement and later as leaders of the FPO resistance in Vilna. The farewell was difficult.

"Who knows whether we will meet again?" Glazman told his friend. "In every situation and under any condition, remember who your quarry is. From this you should draw strength and courage to take a stand in these difficult times."

"Upon these words we separated," remembered Lazar, many years later. "I to go to [the] Rudniki, he to take a journey from which he would not return."

Indeed, within days of the team's departure, two major events occurred that had serious consequences for all the Jews taking refuge in the Narocz Forest. First, following an inspection of the Voroshilov Brigade by Belorussian Communist officials, it was decided by the Soviet partisan command that the Jewish unit be disbanded. They asserted that Nekamah was in violation of partisan rules that did not permit detachments to be established on a "national basis." In fact, Markov had already weakened the unit by demanding that several submachine guns given to the Jewish fighters by Ziman be relinquished. The Jewish partisans had no choice but to comply with the order.

Nevertheless, Norman Shneidman, one Jewish fighter who was present, does not believe that Markov was purposely being spiteful or anti-Semitic. "Markov was not to blame for it," he argues. "It was an order from Soviet authorities in Moscow and there was little he could do about it."

The official declaration about Nekamah's fate was made on September 23, 1943, ironically the same day the Nazis selected to liquidate the Vilna ghetto. In a stern speech, Markov lectured the Jews about the realities of partisan warfare. It was unacceptable, he claimed, that some trained fighters — that is, non-Jewish ones — were not adequately armed, while less skilled partisans in Nekamah possessed weapons. To rectify this apparent imbalance and to make more efficient use of men and arms, Markov announced his solution: Those Jews in Nekamah who were able to fight were reassigned into the predominately Belorussian detachment, Komosomolski, while the rest, including the majority of Jewish women, formed a non-combat service and supply detachment. They were to mend clothes, prepare food, repair weapons, and assist the fighters in every and any way possible.

In short order, and much to the dissatisfaction of those Jewish partisans deemed to be unsuitable for combat, their weapons, boots, watches, rings, and leather coats were seized. As historian Dov Levin has noted, it was a humiliating experience for all concerned. Adds Norman Shneidman, "it was very disappointing and very pessimistic because some people had to give up their handguns that they had smuggled out of the ghetto."

"Our aim was to fight the Germans, and our only hope of doing so was to prove that we accepted discipline," remembered Abraham Keren-Pez, who had arrived in the Narocz woods shortly before Markov acted. "Sadly, each of us surrendered his pistol and ammunition. That was not the end of the episode, however. Once they had received our weapons, they said, 'Our battle is hard — and expensive. . . . We consequently need supplies of money or valuables . . . or else we cannot meet our [weapons] requirements. . . . It was sheer daytime robbery — as we realized a short while later when we saw that the watches and rings which were taken away from us and our female comrades were adorning the hands of the girlfriends of the non-Jewish commissars and commanders."

Before the Jews could adjust to the enforced changes, the situation in the Narocz woods worsened. Partisan intelligence reports confirmed the rumours that had been circulating in the forest for weeks: that a Nazi force of more than 70,000 troops was preparing for a massive attack on the fighters' base. Outnumbered, the Soviet partisans had no choice but to retreat farther north in the direction of the Koziany Forest. The 200 or so Jews without weapons, however, were not welcome. They were ordered to carry the wounded deep inside the forest to an island surrounded by trees and swamps and wait out the German blockade. Those Jews who attempted to accompany the Komosomolski were shot at on the orders of the unit's commander, Vladimir Shaulevich.

Sacrifices had to be made, and in this case the lives of the Soviet partisans were placed ahead of the defenceless Jews. As Shneidman points out, "When a detachment was trying to break through a blockade, or to move anywhere, and all of a sudden you had fifty women and children hanging on, it impaired the possibility to move. Everyone would have perished. The commander did not want to risk the lives of his men to save these people." Abandoned, the Jews attempted to hide themselves in the swamps, where it was more difficult for the Nazis to search. Nonetheless, the Germans were still able to kill about 130 of them. (Shneidman himself had been sent, with three other Jewish partisans, on a food-gathering mission a few days before the Nazi assault commenced. By the time they returned, their unit had left. They were able to break through the blockade into western Belorussia with the help of a group of well-armed Soviet partisans. These fighters were part of a special team that had recently parachuted into the Narocz woods. Shneidman did not return to the Narocz area and did not see members of the Komosomolski detachment again until after the war.)

Meanwhile, Ziman's Lithuanian Brigade, including the Jewish partisans led by Josef Glazman, was also forced to retreat. To increase the odds of a successful escape, the brigade was divided into smaller groups, and Glazman and the Jews, still poorly armed, were on their own. "Glazman spoke to [Ziman] ten times a day, asking him to provide weapons and protection for the Jewish partisans," write Chaim Lazar and Lester Eckman. "But even though [Ziman] was a Jew, his heart was hard as stone." Finally, on the day Ziman left, he provided Glazman with ten submachine guns and advised him to head north, towards the Koziany Forest.

With the Nazis closing in, Glazman and eighteen fighters started their dangerous journey towards Koziany. In the woods they met another seventeen Jews who joined them. They then encountered a group of Lithuanian partisans led by Motiejus Sumauskas, also known as Kazimieras, a partisan commander and organizer who had arrived in the region with Ziman. He informed Glazman that, owing to Nazi pressure, Ziman had headed west towards the Rudniki Forest and suggested he do the same. The road to Koziany was impossible to break through. Glazman turned his thirty-five-member group around and headed in the other direction.

It was now the first week of October 1943. Glazman was surrounded on all sides. His only chance for escape, he decided, was to attempt to break through the blockade at a railway track that led to Polotsk and then continue on to the relative safety of the Rudniki Forest. The partisans arrived at their destination in the middle of the night, and though the area was crawling with Nazi troops, they successfully made it to the other side. At a spot in the woods, well away from the railway line, they planned to rest during the day and continue their trek when night fell. The date was October 9, Yom Kippur, the Day of Atonement.

Unknown to the Jews, they had been seen by local peasants, who had quickly informed the Germans of their position. Within hours, they were encircled and embroiled in a "cruel and hopeless battle," as Chaim Lazar relates, from which only one young Jewish girl hidden in the bush emerged alive.

"One by one the comrades fell," she later told another partisan. "Everyone knew that the battle was lost and that there was no hope of getting out of the trap. They angrily stormed the enemy but the latter's forces were much greater. . . . The Germans advanced, hoping to capture several of the Jews alive. Finally there remained only three who continued to fight. . . . The three fought to the bitter end, and when their ammunition was just about gone, they turned their guns on themselves and killed themselves with their last bullets." (The girl's name is unknown. She told her story of the battle to another partisan in the Narocz woods, but whether she survived the war is unclear.)

Josef Glazman was only thirty years old when he died fighting for his people. The long and treacherous journey he had bravely taken from the Vilna ghetto to the forest had ended, as it had for so many others, in tragedy and destruction. His resistance activities might be considered futile today, yet he had heeded the inspiring words of his FPO comrade, Abba Kovner, and had not gone "like a sheep to the slaughter." In 1993, on the fiftieth anniversary of Glazman's death, his former comrades and Betarist friends erected a memorial to him in the Jewish cemetery in Vilnius (as the Lithuanian city is now called).

■ ■

More than a century earlier, Napoleon's great army had marched through the Rudniki Forest on its way to Moscow. Its path, which traversed the 60 kilometres of the *puszcza*'s length, was forever after called the French Way.

"Those traveling the French Way," reflected Chaim Lazar, who arrived in the Rudniki with other Jewish partisans in the fall of 1943, "can get the impression that they are in a sparse wood. But if you stray from the path several meters in either direction, the forest begins to grow thicker. Your feet sink in muddy swamps, full of rotting leaves and tree trunks, and inhabited by a whole kingdom of insects and mosquitoes. Here you can find places where even in broad daylight no sun rays penetrate the thick branches. . . . The wild and uncorrupted nature takes your breath away. This was the site of our new base."

Lazar and the four Jewish fighters who had made the trek from the Narocz with him were not the first Jews to take refuge in the Rudniki. Lying less than 50 kilometres from Vilna, the Rudniki was more accessible than other forest areas in the region, and by the spring of 1943 it was already home to a small contingent of Soviet fighters.

For Jews like those in Yechiel's Struggle Group (the Vilna ghetto resistance organization that had maintained its independence from the FPO), who wanted to take their fight from the ghetto to the forest, escape to the Rudniki made the most sense. In early September 1943, seventy of its members fled to the woods seeking an alliance with Soviet partisans already there. They were led by Elhanan Magid, Shlomo Brand, and Nathan Ring. Like most newly arrived Jews however, they were poorly armed, and the Soviet commander, a Captain Alko, was not willing to take more than twenty of them. Refusing to break up their group, they established their own base a short distance from Alko's detachment.

Less than three weeks later, following the liquidation of the ghetto, more Vilna resistance fighters from the FPO, including groups led by Abba Kovner and Heena Borovska, successfully made the short journey to the forest and arrived at the Yechiel Struggle Group's base. The two rival factions, now numbering about 140, joined together, though as Yitzhak Arad points out, "the antagonism between the two organizations, which stemmed from ghetto days, had not disappeared."

The main point of contention was whether to seek affiliation with the Soviet-Lithuanian movement, the position favoured by Kovner and the FPO fighters, or to stay loosely aligned with Alko's group, the option supported by the Yechiel men. In the end, Kovner's persuasive powers and personality won out. He was installed as leader of the Jewish unit and the decision was made to attempt to join the Soviet-Lithuanian partisans.

Security and survival came first, however. Concerned about the vulnerability of the base, Kovner and his officers ordered that it be relocated deeper into the forest to an area less likely to be discovered by Nazi patrols or local collaborators. They selected one of the many islands in the swamps of the Rudniki, which was accessible only by a log bridge that the fighters constructed. They also built huts for themselves out of branches, leaves, and mud.

Soon, more Jews, those who had been hiding in small groups or alone, found their way to the base, as did eighty who, with the assistance of the partisans, had escaped from the Kailis labour camp near the Vilna ghetto. Thus, by early October 1943, there were approximately 250 Jews living in the proximity of the swamp island, and the numbers were growing each week. Initially, the Jewish resisters were divided into two units; Avenger, led by Kovner, and To Victory, commanded by Shmuel Kaplinski. In time, two more detachments were established: Death to Fascism, under Yankel Prenner's command, and Struggle, led by Aharon Aharonovits, an FPO member who had been one of the Kailis labour camp escapees.

It was about this time that Henrik Ziman, or Yurgis, arrived from the Narocz woods to take charge of the Soviet-Lithuanian partisan units in the Rudniki. He was impressed by, though concerned about, the Jewish presence in the forest and its possible negative impact on Soviet and Lithuanian fighters. As Alex Kremer, a Jewish partisan with the Avenger unit, remarked, "It was the Lithuanian Brigade but there were very few Lithuanians. The majority were Jewish." There was no question that Communism was the ideology of choice in the forest and that politics continued to matter — despite the fact that all factions faced a common and brutal enemy. Kremer, for example, who had been a member of Betar and came from a wealthy family, purposely avoided drawing attention to himself.

Still, anti-Semitic acts and potential violence against Jews were the last things Ziman wanted, as he made clear in a meeting with Kovner. For his part, the Jewish resistance leader wanted only to avenge the death of his brethren and was not worried about upsetting nationalist sentiments. Thus, he accepted Ziman's authority and the Jewish detachments were officially made part of the Lithuanian partisan movement. Although they were not disbanded like Glazman's Nekamah had been, changes in the command structure of the detachments made during the next year altered the distinct Jewish character of the units in a limited way.

The link with Ziman and the Lithuanians did not automatically mean that the Jews suddenly received better weapons or more ammunition. On the contrary, their arms situation remained precarious for the duration of the war. But that did not stop them from undertaking many sabotage missions — everything from cutting telephone wires to destroying trains and rail track.

According to historian and former partisan Dov Levin, about 850 Jews participated in 22 of the 92 detachments that made up the Soviet-Lithuanian movement. (This represents about 10 percent of the total membership and includes the Jews in the four Vilna detachments.) There were also *otriady* composed of Jews from Swieciany, Kovno, and surrounding towns and villages. Fighters in these 22 detachments were responsible for derailing 461 trains (of a total of 577), destroying 288 locomotives (of a total of 400), and injuring or killing 6,633 enemy soldiers (of a total of approximately 14,000).

More specifically, Kovner's Avenger unit, in conjunction with To Victory and Death to Fascism, was involved in 39 operations from

October 7, 1943, to July 8, 1944. Avenger's partisans destroyed 315 telephone and telegraph poles, collapsed 5 bridges, derailed 33 train cars, and destroyed more than 300 kilometres of railway track. The unit also participated in the liberation of Vilna in July 1944, as did all the Vilna detachments, though by then the groups were more mixed.

The size of the Jewish units was changing as circumstances dictated. In early November 1943, for instance, 111 fighters (of which 36 were women) from the third and forth detachments were sent by Ziman to establish a base farther south in the Nacha Forest. Typically, the group, led by Berl Szeresznyevski, had to share eleven rifles and two submachine guns in what turned out to be an unsuccessful mission.

Many Jews, like Leon Kahn, fled to the Nacha woods in 1942 and early 1943. In time, some joined the Leninski Komsomol Brigade, which was organized by Belorussian parachutists. Their leader, an officer named Stankevitch, gathered together the various independent POW groups, introduced military discipline in the forest, and fashioned them into an effective fighting force. Much to the dissatisfaction of the Soviets, however, dozens of Jews — Leon Kahn's father and sister among them — lived in a family camp not far from the brigade's main base.

The arrival in the area in late 1942 of the Polish Home Army, or AK, which declared war on Nazis, Soviets, and Jews, made life difficult for both the fighters and the members of the family camp. In particular, taking food from uncooperative peasants who were now protected by AK soldiers became a dangerous challenge. To make matters worse, in mid-June 1943, the Germans launched a massive operation to clear the Nacha of partisans. The strategy worked. Fighters of the Leninski Komsomol Brigade quickly departed for the safer confines of the Yureli Forest, north of Grodno. During the siege, Leon Kahn was able to guide members of his family and other Jews out of the line of fire, but many civilians were left behind without weapons or food. Within days, these Jews were slaughtered by Nazi police, soldiers, and local peasants waiting to ambush them.

Hence, when the Vilna Jews from Rudniki arrived in the Nacha Forest five months later, the situation was not good. With hostile peasants unwilling to help them, AK soldiers ready to shoot at them, and no organized Soviet partisan operation, they rightly concluded that establishing a base in the Nacha woods was ill-advised. Their only option was to return to the Rudniki. Only a small team of about twenty partisans was left behind to continue the reconnaissance operation. They, too, eventually returned to their Rudniki base.

Jews from Kovno and nearby villages also made their way to the Rudniki Forest. Through the daring work of a Jewish Communist operative named Gesja Glazer, the Jewish underground in the Kovno ghetto — the Yidishe Algemeyne Kamfs Organizatsye, or General Jewish Fighting Organization (JFO) — was able to make contact with Ziman and the Soviet-Lithuanian partisan movement. Glazer, known by the codename Albina, slipped undetected into the Kovno ghetto in early September 1943, and arranged for a contingent of Jewish fighters to depart for the Augustov woods. This initial operation, however (as we learned in Chapter Four), ended in disaster, as many of the Kovno Jews were ambushed, captured, or killed.

In November, an attempt was made to flee to the Rudniki Forest. This time, the escape plan worked brilliantly. JFO leader Chaim Yellin, a slight man, had commandeered several trucks and paid Lithuanian drivers to operate them. Using false papers, he was able to bring out a large group of resistance fighters for "night-shift work." Instead, they were driven to within 40 kilometres of the woods, where they were met by partisans who guided them the rest of the way without incident. More escapes followed during the next few months, with about 250 Jews in total, many armed with pistols and rifles, reaching the Rudniki bases. Eventually, the Gestapo learned of the escapes and in the spring of 1944 ambushed a transport in which dozens of Kovno Jews were murdered.

The young fighters who arrived safely in the forest joined the Kovno Brigade under Ziman and formed three detachments: Death to the Occupiers (or Invaders), led by Constantine Rodinov, a Lithuanian Communist; Vladas Baronas, established in January 1944 and commanded by Karp Ivanov-Seimokov; and Kadima (Forward), organized two months later and led by a Captain Tziko. Kovno Jews served as commissars and staff officers in each unit and participated in many successful sabotage missions. Soon after it was organized, for instance,

Death to the Occupiers was involved in an attack on a German garrison in the town of Zhagarin. "Taken aback, the Germans began to run away from the village," recalled two of the fighters who participated. "The partisans put the barracks to the torch, blew up the water tower and the railway station, destroyed the railway engine garage, put two railway engines and a number of full and empty railway carriages out of commission, dismantled a considerable length of railway tracks, and threw the rails into the marshes. They also blew up two wooden bridges for good measure."

Not all operations, of course, were as successful. In early 1944, six partisans from Death to the Occupiers were headed for a train station at Kaisiadorys, east of Kovno. The group included Shmuel Martovski and Matis Goldberg, both twenty-two years old, Solomon Abramovitch, thirty-six, and Itzik Miklashevski, twenty-one. They decided to rest at the village of Zhalyon but, unknown to them, had been seen by a local collaborator, who informed the German police of their position. Within minutes, they were under attack by superior forces. In the battle that ensued, all six fighters were killed. To instil fear into the local population, the Nazis took the six Jewish bodies and hung them nude from the gallows in the nearby village of Anoshkis.

Perhaps the most noteworthy group of Kovno Jews to become Rudniki partisans were the handful of survivors of a bold escape from the Ninth Fort, the prison and killing ground on the outskirts of the city where more than 50,000 Jews were slaughtered. In June 1942, the Nazis had implemented what became known as *Aktion* 1005, a secret plan to conceal their mass killings from the rest of the world.

Hundreds of prisoners, mostly Jews, were forced to dig up bodies at mass grave sites throughout the occupied territories. Under the watchful eye of Nazi guards, they extracted gold from the teeth of the corpses and rings still on fingers, and then burned them on large pyres. At the Ponary, outside Vilna, noted historian Reuben Ainsztein, "each pyre contained up to 3,500 corpses and burnt from seven to ten days." After the fires had stopped, any remaining bones were crushed and the ashes "mixed with sand and spread over the area of the killing site." This system for getting rid of any trace of the victims was designed by

SS Col. Paul Blobel, an architect by profession. At each site, the Jewish labourers were supervised closely by police squads designated as Sonderkommando 1005 units. The Nazis were sworn to secrecy and the prisoners were killed when their work was finished.

At the Ninth Fort, the excavation and burning of bodies began in September 1943 and was nearly completed by the end of December. The sixty-four prisoners (only four were not Jewish) employed in this gruesome task were locked in cells each night and had no misconceptions about their ultimate fate. They quickly came to the conclusion that their only chance for survival was to escape — as impossible as it seemed. The leader of the group was Abba Diskant, a resistance fighter who had been captured and sent to the Ninth Fort while returning from the Rudniki Forest to the ghetto in order to bring out more Jews. Another prisoner, Pinchas Krakinovski, a locksmith, worked diligently to make keys that could open their cell doors.

The men patiently waited until Christmas Eve, hoping the guards would be drunk and preoccupied. When the night finally arrived, they used Krakinovski's keys to free themselves and then, using a ladder they had made out of timber and hidden, scaled a six-metre high concrete wall. While all sixty-four of them made it out of the fort, many were later killed by Nazi patrols. Only fourteen survived to tell their remarkable story. This small group reached the partisan base in the Rudniki Forest and joined the Kovno unit Death to the Occupiers.

SURVIVAL

We were doing our best to survive, even to resist, but no one in our group expected to come out alive from that hell. The main thing was not to be taken alive by the Germans, not to submit to their questions, their torture, and a passive death at their hands. We were always armed and had an understanding that if we were ambushed, we would fight until we were killed. If need be, we would shoot one another rather than be captured. It was inevitable that we would die — but death would come on our terms.

— JACK SUTIN

"EVERY DAY WE COULD EXPECT TO BE ATTACKED"

Some nights, for a few moments, it was possible to forget the war. To forget the tragedy, the madness, the death of loved ones. Around the smoldering campfire, both Soviet and Jewish partisans sang Yiddish and Russian folk songs and reminisced about better times. "Someone would fry *latkes* [potato pancakes] and boil water for tea," recalled Shalom Cholawski, who was in a partisan unit in the forests of Polesie. "A long-lost feeling of *Yiddishkeit* would float back to us, stroking our memories. We sat together, all brethren welcome, and shared stories of our Jewish community back home. We would speak of the *shtetl* as if it were still thriving and bustling."

On such occasions, there was usually *samogon* — home-made raw vodka, 98 proof — to pass around, along with thick cigarettes made of dried green tobacco leaves or whatever else was available (the chopped-up roots of sunflower plants were popular as well). Soviet partisans preferred *makhorka*, a cheap-cut tobacco that had been a favourite of Russia's lower orders since before the revolution. *Makhorka* rations were usually part of every airdrop, a gift from partisan headquarters in Moscow. Both the liquor and the cigarettes were harsh, but they provided a momentary distraction from the conflict.

Daily life in the forest was reversed. The partisans almost always slept during the day, when moving about the forest was riskier and the chances for detection greater. Sabotage missions and food acquisitions were routinely conducted in the dark, and even those Jews who had never before spent much time in the forest learned to traverse long distances through thick bush using only the stars as a guide.

Communal cooking and eating were also done late into the night so that the smoke from fires could not be seen in nearby towns. Every partisan carried a metal or wooden spoon in his boot to dip into the large pot or bowl of bland meat and potato or cabbage soup (salt was a rare and precious commodity during the war) that more often than not was served for breakfast, lunch, and dinner. "You reached, dove, put your spoon in, and took what you wanted when you wanted it," explained Charles Gelman, who fought in the woods near Kurzeniec. Bread and biscuits usually accompanied each meal; some survivors also remember eating chunks of meat fried in fat or, during leaner days, a "thick clay-like" concoction of water and flour known in Russian as *zacierke*. The more ingenious partisan and family camps had cows for milk and prepared sausages and other delicacies.

Apart from the ever-present danger of Nazi raids, it was the seasons that dictated day-to-day life. Summer was best for travel and sleeping outside, though the heat was often unbearable and the mosquitoes and bugs a terrible nuisance. The fall and winter brought cold weather, with temperatures dipping well below zero. Because the snow held tracks, leaving the forest during the winter in search of food was extremely dangerous. Only during a storm, when the winds would sweep over the tracks, was it possible to move about. And even then, the snow was so deep in spots that travelling any distance was difficult. There were wolves and other animals to watch for as well.

For these reasons, in some forest areas, partisans, both fighters and civilians, remained hidden for a good portion of the winter months — like bears in hibernation. Those in more organized camps ensured that there were enough provisions — potatoes and meat — to see them through the winter, but many Jews in makeshift family camps, vulnerable and alone, often went hungry. "We ate what we could scavenge," remembers Jack Sutin of his first winter with a few friends in the Naliboki *puszcza*. The food situation for a group of Jews from Slonim was so bad that they caught and ate half-starved stray cats that had wandered into the forest looking for food.

The snow, on the other hand, did provide a ready water supply that could be boiled for soup and tea. At other times of the year, water could be collected when it rained or drawn from a nearby lake or stream. Most often, however, the inhabitants of the woods had no choice but to drink an algae-filled liquid that was dug out of a deep hole in the muddy ground. "Sometimes we would come across little patches of dirty rain water, alive with bugs and worms," writes Faye Schulman. "It did not matter — we were so thirsty we would drink anything. This was when a hat came in handy. I would fill my hat with infested water, then spread a piece of gauze from my first aid kit over one end of my hat and drink the water through this make-shift strainer. I didn't know what I was swallowing, but at the moment I didn't care." Lazer Zelkowicz did the same thing for his children. "The water was black as coal," recalls his daughter, Gitel. "My father would take his handkerchief and wring the water through the cloth for us to drink."

■ ■

A partisan rarely, if ever, removed his boots. Next to his weapon, they were his most precious possession. As Liza Ettinger, a Bielski partisan, rightly suggested, "It is not an exaggeration to say that a shoe [or boot] meant the chance for life." It was impossible to flee or fight with your feet wrapped in rags. Sturdy leather boots were a necessity.

A partisan slept in his clothes, guarded his weapon with his life, and was prepared to travel at a moment's notice. "We never remained long in one place — one day, or two at the very most," remembered Nahum Kohn, a Jewish partisan in the forests of Volhynia who eventually joined one of Medvedev's detachments. "We moved according to our instincts. You develop that kind of instinct in the woods. Sleeping comfort was not too important, since we rarely slept in the same place twice."

Jewish family groups tried to follow similar rules, but such mobility was hard to emulate. With women, children, and the elderly to be concerned with, moving from one spot in the forest to another — or from one forest to the next, as was often the case — was more problematic. By April 1943, Tuvia Bielski's family camp, which was growing each day, had yet to find a permanent base. Warned about an imminent German raid, the 300 members of the camp were given twenty-four hours' notice about another move. Yehoshua Yaffe described the hurried relocation like this: "Every day we could expect to be attacked. We received information that the Germans had been informed of our whereabouts. . . . We packed our things, loaded our rucksacks, folded our blankets on top, and set out on our way. The night was cloudy . . . our thoughts were gloomy. . . . In our wanderings from forest to forest, from base to base, we lost many people. . . . During the day snow melted. . . . We had to walk kilometers upon kilometers. . . . Our feet got stuck in the mud. . . . Everything was damp and wet."

This lack of mobility was only one characteristic among several that distinguished forest life in a family camp from that in a fighting unit. Family camps, or civilian camps as the Soviets called them, were a uniquely Jewish experience during the war. In most cases, Polish and Ukrainian women and children were not forced to flee to the woods to save their lives. Only Jews, faced with annihilation, took this precarious route to survival. With few weapons to defend themselves and faced with hostility from all quarters — including most Soviet and Polish partisans, who regarded these Jews as a nuisance not to be tolerated — Jewish families seeking refuge in the forests of eastern Europe confronted death each and every day.

While the two most famous and well-organized family camps in the Belorussian Naliboki Forest — those led by Tuvia Bielski and Shalom Zorin — rescued approximately 2,000 Jewish men, women, and children, thousands more, like the Jews in the Parczew Forest, perished from disease and devastating Nazi raids. Despite the presence of a competent fighting unit led by Chil Grynszpan, only 200 of the 4,000 Jews who escaped to the Parczew Forest remained alive when the war ended (as we learned in Chapter Eight). Similarly, in a family camp organized in 1942 by 370 escapees from towns near Slonim, only twenty walked out of the forest in 1944.

The experiences of Jews from Parczew and Slonim were more typical than, for example, the relatively high survival rate of the Bielski camp, which lost only about 50 of its 1,200 people. (This attrition rate of just 4.2 percent compares with rates that ranged from 30 to 50 percent for Soviet and Jewish fighting units.) The reasons for this remarkable statistic were varied, but they included Tuvia Bielski's shrewd and astute leadership and his success in making his camp an indispensable service depot for Soviet partisans.

The exact number of Jews who successfully reached the forests is unknown. But two facts can be asserted with some precision. First, the majority of Jews who lived in any kind of family camp, even for a short time, originated from the small ghettos in the areas closest to the woods; Jewish family groups from the larger cities — apart from Jews from Minsk, who were, as Yitzhak Arad has pointed out, "the exception" — were less likely to make the difficult journey or view the woods as a potential refuge. Second, and more significantly, many more Jews were killed than the 10,000 or so civilians or family camp members who emerged from the eastern European forests when the Red Army liberated the region in mid-1944.

At any one time between 1942 and 1944, there may have been more than a hundred different family camps of varying sizes, though only a handful survived the war intact. Some were no more than a few tree huts or holes in the ground occupied by a dozen half-starved and diseased fugitives and orphaned children with little chance for long-term survival. At the mercy of the elements, the local inhabitants, and the Nazi police, most of these Jews were dead within months or often weeks of their arrival in the forest. Others were so discouraged by the harshness of life in the woods that they actually returned to the ghettos. There were arguments, apprehensions, complaints, recriminations — even thoughts of suicide.

"Yentil cried and blamed me for bringing her to the woods," relates Byrna Bar Oni about life with her sister in the forest near Slonim. "'Byrna, you're responsible for my misery. It would have been easier to be killed by the Germans in the ghetto. We'll not survive the war — I nor my children. So why suffer? In the ghetto death comes quickly; in the ghetto you do not die alone, the community dies with you. . . .' I would try to comfort her, to convince her to weather the hard times. 'After the storm, good weather comes,' I said. 'You do have a reason to live — you have your son and daughter.'" But months later, Yentil and her two children were dead, the victims of Nazi attacks in the forest.

This story, told by one partisan about a group of Jewish families he had met in late 1942 in the woods near Lublin, was equally common. "[The] Germans and Poles came into the woods with their dogs," he recalled. "The dogs started sniffing out the Jews hiding in the forest and the Germans shot them. There were many Jews who were safely hidden in the depths of the forest, but they panicked because of the dogs and the soldiers and abandoned their shelters. They ran for the fields, where the Germans shot them all."

Not far away, in the Skorodinica Forest, Harold Werner, who had stopped to rest at a family camp that was home to seventy-five Jews, was nearly killed in a Nazi raid that took the lives of thirty Jews. Finding himself alone with a ten-year-old boy, he hid for more than ten hours in a deep swamp with Germans swarming the area.

Lois J. was fifteen years old when she escaped from the Vilna ghetto in 1943 and fled to the Narocz Forest. She arrived at a camp where about 300 Jews lived a miserable existence. The people she met were deprived of both food and water, and had built few shelters. "Everyone was black from the fire and the children were crying all the time. We wanted to go back to the ghetto." In fact, she remained and survived the war in the forest despite the lack of food and the attacks by German police.

In the fall of 1943, on his travels in the Koziany Forest as a member of the Chapyev Brigade, Yitzhak Arad discovered a small Jewish camp that was home to six families from Jody. Unlike a partisan base, which would have been guarded by a ring of security details, this particular family camp had no one standing watch. The twenty people Arad found were a sorry sight.

"Their clothes were torn and patched, the children were in tatters, with rags around their feet instead of shoes," he writes. "Two people had arms, one a rifle, and one a revolver." The weapons had made little difference. When the camp was first established a year earlier, it had been a hiding place for fifteen families who had escaped from Jody. But half the group had died the preceding winter from Nazi attacks and sickness. To make matters worse, Soviet partisans had robbed the Jews of food and supplies, and the head of the Spartak Brigade, the Soviet partisan group in charge of the area, had "forbade them to requisition food from farmers, promising to supply their needs, but the promise was not fulfilled." All these Jews had to eat were the few potatoes they could dig up from the fields. Arad was naturally upset by their predicament, and assured them he and other Jewish partisans would try to assist them.

Support from Jewish partisans who were members of combat units stationed in the area, along with partial toleration from Soviet commanders and local peasants, often determined the fate of a family camp. The young Jewish fighters, of course, were desperate to help the families, many of whom were their own rescued parents and siblings. They were not about to let them starve to death. Thus, whenever it was possible, they brought them food, clothing, and information about potential trouble.

"If there is anything my friends and I are proud of from that time in the forest," asserts Peter Silverman, "it was that our biggest achievement was saving Jews." Despite the restrictions imposed by his Spartak commander (in addition to the order regulating the acquisition of food from local farms, for example, all the family camps near Spartak bases in the Koziany Forest were required to be outside the perimeter of the partisans' guard posts) Silverman did whatever he could to help his father, aunts, cousins, and other members of the camp.

Still, he concedes that the Jewish families in the camps were often "left to the mercy of God." Most Soviet commanders were not about to risk their lives and the lives of their men to rescue Jewish women and children. "We Jews felt that it was a great achievement to save a woman, a child," adds Jacob Greenstein, a partisan in a Soviet-Jewish detachment in the Naliboki Forest. "We knew what would happen to them. But the Russian partisans did not understand that."

"THE FOREST IS FOR PARTISANS, NOT FOR JEWS"

When it comes to Soviet attitudes and behaviour towards Jewish civilians in the forest, generalizations are again impossible. While Soviet partisan leaders such as Fyodorov, Sobiesiak, and Konishchuck went to great lengths to protect and ensure the survival of the Jewish family camps that were located in forest regions under their command — even making good use of the camps as service centres for laundry, tailoring, weapon repair, and food preparation — other Soviet fighters regarded the Jewish civilians as an unacceptable burden. As one Belorussian fighter declared, echoing a widely held view: "The forest is for partisans, not for Jews and their families. The Jews should go back where they came from." Routinely, Jews were blamed for bringing the Nazis into the forest and for alienating local peasants by stealing their food. Though valid, the charges were not as black and white as the Soviets made them out to be.

When Yitzhak Arad visited the small family camp in the Koziany Forest, he had been accompanied by a Soviet fighter named Vasia. After they left the camp, Vasia had told Arad: "Those Jews are charity cases. The forest is a place for people who fight. There is no room here for men with wives and children who worry only about themselves." Arad had then asked the Russian what he thought the Jews should do and where should they go. "Let them go wherever they want," Vasia had declared, "but they must clear out of the forest."

Victor Panchenko, the twenty-five-year-old head of Octiaber, a Soviet fighting unit stationed in the woods near Novogrudok, felt the same way — and he was prepared to do something drastic about it.

A lieutenant in the Red Army, Panchenko was charismatic and popular with both his men and the local Belorussian population. He listened attentively to complaints from many peasants in the area that Bielski's group of *Zhydy* was stealing the farmers' food and supplies. The partisan commander believed every word of it, and the fact that his own men were also taking what they needed from the Belorussians was beside the point. The order was given that Bielski and his camp of Jewish fugitives be shot.

■ ■

The Soviets referred to such food acquisitions, or economic actions, as they were also called, as *bambioshki.* These night missions, in which eight to ten partisans ventured onto local farms to take what they needed, were a dangerous but obviously essential aspect of life in the forest. Next to protecting the base or camp from attack, the partisans spent most of their time obtaining sufficient food supplies, an activity that required careful planning. Emerging from the forest was always risky, and despite a generally reliable intelligence network, Soviets and, particularly, Jews never knew what to expect when they arrived at a farmhouse in the middle of the night in search of bread and meat. Ambushes were frequent, and more than one food-gathering expedition ended in bloodshed.

Some peasants did not have to be coerced into sharing their often meagre supplies — a dentist in the Polish village of Lipnica Gorna, near Cracow, for example, baked bread for Jews hiding in the forest — though admittedly they did not have much of a choice. As Nahum Kohn puts it, "We didn't ask for permission." With guns aimed at the farmer and his family, partisans like Kohn took what they needed and sometimes used the farmer's own wagon to deliver the food and provisions to their forest bases.

Boots and sheepskin coats, needed for the long and cold eastern European winters, were prized possessions taken by partisans from many farmhouses. Equally popular were pigs. While a minority of Jews, like Faye Schulman's brother Kopel, a rabbi, insisted on adhering to all rules of *kashrut,* or kosher observance (surviving mainly on a diet of potatoes), most ate whatever was offered, and pork was more easily preserved than beef. "Once we found a pig, we would kill it on the farm, quarter it, and transport it to the base by wagon," writes Harold Werner about his *bambioshki* experiences. "Most of our group who were from the villages knew how to cut up a cow or pig, and some of them had been butchers before the war. They also knew how to make sausages, which were considered a special treat." Portions of the meat were salted, wrapped in burlap sacks, and buried in various locations for use during emergencies. Months later, Werner notes, the pork was still edible.

Werner, Kohn, and other partisans justified their "economic actions" as a necessity of war. And, indeed, what other options were available to them? Jewish men in the family camps, many of them teenagers who were armed with the group's few weapons, were given the enormous responsibility of finding food for hundreds of people. They had to either confiscate what was required or starve to death.

There was, nonetheless, a fine line between requisitioning food and stealing it — a distinction not lost on Tuvia Bielski. "Although I was very careful about preventing outright robbery, it would be quite difficult to pinpoint the line which divided that requisitioning which sustained our lives, and outright robbery," he explained in his memoirs. "The code of the partisans provided: all that is essential is permitted; but the appropriation of anything superfluous, anything, that is, which can be classified as luxury or more-than-necessary, is considered robbery. Of course, the partisan's conception of the difference between appropriating and robbing was not the same as that of the farmer. . . . Neither was his concept of right and wrong similar to that of the partisans. And the concept of the one who gives the order is not the same as that of the one who obeys it."

To alleviate these ethical concerns, adhere to Soviet rules, and not antagonize the peasants to the point that they would turn to the Nazis for assistance, the Jewish partisans tried to target wealthier farmers or collaborators who deserved to be punished. They made a habit of not visiting the same farmer often and sometimes travelled distances of 20 kilometres or considerably more to take food from peasants outside of their immediate area. Such *bambioshki* could take weeks and placed the partisans who were transporting the food back to their camps in grave danger. With the willing cooperation of informers, Nazi police often heard about large food acquisitions as soon as they happened. For this reason, states Nahum Kohn, "experience taught us that by the second day we had to be 25 to 30 kilometers from where we had been the previous day, because the Germans were constantly searching for us."

Still, there were many unforeseen problems. So many provisions were taken from farmers around the Narocz Forest, for instance, that by the middle of the winter of 1943, their shelves and storerooms were bare. Farther north, in the villages near the Koziany Forest, the Germans, frustrated by their inability to stop partisan sabotage actions, chose an inventive way of dealing with the fighters: They burned all the villages and farmhouses close to the forest, so that the partisans would have to travel far to replenish their food stocks.

Leib Reiser, of the Leninski Komsomol detachment in the Nacha Forest, had other worries. "In order to avoid misunderstandings, I, as commander of my group, allowed my comrades to take from the farmers only the bare necessities of life — bread, potatoes — but took meat only from a farmer who had more than 3 kilograms," he remembered. "Unfortunately, among the Jews there were found some underworld figures, who took from the farmers meat, chicken, clothing and even things that were absolutely not necessary to sustain life. In these cases, I was told by the head of the *otriad* that I must not allow this to happen." On one occasion, Reiser had to come to the defence of three Jews, Pesach Mannes, Zalman Miednitsk, and Berl Miller, who had been accused by the Soviet commander of looting. Only Reiser's timely intervention prevented the three from being executed.

■ ■

Faced with a similar situation following Victor Panchenko's order that his camp be wiped out, Tuvia Bielski used his ingenuity to save the lives of his group. He decided, as he stated, "to meet the threat head on." Bielski arranged a meeting with Panchenko in order to clarify his position and refute some of the charges. Accompanied by three nervous armed Jewish fighters, Bielski began the discussion with the Soviet leader by asserting what he believed to be his status as a partisan commander. (In the summer of 1942, the Bielski group had adopted Zhukov as the official name for its *otriad*, in honour of Marshal Grigori Zhukov, commander of the Soviet western front. The name was not, however, recognized by Soviet partisan headquarters.) "We are not bandits," Bielski declared. "Moreover, if you are a true Soviet citizen you must know that our Motherland requires that we struggle together against the German-fascist enemy. And our Motherland makes no distinction between loyal, obedient citizens on the one hand, and undisciplined gangs bent on sabotage and destruction."

Panchenko insisted that members of Bielski's camp "had been robbing villagers" and must pay the penalty. But Bielski countered by proposing a plan: He and Panchenko, along with a group of their men, would go to one of the Belorussian peasants in the area who had made the accusations against the Jews. The Jewish commander was well aware that no one had bothered this particular farmer for food for several days. As Bielski related in his version of these events: "We rapped on the window, and one of us asked him for bread. He answered in a whining voice, 'There is no bread, beloved brothers, the Jews were here and they took everything. They robbed us and went.' Victor was livid with rage. He drew his gun. 'I'll murder the son of a bitch.' I restrained him. 'You'll have plenty of time for that later.'"

The partisans entered the peasant's house and confronted him with their ruse. The Belorussian shook with fear when he learned that Tuvia Bielski was standing before him. "From now on," Panchenko told the farmer, "if a partisan fighter comes to you, pay no attention to the fact that he may be a Jew, or a Russian, or a Pole. Give him everything he asks for. Give him food, give him boots, and even a fur coat if necessary."

The Soviet commander, convinced that Bielski and his Jewish group were following the rules, decided to divide the region up between them. The Bielski *otriad* was to take food from farms in the vicinity of Lida and Novogrudok only, while Panchenko and his men were to gather supplies from peasants slightly farther south, near Zdzieciol. "We did not enter his villages, and he kept out of ours," added Bielski. Thereafter, the two partisan leaders developed a friendship that gave the Jews more credibility among other Soviet partisans and some much-needed respect and aid from local peasants. The two detachments successfully conducted many sabotage raids together, and Panchenko shared with the Jewish leader any pertinent information about Jewish fugitives.

"LIKE SQUIRRELS, HIDING IN A HOLE"

Depending on the season and locale, partisan brigade camps might be spread over a 25-kilometre area, with each *otriad* having its own site. In the early days of the war, both fighters and family-camp members erected small camouflaged shacks from tree branches and whatever other material was available. Peeled bark was used for the roof and straw for the floor, though this was hardly any protection against the rain and the endless onslaught of bugs. Some partisans, no matter what the season, slept on a bed of tree branches laid out on the ground. On winter mornings, Faye Schulman recalls, "we would find ourselves frozen to the ground."

Among Soviets and Jews, the most popular and widely used type of shelter in the forest was called a *zemlianka*, which was essentially a bunker dug into the ground or the side of a hill. The best built *zemlianki* were not fully underground, but had steps to an entrance above the surface. They were constructed with wooden walls and floors, and were large enough to accommodate twenty to thirty men and women sleeping on straw beds. A makeshift wood-burning stove, with a chimney built from tin cans or bricks and other material scavenged from burned-down peasant homes, provided heat during the winter nights. Oil lamps with rag wicks were used for light, and space was made for food storage.

Beside each bunker at some camps, a second hole was dug to serve as a latrine. "We couldn't relieve ourselves outside, because any farmers passing through the woods would have noticed the human waste," explains Jack Sutin. In his *zemlianka*, a small window gave access to the latrine. "We would relieve ourselves in small pots and empty the pots into that second hole through the window, which we stopped up with rags when it was not in use," he adds. "That was our toilet-flushing system."

Even the Nazis were impressed by the partisans' resourcefulness. "The bunker was solidly built," reported one German lieutenant who discovered a partisan camp during a raid in February 1942. "The walls were made of five to six inch logs, extending only about a foot above the level of the ground. The dugout was covered with earth, with only the entrance and window left uncovered. The roof was supported by two log beams and covered with a foot of ground. . . . The bunker on the inside measured about twenty-six feet in length, sixteen feet in width, and six feet in height. Nearby we found a supply of firewood, a kitchen dugout, and a well. The small stock of food was worthy of note."

Still, no matter how well they were designed, the *zemlianki* were notoriously cold and damp in the winter and hot in the summer. They were, historian Earl Ziemke has pointed out, "barely tolerable living quarters. In the spring and fall, if the bunkers did not fill up with water, they were certain, at least, to be damp and muddy. In the winter, they could be heated only at a risk of revealing their location. In the daytime they were never heated; and at night, as long as snow was on the ground, fires were lighted only for cooking, in order to avoid smoke stains on the snow which could be detected from the air."

Some partisans, like Sam Gruber, found the *zemlianki* claustrophobic and would sleep outside or risk staying at nearby farms to avoid living in a hole in the ground. Indeed, particularly during the winter months, existing day after day in a *zemlianka* left much to be desired. Jack Sutin aptly describes it like this: "We basically lived like squirrels, hiding in a hole. As you can imagine, the air in the bunker stank like hell. On nights when it was snowing or otherwise very dark, we would lift open the cover of the bunker a bit. Otherwise, we would sit in our hole."

Over time, forest inhabitants did, of course, adapt to such harsh living conditions. But newcomers, even those who had experienced the terrible rigours of the ghetto, found it unbearable. Rochelle Sutin (then Schleiff), who arrived at her future husband's camp after her escape from Stolpce in November 1942, was no exception. "The first time I entered Jack's bunker," she recalled in her memoirs, "it was through a hole in the ground with a square cover. You slid into the bunker. Inside it was very dark. And with twelve people inside there, you can imagine the air . . . so stale. Almost at once I got so sick to my stomach that I thought I would pass out. I had to get back outside immediately, just to catch my breath. The stench was terrible. None of the group members bathed — there was no way to do so in the cold weather. All of them were full of lice and vermin. Eventually I learned to stand it, but in the first days I was sick continually, nauseated and fainting, running in and out of the bunker just to keep from vomiting in their midst." Accustomed to life in a *zemlianka,* the other members of the group mistakenly thought that Rochelle was ill because she was pregnant.

Less than a year later, life improved for Jack and Rochelle when they joined Shalom Zorin's larger family camp. At Zorin's base in the Naliboki Forest, the *zemlianki* were of a higher quality and were constructed so that about one-half of the bunkers were above the ground. As Rochelle recalls, "it was a major change — you lived less like an animal and more like a human."

■ ■

One aspect of forest life that Rochelle Sutin and other survivors did not adjust to was the body lice. It was nothing short of a plague. "If you put your shirt or sweater on the ground," remembers Gitel Morrison, "it would walk by itself." Despite their efforts to remain clean and practise good hygiene, the partisans were engaged in an ongoing battle that was not won until the war was over. Baths of any kind were infrequent and clean clothes almost non-existent. Moreover, the close quarters of the *zemlianka* made it next to impossible to control the easily transmitted *Pediculosis corporis* — the medical term for body-louse infestation — caused by unhygienic living conditions. Hence, at most partisan and family camps, the lice had a picnic.

"They crawled into our long hair which we couldn't cut for lack of scissors," stated Byrna Bar Oni. "We found it difficult to sleep nights because, though we were fully clothed, the lice managed to crawl all over us and bite us. Every night we made a fire, took off our clothes and held them above the flame until the heat made the lice drop into the fire. But it was a losing battle. As soon as we lay down, we were again covered with them."

Rochelle Sutin has similar memories. "We used to take turns slipping out of the bunker hole, taking off our clothes, and squeezing off the lice, which we were full of," she writes. "They would get into your pubic hair, under your armpits, around your eyes. . . . One day, I recall I woke up and sensed that my eyelids were heavy. I put my fingers up to feel and there were little black bumps all along my eyelashes. I went outside, taking with me a straight pin and a tiny mirror that we all shared. I poked these out one by one. . . ."

Picking the lice off by hand or burning them over a fire were at best temporary cures. The partisans and civilians tried nearly every remedy they could think of: they rubbed their hair with kerosene when it was available; bathed in rivers; constructed steam and sauna houses using heated stones and water; washed their clothes in boiling water; tried freezing the lice off their clothes in the winter; put their clothes in ant hills so that the ants would eat the lice; and at the Bielski camp, Jews followed the advice of the camp nurse, Riva Reich, and wiped their bodies with urine (the acid in the urine killed the lice).

But nothing would make the lice permanently disappear. A sauna treatment, for example, provided temporary relief. Yet, as Leon Kahn explains, "we could wash off the surface of our skins, [but] the microscopic eggs embedded in our pores were in a constant state of reproduction and we could not rid ourselves of them."

In March 1943, in the woods near Wlodawa, Harold Werner and his friends were fortunate to meet a friendly peasant elder who had learned about a successful cure for lice during his stint as a Russian soldier in the First World War. The formula he prescribed was a combination of egg white and mercury, which was still possible to find in some village pharmacies. Once the mixture was made, Werner notes, "a strip of heavy felt was dipped into this mixture to absorb it and then left to dry. The felt strip was worn diagonally across one's chest, and after a while it was switched to run in the opposite diagonal direction. This formula took care of the lice not just temporarily, like the flame of the fire, but also eliminated the lice eggs so that they did not hatch."

It was more than the discomfort, the constant itching and scratching, that made lice a serious menace in the forest communities. The insects also carried a deadly typhus infection. With antibiotics and delousing, typhus, rare today in western countries (the last epidemic in the United States was in 1921), can be cured without too much trouble. But no antibiotics were available in the forest, and the disease — as it had done in the region before the war as well — took its toll. The Grishin Regiment, for instance, a large unit under the command of Lt. Sergei Vladimirovich Grishin, which was composed of escaped Red Army POWs and operated in the Smolensk region north-east of Minsk, lost 261 men (38 percent of its regiment) in 1942 to illness. Nearly all the partisans died from an unidentified epidemic (most likely typhus) during a four-month period beginning in August. In comparison, that year only 52 Grishin fighters were killed in action and 20 lost through desertions.

Once the disease was contracted, it spread quickly. Partisans went to great lengths to halt its grim progress. At Aleksei Fyodorov's base camp in the forests of the Chernigov region, the unit's gunsmith, Gorobets, combated typhus by building a steam clothes-cleaning machine from an abandoned gasoline drum. During the winter of 1942, at another Soviet partisan camp farther north in the Bryansk Forest, newly arrived female doctors from Moscow, who were brought in to deal with the medical emergency, improved the camp's nearly non-existent sanitary system. But they did not work fast enough: one of the doctors and a nurse became ill a short time after their arrival. The epidemic died out only when the camp was razed and new shelters built.

Rubin Pinsky's experience with typhus was all too common. Pinsky had escaped from the ghetto in Zdzieciol during the summer of 1942 and joined a Jewish partisan *otriad* initially led by Hirsh Kaplinski. During the early part of the winter of 1943–44, Pinsky became ill with typhus. His fever kept rising to the point that he was delirious — a common side-effect of the disease. His only chance for survival was to rest so that his fever would go down. But, as fate would have it, his unit had received orders to relocate. His commander waited a few days, hoping that Pinsky's condition would improve. When it did not, the decision was taken to leave him there. His sister, Chasia, who had escaped to the forest with him, refused to abandon him, and the leader of the detachment gave her permission to stay. The consensus among the unit was that Rubin and Chasia were as good as dead.

Camouflaged in a small *zemlianka*, Chasia attempted to nurse her brother back to health with little more than melted snow and a few blankets for comfort and warmth. Yet nothing she did seemed to make a difference, and Rubin remained very sick. Desperate, she left him alone and visited a friendly farmer, who provided her with a few litres of pure alcohol. As Rubin's son Bernard relates in a history of his father's life, "[Chasia] sat beside Rubin and put his head in her lap, and started to force-feed him the alcohol. She had no medicine but she knew that alcohol kills disease. She also knew it could help break the fever. For three days, she force-fed him, alternating alcohol with food and water. Chasia did not move the whole time. Rubin got worse, but then, miraculously, the fever broke. He slowly recuperated and within a week, they were able to move [and rejoin their partisan group]. . . . My father owed his life to Chasia."

Typhus was only the most serious illness to strike the forest inhabitants. They were bothered by a wide range of ailments, mostly related to their diet and poor living conditions. The fact that they could rarely wash or change their clothes made matters worse. During the winter of 1943–44, the Bielski camp suffered a terrible bout of typhoid fever that affected more than a hundred people. A quarantine was set up in a remote *zemlianka*, and the patients were gradually nursed back to health on a diet of "boiled water and melted snow" by the camp's doctor and nurses.

Skin and mouth problems were common throughout the war. Partisans and civilians suffered from toothaches, scurvy, rheumatism, boils, gum diseases, and fungal infections. Often the pain was unbearable. Sonia Ostrinsky developed a large boil in her throat and, until it burst, was nearly incapacitated.

Jack Sutin was afflicted with "red and raw" boils that covered his body from his head to his toes. He was unable to wear shoes and endured three months of near torture. The boils affected him so badly that he contemplated suicide. "If you so much as touched them," remembers his wife, Rochelle, who tried to comfort him, "yellow pus as thick as honey would run out of them. His body was a bundle of bones and pus." Finally, after what seemed like an eternity, the Sutins and others discovered that bark from a birch tree, when burned into a "thick black sap," healed the infection. "The birch tar was so thick," adds Jack, "that after the infections started to clear up, it was a real problem to wash the tar off. And even after the tar came off, I had red circular spots on my legs for years."

There was indeed no lack of ingenuity at partisan camps. Boiled milk injections helped cure boils and fungi. According to Nechama Tec, "a patient injected with milk would develop a fever and the body would then mobilize its immune system to fight the infection." Zelik Abramovich, a Jewish pharmacist who served as a doctor in Fyodorov's brigade, cured gum disease and scurvy by having his comrades drink a brew of boiled pine needles (at Leon Kahn's camp, it was boiled clover). Abramovich also experimented with boiled grass "steeped in alcohol." Both seemed to have the desired effect.

Old-fashioned improvisation worked as well. When Commander Fyodorov suffered from a toothache, his gunsmith, Gorobets, used a pair of blacksmith's pliers to solve the problem. "He pulled out the teeth in one jerk," recalled the Soviet partisan leader. "I fell asleep almost at once and woke up twenty-four hours later a new man, refreshed and unusually gentle." More serious was the case of Grigory Masalyka, another fighter in Fyodorov's brigade. After successfully blowing up a truck transporting Nazi officers, Masalyka was wounded in his left hand but paid no attention to it. Two weeks later, Fyodorov states, "his arm had turned black to the elbow." Amputating his hand was the only way to save his life. The successful operation was done with a hacksaw by Gorobets, the talented gunsmith. No anesthetic was available, though Masalyka probably was able to drink some vodka to dull the pain. Nevertheless, according to Fyodorov, the fighter did not cry out, "an example of boundless courage and iron endurance" in the commander's view.

"WE WERE NOT SITTING THERE FLIRTING"

One night, only a few weeks after he had escaped to the forest from the Mir ghetto in August 1942, Jack Sutin had a dream. In it, he heard his mother tell him that Rochelle Schleiff, a girl he barely knew from before the war, would come to him in the forest. So powerful was this dream, that Sutin, much to the consternation of the rest of his group, insisted on saving a spot in the small bunker for Rochelle's impending arrival. His friends thought he had gone mad.

Three months later, he was vindicated. Amazingly, Rochelle, who had escaped in September 1942 from Stolpce, made contact with a woman named Fania who had heard about Jack's dream. She brought Rochelle to Sutin's camp. "It was unbelievable," declares Jack in his memoirs. "What I felt when I first saw Rochelle standing there was that my dream had not lied to me. Someone, something, was watching over us. Rochelle and I had been fated to meet."

Rochelle's earliest memories of Jack are not quite as romantic. Even when they were introduced, she did not remember who he was. Dressed in a sheepskin coat, with a fur hat and rifle, he appeared to her as a "wild man." At eighteen, she assumed his invitation to live in his bunker was nothing more than a request to have sex. Yet, alone and afraid, she had few options. In fact, Jack Sutin turned out to be Rochelle's knight in shining armour. He protected her, ensured that she had food, and found her new clothes. First they were simply friends, yet the dangerous times eventually drew them closer together. In their joint memoirs, Rochelle explained the transformation as follows: "It took a while for us to get to know each other — two strangers put together into a hole. But we lived through so many terrible and dangerous moments together. We felt like two soldiers on the front lines. It was a crazy setting for any kind of love. But you grow closer each time you live through moments of hell like those. You have that in common with the other person and with no one else. And you had no idea what would happen tomorrow." On December 31, 1997, Jack and Rochelle Sutin, now living in Minneapolis, Minnesota, celebrated fifty-five years together.

■ ■

The Sutins were by no means the only two people to find comfort, companionship, compassion, love, and even pleasure in the forest. By all accounts, and as strange as it might seem under the circumstances, sex between consenting adults regularly took place in *zemlianki*. It was often, as in the case of Jack and Rochelle, a question of facing the daily hardships together rather than alone. "Sex meant something different in the conditions in which we were living," explains Jack Sutin. "It was a way to feel some kind of pleasure and to forget the misery for a while. But what you would call a romantic atmosphere did not usually exist." Leah Johnson, a Bielski camp survivor who met her husband, Velvke, when he came to the aid of her family and others during a major German assault on the Naliboki Forest in 1943, is adamant on this point. The image of wild sexual escapades taking place in *zemlianki* while Jews still in the ghettos were being starved and beaten to death, she says, is a gross distortion. "We were not sitting there flirting," she declares. (Still, Rochelle Sutin, a lovely and lively woman who does not mince her words, put it like this: "Nature takes over. [The men] didn't care where they were. The lice were crawling, the bugs were buzzing, and they were doing their own thing.")

Two key factors pushed men and women together in the forest. First, life was precarious and uncertain, and partisans were consumed by the thought that they would be dead by the time the sun set. Second, female resisters were dogged by the dilemma of being a woman and a Jew on the run. Survival in the woods was difficult enough for an armed male partisan. A Jewish woman alone (and usually without a weapon) was defenceless against Nazi raids, rape and attacks by unfriendly partisans, and starvation. Rochelle Sutin, for one, claims that without Jack's help and protection, she would have either returned to Stolpce and a certain death or attached herself to a non-Jewish fighter, as was also common.

Fear and the need for protection also sealed the life-long relationship between Sulia Wolozhinski (Rubin) and Boris Rubizhewski (later changed to Rubin), two young Jews from opposite backgrounds who would have never met if not for the tragedy of the times. Sulia, who had escaped from Novogrudok and reached the Bielski camp in late 1942, persevered against tremendous odds. At seventeen, she did not know how to start a fire or cook; she did not even know how to speak a good Yiddish, the language of the forest Jews. She was a bit of a lost soul, barely making it through each day. "Night after night I cried," she recalls, "and wondered, 'Why did I leave my family?'" Her greatest fear was loneliness. "When I came to the forest, I was never afraid of being alone, but I was always afraid of loneliness," she remarks. "If I would have died, there would have been no one to bury me."

In time, Sulia gradually adapted to her new surroundings, though it was a challenge. She took her turn at guard duty, learned how to use a gun, went on sabotage missions, and most important met Boris. Slightly older, he had been born in a small village near the Naliboki Forest. His father, Solomon, an orthodox Jew, operated a general store and provided for his wife and nine children. Unlike Sulia, Boris did not have much schooling and was hardly refined in the manner of the Jews found in the larger cities. But he was accustomed to the nearby forest, knew the local peasants in the area, and when faced with the Nazi terror in June 1941, was determined to survive as well as seek revenge.

Like the Bielskis, Harold Werner, and others, Boris disobeyed the Nazi order to relocate to a ghetto in a nearby town. He immediately fled to the forest with his brother Volodia, although many members of their family, including their father, were killed. (Boris's mother had died before the war.) Armed with rifles and knives, the two Rubizhewski brothers met other Jewish fugitives and established a small partisan group. In addition to participating in some early sabotage missions, they attempted to rescue Jews from the ghetto in Dworzec. However, caught in a ghetto *Aktion*, Volodia was murdered and Boris barely escaped alive. He returned to the forest, where he coincidentally encountered his older brother, Izaak. This led him to the Bielski camp — and to Sulia — where he served as one of several young armed fighters without whom the Jewish families at the camp would have undoubtedly perished.

After considering her options, Sulia accepted Boris as her boyfriend — her *tavo* in the parlance of the Bielski camp — and then as her husband.* She moved into his more comfortable *zemlianka*, but did set down certain conditions that defined their relationship. "I made it clear the day I came to Boris," she writes in her memoirs, "that I would never sleep with him in this 'public' hut; I would not bare my most private life

---

*Nechama Tec explains that "a newly acquired lover was called a 'Tavo'. It is a Hebrew word, a masculine address, that within the context could be translated into 'come here.'" (See Tec, *Defiance*, 159.)

to so many witnesses and become the subject of crude remarks and jokes afterwards." At the same time, she recognized how significantly her life had been altered now that she had a *tavo*. "I was no longer an intruder or outsider. I had my place, and I wasn't alone any more."

Through a courier, Sulia sent a letter to her parents in the Novogrudok Court House ghetto, telling them that she had been "married." Her father wrote back with his approval, but Sulia's mother, Anne, a dentist, indicated that she had hoped for a higher-quality man for her daughter. "She wrote that she could understand a woman selling her body to survive, but I had sold my soul," Sulia recalled many years later. She never heard from her parents again. Before Boris could rescue them, they were murdered.

Many Soviet partisans were also interested in Jewish women, since it was a sign of status for a fighter to have a young woman at his side. At the same time, many Jewish women were drawn to Soviets for protection and love. This was the case with a woman at the Bielski camp, for example, who fell in love with the Russian partisan commander, Victor Panchenko. So smitten was the woman with Panchenko, and he with her, that she moved to his base and shared his *zemlianka*. The relationship ended only when the woman was upset by episodes of anti-Semitism perpetrated, and then boasted about, by men in the *otriad*. Panchenko assured her that he would deal with the problem, but never did. Unhappy, she returned to the Bielski camp, though she and Panchenko stayed close friends until the war ended.

While incidents of rape and violence against Jewish women by non-Jewish partisans took place, survivors of the forests also point out that Jewish and Russian women were valued and respected as nurses, cooks, and seamstresses. Of course, men and women had clearly defined roles, and these were more or less adhered to in the forest. Soviet and east European society, before, during, and after the war, was conservative, traditional, and male-dominated. Nechama Tec points out, for example, that even if a woman arrived at the Bielski camp with a weapon, it was nearly always taken from her. "Guns belonged to men, not women — this was the law of the forest," Tec writes. Few people questioned this principle of partisan wisdom.

Still, this did not mean that women's contributions were not appreciated. Aleksei Fyodorov wrote of Dossia Baskina, a Jewish nurse who fought alongside him: "There was virtually no battle in which she did not take part. She would bandage the wounded under a hail of enemy bullets and evacuate them from the field of battle. In this manner she saved the lives of forty-nine wounded fighters and officers."

Despite the fact that she was often the only woman among fifty Soviet fighters, Faye Schulman kept her distance and was rarely bothered. In her particular Soviet brigade, sex between male and female partisans was not permitted, although this does not seem to have been a widely followed policy among Soviet *otriady*. In fact, those guilty of breaking this rule were given an automatic death sentence. But such infringements were rare, according to Schulman. "Sex was not a major issue in our group," she suggests. "We didn't think in terms of men and women, boys and girls. We treated each other as equals. There were no special privileges for women; we were all partisans and we knew that death in war did not spare anyone."

But some women cheated death only to face a new enemy: pregnancy. This was, to use Rochelle Sutin's words, nothing less than "the kiss of death." In a *zemlianka*, there was only one kind of real contraception and that was abstention. Yet, given the fragile nature of life, people did not think too far ahead. At the same time, giving birth to a child in the forest was fraught with danger, though it did happen. As Rochelle Sutin remembers, "One of the girls in a nearby bunker gave birth during that winter [of 1943]. As soon as the baby was born she placed it on a rag outside on the snow so that it would die right away and not suffer." Other former partisans recall a few newborns surviving, including a set of twins born to a woman at the Zorin family camp.

Accidents did happen, and as a result, physicians at the family camps, including those with minimal or no gynecological training, often performed abortions under the most primitive of conditions. One Russian female doctor from Minsk named Katia helped many women, like Sulia Rubin, through difficult traumas at the Zorin camp.

Rubin became aware that she was pregnant, she also learned that her older sister, Rita, had been captured and killed attempting to escape from the Novogrudok ghetto in November 1943. Devastated, Sulia withdrew into a deep depression. She even tried to self-abort the fetus, but her attempts failed. She finally sought an abortion from Katia, though it was a painful procedure. "No anesthesia — nothing," she writes. "Like a grunting animal I lay there in this ripping pain until it was over. I was there five days, bleeding heavily." Soon Sulia recovered from both her physical ordeal and her depression, determined, she says, "not to wallow in self-pity." This was a sentiment shared by many Jews in the family camps of the Naliboki *puszcza*.

SHTETLACH
IN THE NALIBOKI

Nothing else matters but this: If not for Tuvia Bielski, we would all be dead. It is as simple as that.

— GITEL MORRISON

"A GORGEOUS MAN ON A WHITE HORSE"

By late 1942, the vast forests and swamplands of Belorussia were crawling with Soviet and Jewish partisans. Estimates put the number of fighters anywhere from 70,000 to more than 100,000, and this would triple before the war was over. Gradually, more and more areas came under partisan control, though the Nazis did not surrender their positions easily. Bloodshed devastated both the people and the land. "Our village," said one Belorussian peasant, "was for a while in German hands in the daytime and in guerrilla hands at night."

The largest group of partisans and Jewish civilians sought refuge in the great Naliboki *puszcza,* approximately 414 square kilometres of primeval wood and swampland that extends from the right or northern bank of the Niemen River, north-east of the town of Novogrudok, to an eastern tip not far from Minsk. The forest gets its name from the town of Naliboki, located in the south-east section. Where tributaries of the

Niemen cross the forest, small "islands" exist in a sea of swamps that fugitives ran to in times of extreme danger. At the start of the Second World War, predominately Jewish towns and villages were situated on all sides of the *puszcza*, or were within a few days' walk. Jews fled to the Naliboki from the ghettos in Novogrudok, Mir, Iwje, Lida, Baranowicze, and many more. Eventually, the forest became the base not only for dozens of Soviet and Jewish fighting detachments, such as Iskra, Ponomarenko, Voroshilov, First of May, and Sokolov, but also for Jerusalem, or Jew town, as the peasants called the huge family camp established by Tuvia Bielski and his brothers.

■ ■

In the young teenage eyes of Gitel Morrison, Tuvia Bielski was "a gorgeous man on a white horse." Declares Leah Johnson, another of the 1,200 Jews who owes her life to Bielski and his two brothers, Zus and Asael: "When we saw Tuvia Bielski, we knew that we were alive. He was a powerful man, a good man, a gentle person. By Tuvia's wisdom we survived." Daniel Ostaszynski, the one-time head of the Novogrudok Judenrat who escaped to the forest in 1943, told Nechama Tec that Bielski was "a meteor. . . . Somehow Tuvia sensed that we were all in the same boat. He understood that we had to help each other and that by helping each other we had a better chance to live."

Who knows what motivates any person to risk his life for others? No one held a gun to Tuvia Bielski's head, ordering him to rescue 1,200 Jews from the ghettos or to offer fugitives he did not know a safe haven in the forest. No one, moreover, coerced him into finding food for hundreds of people each day for more than two years. He and his immediate family could certainly have hidden by themselves at a peasant farm. The Bielski brothers, simple Jews from a rural village, were acquainted with many local Belorussians and Poles. Life-and-death risks did not have to be taken.

Choices, however, were made. For reasons of the heart, Tuvia and his brothers opted to become the protectors of hundreds of helpless individuals under the most extreme of conditions and in the most dangerous of times. "Tuvia Bielski was filled with the national pain and the national love, the pain and love for the Jews," observed Abraham Viner, a Bielski survivor. "He devoted his soul, his brains, and everything else to the rescue of Jews. He saw a chance, a great opportunity, in his ability to save. He was grateful that he could save Jews. For him it was a privilege."

■ ■

By October 1942, when Tuvia had already made peace with Victor Panchenko, the Russian partisan commander who had wanted to annihilate him and his group, the Bielski *otriad* consisted of approximately 200 people. Always moving, the group travelled in the woods not far from Novogrudok, wary of setting up a permanent base.

Determined to save the small minority of Jews still alive in Novogrudok and surrounding ghettos, Bielski dispatched young men like Jacob Druk, Irving (Yitzhak) Resnik, Israel Yankielewicz, and Ike Bernstein to rescue Jews who wanted to escape. Bernstein, born in 1924 in the village of Ivenets, had escaped from the Novogrudok court-house ghetto with two friends in the late summer of 1942. He recalls being ordered by Tuvia to return to the town and take out a few of the Bielski family's relatives, which he did. But another ten to twelve desperate Jews followed him to the camp. "What could I do?" he asks. Though each new person was another mouth to feed and another body to shelter — a reality often resented by those who were already there — Tuvia welcomed each and every one of them with open arms.

Though few survivors will speak openly about it today, the fear and terror of the Nazis sometimes created an atmosphere of selfishness. In her 1993 book on the *otriad*, Nechama Tec suggested that many of the Jews at the Bielski camp were "absorbed in their own survival [and] did not identify with the overall plight of the Jewish people." No matter, Tuvia and his brothers, who ruled the camp with discipline and military authority, established an official policy of acceptance of all Jews they encountered. As they went back and forth from the ghettos, eluding Nazi patrols and collaborators along the way, Bernstein and other armed young Bielski partisans, most about eighteen and nineteen years old, often found small groups of Jews hiding by themselves. They too were brought to the camp, as Tuvia had ordered. In late 1942, a special rescue mission saved about 150 Jews from the ghetto in Iwje, north of Novogrudok, only days before the Nazis planned to liquidate it.

At approximately the same time, in December 1942, the Bielski camp, and Tuvia in particular, suffered a tragic set-back. Word had reached Bielski that the Germans were planning a major offensive against them. One night, Tuvia ordered a total relocation closer to the woods near Iwje. The winter weather was already bitter and the new temporary camp inadequate. A few weeks passed and the Nazi attack did not transpire, so Tuvia allowed his group to go back to their more comfortable bunkers in the Zabielowo Forest, farther south. Everyone immediately made the return journey, except for a dozen people who, with Tuvia's permission, decided to rest for a few days at two farmhouses owned by friendly Belorussian peasants. This group included Zus's wife, Sonia Bielski; Asael's wife, Chaya Bielski; Tuvia's wife, Sonia; her sister, Regina Ticktin; Regina's son from her first marriage, Grisha Meitis; Israel Kotler; Lova Volkin; and Shimon Bernstein (Ike Bernstein's younger brother), who was recuperating from frostbite on one of his feet. Tired, most of them went to sleep soon after they arrived at the farms.

They should have been more cautious; informers were everywhere. Moreover, the Germans were fully aware of the Bielski brothers' movements in the woods and the fact that they were protecting hundreds of Jewish fugitives. A bounty of 50,000 marks (about US$20,000 in the exchange rate of the day) had already been placed on Tuvia's head. Later, the amount was doubled. If Nazi police officials in the area had had their choice, they would have captured Bielski alive, tortured him for information, and then publicly executed him as an example of what happens to Jewish "bandits."

Chaya Bielski saw them first. Sensing danger, she had stepped outside into the cold for a moment to look for potential trouble or for lost escapees from Iwje. Suddenly, the two farmhouses were surrounded by German and Belorussian police. Chaya screamed and panic ensued. Sonia Bielski, Zus's wife, was hysterical. She ran into the adjacent field and stumbled into a hole used to store potatoes. "Go save yourself," she yelled to Chaya. "Leave me!" But Chaya would not abandon her sister-in-law. Before the Germans could fire a round, Israel Kotler began to shoot his rifle and the other armed men joined in. But it was a lost cause.

Chaya helped Sonia out of the hole and ran into the forest behind Israel Kotler. They were the only three to survive. In moments, everyone else perished in the battle, including Tuvia's wife. When it was over, the Germans burned the two peasant huts to the ground. Only Lova Volkin was captured alive. According to one account, told later to Chaya Bielski by a Belorussian policeman, the Nazis brutally tortured him. "They pulled his nails out one at a time, cut off his fingers, and gouged out his eyes. But he would not talk. He did not open his mouth [and tell them the location of our camp]. Then they hung him in the town centre of [Novogrudok] and put two signs on him: This is what will happen to every Jew who leaves the ghetto."

Word of the attack and killings soon reached Tuvia and other members of the *otriad* back at their camp. When it was safe, Bielski and his men conducted an investigation of the site. The rumours were true: his wife and nine others were dead. Devastated by the loss of Sonia, Tuvia, according to Tec, began drinking vodka heavily and became very depressed. In time, however, the effect of the tragedy passed, and the thirty-seven-year-old commander soon found comfort with the considerably younger Lilka Ticktin, then about eighteen years old, the daughter of his brother-in-law, Alter Ticktin. She became Tuvia's third wife and remained with him until the day he died.

■ ■

The winter of 1943 was difficult for the growing Bielski group. By February, the *otriad* had increased to approximately 300 people — that number would nearly double by start of the summer of 1943 — and finding food for so many became more of a challenge. *Bambioshki*, or food missions, were always dangerous, a reality of life in the forest which was reinforced that month when an accident occurred that could have cost the lives of hundreds. Returning by sleigh from a food-gathering mission on a farm near Novogrudok, several of Bielski's young men brought with them a freshly killed cow or chicken. But, as Sulia Rubin recalls, it was not wrapped properly and, unbeknown to the partisans, dripped blood all the way back to the Bielski camp. The trail was easy to follow, and the police did not hesitate to take advantage of this mistake.

Sulia had just left her guard post the next morning when she heard the first shots. "We were no match for a well-organized police company," she writes. "We did not know how many there were, but we couldn't risk finding out. Quietly, and as quickly as possible, we ran out. . . . I just followed the footsteps in the snow until I caught up with the retreating partisans. . . . We cut out safely from [Zabielowo] and gathered in nearby bushes."

On this occasion, the Jews were lucky. Even the elderly guard whom the police believed they had killed escaped relatively unharmed. For the remainder of the winter, Bielski kept moving his group on a regular basis, which made it impossible to build proper bunkers. Then, in the spring, yet more tragedy.

Feeling that he was not doing enough for his family, Alter Ticktin, then forty-nine years old, convinced his brother-in-law (and new son-in-law) that he should be permitted to go on a food expedition led by Avraham Polonski. Reluctantly, and despite the objections of Lilka Ticktin Bielski, Tuvia agreed to let him go. The mission proceeded without incident and the group loaded up their wagons with confiscated supplies. About 5 kilometres from Novogrudok, they decided to rest for a day at the home of a Belorussian peasant known to Polonski. The farmer's name was Bielus. The peasant greeted his Jewish friends warmly, but it was all an act. As soon as he saw the Jews approaching, he had sent one of his sons to bring the police. By midnight, the house was surrounded.

"When our friends woke up in surprise, it was too late to fight," Tuvia later recalled. "They were all shot, except Avraham, who managed to hide in the chicken coop under the stove. When he heard the police and their officers leaving, and the family rejoicing and celebrating its victory, he came out of his hiding place and shouted to Bielus: 'The partisans will take revenge.' Suddenly an ax, wielded by one of Bielus's sons, came down on his head."

When Bielski learned of what had happened, he undertook an investigation of the crime. He found a girl who worked for the Bielus family, and she confirmed the story of the massacre. Then, late one evening, a group of armed men from the *otriad*, led by Asael Bielski, paid a visit to the Bielus farm to exact retribution.

In his memoirs, Tuvia related what took place: "[Asael] surrounded the house at midnight. His thunderous pounding on the door frightened them into opening it. With him were Israel Yankielewicz, Michal Leibowicz, and Pesach Friedberg. They came to the point immediately, declaring that they had come to avenge the blood of their ten comrades. Bielus felt what was coming, and resisted. When the four of them aimed their guns at him, he grabbed the barrels and wrestled with them. Even after he had been stabbed several times, he continued to struggle. Asael shot him and ordered his friends to finish the job. They completed what they had set out to do in the course of a few minutes. The house, the stable, and the barn went up in smoke." With Asael's permission, Michal Leibowicz took a coat from the house and discovered a letter inside the pocket addressed to Bielus from the German commander of Novogrudok, thanking him for his work on behalf of the Nazi fight against the Jewish "bandits."

Further incidents and confrontations with the police and collaborators continued to occur, including one that resulted in the death of eighteen-year-old Yossel Zelkowicz in mid-March 1943. Though the precise details are not known, Yossel was apparently on a routine reconnaissance mission with a dozen other fighters. While leading the group across a road, he encountered a German ambush and was shot in the back. Motel Dworzecki and David Sztein may have been killed with him. Their bodies were taken to a nearby farmhouse, but their distraught families were never able to locate the graves.

Hearing rumours of an impending German assault on the forest area near Novogrudok, Tuvia finally decided, by the early summer of 1943, that he had to find a more secure and permanent location for his camp. He chose a spot for his new base deep in the Naliboki *puszcza*.

OBLAVA

The trek to the Naliboki was long and arduous. Like a modern-day Moses, Tuvia Bielski led more than 600 Jews through the woods and across the

Niemen River on a dangerous journey that took weeks. That so many Jews could travel, even by night, through enemy territory without a major incident taking place is both remarkable and difficult to fathom.

At the bank of the Niemen, recalls Pessia Bairach, "we got into the river. Those who could swim helped those who couldn't. We formed a kind of human chain, and somehow, we reached the other [side]." Her husband, Moshe, adds, "Once we were caught in a terrible rain, even the wagons were stuck. It was awful. It was pouring all night. We were soaked through. Tuvia moved around us and tried to keep up our spirits."

Finally, they arrived at the outskirts of the Naliboki, but the Soviet partisans guarding the area refused to allow them to enter the *puszcza*. According to Pessia Bairach, "it was only after several days of exhausting negotiations that we were finally granted the long-awaited permission."

They walked to a spot deep in the forest, near Lake Kroman, "a breathtaking place with a magnificent view, but [we] were too disappointed and too tired to even pay attention, let alone admire the scenery," remembered Pessia. "It was on the banks of this lake that we built our camp, a camp that consisted mostly of huts." A Soviet fighting group was not too far away, and the lake provided a clean source of water. "Life in the group," stated Tuvia Bielski, "was normal."

■ ■

While the Jews with the Bielski brothers believed they had at last found a safe haven beside Lake Kroman, they were sadly mistaken. Even the vastness of the Naliboki could not halt the Nazis' diabolical scheme to annihilate them. In early July 1943, well aware of the increasing number of partisan and civilian groups hiding in the forest, the Germans set in motion the plans for Unternehmen "Hermann," — the "Herman" Undertaking. The Jews referred to it as "the Big Hunt," or in Russian, an *oblava*, a blockade. (The word *oblava* also means a round-up of suspected persons, but in the context of the partisan movement, it specifically referred to a Nazi assault on the forest.)

At least 20,000 (and perhaps as many as 65,000) German troops, fully armed and mobile, readied themselves for an attack on their great and dangerous enemy: Russian, Polish, and Jewish fighters and an army of defenceless Jewish men, women, and children. The object of any Nazi *oblava* was to surround as much of the forest as possible, plugging up escape routes and forcing partisans into an impossible position from which the only retreat was death. In cases like this, confrontations with the Nazis were futile.

Outnumbered and overpowered, even the best-armed Soviet fighters began to search for a way out of the *puszcza* when the assault commenced. "We received an order," recalled Jacob Greenstein, a Jewish fighter in the Parkhomenko Brigade, "to disperse in [groups of] fives, and not offer any resistance."

Sounds of German guns could be heard at the Bielski camp on the first day of August 1943. Pessia Bairach also remembers the planes of the Luftwaffe circling overhead, scouring the land below for enemy targets. Tuvia had already moved the *otriad*'s base deeper into the forest, but as he recalled, the atmosphere among his people was "tense." A sense of impending doom quickly descended on the camp. "The forest was large, the swamps were deep, there was no place to escape," he wrote. "It was only possible to try to hide." He, Zus, Asael, and the other members of the command tried to remain calm. All around them, groups of Soviet and Polish partisans were in retreat. Not far away, a detachment of Polish resisters had had no choice but to fight the Germans and were easily defeated.

"What do you think we should do?" Tuvia asked Kovalov, commander of the First of May detachment, whose base was nearby.

"Stupid question," he told Bielski. "We can't hold our own in open battle. We have to get out of here."

"Where to?"

"The road is open."

"What do you think we should do?"

"As you see fit."

With his brother Asael at his side, Tuvia returned to the camp. "Everybody was tense, waiting for a word from me," he later remembered. "It was imperative to bolster their spirits, to warn them and encourage them at the same time." Standing before his masses, he declared, "We will find a way to escape from the Germans, by courage and quiet." In fact, Bielski later conceded that he was not sure what to do. The First of May Brigade was marching east in the direction of a road near the Shobin River. Following them were Jews from Shalom Zorin's smaller family camp, located a short distance away. But something inside Tuvia convinced him that this was not a safe escape route. He briefly spoke with Zorin about altering his plans, but the Jewish commander refused to listen to him.* He also warned members of his own *otriad* to remain where they were and threatened to shoot anyone who did not obey.

The ability to act rationally under extreme pressure often distinguishes the true leaders from the pretenders. Considering the life-and-death struggle Tuvia Bielski found himself in during those long weeks in the summer of 1943, this may have been his finest hour as a commander. "He stood in front of us all, encouraging and comforting us," states Pessia Bairach. "He had a very special plan of his own that he wished to tell us about and that he had never revealed to anyone before."

The "special plan" Bielski had in mind had in fact been proposed to him by two of his men, Michal Mechlis and Akiva Szymonowicz. Both were familiar with the forest terrain. Mechlis had worked as a forest surveyor before the war and Szymonowicz had been a travelling peddler. They suggested that the *otriad* head for the swamps, about 12 kilometres to the north, and seek refuge on a large island called Krasnaya Gorka. Bielski was sceptical, but he had few options remaining. The order was given.

The departure was quietly proceeding when, suddenly, bullets began flying over the partisans' heads. People screamed hysterically and ran in all directions, some towards a bridge in the same direction as the Soviets and Zorin Jews had gone. It was the last thing Bielski wanted. Pessia Bairach was among the first to start running that way. She had gone a few hundred metres, she relates, "when I suddenly saw Tuvia coming after us, screaming and entreating us to come back and go in the opposite direction." Scared, Pessia snapped. "At that moment, I felt my

---

*It is unclear whether many members of the Zorin group were later killed. While Nechama Tec claims that the Zorin unit "incurred heavy losses" during the attack, Jack and Rochelle Sutin, who were members of Zorin's group, suggest otherwise. (See Tec, *Defiance*, 234, n.63, and Sutins, *Jack and Rochelle*, 129–32.)

anger rising and I started attacking him, but he was so strong and so determined that he managed to take us back to the camp and to prevent us from running towards the bridge."

Back at the base, the camp's cattle and horses were set free. Children were placed on the shoulders of the adults, and everyone carried food and a few belongings. "Those who carried the children marched first, for the swamp became deeper and more muddy from the marching feet," wrote Bielski. "Those who were stronger and those who carried weapons marched in the rear. We marched single file in order not to leave too many footprints. At times we sank up to our waists. Later on, the water became shallower. Three hours we walked and covered three kilometers. Here a drier area appeared and we sat down to rest. Some of our people began to fall asleep despite the wet and the mud. The air was stifling. Again we warned against speaking loudly. . . ."

Although Boris Rubizhewski was familiar with the swamp area, Sulia was not. "I was afraid of the [swamps] and stayed closed to the trees, which seemed to float on top," she recalled. "We sat hugging the trunks of trees and each other, shivering. . . . The shapes of the people, the trees, the darkness were eerie. One did not expect to live; one only hoped not to be caught alive."

In the morning, accompanied by Asael, Mechlis, and two others, Tuvia returned to his base to see whether it had been discovered by the Germans. Yet before they could get very close, shells and machine-gun fire whistled all around them. When the bombardment stopped, they quickly began to run back towards the group. In the distance, they could hear the enthusiastic shouts of the Belorussian police as they arrived at the deserted Jewish family camp. "Hurray! Grab the Jews! . . . Grab the cow!"

As soon as the reconnaissance team rejoined the main group, Tuvia ordered everyone to resume their march. The swamp became deeper still, with the water as high as some people's necks. The members of the *otriad* were hungry and exhausted, but kept moving as they were told. Even the children remained silent. In the confusion, a few stragglers, including Leah (Bedzow) Johnson and her brothers, got lost. Not sure what to do, they rested by a tree until they happened to be found by Velvke Yonson (Leah's future husband), who was then a member of a

Soviet detachment. He remained with them and eventually led them back to the Bielski *otriad*.

Finally, after days of non-stop walking through weeds and filthy water, they found another rest area. Tuvia tied himself to a tree with his belt, to insure that he did not fall into the swamp, and slept. They remained there all night. "The next morning was beautiful," he recalled. "Again we started to march forward, northward, according to the map. We went into very deep water. It was almost impossible to survey the end of the line, to see if everything was in order. We thought: 'Here some will be lost.' After some meters we went up on dry ground onto a pleasant hill — Krasnaya Gorka!"

The swamp island was hardly a paradise or a secure location. Indeed, soon after their arrival, Moshe Bairach, who was on guard duty, heard a rustle in the bush. It was a Belorussian woman who told Bairach and the other sentry on duty that she was lost. As was required, they took her to Tuvia, who questioned her. She claimed that she was from Kleszczyce, a village about 6 kilometres away. Though she was wet and ragged looking, Bielski was convinced she was a German spy. Further interrogation, during which the woman was hit several times, confirmed his suspicions. She confessed that she had been sent into the swamp area by the Nazis to locate the Jews. Unwilling to risk the lives of his group, Bielski ordered that the woman be shot, as partisan law required.

With the Germans only a few kilometres away, food-gathering expeditions were out of the question. Day after day, the Jews sat there, wet and starving. The bombardment of shells was constant, and at night the voices of the Nazi soldiers and the barking of their dogs could be heard, adding to the terror and despair of the partisans. The lack of food, however, was the worst part. People grew weak and depressed. Some members of the *otriad* were so hungry that they ate the rotting meat of a dead horse they found. Others subsisted on wild mushrooms and berries.

Jacob Greenstein describes the situation during the *oblava* in this way: "For fifteen days, the enemy hunted us. Our experiences of those terrible days are truly difficult to relate. For eight days, my wife and I and another Jewish couple lay hidden on a little island in a marsh among tall wild grasses. Completely without food, every day seemed like a year. The hunger was terrible, the heat unbearable. The only thing we had was water. The Germans searched near us, searched the forest, shooting at every step. . . . We were weakened by hunger and the last three nights we could not move. We were ready with pistols to shoot ourselves."

With no alternative, Bielski sent Akiva Szymonowicz and a small team to Kleszczyce, hoping they could find some food. Yet with German troops still swarming the area, burning villages as they moved, Szymonowicz and his men returned empty-handed. The Bielski *otriad* had been in swamps for ten days. Some individuals, Tuvia related, "had a puffiness under the eyes." The camp's doctors explained that this was a result of malnutrition.

After much deliberation, Tuvia decided to send Zus Bielski with eighty armed men to see if a safe passage out of the Naliboki could be found. When two days had passed and Zus and his party had not returned, Tuvia assumed the blockade had ended. Orders were given to leave the swamp island, but this time in groups of forty to sixty people. Everyone was to make their way back to the *otriad*'s former camp in the Jasinowo Forest. Pessia and Moshe Bairach were in the last group to leave, a band of sixty people led by Tuvia and Asael Bielski. "The road was so full of dangers and liabilities that whenever we would stop to rest, Tuvia would put several guards on duty," Pessia recalled. One dark night, Moshe happened to be on guard duty when the order was suddenly given to depart. However, no one told Moshe. Upset, Pessia told Tuvia what had happened, but it was too dangerous to return. "Confused and desperate," states Pessia, "I had no choice but to follow the others."

The group eventually arrived again at the banks of the Niemen River and began crossing in small boats. Some people opted to swim across. Before Pessia could get to the other side, there was shouting that the Nazis were coming. "We started running in all directions," she continues. "The forest was quite a distance from where we were. I hurried to hide in the garden of a farm and I lay in the bushes." When she believed it was safe again, she emerged from her hiding place. Alone and frightened, she walked aimlessly in the adjacent fields. Finally, she found her way back to the river, where she met two other unarmed Jews from the *otriad*. Together they began trekking through the bush, when she heard a woman's voice.

"Wait for me and don't walk so fast! Why are you in such a hurry, Bairach? Don't walk so fast," the woman said.

It was Moshe with another woman. Pessia remembers: "'What an incredible coincidence,' I whispered to myself, and my joy knew no limits." Moshe and Pessia were alone in the woods for about a month, barely able to acquire enough food to survive. On more than one occasion, they met unfriendly Soviet partisans who tried to rob them. "We had to use endless tricks to prevent them from doing so," adds Pessia. Somehow, Moshe led Pessia back to where the Bielski base was being re-established and the two of them rejoined the camp.

JERUSALEM

Soviet partisan headquarters had spoken: the Bielski *otriad* was to be divided up. All civilians were to return to the Naliboki Forest, as part of the Kalinin unit; those young Jews capable of combat were to remain and become part of a new Soviet-led detachment known as Ordzonikidze. Only Zus Bielski, whose talents and knowledge as a reconnaissance leader the Soviets respected, maintained his command position. The wives and girlfriends of the Jewish fighters were also permitted to stay with them in the new unit.

Clearly, the Nazi blockade had upset the order and discipline that Soviet officials in Moscow and in the forests had worked so diligently to establish among the partisans. Now that the immediate danger had passed, the time had come to reaffirm their authority. In this regard, the Soviets reasoned that Tuvia Bielski and his Jews would be better off and out of the way if they were based deep in the Naliboki *puszcza*. Tuvia was not particularly happy with the developments of September 1943 — for one thing, they left him without 180 of his armed fighters — but there was little he could do about it. (On the other hand, as Velvke Yonson, a member of Ordzonikidze, suggests in his memoirs, "because of our [sabotage] exploits, Bielski's reputation rises in the district.") This seemingly indifferent attitude exhibited by the Soviets about the fate of the Jewish family camps was the norm. It had been this way with the Russians from the beginning.

The Soviet partisan high command in western Belorussia, which was led by Gen. Vasily Yehimovich Chernyshev, or Platon, as he was known in the forest, more or less supported the existence of the Bielski camp. But young Jewish scouts, whether on rescue or food missions, continually had confrontations with Soviet fighters — even those who belonged to *otriady* such as Iskra, which included many Jews. "You had to have a loaded gun with you at all times," asserts Irving Resnik. "If you were caught on the road somewhere and the Russians could kill you, they would."

On their way to join the Bielski *otriad*, Jewish escapees from Lida were often robbed and beaten by Russian fighters from Iskra. "One could see hatred for Jews in their eyes," recalled Liza Ettinger about an incident after her escape from Lida in September 1943. That day, the Soviets took Ettinger's toothbrush and a matchbox that contained two gold coins she intended to buy weapons with. She was lucky; some fugitives suffered a worse fate. Furthermore, for the duration of the war, some Soviet partisan commanders, according to Nechama Tec, "used the Bielski *otriad* as a dumping ground for Jews that they did not want [as fighters in their detachments]. Anti-Semitism rather than realistic evaluations was often behind these decisions."

At the same time, one of the key reasons for Tuvia Bielski's enduring success as a Jewish commander was his ability to neutralize the Soviet partisan headquarters' opposition to his camp's existence. He had reasoned and charmed Victor Panchenko, and he did the same thing later with General Platon. (Two other partisan generals worked with Platon: General Sokolov, who was a Bielski supporter, and General Dubov, who regarded the family camp as a burden.) No less important, of course, was the fact that Tuvia was astute enough to follow the Soviet officials' orders — even when he did not agree with them, which was often. When he was told by the Russians that Jews from his group were required to participate in dangerous sabotage operations, he willingly complied.

In the end, what finally guaranteed the Bielski camp's survival — and protected Tuvia from the many death threats he regularly received from Soviet partisans — was its self-sufficiency and usefulness. In particular, Platon emerged as one of Tuvia's strongest allies. He was highly impressed with the resourcefulness of the Bielski family camp members and the establishment of its various workshops following the return to the Naliboki Forest in the fall of 1943.

On one visit to the camp, Platon noticed a group of elderly Jewish men praying. When the general asked Bielski about this peculiar activity, Tuvia was reported to have replied: "They are studying the fourth chapter of the history of the communist movement (a chapter written by Stalin about the philosophy of Marxism)." Platon howled with laughter. He departed more committed than ever to defending Tuvia and his camp from criticism and attack.

It was the general, for example, who intervened on Asael Bielski's behalf. During the restructuring of the *otriad* in the fall of 1943, Asael had been appointed head of intelligence of a Soviet partisan brigade. But he was not happy and decided to rejoin the family camp without permission. Such independent action could have led to an execution before a firing squad. Asael and Tuvia immediately discussed the matter with Platon, and a satisfactory compromise was worked out: Asael could remain with his brother and the Jewish families, providing he would join other guerrilla units on sabotage and combat missions. Thus, the matter was resolved without too much trouble.

■ ■

General Platon was right. The Bielski camp in the Naliboki Forest, called Jerusalem, was indeed something to behold. When Liza Ettinger arrived at the Bielski camp with a group of twenty Jews from Lida in September 1943, she was astonished by what she saw. "Although we had heard much about it beforehand, still our first meeting with reality was a surprise for all of us," she recalled. "It all seemed like a fantasy from another world. The same people — flesh and blood — but stronger and freer. A kind of gay abandon filled the air; biting, frank talk spiced with juicy curses; galloping horses and the laughter of children. . . . Suddenly

I saw myself as an extra in a Wild West movie with many participants. I didn't know whether to laugh with everyone or cry alone."

Under the supervision of Tuvia Bielski and his *shtab*, or staff, a viable camp was built. It resembled a forest *shtetl* more than it did a military base. Tuvia's staff included his two brothers, Asael and Zus (when he regularly visited from Ordzonikidze camp); Lazar Malbin, his competent but, according to some survivors, hard-drinking chief of staff; Quartermaster Pesach Friedberg; Solomon Wolkovisky, chief of special operations; and Leibush Ferdman, chief of sabotage.

As more Jews from Lida arrived prior to the liquidation of that ghetto in mid-September 1943, the camp's population soon exceeded a thousand people. Better bunkers were constructed and the *otriad* became more self-reliant. Tailors, locksmiths, bakers, butchers, and leather makers all set up workshops to make bread and sausages, repair guns, and shoe horses. "You went to work, like in a normal town," says Sulia Rubin. "Life was busy but dangerous." The base was so spread out that, decades later, many survivors discovered that they had been living at the Bielski camp at the same time but did not know it.

The camp was a beehive of activity. Most of the young men were kept occupied on *bambioshki*, especially after the camp's population exceeded 500 people. Many survivors, in fact, argue that the work of these brave boys should not be underestimated. "They were not afraid of anything," declares Sonia Bielski, Zus's wife. "People would have died of hunger. Without these people, there would have been no Bielski partisans."

Jerry Seigel, who joined the Bielski *otriad* with his small independent family group in the spring of 1943, recalls participating in many dangerous food expeditions. "The rule was that you were supposed to deposit all food in the camp's general warehouse," he says with a smile. "But occasionally, I might stuff a piece of cheese or salami in my pocket as a treat for the people in my *zemlianka*."

In October 1943, to prepare for the winter, Liza Ettinger and seven other members of the *otriad* were ordered to go to the abandoned potato fields near the burned-down village of Naliboki. There they stayed in a temporary camp for two months gathering the fall crop. The work was back-breaking and risky. "At first we weren't aware at all of the dangers in store for us," she recalled. "The fields were covered with snow and we were to remove it with our bare hands in order to get to the frozen potatoes. But freezing was not the worst danger. The very exposure in open fields was a security threat from the Germans on the one hand and from the [Soviet and Polish] partisan bands on the other. . . . Thus we were thrown into a condition of constant anxiety."

At the main camp, elderly Jews prayed; some even put on *teffilin* (phylacteries) each morning. The celebrations of such festivals and holidays as Chanukah, Purim, Pesach, Rosh Hashana, and Yom Kippur at the Bielski camp and other partisan and family camps were particularly poignant and painful moments, marking the Jews' time as prisoners of the forests. More than anything, these happy but solemn occasions brought with them a flood of reminders of synagogue and family, of good food and wine, of friends and relatives. Praying amid the tall spruce and birch trees, the Jews knew that their lives would never be the same again.

At one family camp deep in the Parczew Forest, for example, the partisans and civilians in the area gathered together for the Kol Nidre service, a solemn and ancient prayer that marks the start of Yom Kippur, the Day of Atonement. "Abram from Zaliszcze had a very thick prayer book which he had somehow saved," remembered Harold Werner, who was present. "The prayer book contained the Hebrew prayers for all the Jewish holidays. We made a big fire. . . . There were about five hundred people around the fire, and Abram started chanting the sad melody of the Kol Nidre. For all of us, it brought to the surface memories of being home with our families and going to synagogue on this sacred night. Everyone was simultaneously crying and praying, while Abram chanted the Kol Nidre. We had lost our families, and none of us could be sure of our future." As was required, the Jews fasted the following day, and Abram recited prayers from the early morning until dusk.

There were other, more practical matters to consider as well. On Tuvia's order, the camp nurses tried to instil proper sanitary conditions, though given the lice problem, it was not an easy task. Still, a Turkish bathhouse was built and using it became mandatory — with soap made from a concoction of ashes and animal fat. Divided into subgroups, the women of the camp prepared food for their particular unit, looked after the sick, and attended to the approximately twenty-five children who grew up in the woods.

Because so many Jewish children died during the war — 1.5 million in total, including many belonging to families in the camp — the youngsters were naturally accorded special treatment. In late 1943, a woman named Czesia appointed herself the children's teacher and storyteller. "There were no paper or pencils," says Gitel Morrison, who was then about twelve years old. "She taught us with her mind." Gitel and her young friends also occupied their time playing make-believe games. "We would pretend we were liberated," adds Gitel, "and that we were wearing beautiful dresses. One of my girlfriends always pretended that she had a large house with a chandelier. After the war, when I visited her in New Jersey in 1951, the first thing I noticed was the big crystal chandelier in her dining room."

Czesia taught the children holiday songs and occasionally they would give performances. When it came time to celebrate Purim, Czesia and the children decided to put on a holiday play. The weather was still bitterly cold, so a stage was built inside one of the camp's workshops. "We watched the children ascending the stage," recalled Shmuel Amarant, the Bielski unit's official historian. "They sang and recited in Yiddish and Russian. They were dressed in white shirts and red ties, their innocent charm lit up the faces of the dancers and gymnasts."

This unique and precious moment was too powerful for some of the people in the audience who had lost their own children. As the children were dancing, Chaya Bielski recalls, a camp member named Yaktowicz, whose family had been killed, stood up and yelled in Yiddish: "'Where are my children? Where are my children? What am I doing here?' He got into such a state that we all began to weep. The party broke up early, each to his own hut."

For other entertainment, Sulia Rubin received Tuvia's permission to organize an adult singing and dancing group, "an amateur hour," as she calls it. Periodically, they would put on performances that Jewish and Soviet partisans would line up to watch. Gradually, there was a normalcy to day-to-day life at the Bielski camp — and yet there was not.

Children may have been playing and adults going to work each day, but no one in the *otriad*, and certainly not the Bielski brothers, ever forgot for one moment why they were living in the forest in the first place.

■ ■

When he was still living full time at the camp before the *oblava*, Zus Bielski was in charge of reconnaissance; his scouts were ever vigilant and maintained contact with local peasants to keep track of German movements. Regular guard duty was established for everyone capable of doing it, men and women, young or old. During the winter of 1943–44, members of the camp were also assigned to guard duty at a small Soviet partisan airstrip that had been built in the woods, about a day's walk from the Bielski base. As the course of the war changed in favour of the Allies, more and more planes made the trip, bringing much-needed food and medical supplies from the other side of the front line.

Sometimes, however, there were complaints about assignments. "If you told a Jew to go and stand guard," says Sulia Rubin, "he would say, 'Why me? Why not him?'" Harmless griping (or *kvetching*, in Yiddish) of this sort seems to have been rampant in the camp. The constant tension under which the partisans lived led to foolish arguments and whining about duties and responsibilities.

From almost the beginning, Tuvia had insisted on strict military-like discipline. When he gave an order, he expected it to be followed. As in Soviet detachments, failure to obey had dire consequences. "These were not times for weaklings," Sulia Rubin rightly observes, and Tuvia could be tough when he had to be. Though Bielski usually considered the views of others and often sought advice, the Bielski camp was not a democracy. The commander's authority was sacrosanct, and in disputes his word was final.

One result of this was the development of a distinct hierarchy that did not sit well (then or now) with some members of the camp. People were classified by their contributions to the *otriad*, and those that risked their lives on food and sabotage missions were naturally accorded more respect than those who sat waiting for the war to be over. People in this latter group were known as the *malbushim*, the Hebrew word for clothes — the reference probably insinuating that these unproductive

Ben Lungen (right) in his partisan uniform in Munich, Germany, in August 1945, with his friend Max Banschick, a Red Army soldier. Both have medals awarded to them by the Soviets for bravery. — *Courtesy of Ben Lungen*

Jack and Rochelle Sutin, September 1944, after liberation. They are survivors of the Zorin family camp in the Naliboki forest. — *Courtesy of Jack and Rochelle Sutin*

A gathering in Germany in fall 1945 of the Belorussian town of Rubjevich. Nearly all of the partisans survived by hiding in family camps. Top row, far right, is Ben Lungen, and second row right, second from left, is his brother, David Lungen. Asher Lungen, Ben and David's father, is bottom row left, seated on the far right. The sign in Hebrew translates as: "In Memory of the souls of our parents, brothers, sisters, wives, and small children who numbered 700 people, that were killed and slaughtered in God's name and the nation at the hands of Hitler and his defiled collaborators — their names should disappear! In the city of Rubjevich, June 24, 1942." — *Courtesy of Ben Lungen*

Gitel Zelkowicz (Morrison) with her mother, Leska, and her brother Simon, Munich 1947. — *Courtesy of Gitel Morrison*

Gitel Zelkowicz (Morrison) with her father, Lazer, and her brother Simon in Munich in 1947. — *Courtesy of Gitel Morrison*

A partisan reunion in Florida in the late 1970s. Left to right: Morris Morrison, Tuvia Bielski (about 72 years old), Lilka Bielski, and Gitel Morrison. — *Courtesy of Gitel Morrison*

Peter Silverman in Zebrus in July 1997, at a partisan safehouse on the edge of the Koziany forest. — *Courtesy of Peter Silverman*

Peter Silverman and Dave Smuschkowitz at the Minsk Museum of Partisans and World War II Soldiers in July 1997. The weapons behind them are the same kind they used as young partisans. — *Peter Silverman*

Peter Silverman in Jody, Poland, in July 1997 at the Monument for Murdered Jews. — *Courtesy of Peter Silverman*

In the Parczew Forest in Poland in 1996, where Chil Grynszpan's unit fought in the Second World War. The trees are the only witnesses that remain. — *Author's photo*

individuals were like clothes hanging in a closet.

Some of the elderly men and younger men and women who were regarded as *malbushim* did not have many options. "I was eighteen years old in the forest," says Leah Johnson. "Who cares if they called me a *malbush*? I do not feel bad about anything I did or did not do." The members of the Jewish intelligentsia who made it to the woods, especially those who could not adapt into fighting partisans from being teachers and lawyers, often had the most difficulties on a day-to-day basis. From being high atop the social ladder before the war, they suddenly found themselves relegated to the bottom. (People have long memories. Ask most Bielski survivors today, and they are still quick to point out who was a *malbush* and who was not.)

Most members of the *otriad* understood that this top-down structure was essential for the survival of the group. Still, these divisions occasionally led to disagreements and resentment, usually over food and shelter. The members of the command staff and their wives often ate better food than the rest of the camp's population. For a brief time, after the camp had been reorganized in the Naliboki, the *shtab* even had their own kitchen, which split the camp further. As Zus Bielski's wife, Sonia, explains, "When I was with my husband I was afraid of nothing at all. He gave me a gun for protection. I had a good life in the forest. He gave me everything. I did not cook. I was the commander's wife."

Liza Ettinger has a slightly different view. "Clearly there were members of the 'privileged' group who were close to the 'powers that be'. There were social repercussions, but who paid attention to them? People simply adopted the slogan — 'the more one can enjoy himself — the better.' Many things were repulsive to me, especially the shaken human relations. The few of my friends that were left wore a countenance of alienation, and debauchery had its victory. I do not blame, judge or criticize; I simply describe the scene. Today I am not sure whether this behavior wasn't right at the time."

Still, Ettinger concedes, "not all went smoothly. Neither Tuvia's kind heart nor his brothers' courage [was] enough to navigate such a large ship. The constant conditions of pressure often demanded quick solutions that were not always thought out to the end."

When Tuvia was confronted with resistance to his leadership, his first instinct was to fight back. He tolerated much, but would not accept challenges to his authority. For troublemakers, those who took food without permission or were guilty of other minor infractions, there was a *zemlianka* set aside as a *kartzer*, a small prison. The more serious the transgression, the more severe the punishment. In October 1942, for instance, when the *otriad* was much smaller and not yet in the Naliboki Forest, a dozen members (including Quartermaster Pesach Friedberg) attempted to thwart Tuvia's control and become more independent. When he refused to permit this, harsh words were exchanged, tempers flared, and guns were pointed. The end result was that these individuals lost their weapons and were banished from the camp on the threat of death. Only some last-minute pleading by the entire *otriad* reversed the commander's decision, and the episode was resolved more or less amicably.

A year later, in the aftermath of the Nazi blockade, Zus Bielski became embroiled in a heated argument with a partisan named Kaplan. The man had made some unfounded accusations about Tuvia stealing gold from members of the *otriad*, and was guilty himself of being cruel to a woman and her child assigned to his subgroup. Zus shouted at Kaplan, and Kaplan shouted back. This only enraged Zus further and, without thinking, he drew his gun. His brother Asael yelled at him to stop, but Zus ignored him. Kaplan ran and the gun went off. Kaplan dropped. He was dead. "Right away," writes Nechama Tec, "Zus regretted what he had done. Over the years the regret turned to guilt and refused to go away."

Tuvia, too, was known to lose his temper. Ike Bernstein remembers one occasion when he returned from a *bambioshka* tired and needing sleep. But as soon as he laid down on his *zemlianka* bunk, he was told that he had a guard-duty assignment, not something he usually did. He ignored the order and went to sleep. The next morning, Tuvia was told what had transpired and he was angry. He saw Bernstein and began reprimanding him. Moments later, Tuvia was pointing his gun directly at him. Bernstein froze, but before anything more serious occurred, Bernstein's friend and Tuvia's brother-in-law pushed Bielski's weapon to the ground. The clash was over. Both men walked away.

Such incidents were caused by stress, high emotions, and bad tempers. Who would have expected anything different, given the situation? Yet the case of Israel Kesler was much more complex and controversial. Even today, survivors become excited and agitated when speaking about Kesler and what occurred so many years ago in the woods.

A Jew from the town of Naliboki, Kesler, who was about thirty-five years old in 1942, was a bit of a rogue before the war. In and out of Polish prisons, he earned a reputation as a petty thief and a troublemaker. When his wife and children were killed in the first days of the Nazi assault, he fled to the forest. There, he met other Jews on the run, including a young and beautiful woman named Rachel, who became his wife. He soon obtained weapons from local peasants and formed his own partisan unit. By all accounts, Kesler was a competent commander who enjoyed both the power and the prestige his new position brought him. The twenty fighters under him, according to Ike Bernstein, were an "iron group," though they were initially more interested in surviving than confronting Nazis.

Tuvia Bielski first learned of the Kesler group from Victor Panchenko in the fall of 1942. The local peasants had complained to the Russian partisan leader about some Jews "who robbed by night and did nothing during the day." According to Panchenko, they were hiding on a farm in a nearby village. He wanted Bielski to deal with them — or he would.

Tuvia took twenty men with him and they found the farm. At first, Kesler did not acknowledge them, but finally he and his fighters emerged from their hiding places. Bielski recognized several of them. After the two groups shared a meal, Tuvia invited Kesler and his partisans to join his *otriad* (though, as Bielski later conceded, it was more of an order than a cordial invitation). When Kesler hesitated, Bielski became angry. "Then they saw that I wasn't joking, and that I wouldn't change my mind," Tuvia recalled. "They yielded."

During the next year, Kesler became a useful member of the Bielski *otriad*, doing whatever had to be done. Tuvia, among others, forgot about his dubious past and respected his leadership qualities. It's unclear whether Kesler was satisfied with taking a back seat to the

Bielski brothers, but he did demonstrate that he was nearly as committed as Tuvia was to rescuing Jews and keeping them alive for the duration of the war.

When the Nazi hunt of August 1943 ended, Tuvia permitted Kesler and about fifty others to remain in the Naliboki Forest and not accompany the rest of the group to the Jasinowo woods. By the time the "civilian" portion of the Bielski *otriad* was forced to return to the Naliboki, just a month or so later, Kesler's group, which now numbered 150 Jews, had already established a viable and more permanent base. Under Soviet partisan command orders, Kesler's people automatically fell under Bielski's control, though Tuvia allowed Kesler a certain degree of autonomy. Kesler remained commander of his camp, which was located about 2 kilometres from the new Bielski base, with all the responsibilities that entailed.

At some point, Kesler became dissatisfied with the hold Bielski had over him, particularly when it came to dealing with Soviet headquarters. Whether he was motivated by a desire for more power or simply wanted to be totally separate from Bielski is unknown. Behind Tuvia's back, however, Kesler started speaking critically about him with General Dubov, who had never been a fan of the Bielski brothers. According to Nechama Tec, Kesler attempted to bribe Dubov with "gifts of jewelry," lobbied him to support his push to be separated permanently from the Bielski detachment, and worst of all, claimed with no evidence that Tuvia had absconded with gold and money taken from the local population and meant for the Soviet partisan treasury.

When Tuvia learned of Kesler's unfounded charges from General Platon, he was naturally upset. Platon was easily convinced of Bielski's innocence, however, and decided that the size of his camp's population should not be altered further. Undeterred, Kesler continued his campaign for his own detachment. One day, Sulia Rubin remembers, her brother-in-law Izaak "came with news that some people from [Kesler's] group stopped him with a petition. Some names were signed already. The petition was to the Central Partisan Movement for a separate company and cited reasons. . . . It was a typical case of 'ratting' to anti-Semites who were looking only for a reason to disperse us."

Izaak took the petition to Tuvia, whose patience had finally run out. Kesler was promptly arrested and put in the camp's prison. He was tried in a closed trial by Bielski and his staff, and was sentenced to death. The execution was carried out by Asael Bielski before anyone in the *otriad* could object.

The death of Kesler left its mark on the camp community, though most members stood behind their commander's decision. This event, observed Liza Ettinger, "that shocked us at the time and left a scar, can perhaps be understood if judged at a later time. It is possible that this was a necessity under those special circumstances." This seems to be the assessment of many Bielski survivors. The execution, writes Sulia Rubin, was "horrible." She recalls Kesler's wife, Rachel, crying near the *zemlianka* where her husband was being held. Still, adds Sulia, "I don't question that [the execution] was necessary, since [Kesler] was a danger to our survival." Many years later, Tuvia, too, justified the shooting as "a choice between the death of the *otriad* or Kesler's death."

For their part, the Soviet leaders were not particularly happy with Bielski's actions. But while General Dubov shouted and screamed about it, General Platon supported both Tuvia and the verdict of his staff. Soon, the Russians had more pressing matters to worry about.

"HE DANCES LIKE A [COSSACK] AND SINGS YIDDISH LIKE A HASID"

Less than 10 kilometres away from the Bielski Naliboki camp, approximately 800 Jews, mostly fugitives from Minsk and surrounding villages, lived a similar existence. They owed their lives to the resourcefulness and courage of Shalom Zorin, a forty-one-year-old Jewish carpenter from Minsk.

Born in the Belorussian city in 1902, Zorin lived a relatively quiet life with his wife and children until June 1941. As a loyal Communist and a supporter of the Bolshevik Revolution, he had spent three years fighting as a partisan during the Russian Civil War. But he never abandoned his Jewish roots. Watching him celebrate the liberation in the summer of 1944, Shmuel Geler, a partisan, aptly remarked, "A strange man, this Zorin, he dances like a [Cossack] and sings Yiddish like a Hasid."

At first, Zorin followed the Nazis' orders and relocated to the Minsk ghetto in late July 1941. He used his skills as a carpenter to stay alive, often working in the nearby POW camp, home to thousands of starving captured Red Army soldiers. There he met Seymon Ganzenko, a Soviet officer.

On November 7, the first of several major *Aktionen* took place. That day, 12,000 Minsk Jews were slaughtered, including Zorin's wife and children. As was the case with many partisans, this devastating event propelled Zorin into action. Accompanied by Ganzenko, who had escaped from the prisoner-of-war camp, he fled to the forest area 30 kilometres south-west of the city. There the two men were instrumental in organizing the Parkhomenko *otriad*, which eventually grew to 150 fighters and included both Soviets and Jews.

Relations between Zorin and Ganzenko were good until more and more escaped Jews arrived in the forest. Ganzenko, like other Soviets, was not interested in saving unarmed Jewish fugitives. Zorin, for his part, refused to turn them away. Like Tuvia Bielski, he considered the rescue of Jews a higher priority than seeking revenge and combating Nazis.

Soon, heated arguments broke out between Soviet and Jewish partisans. According to Jacob Greenstein, Zorin decided to take matters into his own hands. One night, he took a machine gun and a few rifles, gathered together some Jewish fighters, and decided to establish a family camp. When Ganzenko learned what had happened, he arrested Zorin and sentenced him to death. Only the intervention of Maj. Polkovnik Vasilievitsh, the commander of the Zhukov Brigade and a friend to many Jewish fighters, saved Zorin. The entire matter was brought before General Platon, who ordered that Zorin be allowed to organize Unit 106, a civilian camp that was to be located deep in the Naliboki Forest. By the spring of 1942, the camp began to take shape. Its initial population of about sixty Jews had only fifteen guns.

Zorin contacted the Minsk underground, and guides (many of whom were children and teenagers) were sent to bring Jews, including women and children, out to the forest. Though many perished along the way, the *otriad* gradually grew. By the summer of 1943, there were probably 300 to 350 Jews living there.

News of the establishment of Unit 106, or the Zorin *otriad*, as it was usually called, also reached Jews in nearby villages. Hiding on a farm with his father and cousin, David Lungen, Ben's brother, then fifteen years old, was brought to the camp with about thirty others. In June 1943, Jack Sutin, who was still in charge of a small camp in the woods near Mir, happened to encounter one of Zorin's young fighters out on a reconnaissance mission. He invited Sutin and his group to visit the Zorin camp and remain there if they wished. The long walk into the Naliboki bush took two days. Impressed by both the security and the living conditions Zorin offered, the Sutin group decided to stay.

■ ■

Zorin was tall, handsome, and strong. He rode through the camp on a striking palomino horse, accompanied by the beautiful twenty-year-old Russian woman he had selected to be his new wife. The two were, in Rochelle Sutin's words, the "royal couple." As was the case with the Bielski *otriad*, Zorin's camp was hierarchical in structure and everyone had his place. Zorin was clearly the commander and his wife "the queen." Adds Sutin, "They would ride by and we would wave and smile. We knew that our lives depended upon them. Zorin was a good commander and he took care to save the lives of as many Jews as he could. But *his* way was the way things went, and his woman had great power as well." If any fine clothes or goods were brought back from food- and supply-gathering missions, she usually got them.

Anatoly Wertheim, a Jew from western Poland who had escaped with his family to Stolpce in 1939, served as Zorin's chief of staff for most of the war. It was his job to ensure that the camp was secure and ran smoothly. The base was surrounded by six guard posts and everyone, including teenagers like David Lungen, took his turn at four- to six-hour guard-duty shifts. Anyone approaching the camp who could not give the required password was shot at — no questions asked. Wertheim also assigned individuals to food, supply, and sabotage missions (the last were usually joint operations with Soviet units). No one refused a direct order. "When they told you to go out on a food raid, you went no matter how you felt about it," comments Jack Sutin. "It was a very regimented form of life compared to the small group structures we were used to."

To keep the peace with the sceptical Soviets in the area, who often accused the Jews of stealing food from the peasants, Zorin transformed his camp into a viable service depot, as Bielski had done. There were workshops for all tradesmen: cobblers, blacksmiths, and carpenters. A sausage factory and bakery prepared forest delicacies, and Dr. Epstein, with a minimum of medical supplies, ran a small hospital.

For Jacob Greenstein, a Parkhomenko partisan, the most vivid memory of the Zorin camp was of the orphaned children. By 1944, there were about seventy youngsters "whose needs were tended twenty-four hours a day." Even a Soviet partisan official like Vladimir Tsaryuk was, according to Hersh Smolar, "moved to tears when he saw the young children in the camp. He proposed that we send a company of partisans to his region to collect food from the local peasants and bring it back for the Zorin [detachment]." A school was organized for the children, and they celebrated Soviet and Jewish holidays with plays and games.

But, at least in one case, a child who violated a command ruling paid the supreme penalty. With Nazis swarming the area, Zorin had given orders that no one leave the base. One hungry young boy, eleven or twelve years old, went blueberry-picking. When he returned, both Zorin and Wertheim confronted him. They were angry because the boy could have been caught or followed, and thereby endangered the lives of the entire group. They decided that he was a liability. From a short distance away, Rochelle Sutin watched what happened next. "They took the boy out to the bushes and shot him," she says. "If he had parents, maybe they would not have done it. It was terrible — a terrible demonstration of their power."

As it had been for the Bielskis, the worst period for the Zorin camp was the Nazi blockade of August 1943. On the commander's order, the bunkers and workshops were abandoned. At first, everyone ran in the same direction. Immediately, Rochelle Sutin, for one, realized that this was a mistake. The "beaten path of grass" the Jews left in their wake would be easy to follow, and the Germans would quickly find them. The five in her group, including her husband, Jack, and his father, Julius, decided to run in another direction. "Soon we went off to the right, straight into a thick and heavy part of the swamp," relates Rochelle. "Very quickly the water came up to our chins. We stood in it and remained as still as we could. We had to hold onto each other, in a kind of human chain, to keep ourselves from slipping or sinking."

With the Germans close by, the Sutins were forced to remain in the swamps for nearly two days. All the while, leeches attacked their faces and bodies. Finally, when the gunfire grew more distant, they were able to emerge from the filthy water. "Our feet looked like elephant feet. Our clothing stank from mud and rot. We couldn't stand ourselves," remembers Rochelle.

Lack of food became a serious issue for the Sutins' group, as it did for other Jews hiding in the Naliboki swamps. They, too, ate rotting meat from the carcass of a dead horse, and subsisted on mushrooms and berries. One day, they were able to kill a rabbit and found a dead chicken. With some potatoes and beets gathered from nearby fields, Rochelle cooked a chicken soup.

By the end of August, survivors of the Zorin *otriad* had regrouped at their original base. Miraculously, it remained as they had left it; the Nazis had not discovered it. With Zorin and his staff in charge again, the camp prepared for the coming winter — the last they would have to spend in the *puszcza*.

SABOTAGE

Suddenly there was a great roar and a crescendo of crashing metal as the cars began to slam into each other. . . . The giant locomotive was lying on its side like a wounded monster, emitting torrents of steam. . . . I heard shots in the rear. There were German soldiers firing at our men, who were trading shot for shot. The two oil tanks lay directly opposite the depot. "Blow them up!" I shouted to Dvoretzki as I ran past him, along the side of the cars, for cover. . . .
— Sam "Mietek" Gruber

The Work of the *Podrivniki*

Fittingly, the mine, a charge of 12 kilograms of TNT, was placed on a railway track on the outskirts of Swieciany, near the death pit close to the Polygon, where thousands of Jews had perished. Painful thoughts about this slaughter, which claimed his seventy-five-year-old grandmother, and his four-year-old cousin, went through Yitzhak Arad's head as he participated in his first of many sabotage missions.

It was spring 1943. Known in the forest as Tolka, seventeen-year-old Arad was a new recruit of the Vilnius Unit, a small Soviet-Lithuanian *otriad* that was attached to the Djalgiris Brigade. He had been assigned to a sabotage team made up of four other partisans. Their target was a train delivering German troops and supplies to the north-east front lines. It was not going to finish its run.

It took the group a day to reach their destination. They travelled through the Cerkliszki Forest and rested until dark at the hut belonging to a Lithuanian forester they knew and trusted. As soon as it was dark, they approached the rail line and carefully laid the mine under the track and between two ties that were located on a high embankment. Once the engine triggered the charge by passing over the sensitive pressure-detonator, the rest of the train would be derailed. "When a train is blown up on a raised embankment," Arad points out, "the cars plunge down the side, vastly increasing the injury to enemy personnel and damage to equipment."

This was precisely what occurred. Once the mine was set, Arad and his comrades scampered back into the forest. They could hear a German patrol that was also in the vicinity. The train chugged closer. "We paused on a slight rise in the ground and waited," he remembered. "Momentarily it seemed to me that the train had passed the mine without setting it off. Doubt assailed me. Was the mine or the detonating mechanism defective? Had the effort and risk been in vain? Perhaps . . . and just then a great flash illuminated the entire Polygon area, followed by a tremendous explosion. We heard the sound of cars colliding and then falling, and a number of shots were fired. The patrol was apparently shooting in the direction of the forest. We were ecstatic. This was the first train we had derailed. The Polygon was having its revenge on the Germans."

■ ■

Rarely a week went by in 1943 and the first six months of 1944 without a partisan sabotage action taking place somewhere in eastern Poland, Belorussia, and the Baltics. (Officially, the three Baltic states and the western part of Belorussia were known as the Reichskommissariat Ostland. The southern administrative area of the Nazi-occupied Soviet Union was the Reichskommissariat Ukraine.) And most, like the operation Yitzhak Arad took part in, were aimed at destroying railways in an attempt to halt the movement of Nazi troops and supplies to the front lines. Partisan sabotage activities were also directed at other modes and means of transportation — trucks, roads, and bridges — as well as at German communication systems, mainly telephone poles and wires. In other words, anything that wreaked a bit of havoc on the enemy — the more Nazis killed the better — was pursued to the limit.

■ ■

The roads and highways of the Soviet Union never had been adequate, and after two years of war, they were in such terrible condition that relying on them had become risky. In spots, the concrete or asphalt had turned to rubble, and during rainstorms, the mud made some roads impassable. The only practical military solution for the Germans was a near-total reliance on trains. But in their rush to conquer the east, the Nazis had not bothered to take the time to adapt their own engines for Russia's severe winter temperatures. The result was a lot of breakdowns at a time when the delivery of supplies to the front was paramount. On these occasions, any partisan sabotage of the Soviet railway network could seriously hinder the German war effort.

In February 1943, central partisan command in Moscow attempted to introduce some much-needed order into behind-the-line sabotage operations by providing brigade leaders with specific targets and detailed instructions on how to successfully accomplish each mission — right down to the number of men required for the job and where to plant the explosives.

Even before central command gave the order, however, partisan leaders kept their fighters busy. In the Bryansk area, for instance, from May 1942 to April 1943, there were a total of 1,019 railway sabotage actions, or approximately 85 per month. More than half were success-ful, though just how much actual disruption they caused to Nazi operations is not known. The fighters may not, in fact, have had much of an impact on the war at the front, but they certainly did give the Germans something to worry about. More security forces were added and more time was allocated to stopping the partisans — time and effort that, from the German point of view, could have been better utilized winning the battle against the Red Army.

"In 1942, our demolition operations were as yet weak; we were just learning," partisan commander Aleksei Fyodorov noted. "It was a different matter in 1943 and 1944, when we began working according to a schedule and derailed as many as ten trains in one day." Moreover, Fyodorov adds, one notable consequence of these night-time raids was that the Germans were forced "to cancel night traffic and reduce the daytime schedule to eight and at the most ten trains."

As the war in the east turned against Hitler in 1943, and Red Army pilots were able to fly more easily over enemy territory, the partisans' supply of explosives increased and so did the number of demolitions. In Belorussia, German security forces reported 626 attacks in April, and 841 by June. Later in the year, the increased partisan activity was reflected in Nazi reports for the Ostland region. During a two-week period in November 1943, from the thirteenth to the twenty-eighth, the partisans destroyed approximately 110,000 kilometres of track — from Tallinn in Estonia to Minsk in Belorussia and everywhere in between.

This excerpt from the operations diary of a Jewish partisan unit in the Rudniki Forest describes a typical workload during 1943 and 1944 (in total, thirty-nine operations are listed between October 7, 1943, and August 7, 1944):

1. October 7, 1943: "Destruction of telegraph link along the Grodno-Vilna road in the section between Pirciupie and Tetiance. More than 50 telegraph poles were sawn through, the wires were cut and the insulators broken [35 fighters participated, led by Yitzhak Czuzoj and Aron Aronowicz]."

5. October 29, 1943: "Sabotage operation in the city of Vilna: Four transformers and a mechanical water conveyor were destroyed with the aid of English mines [4 fighters participated, commander not listed]."

14. December 31, 1943: "A train was blown up on the railroad from Vilna to Grodno, near Landwarow station. The engine and twenty-one cars carrying troops were derailed. The train had

been on its way from Warsaw to Vilna [6 partisans participated, led by Abba Kovner]."

28. May 10, 1944: "Ambush on the Grodno road in the section between Pirciupie and Zygmunciszki. Two units, 'Avenger' and 'To Victory,' took part. Eleven Germans were killed. Booty captured: 6 rifles, 4 hand-grenades, throwers, and 2 'Degtyarov' machine guns [3 partisans participated, led by Elhanan Magid]."

38. April 7, 1944: "Trains blown up on the Vilna-Lida railroad line. One engine and cars carrying men and supplies were derailed [30 partisans participated, led by Shlomo Brand]."

One of the more successful assaults occurred late in the night of March 7, 1943, when about 600 Soviet (and presumably some Jewish) partisans destroyed a railway bridge crossing the Desna River on the line between Gomel and Bryansk. For several days afterwards, supplies meant for the second Panzer division were disrupted at the precise moment when the German army was preparing to launch a major offensive on Kursk. Still, it must be admitted that such successful partisan actions were more of an aggravation for the Germans than an impediment to their war efforts. The Kursk offensive, for example, was not delayed as a result of the attack on the Desna River bridge. In short, the partisans hurt the German army, but as one historian put it, "the damage was never decisive."

Far from the front, of course, the partisans had no idea what the actual impact of their missions were. And even had they known, it would have made little difference. Their chief objective, as noted, was to disrupt, hinder, distract, and if possible, destroy the enemy. Each blown-up train, each demolished telephone pole, and each dead Nazi soldier was as much a moral victory for the fighters as a military one. As they stood on the edge of the woods watching the demolition of a German train, few Soviet or Jewish partisans stopped to ask themselves whether this particular action made a major contribution to the war effort. At that glorious moment, they didn't care.

■ ■

If you didn't know better, you would have thought it was a yellow bar of soap. The Russian word for it was *tol*. It was as hard as soft wood but could be shaped. (It also tasted terrible, as Peter Silverman discovered when he accidently put some *tol* in the same pouch as a chunk of bread. Hungry, he still ate the bread and is amazed to this day that he did not become ill.) *Tol* could be thrown into a fire, shot at, and tossed around, and nothing would happen. But properly detonated and placed in the right spot, *tol* could destroy a train engine and blow up a bridge.

A type of high explosive similar to plastic (pronounced *plas-tique*), *tol* was essentially a piece of trinitrotoluene, or TNT. It was also the partisans' explosive of choice. Soviet explosives experts were routinely parachuted into the forests behind the lines so that they could conduct training seminars on demolition. As Peter Silverman recalls, there were two simple rules that he was taught to follow: First, the *tol* had to be kept out of the hot sun, which weakened its chemical composition; and second, it was mandatory on missions that one man carry the *tol* and another the small detonating device. Soon, many young Jewish men and boys were recognized explosives experts called *podrivniki*, or dyna-miters. It was a job that required, Jack Sutin says, "great skill and nerve." More than one Jewish partisan died laying a mine, from either a prema-ture detonation or, more often, a Nazi ambush.

At first the *tol* was simply placed beside the rail, but once the Germans caught on to the partisans' strategy, it had to be carefully buried under the ties. A small pencil-size hole was then cut into the *tol* and the detonator, pure dynamite, inserted. Often, the detonator itself, about the size of a small cassette recorder, was set off manually. Fighters hiding perhaps 300 metres away pulled, lit, or ignited (using a battery-powered circuit) a special detonator cord. Alternatively, and less risky for the demolition team, the detonator could be activated by a spring mechanism. The train engine would pass over the spring, setting off the detonator, which in turn activated the charge.

In the last year of the war, the British supplied their Soviet allies with more efficient magnetic mines with timer mechanisms, which were utilized successfully in sabotage missions. "They looked like cigar boxes with a pencil-like timing mechanism sticking out the top," remembers

Leon Kahn. "By turning this device the required number of times, we could make the bombs detonate two to ten hours later. . . . They worked like a charm."

"VICTORY WILL GO TO THE STRONG, AND STRENGTH IS ON OUR SIDE"

The war in the east was supposed to have been over by Christmas, 1941. So confident were Hitler and his Nazi commanders of an easy victory in the Soviet Union that they did not anticipate or properly plan for trouble from a rear guerrilla army — let alone a three-year war of sabotage and surprise attacks by partisans. Then, to compound the miscalculation further, the Führer, paranoid and distrustful to the end, refused to permit the army to take charge of the anti-partisan fight.

On a day-to-day basis, combating the partisans was generally the responsibility of the Ordnungspolizei, or Order Police. Although they were assisted by local police units (and were answerable to the Higher SS and Police Leaders who, in turn, were answerable to Himmler), over-all strategy was shared between various Nazi civil, military, and police organizations. These included the Reichskommissariat, under Alfred Rosenberg, Reich minister for the occupied territories of the Soviet Union; the Oberkommando der Wehrmacht (OKW), or Armed Forces High Command, under Wilhelm Keitel; the Oberkommando des Heeres (OKH), or Army High Command, in theory subservient to the OKW; and finally, the SS and police forces.

During the many large blockades undertaken to rid the forests of partisans, cooperation and joint actions between these factions was possible. Yet, given their divergent priorities — the generals were naturally concerned more with military success, the SS with security and racial issues and the spreading of Nazi doctrine — relations between them were often characterized by petty disputes and power struggles.

In particular, the brutality and terror inflicted on the local population by the SS and, to a certain extent, the Wehrmacht pushed the peasants closer to the partisans than they needed or probably wanted to be, considering their general antagonism to Communism. Taken together, the Nazi infighting, the lack of centralized control in dealing with the partisans, the huge geographic area they were attempting to conquer (about 2.6 million square kilometres), and the harsh rule of the occupation all undermined the Nazi goals and allowed the Soviet and Jewish fighters to continue their battle until the Red Army arrived. In short, the partisans may not have been able to single-handedly stop the German onslaught, but neither could the Nazis defeat the "gangs," "robberbands," and *banditen*, as they referred to them — no matter how hard they tried.*

■ ■

The Nazi high command's first reaction when faced with the nascent partisan movement in the fall of 1941 was to strike back, and with their usual brand of ruthlessness. "The Führer has now given orders that we take action everywhere with the most drastic means in order to crush the movement in the shortest possible time," an OKW directive of September 16 declared. "In this connection it should be remembered that a human life in unsettled countries frequently counts for nothing, and a deterrent effect can be attained only by unusual severity. The death penalty for fifty to one hundred Communists should generally be regarded in these cases as suitable atonement for one German soldier's life."

Hence, a vicious cruelty and an attempt to match the partisans' mobility and resourcefulness defined the Nazis' early anti-partisan strategy. In quick order, they organized small, partisan-like commando groups, the Jagdkommando, whose task it was to guard trains and attempt to infiltrate the forests. They also recruited local informers — the Vertrauensleute, or V-men — who served them very well as spies. These collaborators provided the Germans with valuable intelligence,

---

*The fight with the partisans remained a thorn in the side of Nazi officials in Berlin, though as historian Matthew Cooper argues, they may have "exaggerated the threat." On March 6, 1942, Hitler's chief of Propaganda, Joseph Goebbels, wrote in his diary, "The partisans are in command of large areas of unoccupied Russia, and are conducting a regime of terror there." Ten days later, he added, "The activity of the partisans has increased noticeably in recent weeks. They are conducting a well-organized guerrilla war. It is very difficult to get at them because they are using such terrorist methods in the areas we occupy that the population is afraid of collaborating with us loyally any longer." (See Cooper, *Nazi War against Soviet Partisans*, 78.)

often infiltrating partisan camps and then leading the Nazi police right to their unsuspecting prey.

Indeed, from the beginning, the Nazi intelligence was superb. Their eyes and ears were everywhere, and it seemed as if there was nothing they did not know. Through the work of the V-men, intercepted radio messages, and information obtained by interrogation and torture of captured fighters, they knew their opponents' names, ages, camp locations, weapon strength, and even the type of explosives they used for sabotage operations.

This Nazi thoroughness was evident in Kommando Order #42, a concise November 18, 1941, memorandum from Himmler to his Higher SS and Police Leader representatives and also distributed to district police officials. Entitled "Concerning the Fight against the Partisans," it contained detailed and accurate information about the Soviet partisan movement's size, training methods, leadership structure, and goals. For help in identifying the guerrillas, the memorandum was even more specific: "All persons with very short haircuts and who are not in the territory stated on their identification papers are suspicious. These are typical of members of the Red Army. . . . Beware also of people who are in the correct territory who characterize themselves as 'workers'. This often concerns itself with high party functionaries who have camouflaged themselves among the population of the occupied territories. Women and children are to be paid the utmost attention, as they often serve as carriers of military information; they are also responsible for the assignment of providing communication between individual partisans units, such as the timely transmission of current and planned opposition actions."

Few questioned or disagreed with Himmler's call for vigilant action against the Soviet guerrillas — captured partisans were routinely interrogated and then shot or hanged — but there was some discussion among the military and the police regarding the treatment of the local population. Any impulse, however, towards leniency or compassion, even on the grounds that it would encourage local support of the Nazi regime, was quickly dismissed. When a report from the OKW propaganda section suggested that "force, brutality, looting and deception should be avoided to win over the population," Gen. Alfred Jodl scribbled in the margin: "These are dangerous signs of despicable humanitarianism."

Thus fear, not understanding, was to characterize the Nazis' fight with both the partisans and those who aided them. The guidelines issued by the Higher SS and Police Leader's office in Riga in September 1941 put it like this: "Each inhabitant must be clear that through acts of sabotage, through abetting, through unauthorized possession of weapons, through housing or supporting enemy partisans, they forfeit their lives." Keeping, too, with their policy of collective responsibility, which had been employed so ruthlessly in the ghettos, the Nazis made the local peasants pay dearly following a successful partisan mission in their area. In the Ukraine, for example, as punishment for partisan sabotage actions, civilians were routinely hanged on telephone poles beside rail sidings. Nazi reports from Kiev in late 1941 also note that hundreds of locals were shot following "acts of sabotage."

Any action, whether it was burning a village to the ground or murdering women and children in front of the husbands and fathers, was deemed appropriate in anti-partisan directives. This was the way Hitler wanted it. He took the fight with the partisans seriously, regarding it as a struggle much like the "struggle in North America against the Red Indians." And as had been the case with the Indian wars in the United States, the eventual outcome was never in doubt. "Victory will go to the strong," Hitler declared in August 1942, "and strength is on our side."

Months later, in December 1942, the Führer's patience with the partisan problem had run out. Through his OKW commander, General Keitel, Hitler issued the following order, which more or less defined the Nazi battle against the partisan "bandits" for the duration of the war: "If the repression of the guerrillas in the East, as well as in the Balkans, is not pursued with the most brutal means, it will not be long before the forces at our disposal will prove insufficient to exterminate this plague. The troops therefore have the right and the duty to use, in this struggle, any and unlimited means even against women and children, if only conducive to success. . . . Scruples of any sort whatsoever are a crime against the German people and against the front-line soldier who bears the consequences of attacks by guerrillas and who [cannot understand why] any regard [should be] shown to [them] or their associates."

"FIGHTING THE BANDITS"

Methodically, the Nazis tracked the partisans' every move. They prepared their troops with simulated training exercises that included maps and information on weapons and tactics, and taught them how to evaluate and anticipate partisan actions. They catalogued operations on trains and maintained daily reports on each and every village the resisters occupied. They researched and wrote extensive booklets on the partisans, summarizing the movement's history, strength, and objectives. "The goal of these partisans," one such survey noted, "is the creation of their own front line. Along these lines, they will sabotage *Wehrmacht* material transports, attack Ukrainian auxiliary police, do away with mayors who are friendly to the German cause or perpetuate acts of terror on the civilian population dressed in German uniforms." The Nazis even employed some elementary psychology. An order from Himmler at the end of July 1942 banned the use of the word "partisan" (*partisanen*) in official documents; thereafter, the fighters were to be referred to as "bandits," "robberbands," "terrorists," and "criminals."

In spite of these various efforts, however, they were unable to stop the guerrilla war and they grew frustrated — a frustration that produced more widespread terror and unspeakable violence. (The Nazis' distorted logic, of course, always surmised that such harsh measures worked, when in fact the opposite was true.) Not surprisingly, there were no limits to Nazi reprisals. In January 1942, the following announcement was circulated throughout Latvia by SS Obersturmbannführer Strauch: "The inhabitants of the village of Audriny, in the Rezhetz District, concealed members of the Red Army for over one-quarter of a year, armed them, and assisted them in every way in their anti-government activities. As punishment I ordered the following: That the village of Audriny be wiped from the face of the earth."

Jews still alive in the ghettos also suffered the Nazis' wrath. "The Germans were afraid to enter the woods, but they had to pacify the area," recalled partisan doctor Michael Temchin, about the region near the ghetto of Grabowiec. "They had to show some results of their work, and so they found an easy way out. Every so often they would select at random several Jews, mostly newcomers to the town, and shoot them publicly, announcing that these had been 'bandits'. Later, they did not even bother to look for newcomers. They simply assembled Jews at random and executed them in order to 'set an example'."

Similarly, in late December 1942, the gendarmerie in Grodno learned of the partisan killing of Heger Najorny, a forester who worked for the Germans as an informer. Both Najorny and his wife had been shot. In retaliation, the Germans rounded up twenty-five Jews in the Grodno ghetto and executed them.

As Hitler grew more concerned about the war in the east, he demanded that the partisans be dealt with even more harshly, so that this thorn in the Nazis' back side would cease to exist by the winter. To achieve this goal, he gave Himmler "sole responsibility" for crushing the movement. The SS chief, in turn, appointed one of his trusted Higher SS and Police Leaders, SS Obergruppenführer und General der Polizei Erich von dem Bach-Zelewski, to the position of Plenipotentiary for the Combating of the Partisans in the East (*Bevollmächtigte für die Bandenbekämpfung im Osten*). Within six months, he was promoted to Chief of Anti-Partisan Formations (*Chef der Bandenkämpfvergande*).

Regarded by Hitler as "one of the cleverest persons," a man he could depend on "for the most difficult tasks," Bach-Zelewski had rapidly risen through the ranks of the SS from the moment he joined it in 1931 at the age of thirty-two. Appointed Higher SS and Police Leader for Central Russia following the June 1941 invasion, he was responsible for co-ordinating the mass murder of hundreds of thousands of Jews, a task, according to the SS physician who treated him for a nervous disorder, he apparently found onerous. While Himmler held Bach-Zelewski in equally high esteem — though the Reichsführer hardly appreciated his Police Leader's suggestion that the killing of Jews be halted — he was not prepared to relinquish the power Bach-Zelewski required to combat the partisans. As a consequence, the Nazi campaign against the guerrillas continued to be carried out in a "chaotic manner," as Bach-Zelewski later testified at the Nuremberg trials.

The Nazis were consistent, though, in their treatment of the local population and captured fighters. There was to be no mercy shown for partisans or their sympathizers. If anything, the brutality intensified. Public executions of suspected partisan supporters were frequent throughout the occupied territory. In essence, the Nazis began to treat the peasants as they had already treated the Jews. SS men would arrive at a village or town, round up suspected partisan collaborators (no matter how weak the evidence), execute them, and burn their village to the ground.

In the spring of 1943, the SS and local police descended on one small town near Smolensk. After quickly rounding up and shooting twenty-three men in the town square, they turned on the mayor. One Belorussian policeman who accompanied them on this so-called anti-partisan mission later reported what happened next:

> The SS officer rounded on the mayor, telling him that he was not merely a collaborator, but a full bandit. But first he would admit where the bandit camp was. The mayor refused, quite probably because he did not know. The SS officer then had one of the young girls brought before them, and told the SS [sergeant] to perform. I find the following incident impossible to recount. The result was that the girl, stripped naked, had one of her breasts cut off. The mayor still refused to talk. The girl was then shot in front of him, and the SS officer fired a few indiscriminate rounds into the group of women, felling two or three. The final refusal to provide the information caused the execution of the mayor by slow hanging and the death by shooting of the rest of the inhabitants.

Such terror and savagery had its limitations, a point not lost on Hinrich Lohse, the Reichskommissar for the Ostland. After reading a detailed report about one large anti-partisan operation carried out during the first three weeks of June 1943, when thousands of civilians were killed but only a few hundred weapons discovered, Lohse wrote to Alfred Rosenberg. "I myself do not think that locking men, women and children in barns and then setting fire to the latter is a suitable method for combating partisans," he asserted, "even if one wishes to exterminate the population."

Bach-Zelewski, however, viewed the situation differently. Commenting to Himmler on the same operation, the Chief of Anti-Partisan Formations said: "The gravity of the battle and the number of our own losses, furthermore the fact that the local population supported partisan operations, fantastically and voluntarily, especially by the laying of mines on our rear lines of communication, demand elimination of all human consideration of this population."

■ ■

For Hitler, such efforts were still not sufficient. Enraged by the inability of the police and the army to stop the peasants' support for the partisans, he decided in July 1943 that the entire population must be evacuated "from the partisan-ridden territories of the northern Ukraine and the central Russian sector." As impractical and impossible as this idea was (in fact, it was never fully implemented), Nazi officials were kept busy for weeks drawing up plans for this proposed massive relocation.

At the same time, the Nazis attempted to achieve Hitler's overall goal of total annihilation of the partisan movement with dozens of large-scale blockades. Supported by airplane reconnaissance, thousands of German troops entered the woods in search of their prey, but they did not find it easy going. As the fighters and Jewish civilians already knew, during the winter, the snow was deep and often impassable; in the summer, the bugs and swamps horrific. Also, the partisans knew the terrain, but many of the Nazis did not.

Sometimes, in treks that took twenty-four hours or more, partisan bands, on learning of an impending Nazi assault, retreated deep into the swamps or in the direction of other forest areas. Close calls were common. In October 1943, for instance, during the second blockade of the Koziany Forest, near Jody, Peter Smuszkowicz, a member of the Soviet Ponomarenko Brigade, was forced with his comrades to flee 90 kilometres to avoid confrontation with their well-armed German enemy. "We walked day and night without stopping until we reached a small forest and swamp near the town of Germanowicz. . . . We decided to spend a day there and rest," he recalled. "Daylight brought the realization that we were completely surrounded by Germans and collaborators. Orders were given that everyone must lie quietly in the mud, without food or water. We were all exhausted. A few German reconnaissance planes flew overhead and we could hear German soldiers talking and yelling all around us." With two of his friends, Smuszkowicz managed to escape detection by constantly moving from one hiding place to the next. Many other Soviet and Jewish fighters were not as fortunate.

Yet everything did not always go the Nazis' way. The Germans found it difficult to defend against "hit-and-run" tactics carried out in the deep bush, and more often than not came upon partisan camps only to find them already abandoned. They could do nothing but destroy the bunkers in a fit of rage. "It was our experience that Russian forces, once they were driven into wooded and swampy areas, were extremely difficult to attack by normal means and could hardly ever be completely destroyed," conceded Gen. Franz Halder of the OKH. "On countless occasions, we were confronted with the fact that the Russian was able to move about in these impenetrable forests and treacherous swamps with the certain instinct and sense of security of an animal, where any soldier reared and trained in a civilized country of the West was severely restricted in his movements and placed at a disadvantage."

Operation Hornung, which was carried out from February 8 to 26, 1943, in the southern Pripet Marshes region, was typical. Thousands of Nazi troops and police swarmed the woods in anticipation of a great victory over their guerrilla foes. While 2,200 partisans were killed in action and thousands more captured and executed, the results, in terms of the number of weapons taken, were hardly impressive. The Germans seized only 172 rifles, 14 pistols, and 2 heavy machine guns.

A police report on the action, in fact, pointed out that though the Nazis were better armed, the partisans were better acquainted with the territory. It was futile, the author of this report argued, to send a reinforced battalion into an unknown area with no roads or footpaths. The police official recommended that the Germans bomb all partisan camps and villages from the air, which became more common in the fall of 1943.

In a blockade operation, like the ones in the Naliboki Forest, it was the local population in the villages adjacent to the forests (whose homes were razed and fields burned) and the members of Jewish family camps who suffered the most. More than 3,000 Jews, for example, perished in Operation Hornung. A month earlier, in Operation Hamburg, 2,658 were murdered during an attack in the forests near Slonim. The fortunate few who survived such attacks were able to hide in holes in the ground or in swamp water that was up to their necks. But tens of thousands were slaughtered.

From August 1 to December 1, 1942, for example, according to data prepared by the Higher SS and Police Leader's office responsible for southern Russia, the Ukraine, and the Northeast, 9,901 partisans were killed in Nazi operations, 14,257 "accomplices of guerrillas and guerrilla suspects" were executed, and 363,211 Jews were murdered in forest raids. The Nazis, on the other hand, claimed that they lost only 174 men and had 132 wounded. Interestingly, the same report also notes that the vast majority of weapons seized by the Germans from the partisans were small arms (1,903, compared with 55 mortar weapons and 174 automatic weapons).

■ ■

The existence of Jews in the woods, particularly those who were fighters and saboteurs, posed a particular problem for the Germans. It was as if any Jewish attempt to survive and resist was regarded as a major set-back. In Nazi reports and communiqués, Jews were always listed in a separate category and were rarely, if ever, accorded partisan or "bandit" status. They were, instead, "Bolshevik Jewish sub-humans" (*untermenschen*) who had no right to live. Nazi police wrote with great disdain about discoveries of "Jew camps" (*Judenlager*), where poorly armed Jews spent their days "plundering" for food. Curiously, when questioned at Nuremberg after the war, many Nazi officials denied that Jews were involved in the partisan movement. There were, claimed Alfred Jodl, "next to no Jews among the partisans."

During the conflict, assessments were slightly different. "In all the clashes with the partisans in [Belorussia] it has proved that Jewry, both in the formerly Polish, as well as in the formerly Soviet, parts of the District General, is the main bearer of the partisan movement together with the Polish resistance movement in the East and the Red Army from Moscow," wrote Wilhelm Kube, the Generalkommissar of Belorussia, to Hinrich Lohse and Alfred Rosenberg in July 1942. "In consequence, the treatment of Jewry . . . is a matter of political importance owing to the danger to the entire economy. It must therefore be solved in accordance with political considerations and not merely economic needs." For this reason, Kube added, 55,000 Jews had been "liquidated" near Minsk in past weeks, including Jews from Lida and Slonim.

Such acts of terror did not halt the Jewish escape to the forests or quench the young Jewish partisans' need for revenge. Stocked with *tol* and other explosives, the fighters continued their daring sabotage operations with the aim of destroying the entire Nazi transport system to the front lines. But it was not an objective easily achieved.

BATTLE OF THE RAILS

The so-called Battle of the Rails began in earnest in early August 1943. With the Red Army slowly pushing the Germans west towards the Dnieper River, officials at central partisan command ordered a massive simultaneous sabotage assault. The goal was nothing less than the destruction of 213,000 rails, most located in Belorussia. More than 150 brigades, comprising nearly 100,000 fighters, were to be employed in this assault.

In fact, such a comprehensive and mammoth attack was beyond the scope and capabilities of even the best partisans — not to mention that their supply of explosives was limited. Still, the demolitions, which started on August 3 and continued unabated for the next four months — spreading to the northern and southern regions of the front — certainly grabbed the Germans' attention.

In the month of August alone, the chief of transport for Army Group Centre reported that 1,392 incidents had taken place (compared with 1,114 in July), with an average of 45 demolitions per day. "Within two nights," the chief noted, "the six to seven thousand miles of track in the area were cut in 8,422 places, while another 2,478 mines were detected and removed prior to exploding. Several lines could not be put back into operation for a considerable time." The Nazis discovered as well that locals who had volunteered to protect the railways now "made common cause with the partisans and took German weapons along with them."

But far from being defeated, the Nazis, as historian Matthew Cooper has shown, repaired the rail ties as fast as the partisans could destroy them. Often the fighters spaced their attacks too far apart, allowing the Germans time to recover. And a lot of the partisans' hard efforts were directed at less important feeder lines, as opposed to more vital supply arteries such as the Brest-Litovsk–Minsk–Smolensk line. Indeed, despite the overwhelming nature of the partisan assault, the Germans were able "to keep open their lines of supply and evacuation in all parts of the East. Their armies at the front suffered from other far greater disabilities than those inflicted on them by partisans." The winter weather also considerably cut sabotage operations — there were only 795 during December — and the Nazis devised new methods for detecting mines and flushing the partisans out of their forest retreats.

It was a ruthless battle of brawn, wits, and treachery; a deadly game of chess in which only the victor remained alive. Unwilling to accept partisan interference in their quest to rule the east, the Nazis were relentless in trying to stamp out their elusive enemy. At first, they guarded the rail lines and used inspector railcars mounted with bright lights and machine guns that travelled ahead of the trains. When that did not achieve the desired results, they appointed "battle-tested" officers as train commanders and sent empty flat cars ahead of real transports so that they would trigger and absorb the blast. But the partisans countered with timers that were triggered once the empty cars had gone by. When the Nazis used dogs to sniff out hidden mines, the fighters covered the tracks with gunpowder to throw the animals off the scent. In another example of partisan ingenuity, in the fall of 1942, Soviet fighters set off a mock demolition about 1,500 metres north of the Seltso-Rzhanitza railway — the intended target. This sent the security force guarding the tracks off on a wild-goose chase, and the partisans were able to destroy part of the rail line.

The Nazi police also tried spraying the crushed rocks between the ties and the rail with white paint. This way, the Germans reasoned, they would be able to detect more easily if a mine had been buried. But the clever partisans soon figured out a way to counter this security measure as well. It was, Leon Kahn explains, painstaking work, but it did the trick. "We learned how to carefully collect the rock," he states, "excavate a hole to bury our mine, carry away the excess dirt in our jackets and replace the rocks one by one, white side up. The soil was dumped in the forest and carefully covered in moss." This entire procedure took about thirty minutes, a short time for the men planting the mine but, says Kahn, an eternity for the few fighters guarding them.

While the Germans became quite competent at discovering many of the mines laid by the partisans — in the Bryansk area, for instance, from May 1942 to April 1943, they prevented 523 of 1,019 demolitions, or 51 percent — they were far from satisfied. Eventually, they forced large numbers of POWs and peasants to create security zones around the tracks, often measuring 2 to 5 kilometres, by clearing thousands of trees. Official passes were required to get close to the rail lines and persons discovered near the tracks without the proper authorization papers were shot. By this time, however, as Peter Silverman points out, the partisans were using "delayed-action timers." Hence, despite the increased number of security patrols, the fighters were still able to conduct missions late into the night at unguarded areas. The mines could be planted and the partisans long gone before the Nazis returned to witness the detonations.

A similar move-and-countermove battle was played out with telephone and telegraph poles and wires. The partisans sawed the poles and cut the wires, and the Nazis immediately repaired them. Then, to try to stop this sabotage altogether, the Germans hid a trip-wire in each pole, which was attached to a mine that would explode if the pole was moved. "As we always worked in the dark," Leon Kahn adds, "we couldn't be sure which poles were mined, but we resolved this problem by recruiting men from nearby villages to cut the poles. By choosing only those who had been hostile to the partisans and the Jews, we forced the Germans to kill or injure their own sympathizers and collaborators. . . .

The Germans . . . soon stopped booby-trapping the telephone poles."

Along the same lines, the partisans often forced local civilians to camouflage an attack. They would order a group of men, women, and children across a bridge they intended to demolish. Believing them to be harmless, the Nazi guards on duty would ignore them. Then, from behind the civilians, the fighters would spring up and deal immediately with the security detail before the guards knew what was happening. The mine was then planted, the civilians would flee, and the bridge would explode.

■ ■

During early 1944, on the heels of the continuing German retreat, partisan sabotage activity on the rail lines increased. In the central sector, 841 operations were carried out in January, compared with 1,052 in May. By this time, many *otriady* were equipped with anti-tank guns, which the fighters used to destroy locomotive boilers. In particular, sabotage missions south of Pskov during January and February severely hindered Nazi supply routes and greatly helped the Red Army "breakthrough."

In the spring, more than 18,000 partisans disrupted German transportation on rail lines leading out of Bryansk, while farther west in Belorussia, another 20,000 targeted the important rail links between Minsk and Gomel, and Brest-Litovsk on the banks of the Pripet River and Baranowicze, south-west of the Naliboki Forest. In the latter area, the fighters' actions blocked the Brest-Litovsk–Baranowicze rail line for nearly six days and disrupted rail traffic for more than a week. Soviet and Jewish partisans also assaulted trains, roads, and transports in the areas surrounding both Minsk and Bialystok. It was the same story in eastern Poland, as partisans there also intensified their operations. In the district of Lublin alone, the Nazis recorded eighty-seven separate incidents of partisan activity from May 16 to 19.

By mid-June, fighters in Belorussia were geared towards aiding Marshal Grigori Zhukov and the Red Army's great offensive. During the nights of June 19 to 21, two days before the decisive assault on the weak and deteriorating German Army Group Centre began, the partisans throughout the region launched their greatest combined operation. In one bold action, they put all Nazi rail service out of commission, with more than 10,000 separate demolitions. For at least forty-eight hours, barely a train moved anywhere in the central sector. The Germans were prevented from dispatching further troops to aid their beleaguered soldiers, particularly the 3rd Panzer Army. "Here for the first time," suggests Matthew Cooper, "the partisans had a direct effect on the outcome of a major battle." He adds, however, that the partisans' contributions, though significant, probably did not alter "either the strategic balance or the outcome, [for] the forces facing the Germans were, at that stage of the war, simply too overwhelming."

If Himmler realized the end was near, he hardly showed it. A month earlier, on May 3, 1944, his office had issued a memorandum detailing how German soldiers could earn commendations and awards for battling the partisans. Yet it was a little too late. Promises of gold, silver, and bronze medals were not going to prevent the partisans from gaining control over an ever-widening territory — and were certainly not going to stop the Red Army from moving west.

A PERILOUS LIBERATION

We found it hard to accept the fact that we were to leave the forests. The sufferings, dangers, and battles that we had experienced in the forests now bound us to these dark masses. The forests had once terrified us, but now they blessed us with the feeling of security. We had spent two years less two weeks in the forest. . . . Here in the forest, hope still whispered; the outside promised uncertainty and loneliness. It seemed that once again I was being forced to flee from my home.

— SHALOM CHOLAWSKI

THE YEAR OF THE "TEN VICTORIES"

They waited. In the family and partisan camps throughout the forests of Belorussia, Lithuania, the Ukraine, and eastern Poland, fighters and civilians waited patiently for their Soviet liberators. They had heard the rumours in the villages and received promising reports on their crystal radios. Soon, the soldiers of the Red Army would arrive, pushing the Nazi horde back from whence they came. Soon, they would be free again.

Such freedom, however, was not achieved easily or without the spilling of more blood. The Germans, obedient to the end and dedicated to preserving the glory of the Nazi state that had been carved out of the eastern territories piece by piece during the past three years, did not surrender without a vicious fight. The stunning military defeats did not halt attempts to annihilate European Jews. In the few remaining ghettos and work camps, in confrontations in the forests, and most tragically, in the death camps, the Nazis could not kill Jews fast enough.

On January 18, 1945, ten days before the Red Army finally walked through the gates of hell at Auschwitz — under the sign, forged in cold iron, that bore the haunting words *Arbeit Macht Frei* (Work Makes One Free) — the Nazis relocated about 58,000 of the camp's inmates by forcing them on an infamous "death march" into Germany. The last public execution at the camp occurred on January 6, 1945. Four Jewish women who had assisted in a failed uprising were hanged.

Months earlier, Soviet soldiers had liberated Majdanek, the dreaded concentration camp near Lublin. The war correspondents who accompanied the soldiers were able, for the first time, to send out pictures to the world that confirmed the horrors of the gas chambers and crematoria. Hitler reportedly responded with anger at "the slovenly and cowardly rabble in the Security Services who did not erase the traces" of the death factory before their hasty departure.

The Nazis had exhibited the same relentlessness during the spring of 1944, as they desperately tried to clear the forests of partisans in case they were forced to retreat. Jews discovered hiding or in family camps were dealt with immediately. The imminent collapse of the Nazi empire made no difference. In June 1944, in eastern Galicia, SS soldiers found a young Jewish woman hiding on a Ukrainian farm. Demanding that she give them information about the partisans, they beat her, tortured her, and set dogs on her, which nearly ripped her apart. When they were satisfied she could not tell them anything, they put her on a train bound for Auschwitz. She eluded certain death by jumping off the railcar and hiding until the Red Army arrived.

In the Parczew Forest, the Germans ran several large anti-partisan

actions from April through June. And while they inflicted much damage, they were unable to gain control of the woods. Farther south, on
June 9, Operation Sturmwind began. It was the "largest anti-partisan
campaign in Poland," involving three Wehrmacht divisions, a cavalry
regiment, several units of the Order Police, and an air force bomber
squadron. In all, 25,000 German troops were positioned against the
5,000 Soviet, Polish, and Jewish partisans in the Lipsk and Janow forests.
During this two-week campaign, the Nazis had better success than
in the Parczew Forest. Thousands of partisans perished in what
had become a pointless struggle for the Germans. Hundreds of Jewish
fighters and civilians died in battle only weeks before the Red Army
regained control over the area.

■ ■

From Stalin's point of view, if 1943 had been the *perelom*, the year of the
turning point, 1944 was the year of the "ten victories." The first of these
victories occurred in mid-January, when the Soviets broke the blockade
of steel that had encircled and starved Leningrad for so many
months, signalling the beginning of the Red Army's slow march to
Berlin. In April, the port city of Odessa was liberated. The massive
eastern front line, which stretched from Estonia to the southern
Ukraine, was pushed westward across the Dniester and Bug rivers into
partisan-controlled territory.

The massive offensive into Belorussia and eastern Poland began on
June 23, the third anniversary of the Nazi attack. Swiftly, the Soviets
took Vitebsk and Bobruisk, killing and capturing tens of thousands
of Nazi soldiers on their way west. On July 17, as a sign of power,
the Soviets paraded 57,000 German POWs, including many officers,
through the streets of Moscow. Other captured Nazis were not as
fortunate. For many of them, there was no mercy. They received the
same brutal treatment they themselves had meted out. One young
partisan, Ralph F., recalls watching Soviet soldiers carve a hammer and
sickle into the back of a captured SS man before they shot him.

The Red Army pushed back the German front lines, ably assisted by

Soviet and Jewish partisans who continued their rear actions, attempting to halt the massive German retreat. The Nazis, now disorganized and on the run, fled into the forests. They sought refuge, but instead marched into the partisan firing line. Jacob Greenstein, one of the thousands of fighters near Minsk, remembers that during a five-day period in early July, his brigade captured 25,000 German soldiers.

The partisans did not let up for a moment. "Long columns of German trucks and tanks kept moving westward from the approaching front," writes Harold Werner, who in July 1944 was a member of Chil Grynszpan's unit in eastern Poland. "The Germans were now retreating en masse. They were not only using the highways but also the side roads, fields, and wooded trails. For a two- or three-week period, we were constantly ambushing their columns, especially on the wooded trails. Our PTRs [anti-tank guns] came in very handy. Many of the German tanks went up in flames from their armor-piercing shells. The German tank crews would then jump out of their burning tanks, only to be met by our fire."

The Soviet army took Minsk, which had been burned and destroyed like cities and towns throughout the region, on July 3. Hersh Smolar, one-time leader of the Minsk ghetto underground, was among the partisans who followed the soldiers into the city. "Returning to our liberated native city, we walked like mourners following a coffin," he later recalled. "No longer did we have any hope of perhaps meeting someone there that we knew. The casualties we had suffered, while all the other partisan detachments came out without a scratch, oppressed the spirit of the Jews who . . . had regained the confidence that they would live to see the day of vengeance against the Nazi enemy." Of the 80,000 Jews in Minsk in 1941 (a figure that, as a result of deportations, had increased to 100,000 by that summer), approximately 5,000 remained alive, most surviving either as partisans or as members of Shalom Zorin's family camp.

Soon, Minsk resembled, in Smolar's words, "a tremendous partisan camp." Men lived on the streets as they once had in the forest, dressed in uniforms of every kind and variety, including German uniforms taken from executed prisoners. "High in the clear summer sky floated the smoke of partisan campfires," he relates in his memoirs. "On sticks and iron rods using large scorched kettles, in which partisans — as if they were still in the forest — were cooking something 'to tide them over.' And in accordance with partisan customs we sat down among a group of men completely unknown to us and stuck our inseparable companions — our spoons — into the common kettle of stew."

Outside the city, the countryside resembled a desert. Before their retreat, the Germans had destroyed everything they could. Cities, towns, villages, and farms were all laid to waste. "The destruction in the cities was appalling," according to British journalist Alexander Werth. "Nearly all the factories and public buildings had been destroyed, and at Minsk the majority of all other houses had been burned down, too."

"OUR JOY WAS INDESCRIBABLE"

The Red Army and partisan pursuit of the Nazis had dire consequences for many Jews anxiously awaiting their day of liberation. Their hearts were filled with revenge and sorrow, and they allowed themselves to think about the future. "For the first time since the Germans had arrived in eastern Poland," says Jack Sutin, a fighter at the Zorin family camp, "we started to feel a real hope that they might be driven out and that we would be alive to see it happen."

But times were dangerous. At one family camp in the Lipiczany Forest, dozens of Jews hid in deep bunkers so that roving bands of Nazis, still determined to kill as many Jews as they could while they retreated, would not detect them. These Jewish men, women, and children hid quietly with only a few string beans to eat between them. "As a camouflage, we dragged two dead bodies over the entrance," one eleven-year-old boy who had escaped from Zdzieciol recalled. "The stench was terrible. Even the German dogs would not go near them." Many more young Jews — like Bebale Weisman, who with her father, Chaim, had survived countless raids in the Parczew Forest — were murdered in the last few weeks of the conflict. With the death of his daughter, Chaim had lost his entire family, his wife and all five children, in the forest.

These tragedies and senseless killings occurred not only in the forest regions, but also throughout Nazi-occupied Europe. As historian Martin Gilbert states, "rescue and slaughter marched hand in hand during the twilight days of the Reich." If Jews still lived, the Germans continued the slaughter as if they were still in control. Days before the Soviet liberation of the eastern Galician city of Przemsyl, for example, the SS discovered a Polish family that had been hiding a six-year-old Jewish girl. After the Nazi policemen whipped the young child, she and the Poles who had helped her were shot.

To make matters worse for the Jews in the woods, they also had to watch out for AK soldiers (possibly aligned with the fascist NSZ) and the Ukrainian fascist Banderovtsy. These factions were intent on using the end of the war and the chaotic conditions that accompanied it to rid their respective territories of both Soviets and Jews. The Soviet partisans, following orders from Moscow, were just as eager to destroy the Polish underground, but the Russian fighters could and did defend themselves as well as take aggressive action to ensure Soviet domination. The Jewish civilians and partisans were more vulnerable, and many were slaughtered in bloody clashes with the AK and the Banderovtsy — just as Leon Kahn's sister and father had been in October 1943. In early 1944, the Polish Home Army wiped out a Jewish group led by Yaakov Rochman near Kleszow, south-west of Warsaw. A small *otriad* in the Wyszkow Forest, north-east of the Polish capital, was also destroyed.

Yitzhak Arad recalls one particular confrontation with the AK that took place early in March 1944: "A Polish force of hundreds of fighters surrounded the fifty-man Kostas Kalinauskas unit of our brigade. The battle, near the village of Maironi in the vicinity of Podrodzie, went on for several hours. About half the partisans fell, among them the commander of the unit. . . . The Poles murdered all the wounded who remained in the field."

Farther west, in Warsaw in August, about a thousand Jews, in hiding or labouring as slaves in the city, joined with the Polish fighters in their uprising against the German regime. Hundreds died in battle. The

Poles, who felt that there was "no place for Jews in liberated Poland," murdered many Jews themselves. In one reported case, AK soldiers preposterously accused three Jews of being Nazi spies. Two of the Jews managed to flee, but the AK killed their friend, Yeshieh Solomon, in a barrage of gunfire.

At the Bielski and Zorin family camps in the Naliboki *puszcza*, the spring of 1944 was equally tense. In April, the Bielski Jews celebrated their last Passover in the woods with a "primitive, mostly burned" *matzoh* baked in their makeshift ovens. The children asked the traditional four questions about the Jews' biblical exodus from Egypt and the uniqueness of Passover, then ate some soup. Future Passover family gatherings, or seders, they prayed, would be different.

Jews, in small groups or alone, continued to arrive at the forest family camps. None was turned away. Among those who joined the Bielski *otriad* only months before the end of the war was fourteen-year-old Willy Moll. Months earlier, he had been caught in an *Aktion* during the liquidation of the Lida ghetto. An SS soldier pushed him and others against a wall. Willy was prepared to die. He still shudders when he thinks about the incident more than five decades later. "It was," he says, "the worst moment of my life."

Instead of killing Willy, the SS put him on a train bound for the Majdanek concentration camp. When the train made a brief stop, Willy jumped from the car and hid in the fields until the train continued on its way. Wandering at night, he found a Polish farmer who allowed him to hide in a hole in the ground under the farmhouse. He remained there for several months until he sensed he was in danger from the farmers' two sons, who had decided to join the AK. He fled east towards the Niemen River, where he happened upon two Soviet partisans. They took him to a camp where other Jews agreed to take him to Bielski's in the Naliboki. There, Willy was reunited with other survivors from Lida. They made room for him in their *zemlianka*, where he worked as an assistant to the camp's carpenter.

As they waited for the Red Army to arrive, the young Jewish fighters, along with the Soviets in the area, guarded the family camps against retreating Germans. Both Zorin and Bielski wanted to catch as many as possible. Many enemy soldiers were killed, but the partisans also captured several Nazis and brought them back to the family camps, unleashing a wave of emotion and hatred among the Jews.

At the Bielski camp, the guards apprehended three young SS soldiers who were fleeing into the forest and took them to Tuvia's headquarters for questioning. A crowd of a thousand quickly encircled the hut. Bielski stepped out of his headquarters and ordered the people to be quiet while he did his work. Inside, the Nazis begged for their lives. "I will never forget it," remembered Eliezer Engelstern, who watched the spectacle beside Tuvia and his staff, "how on their knees the SS men were begging for their lives. They pleaded for mercy because they had children at home. They swore that they were not to blame for anything that had happened to the Jews."

One blond Nazi was delivered to the crowd. A Jew named Pupko plunged a knife into the prisoner. The other soldiers were also killed (depending on whose version is accepted, they were either shot or hanged). According to Liza Ettinger, who witnessed this spectacle, "little Yossi (about three) came with his grandfather and beat the criminal with his cane, shouting 'Revenge! For my mother! For my father!' It was a horrible sight that embodied in one minute all the depth of the terrible holocaust of the Jewish people. The young Nazi did not surrender until the last moment. The other two who witnessed what had happened did not beg for mercy. Heads held high, they walked to their fate — faithful to their education and proud of their deeds. As for me — I ran away because I could no longer bear the sight of another deed of vengeance."

It was the same scenario at the Zorin camp. Following a battle, the partisans took two Germans prisoner. They, too, according to Jack Sutin, who was among those who interrogated them, begged for mercy and waved photos of their families before the Jewish partisans' eyes. Meanwhile, another five prisoners were brought into the camp and immediately the Jews surrounded them, screaming and shouting. Rochelle Sutin was, as she recalls, "one of those shouting people. We were so bitter [and] so full of anger."

Many survivors felt that the captured Nazi soldiers and Polish policemen — murderers of Jewish children and the elderly — got what they deserved. Rochelle continues:

Everyone started beating them, with rifle butts, fists, boots. We beat them to mush. I remember that they were lying on the ground just barely breathing. And I . . . I don't think I could ever do it again. . . . I came up to one of the German officers who had his legs spread. I started to kick him again and again in the groin. I was kicking and screaming, 'For my mama! For my tate [daddy]! For my sisters!' I went on screaming out every name I could remember, all my relatives and my friends who had been murdered. It was such a release! . . . When I think back, I'm not sorry for what I did. I don't think I could do it again now. But at that moment, we were all so filled with anger, anxiety, bitterness. Seeing the enemy in our midst was all it took for us to explode. We had been forced to live like animals and for that moment we became animals.

But the war was still not over. In early July, with the Red Army still firing their guns, battles broke out between the partisans and the Germans. Velvke Yonson, a member of Ordzonikidze (the fighting *otriad* that had split from the Bielski family group in the fall of 1943), described one confrontation as follows:

Suddenly thousands of Germans are upon us. A terrible life and death struggle ensues. I shoot my machine gun without a stop. I can see my bullets fell scores of Germans. My artillery is hot, but there is no time to stop. The battle has been raging for four hours. Hundreds of Germans lie dead. The fallen are replaced. Suddenly I am attacked by about 30 Germans. Rather than fall into their hands, I pull the ring of my hand grenade and am prepared to do away with myself. A comrade on my left flank throws a grenade and starts to shoot. Only eight wounded Germans are spared that counterattack. We also suffered many casualties, dead and wounded. The Germans cannot break through our side and throw their might against Bielski's camp and there they are successful, although they suffered heavy losses. Bielski's partisans also lost many men.

In the early morning of July 9, a small group of German soldiers were able to penetrate the family camp's guard posts undetected. Before the Jews could mount a proper defence, the Nazis had shot several of them and thrown grenades into a few bunkers. Eventually, Bielski and other partisans in the area arrived, firing their guns. The Germans were killed, but nearly a dozen Jews also died in the *otriad*'s last fight with the Third Reich.

Close by at the Zorin camp, another battle raged. Six of the *otriad*'s fighters were killed and eleven were seriously wounded. Zorin was hit in the leg and collapsed in agony. Later he was taken to a Minsk hospital, where doctors were forced to amputate the leg to save his life. Before he was taken away on a wagon, he bid farewell to his people in a moving and tearful speech. Jack Sutin later wrote this account of Zorin's speech for a Yiddish newspaper:

"Dear friends, we were together for a long time, and I was always proud of your heroic deeds and sacrifices. Together we have suffered, found, cried, and shared good times." [Zorin] wiped his tears, relaxed a few seconds, and continued.

"In a few hours we will finally be liberated. We will disperse in different directions, forget each other, and probably never see each other again. It looks like I will remain an invalid for the rest of my life. Please don't forget me. Please stay in close contact with me. You are my family."

He could not continue. Tears covered his face, and all of us cried together.

The next day, as the Jews buried their dead friends, the Red Army soldiers entered the camps. "Our joy was indescribable," wrote Velvke Yonson. "After so many years, we were finally free." And yet, as Shalom

Cholawski reflected on the meeting with the Soviet soldiers near his home town of Lachowicze, "the tremendous waves of joy that flooded the heart could not remove the feeling of deep sadness; if only they had come two years earlier! Now that the day of liberation was here, there was no one left to be free."

■ ■

That morning in July, as the 1,200 Jews at the Bielski camp prepared for the long trek back to Novogrudok, Tuvia Bielski, in one of his last orders as a partisan commander, told his people to take only what they could carry. The Soviets demanded that the Jews destroy the camp so that anti-Communists would not be able to use it in the future. The Jews complied. As Nechama Tec notes, "the camp resounded with destruction and explosion."

Naturally, Bielski did not want any trouble with the Soviets and was wary of renegade Nazis wandering around the forest. The anticipation of the march to freedom was great but the mood was tense. "Our great hour had come," recalled Liza Ettinger forty years later. "We were on the threshold of a new historic period for our people and for the whole world. This was a breathtaking moment from the viewpoint of its emotional force. Even today when I come to reconstruct it I stand excited and in awe as then." As they prepared to depart, however, the survivors also talked about the "realistic struggle" that awaited them. Where would they go? How would they survive without their families? After two and three years of living one hour to the next, making long-range plans seemed unnatural to them.

A Jew named Polonecki, a new arrival to the camp, decided to load a wagon with goods (according to some testimonies, Polonecki had left his possessions with a Belorussian farmer and had retrieved them). What happened next is not entirely clear. There was an altercation between Polonecki and Tuvia Bielski. The commander insisted that Polonecki leave the wagon and goods behind. When Polonecki refused, someone (perhaps Bielski, depending on whose version you accept) shot him.

This needless death upset many members of the group. "For days, a constant reminder — the crying of the dead man's widow — followed the mass of subdued marchers," adds Nechama Tec. "Upset about the present, anxious about the future, overcome by sadness, they moved on."

"YOU'RE STILL ALIVE!"

As the Jews finally returned to Novogrudok, Slonim, Lida, Mir, Jody, Zdzieciol, Radun, and the many other towns and villages they had escaped from, a deep collective depression afflicted them. "When the liberation occurred, we knew we had survived, but then the reality of the past three years hit home," explains Peter Silverman. "We did not yet know about the concentration camps. It was all very depressing. We went to Jody and found that most of it had been burned down."

They had no jobs, no money, and little hope. Their Polish and Ukrainian neighbours were certainly not happy to see all these Jews emerging from the woods. Many of the Poles and Ukrainians, in fact, had moved into Jewish homes that had been spared destruction, or assumed that possessions left in their care during ghetto relocations would never be returned to their Jewish owners.

"You're still alive!" they yelled in disbelief. "What do you want? Go away I can't help you!"

In Slonim, Lisa Derman found that her house was still standing. She knocked on the door. A stranger answered. When Lisa told the woman who she was, the stranger assured her that there was nothing in the house that belonged to her family. After she pleaded further, the woman eventually gave Lisa her mother's embroidered slip. It was her only reminder of an earlier and happier life, and she still cherishes it to this day.

Faye Schulman walked out of the forest and into Pinsk — or what was left of it. It was a day she has never forgotten. "It was so heartbreaking. There used to be 30,000 Jews, but now there were not even five," she says. "There were Jewish houses still there, but they were occupied by non-Jews. And most tragic of all, there were no Jewish children left." Faye was forced to return her gun and grenade, her "constant companions" throughout her life as a partisan. Not surprisingly, she felt abandoned and alone. "I felt a loss of identity," she writes. "What would I do with my new-found freedom? Freedom to do what? To go where? . . . The fighting for me had come to an end and I was alive and found myself free. Yet this was the lowest point in my life; I saw no future for myself."

Shalom Cholawski described his return to his hometown, Lachowicze. "Everything as it was. For a second, I think, maybe — as it was? I run to the house. I stand before it, but no door is open, no window. Not a voice is heard." Later he discovered one of his neighbours, a Polish woman, living in the house, surrounded by his family's possessions. He left, never to return.

For Leon Kahn, the war ended in the Lithuanian village of Linitsa on the outskirts of the Lipiczany Forest. "For days after that I wept whenever I was left alone," he later recalled. "Waking and sleeping I found myself overwhelmed by terrifying nightmares re-enacting all the horror of the past [three] years. As if my mind could only now face the reality of it all, I relived all the deaths, heard again the screams, saw the torn flesh and mutilated bodies of my people once more, and underlying everything was the realization that I was truly alone." Weeks later, he was able to visit Eisiskes to confirm what he already knew to be a fact: that his mother had been killed. His family's house had been demolished, as had the town's synagogue. "It was almost as if our family had never been," he adds.

AFTERMATH

They adapted and survived as they had done for the past three years. Many Jewish fighters received medals and thanks from Soviet officials and partisan leaders, and then were immediately drafted into the Red Army and shipped to the front lines. Jacob Greenstein was sent to the Eighth Corps in the Second Belorussian Front and became a tank commander. He survived numerous attacks and reached Berlin to witness the German capitulation. Jerry Seigel, who had been with the Bielski *otriad* at the time of liberation, was transported to a military training camp near Moscow for one month and then dispatched to the front in the northern sector. He was wounded in the leg on October 20, 1944, as his unit pushed into Germany. He went first to a military hospital in Vilna to recover and then to another hospital not far from Moscow, where he spent the remainder of the war recuperating.

At first, Peter Silverman was given a job as a Red Army messenger. Then, mistakenly, he and some of his Jewish friends, all former partisans, were assigned to a poorly armed brigade intended for "collaborators-turned-partisans," individuals who had joined the Soviet cause late in the war and who, to the Russians, could either live or die. Mostly, they died. Only the intervention of a Jewish Red Army major who transferred the Jewish fighters out of this group saved the lives of Silverman and his comrades.

Asael Bielski was not as lucky. In the fierce fighting of the last few months of the conflict, he was killed in Marienburg, Germany, southeast of Berlin. His wife, Chaya, pregnant, eventually left Poland for Palestine with her family. She named her daughter Asaela.

Tuvia and Zus Bielski avoided conscription into the army, but were forced to flee to Rumania along with their wives after they learned the Soviet state police, the NKVD, wanted to question Tuvia about his alleged anti-Communist political views and other incidents that had taken place in the forest. They, too, finally made it to Palestine, where Tuvia fought in the war of Israel's independence. In 1956, Tuvia and Zus and their families relocated to New York City, where Zus owned a taxi cab service and Tuvia bought a few trucks.

Many Jews made their way to Lublin, Poland's provisional capital before the liberation of Warsaw in January 1945. As Sam Gruber remembered, "Lublin became a gathering place for thousands of survivors who had hidden in the forests, bunkers, ghettos, and farmhouses, or had come from the death camps themselves. All these people had flocked to the city hoping to find surviving relatives and friends."

Still other Jews worked for the Soviet authorities in a variety of government positions. Meyer Itzkovitch, for instance, who had fought as a partisan in the Naliboki woods for nearly three years, had a job issuing passports, while Ben Lungen served for a brief time as a clerk and then as an agent-in-training for the NKVD before he was able to escape to the West, and eventually to Winnipeg, Manitoba. In Pinsk, Faye Schulman became the official photographer for the main government-controlled newspaper in Belorussia, *Bialoruskaja Pravda*. She reunited with her two brothers and met her future husband, Morris, before departing for western Europe and then to Canada in 1948.

Leon Kahn became a policeman in the town of Varena, north of Vilna. There, he and a few comrades methodically tracked down and dealt with local Nazi collaborators. In February 1945, Kahn was transferred to another nearby village, where for a brief time he served as police chief. Once the war had officially ended in May 1945, he escaped to Lodz and eventually to Germany, then immigrated to Canada in 1948.

After wandering for several months, Jack and Rochelle Sutin finally wound up in Jack's hometown of Mir. Jack avoided conscription into the Red Army by posing as a dentist. As a young boy, he had watched his mother, a dentist, and figured he could get away with imitating one. His father, Julius, who was a dental technician before the war, helped him. His ruse worked. He did a lot of drilling (without the use of Novocain) on his patients, local farmers, who suffered greatly until a real Russian dentist arrived to assist him in the fall of 1944. Soon after, he confessed the whole charade. The Russian dentist agreed to help Jack so that he would not be dispatched to the front.

Later, the Sutins, like so many other survivors, reached the conclusion that Communist Russia offered few real opportunities for them, and that there was no place for Jews in postwar Poland either. During the summer and fall of 1945, pogroms against Jewish Holocaust survivors broke out in many Polish cities, including Cracow, Lublin, and Sosnowiec. Hundreds were killed. The most notorious act of treachery against Jews occurred in Kielce, south of Warsaw, in early July 1946. The disappearance of a young boy triggered, astonishingly, charges that the boy had been abducted as part of a Passover blood ritual.* This so-called blood libel led to anti-Jewish riots and the deaths of forty-two Jews, several children among them. Many of the rioters were later apprehended and convicted; nine were sentenced to death. The boy had been playing at a farm in a nearby village the entire time.

In the aftermath of the Kielce riot, 100,000 Polish Jews, "more than half the survivors," as historian Martin Gilbert points out, abandoned their Polish homeland forever. They made their way west from deportation camps in Germany, the country that had destroyed their lives. From there, they ventured to western Europe and Palestine, and to North and South America.

■ ■

At precisely the same moment that the Red Army liberated Minsk on July 3, 1944, less than 200 kilometres away the Nazis were quickly disposing of the last Jews of Vilna. With the echo of the Red Army guns in the distance, the SS marched 1,800 of the 2,000 or so survivors to the Ponary death pits, where they slaughtered them. The other 200 were able to hide. A week later, the Soviets reached the outskirts of Vilna and a five-day bloody battle ensued. Desperately, the Nazi troops attempted to flee through the iron ring around the city. The Soviets thwarted their attempts. By July 13, when it was over, 8,000 soldiers of the Third Reich had died and another 5,000 were taken prisoner.

Behind the Red Army, the Jewish partisans came out of the Rudniki Forest to reclaim what was left of their "Jerusalem." In the days preceding the liberation, many had launched their own attacks on the small surrounding villages, driving the Germans out and ambushing as many as crossed their paths. Now, together and free at last, they walked through the ghetto that had imprisoned them.

---

*A 1996 study published by the Polish Educational Foundation in North America has a much different view of the events in Kielce and the treatment of Jews in Poland in 1945 and 1946. Citing numerous Polish testimonies, the authors argue that the trouble in Kielce was most likely planned and initiated by Soviet authorities. The evidence of a larger Soviet conspiracy, however, is largely circumstantial, as historian Tadeusz Piotrowksi concedes and, in my view, not all that convincing. But readers should weigh the evidence and decide for themselves. (See *Kielce–July, 1946*, 5–68.)

Abba Kovner, the young resistance leader, later testified about a particularly stirring find he and the partisans made as they walked carefully through the rubble of the ghetto. A woman emerged out of a small cave in a wall, with a young girl in her arms. The woman said that she had at first been afraid of the partisans because they were dressed in Nazi uniforms. She and her daughter had been hiding in the hole in the wall for almost a year. The entire time, the woman, terrified of German soldiers, had not allowed her daughter to make any noise. Now, the child who had sat so quietly in her mother's arms finally spoke. "May one cry now, Mother?"

EPILOGUE

I am a man with two lives; in one I am called Leibke Kaganowicz of Eisiskes, and in the other I am Leon Kahn of Vancouver. Most of the time my first life is hidden so well behind my second one that few people know it is there.

— LEON KAHN

IF ONLY THE TREES COULD TALK

"So you're a Jew?" asked the driver. Taken aback, the only thing I could do was nod. I had just crawled into the front seat of his white 1989 Mercedes. I had hoped the driver the tour company had hired would be pleasant and could speak English. His question, more like a declaration, was cause for concern.

After all, this was Poland, a country where, prior to the Second World War, relations between Poles and Jews were often strained. Although Poland, the site of the Holocaust, did not plan the Final Solution — that great shame remains Germany's — it did have its share of collaborators, murderers, and informers. They were indifferent as the Nazis marched their Jewish neighbours away, never to return.

I had come to Poland for a few days in May 1996 to witness for myself the cities and towns where generations of Jews had once lived, to obtain a "feel" for the countryside I wanted to write about, and to stand among the trees in at least one forest area where five decades earlier partisans and civilians had fought, trying to survive against the Nazi horde that wanted to crush them.

Obtaining this "feel" was easy. It is, in fact, impossible to go anywhere in Poland without being reminded of the horrors of the Second World War. Of the many sites I saw during my short stay, nothing struck me as much as a hillside monument on the outskirts of the resort town of Kazimierz, north-west of Lublin. After the war, Polish town officials had built a wall of memory from the broken Jewish headstones that the Nazis had callously taken from cemeteries and embedded in sidewalks and roads.

Visiting Poland today is a lot like visiting a museum of lost civilizations. You can still see the remnants of a rich and diverse Jewish culture in old synagogues now serving as restaurants and movie theatres.

As it turned out, our driver, a forty-eight-year-old Pole named Romualt, was a superb guide. He had a wealth of knowledge about Jewish life in every small town we travelled through on the road from Warsaw to Lublin. When we arrived in Lublin, he took us directly to the site of the Majdanek concentration camp.

The barbed wire is still intact. So is the white two-storey house where various German camp commandants and their families lived, while only a short distance away Jewish men, women, and children were gassed to death. Walking through the dozen bunkers still standing at Majdanek, you see how the prisoners lived and you can read about the history of the camp. But it is the last two bunkers that are the most poignant. Each is about 3 metres high and 27 metres long. Down both sides of the bunkers, from floor to the ceiling, are metal cages. Inside are thousands upon thousands of dusty black shoes of all shapes and sizes — including a special section for children's shoes. This image is agonizing, and leaves a lasting impression that humanizes the Holocaust statistics that today are spoken about so casually.

Earlier in the day, before we had reached Majdanek, Romualt had headed for the small town of Parczew, about 140 kilometres south-east of Warsaw. We had left the Sobieski Hotel around nine in the morning. By the time Romualt had navigated his way through the twisting back-roads of the countryside, past Polish peasants still using horse-drawn wagons and scythes in the fields, it was nearly eleven.

In the centre of Parczew, as in the centre of most Polish towns, is the square around which once stood the houses and shops of Parczew's Jews. In 1939, about 5,000 Jews lived here, almost half the town's population. Today there are none. The town's synagogue is now a clothing factory, and its *mikveh* (ritual bathhouse) a movie theatre. Though I did not visit Parczew's former Jewish cemetery, I later learned that in it stands a small monument to Jewish soldiers murdered there in February 1940.

We had a drink of Pepsi at a local bar, and Romualt asked directions to the forest on the outskirts of the town. Before we left, I had Romualt ask the bartender and his wife if they knew anything about partisans and Jews. They had heard the stories, but they had happened, they said, a long time before they were born.

The car ride to the forest took only a few minutes. I tried to imagine what it must have been like in August 1942 for the thousands of Jewish fugitives who fled into the woods rather than be shipped to the Treblinka death camp like cattle for slaughter. But imagination can only go so far. Finally, we stopped on the edge of the trees. Romualt thought it was peculiar that I wanted to take photographs of trees, though he encouraged me to take my time.

Except for the chirping of birds, the air was still and the setting serene. Even when I shut my eyes, it was difficult to envision that, deep in the Parczew Forest, a strong Jewish partisan unit led by Chil Grynszpan fought side by side with Polish and Soviet fighters and protected the Jews of nearby family camps. Only about 200 of the more than 4,000 Jews who had escaped into the woods near Parczew walked out when the war had ended. But for the town's bartender and his wife, and indeed for millions of other Poles, such matters were a lifetime ago, best ignored. If only, I thought as I stepped back into Romualt's car, the tall pine and birch trees could talk. They are the only witnesses that remain.

ALL THE REAL HEROES ARE DEAD

There was a young teenage girl at the Bielski family camp, Gitel Morrison remembered, who had given up on life. She refused to bathe. Covered in lice and diseased, she sat alone in the forest waiting to die. But fate intervened.

One day in early 1945, Gitel, whose family had already returned to their hometown of Lodz, was walking down the city's main street. "I passed this beautiful woman and was certain I knew her. A face, I never forget. I went after her and introduced myself. I asked her about her wartime experiences. It was her. She was the sick girl who everyone would not go near. Now I looked at her in astonishment."

Gitel's recollection and many like it from the years immediately following the war testify to one notable fact: the human body is remarkably resilient. It is like a machine that can be repaired, reconditioned, and restored to its original form. The physical recovery of the concentration camp victims was amazing. They were as close to living corpses as human beings can be. One among thousands was Philip Weiss, then twenty-three years old, who had survived more than two years of hell as a slave labourer for the Nazis. When he was finally liberated on May 5, 1945, by the American army, from a factory near the Mauthausen death camp in Austria, the lower part of his body, from his knees down, weighed more than the rest of him. He spent five months recovering in a hospital and then set out to search for his family. It took him two years to find them.

■ ■

For the survivors of the camps and the forests, mental recovery was equally difficult. Studying the traumatic psychological effects of the Holocaust on the survivors and their children has become the subject of research and academic debate.* Not surprisingly, perhaps, the survivor's

---

*The two most notable and divergent views have been advanced by Bruno Bettelheim and Terrence Des Pres. While Bettelheim, in *The Informed Heart* (Glencoe, Ill.: Free Press, 1960), has maintained that survivors tended to be submissive people, "whose survival was attained at the cost of inner autonomy, humanity and self assertion," Des Pres, in *The Survivor: An Anatomy of Life in the Death Camps* (New York: Oxford University Press, 1976), questioned the "relevance of

ability to successfully adapt and start life over again appears to have
been dependent in large part on their experiences during the war and
on the strengths of their personalities and character. Still, there were
common trends in their postwar healing.

When they first began rebuilding their broken lives, they rarely spoke
of what had happened to them — how they had watched the
Einsatzgruppen murder their families, how they had been herded into
ghettos, how they had survived for two and three years by fleeing
into the forests. Some revisited their experiences by venturing into
the forests of their new homelands. Other former partisans just wanted
to forget. Most, such as Gitel (Zelkowicz) Morrison, had other more
pressing matters to occupy their new lives.

After they had left the forest, Gitel and her family made their way
from one city to the next, from Lida to Bialystok to Lodz, then to
Munich. From Germany, the Zelkowiczes planned to depart for
Palestine, but the quotas for Jewish immigrants were filled quickly. With
the help of North American relatives, they immigrated to Canada in
1948. Gitel's future husband, Moishe (Morris) Chwaiesky (later
changed to Morrison), a former *puszcza* fighter, eventually joined her
in Winnipeg, where they were married in 1949. Gitel and Morris
purchased a small house in the city's north end and began raising a
family. In time, with a lot of hard work, they prospered.

Jack and Rochelle Sutin and their new baby daughter, Cecilia, who
had been born in a displaced person's camp in Munich soon after the
war, immigrated to St. Paul, Minnesota, in 1949, with assistance from
Rochelle's uncle, Herman Schleiff, who had left Europe many years
earlier. Once in the United States, Jack worked his way up from adult-
aged stock boy of the Golden Rule department store to vice-president of
the company within seven years. Meanwhile, Rochelle had another

---

psychoanalytical theory" and focused more on their individual and often "humiliating" personal
experiences. As Hillel Klein of the Hebrew University in Jerusalem has argued, however, "neither
approach allows for the past existence of the survivors and its psychological effect on them, both
as individuals and as a group; a past with special, precious sets of values and traditions. The traditional defenses of Jews . . . which remained viable during the Holocaust experience and were
later utilized in adapting to life as survivors, are overlooked by both authors." (See Klein, "General
Survey, Psychology of Survivors," *EH* 4: 1426–28.)

child, a son named Lawrence, and struggled to learn English. "I watched a lot of television in those days," she says. "Milton Berle and Eddie Cantor were my tutors."

As for their wartime experiences, none of their North American friends and relatives initially wanted to hear about those dark days. Who would believe such wild stories in any event? Who would believe that human beings could live, as Rochelle Sutin puts it, "like animals in the woods"? Adds Jack: "During [the fifties] we met with a number of American Jews, and I have to say it was extremely difficult to talk with them about the Holocaust. Not because we were unwilling or afraid to speak, but because they simply could not understand. Especially when I started to tell them about our time with the Jewish partisans. I had the feeling that they didn't believe what I was saying."

So they, like others, remained silent, troubled in sleep by nightmares of attack dogs and whips, racked by guilt that they alone, among their loved ones, had walked out of the woods to start their lives over again. Many married and had children (some, who had lost their first spouses and families during the war, for the second time) and continued the Jewish traditions that they had been taught in another world, in another time. Fruma (Frances) B., a Bielski survivor living in the United States, keeps a kosher home and lights the candles each Sabbath, but for decades has been troubled by a question for which there is no simple answer: Why did it happen?

As they reached middle age, these former partisans, more able to speak and to cope with their memories than those who had suffered at Auschwitz, Majdanek, Dachau, and the other death camps, began to write their memoirs and deliver public presentations to high-school students. They realized, finally, that it was their duty and obligation to set the historical record straight, as painful as it was. Who else could tell the world about the Jewish people who were nearly obliterated from the face of the earth? Who else could recount the amazing chronicle of their resistance?

Looking back now, it is clear that this resistance was, to use Faye Schulman's words, an "act of desperation." She, like many surviving partisans, believed that her flight to the forest was merely prolonging the inevitable, that death would quickly consume her as it had her family.

And for far too many fugitives, this was sadly the case. It is easy now to suggest that more Jews should have anticipated the Nazi terror, that they should have resisted earlier and not sat patiently behind ghetto walls. Such arguments, however, are elementary. Writes Leon Kahn: "The Nazis found an ally in the eternal tenacity of man's capacity for hope, and the refusal of any human being to believe that an entire nation could be capable of absolute evil. We knew they meant to degrade us, to make us lose faith in God and in ourselves. But that they intended our total extermination was completely unbelievable and, to an extent, still is."

Even the soldiers of the Soviet Red Army who were caught behind enemy lines and became part of, according to a 1969 U.S. study, the "greatest irregular resistance movement in the history of warfare," who had access to weapons, supplies, explosives, and a communication network, and who were led by several brilliant and daring military strategists and tacticians, had limited success against a powerful and insurmountable German enemy. How could the Jews have been expected to fare any better?

In the decades that followed the end of the war, Soviet writers and propagandists created a larger-than-life myth about the country's partisans, about their courageous contributions, missions, and exploits. This myth deeply troubled former partisan commander Aleksei Fyodorov. "After reading newspapers and magazines in Moscow, I saw that the stories about partisan deeds were often inventions," he wrote in his memoirs. "The heroes in these stories were so boundlessly brave and so extraordinary that it was hard to believe they were real human beings. . . . I often regretted that we didn't have a writer in our ranks, who might have truthfully told how the most ordinary of Soviet men and women were battling in the forests, how heroism was becoming an everyday necessity for them."

Heroism, too, in its most basic form, became an everyday necessity for the countless Jewish men and women who, often in a moment of panic during an *Aktion*, took the fateful steps that allowed them to survive. In the whirlwind that seized them and stubbornly refused to let go for three years, they experienced a mixture of emotions: fear, defiance, revenge, self-preservation.

Now, more than fifty years later, their acts of defiance and revenge seem heroic, but heroism was the furthest thing from their thoughts. "All I went through to survive other Jews also experienced," Faye Schulman has written. "There are accounts of suffering far worse than my own. I, after all, survived all my dangerous missions, while thousands of Jewish boys and girls fell in battle, losing their lives heroically fighting for freedom."

Maybe so. Maybe all the real heroes *are* dead, as survivors like Faye Schulman suggest. Still, from the forests of eastern Poland to the woods south of Vilna, Jewish fighters like Chil Grynszpan, Sam Gruber, and Abba Kovner showed remarkable fortitude in the face of overwhelming odds. They also lived to tell their exceptional stories.

Perhaps the experiences of the Jews in the family camps, particularly those who were saved by Tuvia Bielski and Shalom Zorin, deserve special consideration. During the war, such self-preservation was not always appreciated or understood. Resistance meant fighting, and those who did not or could not take up arms were seen as inferior. "Today, when I think about it, not as I was then, a youngster with no children and no responsibility, but as a father with a wife and children, I see the situation differently," reflects former partisan and historian Yitzhak Arad. "From a national point of view, [survival in the family camps] was no less important than the actual fighting. The Germans wanted to exterminate all the Jews [and] anything done to stop this [was] significant."

In terms of sheer perseverance and numbers saved, Tuvia Bielski clearly stands out from the rest of the family camp leaders and saviours. Whether Bielski, who died in 1987 in New York City, operated from a master plan to rescue more than a thousand Jews from certain death in the ghettos and concentration camps remains debatable. Tuvia and his brothers, like most Jewish leaders of the day, were not perfect — far from it. They made mistakes, and often reacted impetuously and not always with the best judgment. But this grave time did not ususally present moments for reflection. As head of a large group of defenceless and fearful people, including hundreds of women, children, and elderly, Tuvia took the various paths that presented themselves and did not stop to ask himself whether he was doing the right thing. Hesitation meant death.

Of course, this debate about Tuvia Bielski's decisions and actions is academic. As many survivors maintain, none of these details truly matters. "Without Tuvia, what would we be?" asks Sulia Rubin. "Nothing. Tuvia gave us the possibility to exist." Sulia and others like her make a strong case. There are probably more than 13,000 descendants of the 1,200 Bielski partisans, and the numbers grow each year.

Without the strength, perseverance, and determination of Jews like the Bielskis, Abba Kovner, Shalom Zorin, Misha Gildenman, Chil Grynszpan, and many more, thousands of these Jewish fugitives of the forest would not be alive today to tell their grandchildren the inspiring and shocking stories of their survival. That is their true legacy, the reason why each and every one of these partisan leaders deserves to be remembered with dignity and honour.

In the war's darkest hour, they did not surrender to the forces of evil. Instead, they lived each day to the next with faith in the memorable words of poet and partisan Hirsh Glik: *Zog nit keynmol az du geyst dem letstn veg* — Never say that you are on your last journey. For them, the journey has never ended.

FOREST REUNIONS

More than five decades later, the forests remain as the Jewish fugitives left them, accessible but still isolated from the nearby cities and towns. Camp sites are now overgrown with trees and brush, yet with a bit of determination they can still be found; monuments to the millions who were slaughtered now stand beside the death pits. Still, many former partisans in North America and Israel have no desire to return to their homelands, places of death and survival. "I will never go back to Poland," asserts Gitel Morrison from her home in Winnipeg. "What is there for me to see? Nothing." She echoes the sentiments of many Holocaust survivors.

But the pressure to show children and grandchildren their roots, as painful as it is, pushes some to make the fateful trip. More than fifty

Bielski camp survivors and their families returned to Novogrudok for a poignant reunion in 1993. The group visited the ruins of the courthouse complex, which once served as the town's ghetto, and ventured into the Naliboki Forest. The few *zemlianki*, barely intact, were as they remembered them: bunkers with mud walls and log roofs, their former homes. And at each spot that marked their time as victims and resistance fighters, they gathered together with tears in their eyes to light memorial candles and recite the Kaddish, the ancient prayer for the dead. They erected a stone memorial, the only lasting sign that Jews once lived in Novogrudok and the surrounding villages.

Peter Silverman and David Smuschkowitz have now returned to their Lithuanian hometown of Jody twice, first in 1995 and then again in 1997 with their children. Both found the experience difficult, but somehow necessary. "It was very emotional and frustrating," recalls Smuschkowitz. "You talk to the local peasants, people we knew as teenagers, and no one is sorry for what happened. Sadly, they don't give a damn whether there are Jews in the town or not."

After the war, neither Silverman nor Smuschkowitz visited the site of the death pits outside Jody where members of their families had been slaughtered. "I don't really know why we did not go there," says Silverman. "Maybe, in those days, we were in a stage of denial. Many survivors have told me they felt the same way. Once, we were only about 50 metres from the mass grave, but we couldn't bring ourselves to look at it." Both men stood by the graves for the first time on their visit in 1995 and recited the *kaddish* prayer.

The nearby Koziany Forest, where they carried out their partisan resistance, is now difficult to enter, but they were able to drive to the outskirts of the woods to show their children. As they stood on the edge of the forest, their sons and daughters found it hard to comprehend the tragic ordeal their fathers had been through. Not Peter Silverman and David Smuschkowitz, however. For them, as for so many other fugitives of the forest, the memory of that terrible time and place remains far too vivid and real, and will always be in their minds, hearts, and souls.

Fugitives like Alex Levin, who survived as a young teenager with a group of ten Jews in a cave in a forest near Rokitno, have found serenity in the forest. Levin still regularly visits woodland areas north of his Toronto, Ontario, home. Asked if he still believes in God after his experiences, Alex responds: "My God is the forest. I survived because of the forest."

SELECTED BIOGRAPHIES

This is a selection of biographies of several of the key characters featured in this book. Some are less well known, while for others more extensive biographies can be found in the *Encyclopedia of the Holocaust* and other available reference sources.

Tuvia Bielski: Born in 1906 in a village near Novogrudok. Bielski and his two brothers, Asael and Zus, organized the largest family camp during the Holocaust, following the Nazi invasion of occupied Soviet territory in June 1941. The Bielskis were responsible for saving the lives of approximately 1,200 Jews. Their main camp was located deep in the Naliboki Forest, west of Minsk, where a small village was constructed. After the war, Tuvia immigrated to Palestine and later moved to the United States. He died in New York City in 1987 at age 81.

Jacob Gens: A controversial police chief and then the head of the Judenrat of the Vilna ghetto. Gens mistakenly believed that making Jews useful would keep them alive, thus he opposed armed resistance and escapes that angered the Nazis. While he did save some Jewish lives, he eventually became the Germans' pawn. In July 1943, he complied with the German demand to hand over Yitzhak Wittenberg, one of the leaders of the Fareynegte Partizaner Organizatsye, or FPO (the United Partisan Organization). Gens was executed by the Nazis on September 14, 1943, at the age of thirty-eight.

Misha Gildenman: An engineer from the town of Korets, Gildenman escaped from the ghetto in September 1942 with his son, Simcha, and organized a successful partisan group in the forests of Volhynia. In the forest he was known as Diadia Misha, or Uncle Misha. Gildenman immigrated to Israel in the early 1950s. He died there in 1958.

Josef Glazman: Resistance leader and partisan from Vilna. Before the war, Glazman, who was born in 1913, was active in the Betar Zionist movement, the youth wing of the Revisionist Party led by Vladimir Jabotinsky. He was one of the founders of the resistance movement in the Vilna ghetto, the FPO, established in January 1942. Glazman led the first group of FPO fighters to the Narocz Forest in July 1943 and helped found the partisan unit Nekamah (revenge). This group was linked with both Soviet and Lithuanian (Communist) partisans. He and his fighters were murdered in an ambush in October 1943.

Yechiel ("Chil") Grynszpan: Born in 1918 in the village of Sosnowica in eastern Poland, Chil Grynszpan successfully organized and led one of the most effective all-Jewish partisan detachments in eastern Europe. Operating from a base in the Parczew Forest region, Grynszpan's partisan unit eventually numbered at least 200 fighters. He aligned his group with the Gwardia Ludowa, or People's Guard, the left-wing Polish partisans. After the war, Grynszpan worked as a police chief in the Lublin area before immigrating to Brazil, where other surviving members of his immediate family lived.

Leon Kahn: Born Leibke Kaganowicz in 1925 in the village of Eisiskes not far from Vilna. After experiencing abuse in the ghetto, Leon escaped to the forest with his younger sister and father (who both eventually perished). He survived the war fighting as a partisan in a Soviet detachment in the forest area north of Grodno. His recollections of wartime experiences can be found in *No Time to Mourn: A True Story of a Jewish Partisan Fighter*. Kahn immigrated to Canada in 1948 and currently lives in Vancouver with his family.

Abba Kovner: Born in 1918 in Sevastopol, Russia, Kovner was an active member of the Ha-Shomer Hatsair youth Zionist movement before the war. He became the leader of the Vilna ghetto underground, the FPO, after Yitzhak

Wittenberg was killed in July 1943. Kovner called on the surviving Jews of Vilna to join the struggle with the immortal words: "Let us not go like sheep to the slaughter." During the liquidation of the Vilna ghetto in September 1943, he escaped to the Rudniki Forest and became a partisan. In the summer of 1944, he helped liberate Vilna. Later, Kovner was instrumental in the organization of the Bricha movement, which helped Jewish survivors immigrate to Palestine. Kovner himself made it to Palestine in 1946 and fought in the ensuing Israeli War of Independence. An accomplished writer and activist, Kovner contributed much to Israeli literature. He died in 1988.

Gitel (Zelkowicz) Morrison: Gitel Zelkowicz was born in Lodz, Poland, in 1930. In 1940, Gitel, her parents, Lazer and Leska, and brothers Yossel and Simon made their way to Lida in Soviet-occupied territory. Following the Nazi invasion, the family was incarcerated in the Lida ghetto. Through Yossel's contacts with the partisans, the Zelkowiczes were able to escape to the forest in the fall of 1942. Gitel and her family survived the war as members of Tuvia Bielski's family camp. Yossel Zelkowicz was killed in the spring of 1943 while on a reconnaissance mission. With the help of North American relatives, the Zelkowicz family immigrated to Winnipeg, Canada, in 1948. A year later, Gitel married Moishe (Morris) Chwaiesky (later changed to Morrison), a former partisan who had also moved to Winnipeg. Gitel currently lives in Toronto; her husband, Morris, died in 1984.

Peter Silverman: Born in 1924 in the town of Jody, north of Vilna. With his cousin David Smuschkowitz and other family members, Silverman escaped to the Koziany Forest in 1942 and eventually joined the Soviet-led Spartak partisan brigade. As a young fighter, he was involved in guerrilla warfare and participated in numerous sabotage missions. Following the war, Peter immigrated to North America and currently lives in Toronto, where he is an active member of the Canadian Society for Yad Vashem. A frequent speaker at high schools, Peter and his cousins described their experiences in their memoirs, *From Victims to Victors*, published in 1992.

Jack and Rochelle (Schleiff) Sutin: Jack Sutin grew up in Mir, and Rochelle Schleiff lived in the neighbouring town of Stolpce. While most members of their families were killed, both managed to escape to the forest not far from Mir. There, in the woods, they reunited, fell in love, and survived. In June 1943, they met a fighter with Shalom Zorin's group who led them to the Zorin family camp, where they remained for the duration of the war. They immigrated to Minneapolis, Minnesota, in 1949. Their memoirs, *Jack and Rochelle: A Holocaust Story of Love and Resistance*, were published in 1995.

Harold Werner: Born Hershel Zimmerman in 1918 in Gorzkow, Poland, Werner was in Warsaw when the war broke out in 1939 and was able to escape east to occupied Soviet territory. When this area also came under German control, Werner survived as a fugitive and later became a partisan in a predominately Jewish unit under the command of Chil Grynszpan in the Parczew Forest region. Werner died at his home in Miami, Florida, in 1990. His wartime experiences are related in his memoirs, *Fighting Back*, published posthumously in 1992.

Shalom Zorin: The leader of the second-largest family camp during the Holocaust. A carpenter from Minsk, Zorin escaped from the Minsk ghetto in late 1941. Eventually, he established his camp for Jewish fugitives in the Naliboki Forest; it had about 800 members by the end of the war. Like the nearby Bielski camp, Zorin's camp also served Soviet partisans as a supply and repair depot. Zorin lost a leg in a battle in June 1944. He died in Israel in 1974 at the age of seventy-two, only three years after he had arrived there from eastern Europe.

NOTES

ABBREVIATIONS

AI   Author's personal interview.

EH   *Encyclopedia of the Holocaust.* 4 vols. New York: Macmillan, 1990.

GFH   Beit Lohamei Haghetaot Archives (Ghetto Fighters' House), Kibbutz Lohamei Haghetaot, Israel.

FVA   Fortunoff Video Archive for Holocaust Testimonies, Yale University.

USH   United States Holocaust Memorial Museum Archives, Washington, D.C.

YVA   Yad Vashem Archives, Jerusalem.

Note: The numbers to the left of the citations below are the page numbers on which the entries appear.

PAGE   PREFACE

xiv   While I am aware of the obvious limitations of oral history . . . See "Historiography of the Holocaust," *EH*, vol. 2, 668–69.

INTRODUCTION: THE FUGITIVES

xxi   "The forest was white . . ." USH, RG-02.133. Liza Ettinger, "From the Lida Ghetto to the Bielski Partisans," (1989), 53.

xxii   The reconnaissance party returned without . . . AI, Gitel Morrison and Simon Zelcovitch (see Selected Bibliography for complete information on all interviews).

xxiii   Half a lifetime later . . . Leon Kahn, *No Time to Mourn* (Vancouver: Laurelton Press, 1978), 144–45.

xxv   But those who dismiss . . . See, for example, Raul Hilberg, *The Destruction of European Jews*, vol. 3 (New York: New Viewpoints, 1973), 1031, and Oscar Handlin, "Jewish Resistance to the Nazis," *Commentary* 34 (November 1962): 398–405.

xxv   The question should not be . . . See Yehuda Bauer, *A History of the Holocaust* (New York: Franklin Watts, 1982), 245–77.

xxvi   "Israeli historians Yisrael Gutman and Shmuel Krakowski, *Unequal Victims: Poles and Jews during World War II* (New York: Holocaust Library, 1986), 103.

xxvi   By 1944, in this vast area . . . For statistics on the Soviet and Jewish partisan movement, see John A. Armstrong, ed., *Soviet Partisans in World War II* (Madison: University of Wisconsin, 1964), 151; Yitzhak Arad, "Family Camps in the Forests" *EH*, vol. 2, 469; and "Partisans" *EH*, vol. 3, 1108–21.

xxvii   In all, about one-third . . . Ezra Mendelsohn, *The Jews of East Central Europe between the World Wars* (Bloomington, Ind.: Indiana University Press, 1993), 5; Neil Ascherson, *The Struggles for Poland* (London: Michael Joseph, 1987), 59.

xxvii   Approximately 75 percent of Poles . . . Gutman and Krakowski, *Unequal Victims*, 2.

xxvii   According to the 1931 census . . . Mendelsohn, *Jews of East Central Europe*, 23–24.

xxviii   In short, Jews were people of the town . . . Moshe Kahanowitz, "Why No Separate Jewish Partisan Movement Was Established," *Yad Vashem Studies* 1 (1957): 154–55.

xxviii   "The Jew treats with aversion . . ." Cited in Edward D. Wynot, "A Necessary Cruelty: The Emergence of Official Anti-Semitism in Poland, 1936–1939," *The American Historical Review* 76, no. 4 (October 1971): 1036.

xxviii   Dmowski's solution to this problem . . . Lucy S. Dawidowicz, *From That Time and Place: A Memoir, 1938–1947* (New York: W. W. Norton, 1989), 172.

xxviii   The National Democrats supported . . . Wynot, "Necessary Cruelty," 1036–58.

xxviii   Successive Polish governments . . . Szymon Rudnicki, "From 'Numerus Clausus' to 'Numerus Nullus'," *Polin* 2 (1987): 246–68.

xxix   Jewish enrolment in . . . Dawidowicz, *From That Time and Place*, 167. "The effect of [Jews'] . . ." Cited in Wynot, "Necessary Cruelty," 1049. "It wasn't so much . . ." Dawidowicz, *From That Time and Place*, 164–65.

xxix   "By that age. . ." Jack Sutin and Rochelle Sutin, *Jack and Rochelle: A Holocaust Story of Love and Resistance* (St. Paul, Minn.: Graywolf Press, 1995), 16; AI, Jack Sutin.

xxx   "Dirty Jew . . ." Martin Gilbert, *The Boys: Triumph over Adversity* (Vancouver: Douglas and McIntyre, 1996), 7.

xxx   "When the teacher . . ." Ibid., 15.

xxx   "In instances when the Jewish . . ." Dawidowicz, *From That Time and Place*, 166.

xxx   "The overwhelming majority of Jews . . ." Yisrael Gutman, "Polish Anti-Semitism between the Wars: An Overview," in Yisrael Gutman, E. Mendelsohn, J. Reinharz, and C. Shmeruk, eds., *The Jews of Poland between Two World Wars* (Hanover, Mass.: University Press of New England, 1989), 102.

xxx   Beginning in 1935 . . . Dawidowicz, *From That Time and Place*, 177–80.

xxxi   They joined Zionist and socialist clubs . . . Celia S. Heller, *On the Edge of Destruction* (New York: Columbia University Press, 1977), 265–73.

xxxi   The Bundists, in particular . . . Ibid., 288.

CHAPTER 1: NAZIS AND SOVIETS

3   "They came like a cloud . . ." Anna Eilenberg-Eibeshitz, "For My Mother," in Jehoshua Eibeshitz and Anna Eilenberg-Eibeshitz, eds., *Women in the Holocaust* (New York: Remember Publications, 1993), 71.

4   "*Wenn Judenblut von* . . ." Ibid., 72. For a slightly different version of the song, see Daniel Jonah Goldhagen, *Hitler's Willing Executioners: Ordinary Germans and the Holocaust* (New York: Alfred A. Knopf, 1996), 500, n. 51.

5   But such were the opportunities . . . Bullock, *Hitler and Stalin* (Toronto: McClelland and Stewart, 1991), 611–12; J. Noakes and G. Pridham, eds., *Nazism 1919–1945: A Documentary Reader*, vol. 3

(Exeter, Devon: University of Exeter Press, 1988), 743–44.

5   "There will probably never again . . ." Ibid., 739–43.

6   "No reason was given . . ." Richard Lukas, *The Forgotten Holocaust: The Poles under German Occupation 1939–1944* (Lexington, Ky.: The University Press of Kentucky, 1986), 3.

6   "When his daughter . . ." Martin Gilbert, *The Holocaust: A Jewish Tragedy* (London: Fontana Press, 1987), 85.

6   As he bent over . . . Ibid., 90.

6   Fifteen-year-old Mary Berg . . . Laurel Holliday, *Children in the Holocaust and World War II* (New York: Pocket Books, 1995), 219.

7   It took twenty-four hours . . . Gilbert, *Holocaust*, 101.

7–8 "We won't waste much time . . ." Noakes and Pridham, *Nazism 1919–1945*, 1055.

8   By a decree of December 1, 1939 . . . Ibid., 1061.

8   Adam Czerniakow, the fifty-nine-year-old . . . Raul Hilberg, Stanislaw Staron, and Josef Kermisz, eds., *The Warsaw Diary of Adam Czerniakow* (New York: Stein and Day, 1979), 106–7.

8   "We must collect . . ." Ibid., 105–6.

9   Somehow Czerniakow, who suffered . . . Ibid., 112.

9   During one such raid in Warsaw . . . Gilbert, *Holocaust*, 100.

9   "One guard called Rudi . . ." Gilbert, *The Boys*, 87–88.

10   "These girls were compelled . . ." Abraham I. Katsh, ed., *Scroll of Agony: The Warsaw Diary of Chaim A. Kaplan* (New York: Collier, 1981), 87.

10   It took Lazer Zelkowicz . . . AI, Gitel Morrison.

11   Estimates put the number . . . Dov Levin, "The Attitude of the Soviet Union to the Rescue of Jews" in *Rescue Attempts during the Holocaust: Proceedings of the Second Yad Vashem International Historical Conference* (Jerusalem: Yad Vashem, 1977), 228–29.

11   "A train filled with Jews going east . . ." Norman Davies and Antony Polonsky, eds., *Jews in Eastern Poland and the USSR, 1939–46* (New York: St. Martin's Press, 1991), 28.

11   Nahum Kohn, a twenty-one-year-old . . . Nahum Kohn, *A Voice from the Forest* (New York: Holocaust Library, 1980), 18–19.

12   In Warsaw, in November, 1939 . . . Yitzhak Arad, *The Partisan* (New York: Holocaust Library, 1979), 16–20.

12   "When they saw us . . ." AI, Gitel Morrison.

13   "Long live the redeemers . . ." Dov Levin, "The Response of the Jews of Eastern Poland to the Invasion of the Red Army in September, 1939," *Gal-ed*, 11 (1989): 95; Davies and Polonsky, *Jews in Eastern Poland*, 16.

13   "These are Messiah's times . . ." Davies and Polonsky, *Jews in Eastern Poland*, 16. See also Jan Tomasz Gross, "The Sovietization of Western Ukraine and Western Byelorussia," in ibid., 66.

13   "We had been sentenced to death . . ." Ibid., 279–80.

13   "I know who the Bolsheviks . . ." Levin, "Response of Jews," 95–96.

14   Historian Jan Gross points out . . . Gross, "Sovietization of Western Ukraine," 73; Bullock, *Hitler and Stalin* , 658.

15   "[Jews] are entering . . ." Davies and Polonsky, *Jews in Eastern Poland*, 13 and 266–67.

15   At Communism's peak . . . Jaff Schatz, *The Generation: The Rise and Fall of the Jewish Communists of Poland* (Los Angeles: University of California Press, 1991), 83 and 95–98.

15   "Jews constituted 25 per cent . . ." Lukas, *Forgotten Holocaust*, 77.

15   Seeing no future . . . Davies and Polonsky, *Jews in Eastern Poland*, 17.

15   "Who cared about Communism . . ." Ibid., 16. See also Levin, "Response of Jews," 101–2.

16   But it was equally true that the Russians arrested . . . Davies and Polonsky, *Jews in Eastern Poland*, 128.

16   Soviet authorities closed . . . Ibid., 22–23.

16   "If you had ten to fifteen . . ." AI, Saul Ihilchik.

16   "Leo Raber, who at twenty-one . . ." AI, Leo Raber.

16   In short, when it came to the Jews . . . Davies and Polonsky, *Jews in Eastern Poland*, 131.

Chapter 2: June 1941

17   "The struggle against . . ." Lucy S. Dawidowicz, *The War against the Jews 1933–1945* (New York: Holt, Rinehart and Winston, 1975), 166.

17   In these initial dark days . . . Ibid., 171.

18   The destruction of Bolshevism . . . Ibid., 166. See also Yitzhak Arad, Yisrael Gutman and Abraham Margaliot, eds., *Documents on the Holocaust* (Jerusalem and New York: Ktav, 1981), 376.

18   "The Jewish doctrine . . .", Adolf Hitler, *Mein Kampf*, Ralph Manheim, trans., (Boston: Houghton Mifflin, 1971), 61–65.

18–19   "The essential aim . . ." Lucy S. Dawidowicz, *A Holocaust Reader* (New York: Behrman House, 1976), 70–71.

19   In preparation for the coming battle . . . Dawidowicz, *War against the Jews*, 161; Arad, et al., *Documents*, 375.

19   The first wave . . . William Shirer, *The Rise and Fall of the Third Reich* (New York: Crest Books, 1962) 1117, and Alexander Dallin, *German Rule in Russia, 1941–1945* (New York: St. Martin's Press, 1957), 3–10.

19   Sixteen-year-old Leibke Kaganowicz . . ." Kahn, *No Time to Mourn*, 17–45, and AI, Leon Kahn.

21   By the evening of June 24 . . . Yitzhak Arad, *Ghetto in Flames: The Struggle and Destruction of the Jews in Vilna in the Holocaust* (New York: Holocaust Library, 1982), 30–35. See also Lucjan Dobroszycki and Jeffrey S. Gurock, eds., *The Holocaust in the Soviet Union* (New York: M. E. Sharpe, 1993), 96.

21   Even before the Nazis . . . On Vilna and Kovno, see Dov Levin, "On the Relations between the Baltic Peoples and Their Jewish Neighbours before, during and after World War II," *Holocaust and Genocide Studies* 5, no. 1: 55–57; Dov Levin, "Lithuanian Attitudes toward the Jewish Minority in the Aftermath of the Holocaust: The Lithuanian Press, 1991–92," Holocaust and Genocide Studies 7, no. 2: 247–48; Arad, *Ghetto in Flames*, 46–47; Dawidowicz, *Holocaust Reader*, 93; Dobroszycki and Gurock, *Holocaust in the Soviet Union*, 195–204; AI, Sara Ginaite.

22   "How do you abandon a house . . ." FVA, Schifre Z., T-11.

22   "No one believed . . ." AI, Sonia Ostrinsky.

22   More telling was . . . Sutins, *Jack and Rochelle*, 32. Also, AI, Abba Gelman.

22   "In those days . . ." AI, Ernie Tessler.

23   They shared their food . . . Sulia Wolozhinski Rubin, *Against the Tide: The Story of an Unknown Partisan* (Jerusalem: Posner and Sons, 1980), 65; AI, Jerry Seigel, Sara Ginaite, Ernie Tessler. On the other hand, it should be noted that several survivors remember watching Wehrmacht soldiers shoot Jews down in the street. AI, Moshe Bairach and Jacob Greenstein. A controversial photo exhibit about the Wehrmacht during the war is currently travelling through Germany. It also attests to many incidents of brutality perpetrated by German sol-

diers. See "Riot erupts over exhibit," *Winnipeg Free Press*, January 25, 1998.

23   On Nazi police and Einsatzgruppen, see Leni Yahil, *The Holocaust: The Fate of European Jewry* (New York: Oxford University Press, 1990), 130–32, 255–57; Dawidowicz, *The War against the Jews*, 167; U.S. War Department, *Handbook on German Military Forces* (Baton Rouge, La., 1990), 180–99; *EH*, vol. 2, "Einsatzgruppen," 433–39; vol. 3, "Ordnungspolizei," 1093; Reuben Ainsztein, *Jewish Resistance in Nazi-Occupied Eastern Europe* (London: Paul Elek, 1974), 223; Goldhagen, *Hitler's Willing Executioners*, 148–53 and 517, n. 63; Richard Breitman, "Himmler's Police Auxiliaries in the Occupied Soviet Territories," *Simon Wiesenthal Annual* 7 (1994): 23–39; Yaacov Lozowick, "Rollbahn Mord: The Early Activities of Einsatzgruppe C," in Michael Marrus, ed., *The Nazi Holocaust: Historical Articles on the Destruction of European Jews*, vol. 3, (London: Meckler Corporation, 1989), 471–91.

23   *Judenfrei* or "free of Jews" was another favourite Nazi term . . . *EH*, vol. 4, 1753.

24   At first only Communist party . . . Noakes and Pridham, *Nazism*, 1091–92; Alfred Streim, "The Tasks of the Einsatzgruppen" in Marrus, *Nazi Holocaust*, vol. 3, 438–39; Yisrael Gutman, *The Jews of Warsaw, 1939–1943* (Bloomington, Ind.: Indiana University Press, 1989), 159.

24   In his affidavit . . . "Affidavit of Otto Ohlendorf," November 5, 1945, Nuremberg Documents, 2620-PS.

25   Under the command of Maj. Ernest Weis . . . Christopher R. Browning, *Ordinary Men* (New York: HarperCollins, 1992), 11–12; Goldhagen, *Hitler's Willing Executioners*, 188; Ainsztein, *Jewish Resistance*, 222–23.

25   "The unit had barely . . . Goldhagen, *Hitler's Willing Executioners*, 188.

25   Seeing this, one member . . . Browning, *Ordinary Men*, 12.

25   When this did not produce . . . Ibid., 12–13; Goldhagen, *Hitler's Willing Executioners*, 189–92; Ainsztein, *Jewish Resistance*, 222–23.

25   Initially the Nazis had hoped . . . Noakes and Pridham, *Nazism*, 1092–93, 1093–94, and 1094; Arad, *Ghetto in Flames*, 67.

26   "They were the strongest . . ." FVA, Frances B., T-959. See also Nechama Tec, *Defiance: The Bielski Partisans* (New York: Oxford University Press, 1993), 27–28.

26   In Stolpce, Rochelle Sutin's father . . . Sutins, *Jack and Rochelle*, 37–38.

26   As had been their practice . . . Yahil, *Holocaust*, 131, 462–63; Michael Marrus, *The Holocaust in History* (Hanover, Mass.: The University Press of New England, 1987), 134–35; Gutman, *Warsaw*, 31.

26   After a Nazi policeman . . . Gilbert, *Holocaust*, 184.

27   The rules changed daily . . . See Avraham Tory, *Surviving the Holocaust: The Kovno Ghetto Diary* (Cambridge, Mass., 1990), 50; Arad, *Ghetto in Flames*, 56; Kahn, *No Time to Mourn*, 23–27; Ilya Ehrenberg and Vasily Grossman, eds., *The Black Book: The Nazi Crimes against the Jewish People* (New York: Holocaust Library, 1980); Peter Silverman, David Smuschkowitz and Peter Smuszkowicz, *From Victims to Victors* (Toronto: Canadian Society for Yad Vashem, 1992), 73–74; Ettinger, "From the Lida Ghetto to the Bielski Partisans," 22.

27   "I stand at the window . . ." Yitzhok Rudashevski, *The Diary of the Vilna Ghetto: June 1941–April 1943* (Western Galilee, Israel: Ghetto Fighters' House, 1972), 27–28.

28   "It is a sleepless, desperate night . . ." Ibid., 31.

28   "The street streamed . . ." Ibid., 32.

29   "Besides the four of us . . ." Ibid., 33.

29   "The first night was hell . . ." Ettinger, "From the Lida Ghetto to the Bielski Partisans," 16.

29   "The [Demokratu or Democracy] square was . . ." Tory, *Kovno Ghetto Diary*, 51–53.

30   "When the light of day arrived . . ." Faye Schulman, *A Partisan's Memoir: A Woman of the Holocaust* (Toronto: Second Story Press, 1995), 66–67.

30   From the start of the German . . . See Silverman, et al., *Victims to Victors*, 82–83; Gutman and Krakowski, *Unequal Victims*, 205–51; Sutins, *Jack and Rochelle*, 37. Also AI, Jack and Rochelle Sutin, Gitel Morrison, Peter Silverman, and Ben Lungen.

31   "One must not waste . . ." David Kahane, *Lvov Ghetto Diary* (Amherst, Mass.: University of Massachusetts Press, 1990), 9–11. See also Tory, *Kovno Ghetto Diary*, 7-9, 14, 50.

31   Holocaust historian Philip Friedman . . ., "Ukrainian-Jewish Relations during the Nazi Occupation," *YIVO Annual of Jewish Social Science* 12 (1959): 274–76.

31   Faye Druk, a survivor of the Lida ghetto . . . AI, Faye Druk.

31   Similarly Eugene Katz . . . AI, Eugene Katz.

31   "Righteous among the Nations . . ." see *EH*, vol. 3, 1279–83. For Zegota, see *EH*, vol. 4, 1729–31.

31   "I saw them kill my [Jewish] neighbour . . ." AI, Adam Goszer.

32   "To ask why . . ." Norman Davies, *God's Playground: A History of Poland*, vol. 2 (New York: Columbia University Press, 1984), 264.

32   "The peasant lifted [his] lamp . . ." Cited Gilbert, *Holocaust*, 200–1.

32   As the group of fifty Jews . . . AI, Willy Moll.

33   Israeli historians Yisrael Gutman and Shmuel Krakowksi . . . Gutman and Krakowski, *Unequal Victims*, 246. For a different view, see Stefan Korbonski, *The Jews and the Poles in World War II* (New York: Hippocrene Books, 1989) 64–68.

33   How can we account for this hateful . . . See A. Zbikowski, "Local Anti-Jewish Pogroms in the Occupied Territories of Eastern Poland, June–July 1941," in Dobroszycki and Gurock, *Holocaust and Soviet Union*, 173–79; Friedman, "Ukrainian-Jewish Relations," 272.

33   "Did you ever see a Jew . . ." AI, Sam Gruber.

34   And the horror and tragedy . . . For Polish Police, see "Polnische Polizei," *EH*, vol. 3, 1178–79.

34   "We're carrying on scientific work . . ." Ehrenberg and Grossman, *The Black Book*, 303.

34   In the same city, a nineteen-year-old . . . Ibid., 304.

35   "For our task . . ." Kahn, *No Time to Mourn*, 31–33.

36   "This decision contained . . ." Tec, *Defiance*, 26–27.

36   October 6 was the first day . . . Arad, *Partisan*, 48–50.

37   In the words of a secret . . . Dawidowicz, *Holocaust Reader*, 70–71.

37   "There was no food . . ." AI, Ben Lungen. See also Yahil, *Holocaust*, 251.

38   The death pits at Vilna . . . Arad, *Ghetto in Flames*, 48, 75; Yahil, *Holocaust*, 277–78.

39   They were, in the words of one Jewish youth . . . Arad, et al., *Documents on the Holocaust*, 400–1; Arad, *Ghetto in Flames*, 192.

39   "We all had to lie . . ." Mina Rosner, *I Am a Witness* (Winnipeg: Hyperion Press, 1990), 59–62.

39   "When a major *Aktion* began in Novogrudok . . ." FVA, Frances B., T-959.

40   Other Jews throughout the eastern area faced . . . See Yahil, *Holocaust*,

256; Arad, *Ghetto in Flames,* 49, 76; Goldhagen, *Hitler's Willing Executioners,* 218, 228–29.

40   Dissatisfied with the inefficiency . . . G. Schneider, "The Two Ghettos in Riga, Latvia, 1941–43" in Dobroszycki and Gurock, *Holocaust and Soviet Union,* 183; Hersh Smolar, *The Minsk Ghetto* (New York: Holocaust Library, 1989), 72–75.

40   From his hiding place . . . Aba Gefen, *Hope in Darkness* (New York: Holocaust Library, 1989), 29.

40–41   Concerned that the work . . . "Affidavit of Otto Ohlendorf," November 5, 1945, Nuremberg Documents, 2620-PS; Goldhagen, *Hitler's Willing Executioners,* 149.

41   "I had to shoot an old . . ." Goldhagen, *Hitler's Willing Executioners,* 219.

41   "Himmler, who attended a mass execution . . ." Gilbert, *Holocaust,* 191; Yahil, *Holocaust,* 259.

41   "Why are you crying . . ." Ehrenberg and Grossman, eds., *The Black Book,* 313–14. Frida Michelson, *I Survived Rumbuli* (New York: Holocaust Library, 1979), 90–92. According to Ehrenberg and Grossman, this episode occured in the Bikernieki Forest. In fact, it may have taken place in the nearby Rumbuli Forest, as Frida Michelson remembered.

42   As efficient as the entire operation . . . See Yahil, *Holocaust,* 259.

43   As late as October 1941 . . . YVA, Testimony of Yehuda Szymszonowicz, 0-33/296; Tec, *Defiance,* 28.

43   The Jews in Jody . . . Silverman, et al., *Victims to Victors,* 75.

43   "The people who were seized . . ." Arad, *Ghetto in Flames,* 199.

43   "The paramount importance . . ." Isaiah Trunk, ed., *Jewish Responses to Nazi Persecution* (New York: Stein and Day, 1979), 10.

43   "To say that when a Jew . . ." Silverman, et al., *Victims to Victors,* 119.

Chapter 3: Partisan Beginnings and Collective Interests

45   "We must show [the Germans] . . ." Ada June Friedman, ed., *Roads to Extinction* (Essays by Philip Friedman), (Philadelphia: The Jewish Publication Society of America, 1980), 367.

45   At sixty-two, Josef Stalin . . . Bullock, *Hitler and Stalin,* 727-29.

46   "The war on the eastern front . . ." Ibid., 726.

46   "Comrades! Citizens! Fighting men . . ." Ibid., 730.

46   To the countless number of Red Army . . . Armstrong, *Soviet Partisans,* 76.

46   In Kiev, Stalin's radio address . . . Aleksei Fyodorov, *The Underground Committee Carries On* (Moscow: Foreign Languages Publishing House, 1952), 15–17.

46   "In the darkness . . ." Arad, *Partisan,* 37.

47   A German report of February 19, 1942 . . . Bullock, *Hitler and Stalin,* 745.

47   These included Jews . . . Armstrong, *Soviet Partisans,* 143.

47   Only about one-third . . . Matthew Cooper, *The Nazi War against the Soviet Partisans, 1941–1944* (New York: Stein and Day, 1979), 33–35.

48   By the end of 1941 . . . Armstrong, *Soviet Partisans,* 151.

48   More often than not, they shot . . . See Schulman, *Partisan's Memoir,* 104–6; Nicholas P. Vakar, *Belorussia: The Making of a Nation* (Cambridge, Mass.: Harvard University Press, 1956), 194–95; AI, Peter Silverman.

48   Jews made up less than 2 percent . . . Dov Levin, "Unique Characteristics of Soviet Jewish Soldiers in the Second World War," *The Shoah and the War* (1992): 234–40; AI, Ben Lungen, Morris Kirshner.

48   Despite Stalin's order . . . Tec, *Defiance,* 66.

48   The Nazis called them "stragglers" . . . Yitzhak Arad, "Jewish Family Camps in the Forests — An Original Means of Rescue," in Marrus, *Nazi Holocaust,* vol. 7, 229–30.

49   But by mid-July 1941, Communist Party . . . Armstrong, *Soviet Partisans,* 528.

49   Prior to Linkov's arrival . . . Ainsztein, *Jewish Resistance,* 282–83.

49   Within time, when the peasants . . . Armstrong, *Soviet Partisans,* 325.

49   This narrow route . . . Ibid., 532.

50   This was a joint operation . . . Cooper, *Nazi War,* 29.

50   As Hitler was forced to concede . . . Ibid., 61.

51   "Active warfare against the Nazis . . ." Yitzhak Arad, "Jewish Armed Resistance in Eastern Europe," in Yisrael Gutman and L. Rothkirchen, eds., *The Catastrophe of European Jewry* (Jerusalem: Yad Vashem, 1976), 492.

51   Its official policy towards Jews . . . See Lukas, *Forgotten Holocaust,* 121–51.

52   Jacob Greenstein, who survived . . . AI, Jacob Greenstein.

52   "We were desperate . . ." Nechama Tec, *In the Lion's Den: The Life of Oswald Rufeisen* (New York: Oxford University Press, 1990), 130.

52   In Vilna and other ghettos . . . Dawidowicz, *War against the Jews*, 386.

53   "Fate suddenly split the people . . ." Rudashevski, *Diary*, 36.

53   This left approximately 20,000 . . . See "Vilna," *EH*, vol. 4, 1573.

53   Meanwhile, on January 20 at a villa . . . See "Wannsee Conference," *EH*, vol. 4, 1593; Gilbert, *Holocaust*, 280–93.

53   As Eichmann later testified . . . See "Wannsee Conference," *EH*, vol. 4, 1593.

54   "We did not know then . . ." Smolar, *Minsk Ghetto*, 72–73.

54   That day, Greenstein and his wife . . . YVA, Testimony of Bella and Jacob Greenstein, 0-33/459.

54   The mass murder of more than 5,000 . . . Gilbert, *Holocaust*, 297; Ainsztein, *Jewish Resistance*, 474.

55   "It was a hair-raising sight . . ." Ettinger, "From the Lida Ghetto to the Bielski Partisans," 25.

55   "The congestion is unbearable . . ." Anna Eilenberg-Eibeshitz, *Remember: A Collection of Testimonies* (Haifa: Institute for Holocaust Studies, 1992), 20–21.

56   "You had only as much space . . ." Sutins, *Jack and Rochelle*, 41.

56   In Vilna, according to . . . Arad, *Ghetto in Flames*, 315.

56   In Kovno an underground hospital . . . Bauer, *A History of the Holocaust*, 187; Arad, *Ghetto in Flames*, 316.

57   The official food ration . . . Trunk, *Jewish Responses*, 13; Arad, *Ghetto in Flames*, 302–3; Bauer, *A History of the Holocaust*, 186–87.

57   In Piotrkow, in central Poland . . . Gilbert, *The Boys*, 91–92.

58   The lack of food . . . Dawidowicz, *War against the Jews*, 228.

58   "The dread of disaster . . ." Pessia Bairach, "In Their Slashing Claws," unpublished manuscript (Tel Aviv, 1958), 10.

58   And in the Baranowicze ghetto . . . FVA, Irving F., T-927.

58   "Heavy drapes were drawn . . ." Eibeshitz, *Women in the Holocaust*, 54–55.

59   "I think to myself . . ." Rudashevski, *Diary*, 67–69.

59   Later, after the war . . . Solon Beinfeld, "The Cultural Life of the Vilna Ghetto," in Marrus, *Nazi Holocaust*, vol. 6, 95.

60   "People laughed and cried . . ." Ibid., 95–96.

60   Herman Kruk, head librarian . . . Ibid., 107.

60   Ralph F., then age twelve, was present . . . FVA, Ralph F., T-110.

61   "I would like to declare . . ." Yahil, *Holocaust,* 263; Grosman, *The Underground Army: Fighters of the Bialystok Ghetto* (New York: Holocaust Library, 1987), 60–67.

62   Leon Kahn recalls . . . Kahn, *No Time to Mourn,* 57–58.

62   "Lacking weapons and military . . ." Dawidowicz, *War against the Jews,* 296.

62   Each day in the Lida ghetto . . . AI, Gitel Morrison.

63   With a wave of his cane . . . Friedman, *Roads to Extinction,* 366–67.

64   Gens was born . . . See "Gens, Jacob," *EH,* vol. 2, 555.

65   "This is the first time . . ." Friedman, *Roads to Extinction,* 366.

65   "I hate them from the bottom of my heart . . ." Rudashevski, *Diary,* 69–70.

65   "He is smiling . . ." Friedman, *Roads to Extinction,* 369–70.

66   A group of young resisters . . . Arad, *Ghetto in Flames,* 396–99.

66   In the ensuing battle . . . Lester Eckman and Chaim Lazar, *The Jewish Resistance: The History of the Jewish Partisans in Lithuania and White Russia during the Nazi Occupation* (New York: Shengold, 1977), 243–45; Arad, *Ghetto in Flames,* 398.

67   He explained his position . . . Arad, *Ghetto in Flames,* 399–400; Isaiah Trunk, *Judenrat: The Jewish Councils in Eastern Europe under Nazi Occupation* (New York: Stein and Day, 1977), 456.

67   In Kovno, Dr. Elhanan Elkes . . . Isaiah Trunk, "*The Attitude of the Judenrats to the Problems of Armed Resistance against the Nazis,*" in Gutman and Rothkirchen, *The Catastrophe of European Jewry,* 435–36.

68   Worse still were the actions . . . See Ibid., 425–50; Shmuel Spector, *The Holocaust of Volhynian Jews 1941–1944* (Jerusalem: Yad Vashem and the Federation of Volhynian Jews, 1990), 230.

68   And in Sosnowiec . . . Friedman, *Roads to Extinction,* 358–59; "Merin, Moshe," *EH,* vol. 4, 972–74.

68   "Many of you think of me . . ." Friedman, *Roads to Extinction,* 370–71.

69   They came, one survivor . . . Arad, *Ghetto in Flames,* 63.

69   In October 1942, for example . . . Friedman, *Roads to Extinction,* 371–72.

70   "In the heritage of Orthodox Jewry . . ." Gutman, *Jews of Warsaw,* 225. See also Friedman, *Roads to Extinction,* 392–93.

71   Survivor Liza Czapnick . . . YVA, Testimony of Liza Czapnick, 03/2309.

Chapter 4: The Ghetto or the Forest

72   "Having access to the world . . ." Schulman, *Partisan's Memoir*, 79.
73   Long before the Nazis arrived . . . Gutman, *Fighters among the Ruins* (Washington, D.C.: B'nai B'rith Books, 1988), 188–89.
74   "The East European urban Jew . . . Ibid., 188.
74   Three generations of . . . Tec, *Defiance*, 5–6.
75   That day, 4,000 Jews . . . Ibid., 33.
75   Meanwhile, Tuvia Bielski . . . Ibid., 41; AI, Israel Levitt.
75   Born in 1918 . . . Harold Werner, *Fighting Back: A Memoir of Jewish Resistance* (New York: Columbia University Press, 1992), 6–20.
76   Initially, Werner and his companions . . ." Ibid., 57–76.
77   Lachva was a small town in western Belorussia . . . See "Lachva," *EH*, vol. 3, 847–48; Gilbert, *Holocaust*, 446–47; Ainsztein, *Jewish Resistance*, 267–68; Gutman, *Fighters among the Ruins*, 190–91; Itzchak Lichtenberg, "Partisans at War," in Isaac Kowalski, ed., *Anthology on Armed Jewish Resistance, 1939–1945* vol. 2 (New York: Jewish Combatants Publishers House, 1984), 592–94. As the timing of the events in Lachva are slightly different in each source, I have relied on the dates given in the *EH*.
78   The courage of Berl Lopaytn . . . Gutman, *Fighters among the Ruins*, 192.
78   The German and Ukrainian police . . . Ibid., 192–93; Ainsztein, *Jewish Resistance*, 268–69.
79   "Underground life is serious . . ." Chaika Grosman, *Underground Army*, 89.
80   "If we had foreseen . . ." Gutman, *Jews of Warsaw*, 143–44.
81   "The Communists had contact . . ." AI, Sara Ginaite.
81   "Are we to desert . . ." Grosman, *Underground Army*, 94–95.
81   "The question at issue . . ." Ibid., 189–90.
82   In Vilna, a resistance . . . Arad, *Ghetto in Flames*, 266.
82   In Kovno, it took until the summer . . . Eckman and Lazar, *Jewish Resistance*, 66; "Kovno," *EH* vol. 2, 826–27; Tory, *Kovno Ghetto Diary*, 462–528.
83   A staunch Zionist . . . Grosman, *Underground Army*, 149, 270–71.
84   These groups united . . . Ainsztein, *Jewish Resistance*, 439–40.
84   The next morning . . . Grosman, *Underground Army*, 275–91;

"Bialystok," *EH*, vol. 1, 212–14.

85   In his memoirs, Smolar related . . . Smolar, *Minsk Ghetto*, 65–66.

85   At the end of March 1942 . . . Ainsztein, *Jewish Resistance*, 475–76.

85   Led by Boris Khaimovich . . . Ibid., 471; Smolar, *Minsk Ghetto*, 63.

86   "In the [Minsk] ghetto . . ." Smolar, *Minsk Ghetto*, 95.

86   "His body was half-burned . . ." Yuri Suhl, ed., *They Fought Back: The Story of the Jewish Resistance in Nazi Europe* (New York: Schocken Books, 1975), 245.

87   "That same night . . ." Smolar, *Minsk Ghetto*, 96; Suhl, *They Fought Back*, 241–43.

87   On New Year's Eve . . . Arad, *Ghetto in Flames*, 231; Abba Kovner, "A First Attempt to Tell," in Yehuda Bauer and Nathan Rotenstreich, eds., *The Holocaust in Historical Experience* (New York: Holmes and Meier, 1981), 81.

87   "One thing is clear to me . . ." Arad, *Ghetto in Flames*, 227.

88   "Jewish youth! . . ." GFH, "Kovner's Declaration," January 1, 1942. See also Arad, *Ghetto in Flames*, 231–32; Kovner, "A First Attempt," 81–82.

88   "His willingness . . ." "Wittenberg, Yitzhak," *EH*, vol. 4, 1657.

89   "It soon became apparent . . ." Arad, *Ghetto in Flames*, 263–70.

90   Guns, grenades, rifles . . . Kovner, "A First Attempt," 82–83; AI, Anna Kremer.

90   As Kovner later recalled . . . Kovner, "A First Attempt," 84.

90   In the view of many Vilna Jews . . . Arad, *Ghetto in Flames*, 254–59.

90   Dated August 11 . . . Holliday, *Children in the Holocaust*, 166.

91   By the new year . . . Arad, *Ghetto in Flames*, 381; AI, Moshe Shutan.

91   He allowed Moshe Shutan . . . Arad, *Ghetto in Flames*, 377–84; AI, Moshe Shutan.

91   "We are faced . . ." Arad, *Ghetto in Flames*, 384; See also Herman Kruk, "Diary of the Vilna Ghetto," *YIVO Annual of Jewish Social Science* 13 (1965): 66–75.

92   According to Chaim Lazar . . . Chaim Lazar, "Joseph Glazman: Portrait of a Fighter," *Publications of the Museum of the Combatants and Partisans* 8, no. 9 (September 1994): 79.

92   It took the intervention of . . . Arad, *Ghetto in Flames*, 349.

93   A massive search for Wittenberg . . . Ibid., 390.

93–94   "We came to Witenberg [*sic*] . . ." Ibid., 392.

94   That night, while in custody . . . Ibid., 392–93.

95   "Jews! Defend yourselves . . ." Ibid., 411–12.

95   "As regards, the revolt . . ." Ibid., 417.

95   Other Jews, those not affiliated with the FPO . . . AI, Norman Shneidman.

96   On September 14, Gens was ordered . . . Michael Okunieff, "Witness to the Execution of Jacob Gens," *Publications of the Museum of the Combatants and Partisans* 8, no. 8 (September 1993): 83–86.

96   "All that he did during his tenure . . ." Arad, *Ghetto in Flames*, 426.

96   The escape began at noon . . . Dov Levin, *Fighting Back: Lithuanian Jewry's Armed Resistance to the Nazis, 1941–1945* (New York: Holmes and Meier, 1985), 237.

97   "Darkness prevails in the tunnel . . ." *Sefer Hapartisanim Hayehudim* (The Jewish Partisan Book) (Israel: Sifriath Poalim, Hashomer Hatzair, 1958), 50–51; Arad, *Ghetto in Flames*, 434; Levin, *Fighting Back*, 237–38.

97   But four fighters . . . Kovner, "A First Attempt," 90.

97   On learning that the guides . . . Arad, *Ghetto in Flames*, 435.

Chapter 5: Escape

99   "If someone tells you that . . ." Tec, *Defiance*, 48.

99   "Escape from the ghetto . . ." AI, Sara Ginaite.

99–100   In the region south of Lublin . . . Shmuel Krakowski, *The War of the Doomed: Jewish Armed Resistance in Poland, 1942–1944* (New York: Holmes and Meier, 1984), 80.

100   Nazi police units . . . Goldhagen, *Hitler's Willing Executioners*, 195. See also Browning, *Ordinary Men*, 122.

100   "People found it hard to make decisions . . ." Yahil, *Holocaust*, 267.

100   "We must flee . . ." Tory, *Kovno Diary*, 304–5.

101   "To leave the ghetto . . ." Silverman, et al., *Victims to Victors*, 107.

101   In another case in the town of Orla . . . Ainsztein, *Jewish Resistance*, 241.

101   "The realization that there were men . . ." Kahn, *No Time to Mourn*, 58.

101   "Mama didn't believe in it . . ." Rubin, *Against the Tide*, 79.

102   Sulia, however, was clever . . . Ibid., 82–97.

102   Undeterred by her close . . . Ibid., 102–4.

103   Motel B. was also in the vicinity . . . FVA, Murray (Motel) B., T-960. See also Tec, *Defiance*, 55–57.

104   The last time Sonia Ostrinsky . . . AI, Sonia Ostrinsky.

105   Not far away in the town of Zoludek . . . Pessia Bairach, "In Their Slashing Claws," 26–31.

106   Hours before the beginning of a major *Aktion* . . . USH, RG 50.030.300, Video testimony of Lisa Nussbaum Derman; and RG 50.030.299, Video testimony of Aron Derman.

107   On Yom Kippur 1942 . . . FVA, Ralph F., T-110.

109   As Rochelle Sutin put it . . . Sutins, *Jack and Rochelle*, 72.

109   As his son Peter later observed . . . Silverman, et al., *Victims to Victors*, 80.

110   Once the killing of Jody's Jews had stopped . . . Ibid., 87–88.

110   Farther to the south-west, in the Radun ghetto . . . Kahn, *No Time to Mourn*, 62.

111   "Our parting will remain forever . . ." Ibid., 69–72.

111   Unlike Leon Kahn, eighteen-year-old Rochelle Sutin . . . Sutins, *Jack and Rochelle*, 71.

111   Still, she was determined . . . Ibid., 73.

112   "Within a minute we could hear . . ." Ibid., 74.

113   They hid in the same spot . . . Ibid., 75.

113   "They were unshaven . . ." Ibid., 77.

113   The German police, remembers Jerry Seigel . . . Jerry Seigel, "My Mother's Dream: The Story of My Personal Survival through the Holocaust," unpublished manuscript (Toronto, 1990), 8–18.

115   For the first six months . . . Velvke Yonson, "I Avenged Our Blood," Sefer Zikaron Lubcz (Remembrance book of Lubcz) (Tel Aviv: Lubcz Survivors, 1971), 347–50.

116   Eighteen-year-old men are not normally described as beautiful . . . AI, Faye Druk, Moshe Bairach, Chaya Bielski, Gitel Morrison.

117   It was after the killing . . . AI, Gitel Morrison, Ignaz Feldon.

117   Tuvia and his brothers . . . Tec, *Defiance*, 41–43.

117   This movement of people . . . Ibid., 42–43.

118   Tuvia was formally made head . . . Ibid., 43.

118   "Would that there were thousands . . ." Ibid., 45–46.

118   "After a time . . ." AI, Simon Zelcovitch.

119   Historian Dov Levin estimates . . . Levin, *Lithuanian Jewry*, 174–75.

119   Jacob Druk, his wife Faye, and their baby son . . . AI, Faye Druk.

119   On one such journey . . . Tec, *Defiance*, 98.

119   In the letter inviting Chaim to join him . . . Ibid., 97.

120   During the war, Jews . . . Tec, *In the Lion's Den*, 81.

120   It was not that Rufeisen . . . Ibid., 87.

120   When Serafimowicz was transferred . . . Ibid., 64–65.

121   "The *zamek* had an eerie atmosphere . . ." Sutins, *Jack and Rochelle*, 51.

121   For nine months . . . Eckman and Lazar, *Jewish Resistance*, 144–45; Tec, *In the Lion's Den*, 89–94, 125.

122   "We had no weapons . . ." Sutins, *Jack and Rochelle*, 51–52.

122   By this time, Oswald was smuggling weapons . . . Eckman and Lazar, *Jewish Resistance*, 145; Tec, *In the Lion's Den*, 137.

122   Oswald planned to fabricate . . .Tec, *In the Lion's Den*, 139–40.

122   Adding to the tension were the reports . . . Ibid., 140.

122   Most members of the *Judenrat* . . . Ibid., 140–45.

123   "On Saturday, I went into the courtyard . . ." Ibid., 145.

123   For those not in the small and relatively well-organized . . . Ibid., 146; Simon Kagan interview.

123   When it was his turn to run . . . Sutins, *Jack and Rochelle*, 61.

124   Furious about the escape . . . See Eckman and Lazar, *Jewish Resistance*, 146–47; Tec, *In the Lion's Den*, 148–90.

124   Later he was forced to take refuge . . ." Tec, *In the Lion's Den*, 192–96; "Rufajzen, Oswald," *EH*, vol. 3, 1311.

124   After the war, Oswald's amazing transformation . . . Tec, *In the Lion's Den*, 226–30.

CHAPTER 6: INTO THE FOREST

127   "On Saturday, January 23, 1943 . . ." Gutman and Krakowski, *Unequal Victims*, 247–48.

127   By the time he caught up . . . Trunk, *Jewish Responses*, 167–70.

129   For a variety of reasons . . .Krakowski, *War of the Doomed*, 16; Ainsztein, *Jewish Resistance*, 440–41.

129   In the Volhynia district alone . . . Martin Gilbert, *The Dent Atlas of the Holocaust* (London: J. M. Dent, 1988), 149, 193.

129   German authorities even instituted a quota system . . . Michael Temchin, *The Witch Doctor: Memoirs of a Partisan* (New York: Holocaust Library, 1983), 89.

129   "There was no uniformity . . ." Lukas, *Forgotten Holocaust*, 26. See also

Trunk, *Jewish Responses,* 224, and Gutman and Krakowski, *Unequal Victims,* 228.

129–30 Day after day, with veiled threats . . . Gefen, *Hope in Darkness,* 33–37.

130 "Most of the one-hundred Jews . . ." Silverman et al., *Victims to Victors,* 83.

130 They truly wanted to help . . . See Lukas, *Forgotten Holocaust,* 127; Fyodorov, *Underground Committee Carries On,* 324–25.

130 "Before the war, they called me goy . . ." Lukas, *Forgotten Holocaust,* 144.

130 "The ironic thing was that . . ." Kahn, *No Time to Mourn,* 75.

131 "Just after dawn . . ." Ibid., 83–84.

131 Fed with anti-Jewish German propaganda . . . USH, RG 53.0024, Reel 4, Fond 655, Opis 1, Folder 1, "Trophy Documents," HQ 108, German propaganda poster, September 1941. See also Browning, *Ordinary Men,* 126–32.

131 "The Ukrainian murderers . . ." Yahil, *Holocaust,* 268.

132 "A large number of Jews . . ." Gutman and Krakowski, *Unequal Victims,* 240. See also Nachum Albert, *The Destruction of Slonim Jewry* (New York: Holocaust Library, 1989), 34.

132 "The peasants were buying scythes . . ." Gutman and Krakowski, *Unequal Victims,* 209.

132 "The German gendarmerie and the Polish police . . ." Ainsztein, *Jewish Resistance,* 247.

133 "He told me in a firm tone . . ." Werner, *Fighting Back,* 77.

133 "The men who participated . . ." Ibid., 77–78.

134 "I looked around at our captors . . ." Ibid., 79–85.

134 In fact, historians Yisrael Gutman and Shmuel Krakowski . . . Gutman and Krakowski, *Unequal Victims,* 220.

134 A 1961 Polish study . . . Lucy S. Dawidowicz, *The Holocaust and the Historians* (Cambridge: Harvard University Press, 1981), 106.

135 These few incidents are just . . . Gutman and Krakowski, *Unequal Victims,* 220–23.

135 Partisans were particularly angered . . . See, for example, Sutins, *Jack and Rochelle,* 97; Rubin, *Against the Tide,* 140–41.

135 Harold Werner and several of his friends . . . Werner, *Fighting Back,* 179.

136 Leib Reiser, a Jew, who escaped . . . YVA, Testimony of Leib Reiser, 016/621.

136   Eugene Katz had escaped . . . AI, Eugene Katz.

136   In late 1942, Bielski . . . Tuvia Bielski, "In the Forests," in Albert Nirenstein, *A Tower from the Enemy* (New York: Orion Press, 1959), 361–62; Tec, *Defiance*, 77–78; YVA, Testimony of Tuvia Bielski, 03/3607.

137   Some months after this incident . . . Bielski, Ibid., 362–63; Tec, Ibid., 102–3; YVA, Testimony of Tuvia Bielski, 03/3607. See also Isaac Aron, "Fallen Leaves," in Kowalski, *Anthology*, vol. 1, 302–8, and Ainsztein, *Jewish Resistance*, 356.

137   In other cases, argues Peter Silverman . . . AI, Peter Silverman.

137   Until the summer and fall of 1942 . . . Arad, "Jewish Family Camps," 231–32; Tec, *Defiance*, 67–68; Trunk, *Jewish Responses*, 472; Krakowski, *War of the Doomed*, 28; Chaim Lazar, *Destruction and Resistance: A History of the Partisan Movement in Vilna* (New York: Shengold, 1985), 141; AI, Peter Silverman.

138   "Although we protested . . ." Werner, *Fighting Back*, 91–92.

138   Alter Dworzecki, for instance, escaped in late April 1942 . . . Bernard Pinsky, "Ordinary, Extraordinary: My Father's Life," unpublished manuscript (Vancouver, 1996), 17–21; AI, Ruben Pinsky; Gilbert, *Holocaust*, 337–38; Arad, "Jewish Family Camps," 232.

138   Hershel Posesorki, a daring young partisan . . . Trunk, *Jewish Responses*, 242–43; Kowalski, *Anthology*, vol. 2, 184–85; Shalom Cholawski, *Soldiers from the Ghetto* (San Diego: A. S. Barnes, 1980), 147.

139   For the duration of the war . . . See, for example, Arad, "Jewish Family Camps," 232–35; Cholawski, Ibid., 123, 147; Spector, *Volhynian Jews*, 305–6; USH, RG–02.142, Donald M. Douglas, "Strangers in the Heartland," unpublished manuscript, (1989), 54.

139   When the Germans began to occupy . . . Ainsztein, *Jewish Resistance*, 304–5.

139   They could make their own bombs . . . Arad, "Jewish Armed Resistance," 498; Spector, *Volhynian Jews*, 228–29.

140   "I shiver just thinking about . . ." Silverman, et al., *Victims to Victors*, 105; AI, Peter Silverman.

140   Even with the newly acquired weapons . . . Ibid., 97–102.

140   A former Jewish officer in the Polish army . . . Krakowski, *War of the Doomed*, 261; AI, Samuel Gruber.

140   They were guided by two Poles . . . Krakowski, *War of the Doomed*, 267.

141   "We saw no reason . . ." Samuel Gruber, *I Chose Life* (New York: Shengold, 1978), 50; AI, Samuel Gruber.

141   "The result was that we had to administer . . ." Gruber, *I Chose Life*, 50–53.

141   Then, with about sixteen other POWs . . . Ibid., 52. See also Krakowski, *War of the Doomed*, 267–68.

142   Days later, their bodies were discovered . . . Krakowski, *War of the Doomed*, 63; Gruber, *I Chose Life*, 54.

142   When Yeheskel Atlas asked . . . Leonard Tushent, "The Little Doctor: A Resistance Hero," in Suhl, *They Fought Back*, 257.

142   In the forest, according to one of the partisans . . . Samuel Bornstein, "Dr. Atlas Platoon," in Kowalski, *Anthology*, vol. 2, 138.

142   Atlas had vowed to say *kaddish* . . . Tushent, "The Little Doctor," 257.

143   The assault on Kozlovshchina . . . Eckman and Lazar, *Jewish Resistance*, 52; Ainsztein, *Jewish Resistance*, 322.

143   In the back of Atlas's mind . . . Eckman and Lazar, *Jewish Resistance*, 55; Ainsztein, *Jewish Resistance*, 323.

144   When the battle ended . . . Eckman and Lazar, *Jewish Resistance*, 54; Ainsztein, *Jewish Resistance*, 322–23.

144   The Soviets had initially planned . . . Tushent, "The Little Doctor," 257.

144   "A violent explosion ripped . . ." Bornstein, "Atlas Platoon," 158.

145   In a battle on September 15 . . . Ibid., 258; Ainsztein, *Jewish Resistance*, 324.

145   One family camp . . . Bornstein, "Atlas Platoon," 137.

145   Consequently, many of the refugees . . . Tec, *Defiance*, 81–82.

146   "Our platoon attempted to move into a better position . . ." Bornstein, "Atlas Platoon," 159–60.

146   In retrospect, historian Nechama Tec . . . Tec, *Defiance*, 82.

147   When the prayers were finished . . . Ainsztein, *Jewish Resistance*, 366; AI, Adam Goszer.

147   "They lived in a beautiful house . . ." AI, Rachel Szternfeld Goldstein.

147   He hoped a group from Korets . . . YVA, Testimony of Simcha Gildenman, 03/4250; Spector, *Volhynian Jews*, 287; AI, Adam Goszer.

148   "If [Hitler] exterminates us . . ." Yahil, *Holocaust*, 267.

148   Gildenman decided to follow . . . Spector, *Volhynian Jews*, 288;

Ainsztein, *Jewish Resistance*, 369.

148   Within a few days, Gildenman and his group . . . Spector, *Volhynian Jews*, 289–90.

148   That October night, Gildenman recorded in his diary . . . YVA, Testimony and diary of Misha Gildenman, 0-33/522.

149   At the outset of the Nazi invasion . . . Friedman, "Ukrainian–Jewish Relations," 265.

150   Bandera's subsequent campaign . . . "Bandera," *EH*, vol. 1, 145–46; "Ukrainska Povstanska Armyia," *EH*, vol. 4, 1531–32.

150   Based in the forests of Polesie . . . Friedman, "Ukrainian–Jewish Relations," 269.

150   In the spring of 1943 . . . Ainsztein, *Jewish Resistance*, 253; Spector, *Volhynian Jews*, 269–70.

151   "When I peered into the house . . ." Misha Gildenman, "Diadia Misha and His Partisans," in Suhl, *They Fought Back*, 269–70.

151   Next, Gildenman freed forty Jews . . . Ibid., 271–73.

151   Of the many stories . . . Ibid., 262–67. See also Gertrude Samuels, *Mottele: A Partisan Odyssey* (New York: Harper and Row, 1976).

152   By May 1942, his original group of fifteen . . . Ainsztein, *Jewish Resistance*, 344–48; Armstrong, *Soviet Partisans*, 26, 128.

153   Once the Soviets had assumed control . . . Ainsztein, *Jewish Resistance*, 368; "Gildenman, Misha," *EH*, vol. 2, 585.

CHAPTER 7: RUSSIANS AND JEWS

155   "We learned early in the game . . ." AI, Peter Silverman.

156   "They killed Jews and raped Jewish girls . . ." Ibid.

157   "We knew we were about to die . . ." Silverman, et al., *Victims to Victors*, 131.

157   "He openly told us . . ." Ibid., 148.

158   "We needed them . . ." AI, Peter Silverman.

158   "On the day any Jewish boy . . ." Silverman, et al., *Victims to Victors*, 162.

158   "Hunting a German . . ." Cooper, *Nazi War*, 91–92.

159   "I do not need . . ." Silverman, et al., *Victims to Victors*, 156, 162.

159   Such was the case with a "frail" . . . Ainsztein, *Jewish Resistance*, 348–50.

160   In fact, few of the Jews . . . Zwi Bar-on, "The Jews in the Soviet Partisan Movement," *Yad Vashem Studies* 4 (1960), 175.

160 "The non-Jew went off . . ." Gutman, *Fighters among the Ruins*, 221.

161 Yitzhak Einbinder from Kurzeniec . . . Joseph Tenenbaum, *Underground: The Story of a People* (New York: Philosophical Library, 1952), 394–95.

161 As historian John Armstrong has observed . . . Armstrong, *Soviet Partisans*, 3–7.

161 In the Spadschansky Forest . . . S. A. Kovpak, *Our Partisan Course* (London: Hutchinson and Company, 1947), 33–36.

162 Local peasants who had fled . . . Cooper, *Nazi War*, 61.

162 "Procrastination and inactivity . . ." Armstrong, *Soviet Partisans*, 671–72.

162 Soviet propaganda continued . . . Ibid., 672–74.

162 "Do you really want to shed your blood . . ." Ibid., 711. See also 713–19.

163 Fyodorov, operating farther east . . . Fyodorov, *Underground Committee*, 503–12.

163 When the plane carrying . . . Kovpak, *Partisan Course*, 75.

163 "Before coming to Stalin's office . . ." Ibid., 76.

163 In the forest, indolence . . . Cooper, *Nazi War*, 61–62.

164 "Fulfill your Partisan oath . . ." USH, RG 18.002 Reel 11, Folder 122, "Fighting the Bandits," a publication of the Reichsführer SS office, Berlin, September 1942, 31.

164 Before Kovpak had left . . . Kovpak, *Partisan Course*, 77–79.

164 Born in 1887 in the village of Kotelva . . . Armstrong, *Soviet Partisans*, 46.

164 As a loyal Ukrainian . . . Kovpak, *Partisan Course*, 7–9; "Kovpak, Sidor," *EH*, vol. 2, 827.

164 A base was established . . . Kovpak, *Partisan Course*, 24–25.

164–65 "We had by no means . . ." Ibid., 12.

165 By early October 1942 . . . Ibid., 82–83; Armstrong, *Soviet Partisans*, 745; Cooper, *Nazi War*, 66.

165 During the winter of 1942–43 . . . Kovpak, *Partisan Course*, 90–101; Cooper, *Nazi War*, 68.

165 "It was not until the Red Army . . ." Cooper, *Nazi War*, 69.

165 "One should not shoot . . ." Armstrong, *Soviet Partisans*, 746–49.

166 In one incident in early July 1943 . . . Ibid., 748–49.

166 More than 50 percent of the fighters . . . Ibid., 145; Cooper, *Nazi War*, 71.

166 In his memoirs, partisan leader . . . Fyodorov, *Underground Committee*, 424–25.

166   German police saw the situation . . . USH, RG 18.002 M84 Reel 11, Folder 121, "Report of Befehlshaber der Ordnugspolizie für das Ostland," Riga, June 30, 1942, 7.

166   Units were given names . . . Cooper, *Nazi War*, 72–73.

166   Beginning in 1942, partisans . . . *The Soviet Partisan Movement* (Washington, D.C., 1969) (A publication of the Center of Military History), 83. (Hereafter CMH, *Partisan Movement*.)

167   "My persistent requests . . ." Armstrong, *Soviet Partisans*, 737. See also 703–4.

167   Earlier in 1943, for instance, Grishin . . . Ibid., 736–37.

167   Partisans who deserted . . . Ibid., 187; CMH, *Partisan Movement*, 141; Cooper, *Nazi War*, 75; Kahn, *No Time to Mourn*, 133.

167   In the interests of the collective spirit of resistance . . . Armstrong, *Soviet Partisans*, 279–80.

168   Far from the officials in Moscow . . . Ibid., 148–49; Levin, *Lithuanian Jewry*, 206.

168   Aleksei Fyodorov, for example . . . Tenenbaum, *Underground*, 411.

168   In the same region, Col. Dimitry Medvedev . . . Ainsztein, *Jewish Resistance*, 371. See also Spector, *Volhynian Jews*, 294, 304.

168   As early as December 1942 . . . Ainsztein, *Jewish Resistance*, 370–80.

169   Two days later, he gave the Skalat Jews . . . Ibid., 380–83.

169   The Nazis regularly sent . . . Cooper, *Nazi War*, 74.

169   The commander of their *otriad* . . . AI, Jacob Greenstein.

169   In other regions, anxious fighters . . . Schulman, *Partisan's Memoir*, 104.

170   The notion persisted among the Soviets . . . See Bar-on, "Jews in the Soviet Partisan Movement," 175; Ainsztein, *Jewish Resistance*, 329; Armstrong, *Soviet Partisans*, 668; Davies and Polonsky, *Jews in Eastern Europe*, 40.

170   One Soviet commander was reported . . . Spector, *Volhynian Jews*, 352.

170   When Irving F. from Baranowicze . . . FVA, Irving F., T-927.

170   There was also talk . . . Tec, *Defiance*, 111; Sutins, *Jack and Rochelle*, 79–80; AI, Moshe Bairach; Schulman, *Partisan's Memoir*, 146.

170   Having seen the bodies for himself . . . Smolar, *Minsk Ghetto*, 128.

171   "We took a Jew into our *otriad* . . ." Tec, *Defiance*, 69–70.

171   "Jewish partisans found themselves . . ." Schulman, *Partisan's Memoir*, 105, 144. See also Levin, *Lithuanian Jewry*, 207.

171   In Silverman's Spartak Brigade . . . Silverman et al., *Victims to Victors*, 157. See also Arad, "Jewish Armed Resistance," 511.

171   No Jew could refuse . . . Silverman, *Victims to Victors*, 148; AI, Ben Lungen, Rubin Pinsky.

172   "We were stunned . . ." Arad, *Partisan*, 114–15.

172   Jewish partisans, moreover, rarely received . . . Smolar, *Minsk Ghetto*, 127. See also Arad, *Ghetto in Flames*, 459; Silverman et al., *Victims to Victors*, 148; Levin, *Lithuanian Jewry*, 208; Albert, *Slonim Jewry*, 348; FVA, Sam F., T-582.

172   When they resisted, the Soviets . . . Spector, *Volhynian Jews*, 305–6; Ainsztein, *Jewish Resistance*, 357.

172–73 One popular joke among the Soviets . . . Smolar, *Minsk Ghetto*, 125.

173   One prominent Ukrainian partisan . . . Armstrong, *Soviet Partisans*, 668.

173   "The [Soviets] tried to minimize . . ." Yitzhak Lichtenberg, "Partisans at War," in Kowalski, *Anthology*, vol. 2, 592–95.

173   The situation in Sara Ginaite's unit . . . AI, Sara Ginaite.

173   Peter Silverman and his friends . . . Silverman et al., *Victims to Victors*, 202. See also Levin, *Lithuanian Jewry*, 205–7; Schulman, *Partisan's Memoir*, 142; Sutins, *Jack and Rochelle*, 117–18; Albert, *Slonim Jewry*, 348.

173   Velvke Yonson's experiences . . . Yonson, "I Avenged Our Blood," 353–54.

174   By early 1943, it was an established Soviet policy . . . Arad, "Jewish Armed Resistance," 511–12; Levin, *Lithuanian Jewry*, 203–10.

174   From any perspective, it made sense . . . Bar-on, "Jews in the Soviet Partisan Movement," 186; Kahanowitz, "Why No Separate Jewish Partisan Movement Was Established," 153–67.

175   Peter Silverman's cousin . . . Silverman et al., *Victims to Victors*, 200.

175   Jewish escapees from Slonim . . . Albert, *Slonim Jewry*, 238; Ainsztein, *Jewish Resistance*, 332.

175   They learned, observed Nachum Albert . . . Albert, Ibid., 238.

175   In early August 1942, Group 51 . . . Ainsztein, *Jewish Resistance*, 332–34.

175–76 Konishchuk, a Ukrainian Communist peasant . . . Ibid., 353.

176   At first, only a small contingent of Jews . . . Dov Lorber, "My Life under Ukrainian–German Occupation," in Jack Porter, ed., *Jewish Partisans: A Documentary of Jewish Resistance in the Soviet Union during World*

War II, vol. 2 (New York: University Press of America, 1982), 194–96; Ainsztein, *Jewish Resistance*, 354–55; Spector, *Volhynian Jews*, 328.

176   For his efforts, Konishchuk . . . David Blaustein, "A Partisan's Testimony," in Porter, *Jewish Partisans*, 87.

176   In late 1942, Kruk's detachment . . . Ainsztein, *Jewish Resistance*, 356–57.

177   "We do to the Russian partisans . . ." Yonson, "I Avenged Our Blood," 354–56.

178   A Jewish bookkeeper named Minich . . . Porter, *Jewish Partisans*, vol. 1, 127.

178   From his base in the Nacha Forest . . . Kahn, *No Time to Mourn*, 85.

178   Nervously, Kahn and his comrades . . . Ibid., 86–87.

179   Faye Schulman's entry . . . Schulman, *Partisan's Memoir*, 84–95.

181   "I lay down under a tall, old tree . . ." Ibid., 99.

181   Schulman's association with her departed . . . Ibid., 107.

181   "I soon found myself able to care . . ." Ibid., 110.

182   In fact, a directive from Berlin . . . USH, RG 18.002 Reel 6, Folder 2, 5, "Directive from Head of the Order Police," Berlin, Jan. 28, 1943.

182   Schulman recalls hearing of one . . . Schulman, *Partisan's Memoir*, 157; AI, Faye Schulman; Levin, *Lithuanian Jewry*, 200–1.

182   In the area near Dedovichi . . . Armstrong, *Soviet Partisans*, 691. See also Fyodorov, *Underground Committee, 323.*

182   "My family was killed . . ." Schulman, *Partisan's Memoir*, 149.

Chapter 8: Partisans

183   "The backbone of the resistance . . ." Rubin, *Against the Tide*, 127.

183   The sick and elderly who were not able to march . . . Browning, *Ordinary Men*, 89–90.

183–84 Hundreds later died . . . YVA, Testimony of Arieh Koren, 03/2019; Krakowski, *War of the Doomed*, 31.

184   In one *Judenjagd*, or Jew hunt . . . Browning, *Ordinary Men*, 123–24.

184   One of those not captured . . . Krakowski, *War of the Doomed*, 32; Werner, *Fighting Back*, 130, 136.

184   The youngest son in a family of . . . Mario Grynszpan (Rio de Janiero) letter to author, April 5, 1997.

184   "It was not only his military training . . ." Werner, *Fighting Back*, 131.

185   Grynszpan was not driven by ambition . . . Mario Grynszpan (Rio de

Janiero) letter to author, May 18, 1997.

185 As a horse trader, he was more familiar . . . Ibid., May 18, 1997; Krakowski, *War of the Doomed*, 32.

185 One of the fighters in Lichtenberg's group . . . Werner, *Fighting Back*, 119–21. In his memoirs, Werner refers to Moshe Lichtenstein, but according to Grynszpan and Krakowski, his last name was Lichtenberg.

185 On Easter Sunday, a force of more than 1,600 . . . USH, RG 15.034, Reel 5, Folder 63, 32, "Report on Parczew Operations," prepared by Lublin SS, March 28, 1944; RG 15.034, Reel 5, Folder 56, 25–28b, "Report and History of Anti-Partisan Operations in Makoschka and Parczew Forests," April 1, 1944; Krakowski, *War of the Doomed*, 37–38; Ainsztein, *Jewish Resistance*, 423.

186 In the aftermath of the German operation . . . Krakowski, *War of the Doomed*, 38; Werner, *Fighting Back*, 135.

186 This was a pattern followed throughout the forest . . . Krakowski, *War of the Doomed*, 7; Ainsztein, *Jewish Resistance*, 410.

187 In the Radom district . . . Krakowski, *War of the Doomed*, 108–13. For further examples of GL-Jewish cooperation, see Ibid., 82–84, 93–94, 104–6; Ainsztein, *Jewish Resistance*, 408–27.

187 Grynszpan today claims . . . Mario Grynszpan (Rio de Janiero) letter to author, May 18, 1997.

187 In one such episode, in June 1943 . . . Krakowski, *War of the Doomed*, 114.

187 On another occasion, three months later . . . Ibid., 92–94.

187 In the forest area north of Lublin . . . Ibid., 66–67, 134, 209.

188 "The day has come to say loudly . . ." Ainsztein, *Jewish Resistance*, 408–9.

188 "Give shelter to fleeing Jews . . ." Ibid., 409.

188 Harold Werner attributed Lichtenberg's negative . . .Werner, *Fighting Back*, 136.

188 Whatever his reasons, Lichtenberg . . . Krakowski, *War of the Doomed*, 36–37.

188 "In order to get there . . ." Werner, *Fighting Back*, 131.

189 "The Germans are moving about the area . . ." Krakowski, *War of the Doomed*, 40–41.

189 "To be sure, there were incidents . . ." Lukas, *Forgotten Holocaust*, 78–81. For some critical comments on the AK, see Bryk, "Hidden Complex of

the Polish Mind," 168–70. The AK did supply a small number of arms to the Jewish resisters in the Warsaw Ghetto. See Krakowski, *War of the Doomed*, 299.

190   The fault for their various hardships . . . Lukas, *Forgotten Holocaust*, 171–73.

190   "Bands of Jews and mixed bands . . ." Arad, "Jewish Family Camps," 227.

190   "It is most typical that the stories . . ." Krakowski, *War of the Doomed*, 137.

190   Yet another dispatch . . . Krakowski and Gutman, *Unequal Victims*, 122–23.

190   This was a selective and distorted . . . Ibid., 123–24; "Bor-Komorowski, Tadeusz," *EH*, vol. 1, 231–32.

191   Stephan Balinski, a veteran of the Home Army . . . AI, Stephan Balinski.

191   In *Unequal Victims*, Gutman and Krakowski showed that . . . Gutman and Krakowski, *Unequal Victims*, 127–33, 216–20. See also Arad, *Partisan*, 16–62; Gruber, *I Chose Life*, 88; Werner, *Fighting Back*, 155–56; Spector, *Volhynian Jews*, 265–66; Kahn, *No Time to Mourn*, 143–50; Trunk, *Jewish Responses*, 303; YVA, Testimony of Jacob Greenstein, 0-33/459. For a contrary view of the AK and its assistance of Jews, see Stanislaw Bura-Karlinski, "Poles Have Brave Record of Aiding Jewish Escapees," Letter to the Editor, *Toronto Star*, July 25, 1992; *Kielce-July, 1946* (Toronto: The Polish Educational Foundation in North America, 1996), 62.

191   In his diary for September 10 and 11, 1943 . . . Gutman and Krakowski, *Unequal Victims*, 128–29.

191   At first, recalled Jacob Greenstein . . . YVA, Testimony of Jacob Greenstein, 0–33/459.

192   AK soldiers in the Rudniki Forest . . . Gutman and Krakowski, *Unequal Victims*, 131.

192   On the other hand, one former member . . . Letter to the Editor, *Toronto Star*, July 5, 1992.

192   "The [Home Army] hated us . . ." Werner, *Fighting Back*, 156.

192   "They were afraid to provoke us . . ." YVA, Eliahu Liberman, 03/1824; Krakowski, *War of the Doomed*, 42.

192   They included an assault . . . YVA, Testimony of Avraham Lewenbaum 03/2080; Krakowksi, *War of the Doomed*, 54. See also USH, RG 15.027M, Reel 2, Folder 12, 14b, "SS Police Reports for the Lublin Area," April

1944. This report notes that "19 Jews had been killed by Polish partisans." Though to be fair, it is not clear whether the Poles belonged to the AK.

193   "Even though we fought the same common . . ." Werner, *Fighting Back*, 193–96.

193   Their contact with the Soviet partisan . . . Krakowski, *War of the Doomed*, 43; Mario Grynszpan (Rio de Janiero) letter to author, May 18, 1997; Werner, *Fighting Back*, 157.

193   "I strained my eyes . . ." Werner, *Fighting Back*, 156–57.

194   By this time, there was no stopping . . . Krakowski, *War of the Doomed*, 47.

194   "[Chil] was extremely popular . . ." Gruber, *I Chose Life*, 117; AI, Sam Gruber.

194   Desperate the Nazi Order Police . . . USH, RG 15.034, Reel 5, Folder 63, 12, "Report from Police in Cholm to Lublin SS"; 16, "SS Police Reports from Lublin, March 22, 1944," RG 15.027M, Reel 2, Folder 12, 34; Lublin SS to Higher SS and Police Leader, April 23, 1944; 46, April 26, 1944; 51, April 27, 1944.

195   "This was," historian Shmuel Krakowski points out . . . Krakowski, *War of the Doomed*, 49–50.

195   In conjunction with this relocation . . . Ibid., 51; Gruber, *I Chose Life*, 136.

195   One morning, Zemsta and several of his men . . . Gruber, *I Chose Life*, 141–43; Krakowski, *War of the Doomed*, 53–55.

196   "We were lying flat in the middle of the field . . ." Gruber, *I Chose Life*, 149–50: Krakowski, *War of the Doomed*, 58–59; AI, Sam Gruber.

196   "I was sick and weak . . ." YVA, Testimony of Avraham Lewenbaum, 03/2080; Krakowski, *War of the Doomed*, 59.

197   "I suppose I am sorry . . ." AI, Sam Gruber.

197   In total, Chil Grynszpan, Sam Gruber . . . Krakowski, *War of the Doomed*, 59.

197   A Belorussian and a loyal Communist . . . Ainsztein, *Jewish Resistance*, 309; Arad, *Partisan*, 112–13.

197   Within a year, Markov's small group . . . Arad, *Partisan*, 113.

197   Night airdrops, guided by large bonfires . . . Joseph Riwash, *Resistance and Revenge, 1939–1949* (Montreal: R and R Distribution, 1981), 57–58. See also USH, RG 18.002 M84, Reel 11, Folder 122, 52, "Police

Report on Airdrops," September 1, 1943.

198   He was dressed, recalled Bernard Drushkin . . . Eckman and Lazar, *Jewish Resistance*, 246.

198   Owing to Glazman's anti-Communist political views . . . Levin, *Lithuanian Jewry*, 184; Arad, *Ghetto in Flames*, 450.

198   A few days after Nekamah's establishment . . . Lazar, *Destruction and Resistance*, 120.

199   "One of our boys returned to the camp . . ." Ibid., 121.

199   "We were welcomed by Glazman . . ." USH, RG 50.030.300, Testimony of Lisa Nussbaum Derman.

199   One of their leaders who had been flown in . . . "Ziman, Henrik," *EH*, vol. 4, 1734.

200   "Who knows whether we will meet . . ." Eckman and Lazar, *Jewish Resistance*, 42.

200   They asserted that Nekamah . . . Arad, *Ghetto in Flames*, 451.

200   In fact, Markov had already weakened . . . Levin, *Lithuanian Jewry*, 184.

200   Nevertheless, Norman Shneidman, one young Jewish fighter . . . AI, Norman Shneidman.

200   The official declaration about Nekamah's fate . . . Levin, *Lithuanian Jewry*, 184–85.

201   "Our aim was to fight the Germans . . ." Abraham Keren Pez, "The Suffering of the Jewish Partisan," in *Pirsumei Muzeyon Ha-Lohamin Ve-Ha-Partizanim* 2, no. 5 (September 20, 1973), 11–13. Cited in Levin, *Lithuanian Jewry*, 244–45.

201   Outnumbered, the Soviet partisans had no choice . . . Levin, *Lithuanian Jewry*, 185; Arad, *Ghetto in Flames*, 452–53; AI, Moshe Shutan.

202   As Shneidman points out . . . AI, Norman Shneidman.

202   Abandoned, the Jews attempted to hide themselves . . . Arad, *Ghetto in Flames*, 453.

202   Shneidman himself had been sent . . . AI, Norman Shneidman.

202   "Glazman spoke to [Ziman] ten times a day . . ." Eckman and Lazar, *Jewish Resistance*, 42.

203   At a spot in the woods, well away from the railway . . . Lazar, *Destruction and Resistance*, 124.

203   "One by one the comrades fell . . ." Ibid., 124. See also Lazar, "Portrait of a Fighter," 76.

204   "Those travelling the French Way . . ." Lazar, *Destruction and Resistance*, 126.

204   In early September 1943, seventy of its members . . . Arad, *Ghetto in Flames*, 454–55; "Partisans," *EH*, vol. 3, 1117.

205   Less than three weeks later, following the liquidation . . . Arad, *Ghetto in Flames*, 456.

205   In the end, Kovner's persuasive powers . . . Ibid., 455.

205   Concerned about the location of the base . . . Ibid., 456.

205   Thus, by early October 1943, there were approximately 250 Jews . . . Ibid., 456–57; "Partisans," *EH*, vol. 3, 1117.

206   As Alex Kremer, a Jewish partisan . . . AI, Alex Kremer.

206   For his part, the Jewish resistance leader . . . Levin, *Lithuanian Jewry*, 204–5.

206   According to historian and former partisan Dov Levin . . . Ibid., 195–97.

207   The size of the Jewish units were changing . . . Ibid., 214.

207   In time some joined the Leninski Komsomol Brigade . . . Ainsztein, *Jewish Resistance*, 312; Kahn, *No Time to Mourn*, 117–20; AI, Leon Kahn and Abraham Asner.

207   Fighters of the Leninski Komsomol Brigade quickly departed . . . Kahn, *No Time to Mourn*, 122–23.

207   Hence, when the Vilna Jews from Rudniki . . . Arad, *Ghetto in Flames*, 458; Levin, *Lithuanian Jewry*, 214.

208   Jews from Kovno and nearby villages . . . "Glazer, Gesja," *EH*, vol. 2, 586–87; M. Yellin and G. Galperin, "The Partisans of the Kovno Ghetto," in Porter, *Jewish Partisans*, vol. 1, 181.

208   In November, an attempt was made to flee . . .Yellin and Galperin, Ibid., 182; Ainsztein, *Jewish Resistance*, 701–2.

208   The young fighters who arrived safely in the forest . . . Yellin and Galperin, Ibid., 182–87; "Kovno," *EH*, vol. 2, 827; Levin, *Lithuanian Jewry*, 188, 195.

209   "Taken aback, the Germans began . . ." Yellin and Galperin, Ibid., 184.

209   In early 1944, six partisans from Death to the Occupiers . . . Ibid., 189.

209   At the Ponary, outside Vilna . . . Ainsztein, *Jewish Resistance*, 706.

209   This system for getting rid of any trace . . . "Aktion 1005," *EH*, vol. 1, 11–12; Ainsztein, *Jewish Resistance*, 704–6; Gilbert, *Holocaust*, 584–85, 612–13.

210   The leader of the group was Abba Diskant . . . Ainsztein, *Jewish Resistance*, 702–3.

CHAPTER 9: SURVIVAL

211   "We were doing our best to survive . . ." Sutins, *Jack and Rochelle*, 67.

211   "Someone would fry *latkes* . . ." Cholawski, *Soldiers from the Ghetto*, 132.

212   On such occasions, there was usually *samogon* . . . Ibid., 88; Smolar, *Minsk Ghetto*, 126; W. Bruce Lincoln, *In War's Dark Shadow: The Russians before the Great War* (New York: The Dial Press, 1983), 123–24; Fyodorov, *Underground Committee*, 309.

212   Sabotage missions and food acquisitions . . . Gruber, *I Chose Life*, 108.

212   Every partisan carried a metal or wooden . . . On food in the forest, see Charles Gelman, *Do Not Go Gentle: A Memoir of Jewish Resistance in Poland* (Hamden, Conn.: Archon Books, 1989), 178; Cholawski, *Soldiers from the Ghetto*, 131–32; Sutins, *Jack and Rochelle*, 65–66; Spector, *Volhynian Jews*, 344–45; Schulman, *Partisan's Memoir*, 169; Pesel Librant, "Family Camp under Max's Command," in Porter, *Jewish Partisans*, vol. 2, 79.

213   "We ate what we could scavenge . . ." Sutins, *Jack and Rochelle*, 65.

213   The food situation for a group of Jews . . . Albert, *Slonim Jewry*, 349.

213   "Sometimes we would come across little . . ." Schulman, *Partisan's Memoir*, 171; AI, Gitel Morrison.

213   As Liza Ettinger, a Bielski partisan . . . Ettinger, "From the Lida Ghetto to the Bielski Partisans," 48.

214   "We never remained for long in one place . . ." Kohn, *A Voice from the Forest*, 35.

214   "Every day we could expect to be attacked . . ." Arad, "Jewish Family Camps," 224.

215   Despite the presence of a competent fighting unit . . . Krakowski, *War of the Doomed*, 59.

215   The experiences of Jews from Parczew and Slonim . . . Tec, *Defiance*, 208.

215   The exact number of Jews . . . Arad, "Jewish Family Camps," 222–23.

216   Others were so discouraged . . . Werner, *Fighting Back*, 96; FVA, Abraham J., T-156.

216   "Yentil cried and blamed me for bringing her to the woods . . ." Byrna Bar Oni, "Life among the Partisans," in Vera Laska, ed., *Women in the*

Resistance and in the Holocaust (Westport, Conn.: Greenwood Press, 1983), 274–78.

216 "[The] Germans and Poles came into the woods . . ." Trunk, *Jewish Responses*, 170.

216 Not far away in the Skorodinica Forest, Harold Werner . . . Werner, *Fighting Back*, 90.

216 "Everyone was back from the fire . . ." FVA, Lois J., T-156.

217 "Their clothes were torn and patched . . ." Arad, *Partisan*, 118–19.

217 "If there is anything my friends . . ." AI, Peter Silverman; Silverman et al., *Victims to Victors*, 158–59, 182.

218 "We Jews felt that it was a great achievement . . ." Tec, *In the Lion's Den*, 184; AI, Jacob Greenstein.

218 When it comes to Soviet attitudes . . . Spector, *Volhynian Jews*, 329–31.

218 As one Belorussian fighter declared . . . Albert, *Slonim Jewry*, 346.

218 After they left the camp . . . Arad, *Partisan*, 119.

218 Victor Panchenko, the twenty-five-year-old head . . . Tec, *Defiance*, 74.

219 The partisan commander believed . . . Ibid., 74; Bielski, "In the Forests," 352–53.

219 Ambushes were frequent . . . Bielski, "In the Forests," 362–63.

219 Some peasants did not have to be coerced . . . Gutman and Krakowski, *Unequal Victims*, 228.

219 As Nahum Kohn puts it . . . Kohn, *Voice from the Forest*, 33.

219 Boots and sheep-skin coats need for the long . . . Arad, *Partisan*, 151.

220 "Once we found a pig . . ." Werner, *Fighting Back*, 133.

220 "Although I was very careful . . ." Bielski, "In the Forests," 352; YVA, Testimony of Tuvia Bielski, 03/3607.

220 They made it a habit of not visiting . . . Sutins, *Jack and Rochelle*, 96–97; Silverman et al, *Victims to Victors*, 176; Tec, *Defiance*, 86, 110; Gelman, *Do Not Go Gentle*, 91–92; Arad, *Partisan*, 151; AI, Peter Silverman.

221 For this reason, states Nahum Kohn . . . Kohn, *Voice from the Forest*, 34.

221 So many provisions were taken . . . Arad, *Partisan*, 151.

221 Farther north in the villages near the Koziany Forest . . . Silverman et al., *Victims to Victors*, 176.

221 "In order to avoid misunderstandings . . ." YVA, Testimony of Leib Reiser, 016/621.

221 Faced with a similar situation . . . Tec, *Defiance*, 43, 217 n. 9.

222 "We are not bandits . . ." Bielski, "In the Forests," 353.

222 Panchenko insisted that members of Bielski's camp . . . Bielski, Ibid., 353–57; Tec, *Defiance*, 74–76; USH, RG 50.030.025, Video testimony of Sonia Bielski; YVA, Testimony of Tuvia Bielski, 03/3607.

223 Depending on the season and locale . . . Armstrong, *Soviet Partisans*, 161.

223 Peeled bark was used for the roof . . . Spector, *Volhynian Jews*, 342–43.

223 On winter mornings . . . Schulman, *Partisan's Memoir*, 165.

223 The best built *zemlianki* were not fully underground . . . Spector, *Volhynian Jews*, 342–43; Tec, *Defiance*, 87; Kahn, *No Time to Mourn*, 114–15; Sutins, *Jack and Rochelle*, 65; AI, Ruben Pinsky.

223 "We couldn't relieve ourselves . . ." Sutins, *Jack and Rochelle*, 66–67.

224 "The bunker was solidly built . . ." Armstrong, *Soviet Partisans*, 161.

224 They were, historian Earl Ziemke has pointed out . . . Ibid., 161.

224 Jack Sutin aptly describes it like this . . . Sutins, *Jack and Rochelle*, 67.

224 "The first time I entered Jack's bunker . . ." Ibid., 89.

225 At Zorin's base in the Naliboki Forest . . . Ibid., 119.

225 "If you put your shirt or sweater . . ." AI, Gitel Morrison.

225 "They crawled into our long hair . . ." Bar Oni, "Life among the Partisans," 274.

226 "We used to take turns . . ." Sutins, *Jack and Rochelle*, 110.

226 Picking the lice off by hand . . . Ibid., 110–11; Spector, *Volhynian Jews*, 346; Tec, *Defiance*, 170–71; Kohn, *Voice from the Forest*, 36; Kahn, *No Time to Mourn*, 78–79; AI, Ben Lungen, Sulia Rubin.

226 A sauna treatment, for example, provided . . . Kohn, *Voice from the Forest*, 78.

226 In March 1943, in the woods near Wlodawa . . . Werner, *Fighting Back*, 113.

227 The Grishin Regiment . . . Armstrong, *Soviet Partisans*, 164, 731–32.

227 At Aleksei Fyodorov's base camp . . . Fyodorov, *Underground Committee*, 422.

227 During the winter of 1942, at another Soviet . . . V. A. Andreyev, "In the Forests of Bryansk," in Kowalski, *Anthology*, vol. 2, 550–55.

227 Rubin Pinsky's experience with typhus . . . Bernard Pinsky, "Ordinary, Extraordinary: My Father's Life," 28; AI, Ruben Pinsky.

228   During the winter of 1943–44, the Bielski camp . . . Tec, *Defiance*, 174–75; AI, Grunya Ferman, Anna Goldsmith, Ruchel Wolfe.

228   Partisans and civilians suffered . . . Tec, *Defiance*, 172; Armstrong, *Soviet Partisans*, 164.

228   "If you so much as touched them . . ." Sutins, *Jack and Rochelle*, 124–27.

229   According to Nechama Tec . . . Tec, *Defiance*, 173.

229   Zelik Abramovitch, a Jewish pharmacist . . . Fyodorov, *Underground Committee*, 421–23.

229   One night, only a few weeks after he had escaped . . . Sutins, *Jack and Rochelle*, 68–69.

230   "It was unbelievable . . ." Ibid., 69.

230   In their joint memoirs, Rochelle explained the transformation . . . Ibid., 108.

231   "Sex meant something different . . ." Ibid., 93; AI, Jack and Rochelle Sutin.

231   Leah Johnson, a Bielski camp survivor . . . AI, Leah Johnson; Jack and Rochelle Sutin.

231   Rochelle Sutin, for one, claims . . . Sutins, *Jack and Rochelle*, 107.

231   "Night after night I cried . . ." Rubin, *Against the Tide*, 117; AI, Sulia Rubin.

232   Like the Bielskis, Harold Werner, and others . . ." Rubin, *Against the Tide*, 121–27.

232   "I made it clear the day . . ." Ibid., 120.

233   "She wrote that she could understand . . ." Ibid., 121; AI, Sulia Rubin. See also Tec, *Defiance*, 160–62.

233   So smitten was the woman with Panchenko . . . Tec, *Defiance*, 98–99; Bielski, "In the Forests," 354.

233   While incidents of rape and violence . . . See Werner, *Fighting Back*, 92; Tec, *Defiance*, 154–55.

233   Nechama Tec points out, for example . . . Tec, *Defiance*, 159.

234   Aleksei Fyodorov wrote of Dossia Baskina . . . Fyodorov, "Partisan Friendship," in Porter, *Jewish Partisans*, vol. 1, 86–87.

234   "Sex was not a major issue . . ." Schulman, *Partisan's Memoir*, 146–49.

234   But some women cheated death . . . Sutins, *Jack and Rochelle*, 108.

234   As Rochelle Sutin remembers . . . Ibid., 108; AI, Jack and Rochelle Sutin.

234   Other former partisans recall a few newborns . . . Tec, *Defiance*, 167; Rubin, *Against the Tide*, 148–49; AI, Sulia Rubin, Grunya Ferman.

234   Accidents did happen . . . See Tec, *Defiance*, 167.

234–35   When Rubin became aware . . . Rubin, *Against the Tide*, 150.

Chapter 10: *Shtetlach* in the Naliboki

237   "Nothing else matters . . ." AI, Gitel Morrison.

237   By late 1942, the vast forests and swamps . . . "Partisans," *EH*, vol. 3, 1113; Vakar, *Belorussia*, 198.

237   "Our village," said one Belorussian peasant . . . Vakar, *Belorussia*, 199–200.

237   The largest group of partisans and Jewish civilians . . . "Partisans," *EH*, vol. 3, 1114. The *Encyclopedia of the Holocaust* lists the size of the Naliboki Forest as 1,158 square miles or 3,000 square kilometres. The *Columbia Lippincott Gazetteer of the World* (1952) describes it, however, as only 160 square miles or 414 square kilometres. As Nechama Tec argues, this figure would seem to be more accurate than the one used in the *Encyclopedia of the Holocaust*. See Tec, *Defiance*, 230 n. 49.

238   Eventually, the forest became the base . . . Ainsztein, *Jewish Resistance*, 316; Bairach, "In Their Slashing Claws," 43.

238   In the young teenage eyes . . . AI, Gitel Morrison, Leah Johnson.

238   Daniel Ostaszynski, the one time head . . . Tec, *Defiance*, 47.

238   The Bielski brothers, simple Jews . . . Ibid., 87.

238–39   "Tuvia Bielski was filled with national pain . . ." Ibid., 47.

239   By October 1942, when Tuvia . . . Ibid., 86.

239   Bernstein, born in 1924 . . . AI, Ike Bernstein.

239   Nechama Tec suggested that many of the Jews . . . Tec, *Defiance*, 49; AI, Faye Druk, Grunya Ferman, Moshe Bairach.

240   In late 1942, a special rescue mission . . . Ibid., 90–91.

240   One night, Tuvia ordered a total relocation . . . Ibid., 90–91.

240   Everyone immediately made the return journey . . . AI, Chaya Bielski, Ike Bernstein; Tec, *Defiance*, 91.

240   Moreover, the Germans were fully aware . . . The story of the attack on the huts is based on AI, Chaya Bielski; USH, RG 50.030.025, Video testimony of Sonia Bielski; "The Bielski Brothers," Film for the Humanities and Sciences (Princeton, N.J, 1996); Tec, *Defiance*, 91–92.

241   Word of the attack and killings . . . Tec, *Defiance*, 92–93.

242   Sulia had just left her guard post the next morning . . . Rubin, *Against*

the Tide, 115; AI, Sulia Rubin.

242   On this occasion, the Jews were lucky . . . Tec, *Defiance*, 101.

242   "When our friends woke up in surprise . . ." Bielski, "In the Forests," 362.

243   In his memoirs, Tuvia related . . . Ibid., 364. See also Tec, *Defiance*, 103.

243   One resulted in the death of Yossel Zelkowicz . . . AI, Gitel Morrison, Moshe Bairach, Chaya Bielski, Ike Bernstein. See also Tec, *Defiance*, 254 n. 4.

244   At the bank of the Niemen . . . Bairach, "In Their Slashing Claws," 34.

244   Her husband, Moshe, adds . . . Tec, *Defiance*, 107.

244   According to Pessia Bairach, "it was only after . . ." Bairach, "In Their Slashing Claws," 34. Her husband, Moshe, on the other hand, suggests that the negotiation to enter the forest took only a few hours. See Tec, *Defiance*, 107.

244   They walked to a spot deep in the forest . . . Bairach, "In Their Slashing Claws," 35; Rubin, *Against the Tide*, 134; Bielski, "In the Forests," 364.

244   In early July 1943, well-aware of the increasing . . . Tec, *Defiance*, 233 n. 31; Bielski, "In the Forests," 364.

244   At least 20,000 German troops . . . YVA, Testimony of Bella and Jacob Greenstein, 0-33/459; Rubin, *Against the Tide*, 137; Tec, *Defiance*, 233 n. 32.

245   "We received an order . . ." YVA, Testimony of Bella and Jacob Greenstein, 0-33/459.

245   Tuvia had already moved the *otriad* . . . Bielski, "In the Forests," 365.

245   "What do you think we should do? . . ." Ibid., 366.

246   "He stood in front of us all . . ." Bairach, "In Their Slashing Claws," 37.

246   The 'special plan' Bielski had in mind . . . Bielski, "In the Forests," 367; Tec, *Defiance*, 118.

246   Pessia Bairach was among the first to start running . . . Bairach, "In Their Slashing Claws," 38.

247   "Those who carried children . . ." Bielski, "In the Forests," 367–68.

247   "I was afraid of the [swamps] . . ." Rubin, *Against the Tide*, 138.

247   In the morning, accompanied by Asael . . . Bielski, "In the Forests," 369.

247   Even the children remained silent . . . Tec, *Defiance*, 120.

247   In the confusion, a few stragglers . . . AI, Leah Johnson.

248   "The next morning was beautiful . . ." Bielski, "In the Forests," 369–70.

248   Indeed, soon after their arrival, Moshe Bairach . . . Ibid., 370; Tec, *Defiance*, 121; AI, Moshe Bairach.

248   Day after day, the Jews sat . . . Bielski, "In the Forests," 371; AI, Chaya Bielski.

248   "For fifteen days, the enemy hunted . . ." YVA, Testimony of Jacob Greenstein, 0-33/459.

249   With no alternative, Bielski sent . . . Bielski, "In the Forests," 371.

249   Everyone was to make their way . . . Bairach, "In Their Slashing Claws," 40; Tec, *Defiance*, 123.

249   "The road was so full of dangers . . . Bairach, "In Their Slashing Claws," 41–42.

250   Soviet partisan headquarters had spoken . . . Tec, *Defiance*, 126–27.

250–51 On the other hand, as Velvke Yonson . . . Yonson, "I Avenged Our Blood," 360.

251   "You had to have a loaded gun . . ." AI, Irving Resnik.

251   "One could see hatred . . ." Ettinger, "From the Lida Ghetto to the Bielski Partisans," 46–47. See also Vakar, *Belorussia*, 165; Tec, *Defiance*, 110–11.

251   Furthermore, for the duration of the war . . . Tec, *Defiance*, 110.

252   In the end, what finally guaranteed . . . Ibid., 151.

252   On one visit to the camp . . . Ibid., 151; AI, Chaya Bielski.

252   During the restructuring of the *otriad* . . . Tec, *Defiance*, 127.

252   "Although we had heard much about it . . ." Ettinger, "From the Lida Ghetto to the Bielski Partisans," 48.

253   Under the supervision of Tuvia . . . Tec, *Defiance*, 44, 267; AI, Ike Bernstein, Irving Resnik.

253   "You went to work, like in a normal town . . ." "The Bielski Brothers," Film for the Humanities and Sciences; AI, Sulia Rubin, Chaya Bielski.

253   The base was so spread out . . . AI, Jerry Seigel.

253   "They were not afraid of anything . . ." USH, RG 50.030.025, Video testimony of Sonia Bielski.

253   "The rule was that you were supposed . . ." AI, Jerry Seigel.

253   In October 1943, to prepare for the winter . . . Ettinger, "From the Lida Ghetto to the Bielski Partisans," 52.

254   Abram from Zaliszcze had a very thick prayer book . . . Werner, *Fighting Back*, 182.

254   On Tuvia's order the camp nurses . . . Tec, *Defiance*, 170–72.

255   Because so many Jewish children died during the war . . . Ibid., 165–66; AI, Gitel Morrison, Chaya Bielski; "The Bielski Brothers," Film for the Humanities and Sciences.

255   "We watched the children ascending . . ." Shmuel Amarant, "The Tuvia Bielski Partisan Company," in *Nivo Shel Adam* (Expressions of man) (Jerusalem, 1973), cited in Tec, *Defiance*, 166.

255   "Where are my children? . . ." "The Bielski Brothers," Film for the Humanities and Sciences; AI, Chaya Bielski; Tec, *Defiance*, 166.

255   For other entertainment . . . Rubin, *Against the Tide*, 154; AI, Sulia Rubin.

256   Regular guard duty was established . . . Ettinger, "From the Lida Ghetto to the Bielski Partisans," 59–60; Seigel, "My Mother's Dream," 20–21.

256   "If you told a Jew to go and stand guard . . ." AI, Sulia Rubin.

256   "These were not times for weaklings . . ." Ibid.

256   One result of this was the development . . . Tec, *Defiance*, 82, 142; AI, Grunya Ferman.

257   "I was eighteen years-old . . ." AI, Leah Johnson.

257   The members of the Jewish intelligentsia . . . Tec, *Defiance*, 142–43; AI, Sulia Rubin.

257   Still, these divisions occasionally led to disagreements . . . Tec, *Defiance*, 139; AI, Grunya Ferman, Chaya Bielski, Israel Levitt.

257   "When I was with my husband . . ." USH, RG 50.030.025, Video testimony of Sonia Bielski.

257   "Clearly there were members . . ." Ettinger, "From the Lida Ghetto to the Bielski Partisans," 51, 56.

258   For troublemakers, those who took food . . . Rubin, *Against the Tide*, 145.

258   In October 1942, for instance, when the *otriad* . . . Tec, *Defiance*, 88–89.

258   A year later, in the aftermath of the Nazi blockade . . . Ibid., 124–25; AI, Moshe Bairach.

258   Ike Bernstein remembers one occasion when he had returned . . . AI, Ike Bernstein.

259   Even today, survivors become . . . AI, Gitel Morrison, Ike Bernstein, Chaya Bielski, Moshe Bairach; Ettinger, "From the Lida Ghetto to the Bielski Partisans," 56.

259   A Jew from the town of Naliboki . . . Tec, *Defiance*, 76; AI, Ike Bernstein.

259   Tuvia Bielski first learned . . . Bielski, "In the Forests," 357–58.

259   "Then they saw that I wasn't . . ." Ibid., 360.

259   During the next year, Kesler became . . . Tec, *Defiance*, 112, 123, 128, 179.

260   When the Nazi hunt of August 1943 ended . . . Ibid., 128–29, 179.

260   At some point, Kesler became dissatisfied . . . Ibid., 178–79; Ettinger, "From the Lida Ghetto to the Bielski Partisans," 56; AI, Ike Bernstein.

260   When Tuvia learned of Kesler's unfounded charges . . . Tec, *Defiance*, 180.

260   One day, Sulia Rubin remembers . . . Rubin, *Against the Tide*, 158.

261   He was tried in a closed trial . . .Tec, *Defiance*, 182–83.

261   This event, observed Liza Ettinger . . . Ettinger, "From the Lida Ghetto to the Bielski Partisans," 56.

261   The execution, writes Sulia Rubin . . . Rubin, *Against the Tide*, 158.

261   Many years later, Tuvia, too, justified . . . Tec, *Defiance*, 184.

261   Watching him celebrate . . . YVA, Testimony of Shmuel Geler, 03/2103; Ibid., 195.

262   That day, 12,000 Minsk Jews . . . Jacob Greenstein, "An Officer and a Saviour," in Eckman and Lazar, *Jewish Resistance*, 229; "Zorin, Shalom," *EH*, vol. 4, 1739.

262   Accompanied by Ganzenko, who had escaped . . . "Zorin, Shalom," *EH*, vol. 4, 1739.

262   Zorin, for his part, refused to turn . . . Greenstein, "An Officer and a Saviour," 229.

262   When Ganzenko learned what had . . . Ibid., 229; Smolar, *Minsk Ghetto*, 129.

263   In June 1943, Jack Sutin, who was still in charge . . . Sutins, *Jack and Rochelle*, 117–20.

263   As was the case with the Bielski *otriad*, Zorin's . . . Ibid., 122; AI, Jack and Rochelle Sutin.

263   Anyone approaching the camp . . . Sutins, *Jack and Rochelle*, 120.

263   "When they told you to go out on a food raid . . ." AI, Jack and Rochelle Sutin.

264   For Jacob Greenstein, a Parkhomenko partisan . . . YVA, Testimony of Jacob Greenstein, 0-33/459; Greenstein, "An Officer and a Saviour," 230; AI, Jacob Greenstein.

264   Even a Soviet partisan official like . . . Smolar, *Minsk Ghetto*, 129.

264   A school was organized . . . "Zorin, Shalom," *EH*, vol. 4, 1740.

264   One hungry young boy . . . AI, Jack and Rochelle Sutin.

264   Immediately, Rochelle Sutin, for one . . . Sutins, *Jack and Rochelle*, 130.

265   "Our feet looked like elephant feet . . ." Ibid., 131; AI, Jack and Rochelle Sutin.

265   Lack of food became a serious issue . . . Sutins, *Jack and Rochelle*, 131–32.

Chapter 11: Sabotage

267   "Suddenly there was a great roar . . ." Gruber, *I Chose Life*, 99.

267   Fittingly, the mine, a charge of 12 kilograms . . . Arad, *Partisan*, 128.

268   He had been assigned to a sabotage team . . . Ibid., 126–28.

268   "When a train is blown up . . ." Ibid., 127–29.

269   The roads and highways of the Soviet Union . . . CMH, *Partisan Movement*, 6–7, 76.

269   In February 1943, central partisan command . . . Armstrong, *Soviet Partisans*, 493.

269   Even before central command . . . Ibid., 495.

270   "In 1942, our demolition operations . . ." Fyodorov, *Underground Committee Carries On*, 468–69. See also USH, RG 53.004 M, Reel 3, Folder 276, "Order from Bialystok of the Kreiskommissar, re: Night Train Travel," May 17, 1943.

270   In Belorussia, German security forces reported . . . Cooper, *Nazi War*, 134.

270   Later in the year, the increased activity . . . USH, RG 18.002 M, Reel 6, Folder 42, 49–60, "Sabotage and Partisan Reports," Riga, November 13–November 28, 1943.

270–71 This excerpt from the operations diary . . . Arad, *Ghetto in Flames*, 463–71. See also USH, RG 18.002 M, Reel 6, Fond R–70, Opis 5, Folder 36, "Reports from Wehrmacht Commander in Ostland on Partisan Activity," December 23, 1942–April 19, 1943.

271   One of the more successful assaults . . . Cooper, *Nazi War*, 64; Armstrong, *Soviet Partisans*, 495–96.

271   The Kursk offensive, for example . . . Cooper, *Nazi War*, 134; CMH, *Partisan Movement*, 210.

272   Soviet experts were routinely parachuted . . . AI, Peter Silverman; Kagan interview; Smolar, *Minsk Ghetto*, 125; Sutins, *Jack and Rochelle*, 124; Silverman et al., *Victims to Victors*, 167.

272   At first the *tol* was simply placed . . . Gelman, *Do Not Go Gentle*, 164–65; Fyodorov, *Underground Committee Carries On*, 473; AI, Peter Silverman.

272   "They looked like cigar boxes . . ." Kahn, *No Time to Mourn*, 130, AI, Leon Kahn.

273   On a day-to-day basis, combating the partisans . . . Cooper, *Nazi War*, 38; "Wehrmacht," *EH*, vol. 4, 1636–37.

273   Taken together, the Nazi infighting . . . Cooper, *Nazi War*, 38–46, 78–79.

274   "The Führer has now given orders . . ." Ibid., 49.

274   In quick order, they organized small, partisan-like . . . Armstrong, *Soviet Partisans*, 502.

274   They also recruited local informers . . . CMH, *Partisan Movement*, 67–68; YVA, Nuremberg Files, N11/1021/E, no. 2455, SS–Gruppen-führer Berger to Himmler, June 17, 1942; USH, RG 53.002, Reel 4, Folder 5, 4–4b, "Report on Jan Haschtila," February 2, 1944.

275   Indeed, from the beginning, the Nazi intelligence . . . See, for example, USH, RG 18.002 M84, Reel 11, Folder 121, 21, "Order Re: mines," July 9, 1942; Folder 122, 20, "Letter to the Wehrmachtsbefehlshaber, Ostland," October 10, 1941; Folder 114, 37–63, "Order Police Report," Riga, July 29, 1942; Folder 121, "Order Police Report," Riga (on the participation of escaped POWs in partisan bands); Folder 122, 52, "OKH Report on Soviet Plane Air Drops," September 1, 1943; RG 18.002, Reel 11, Folder 122, 26, "Schutzpolizei Report," Riga, November 1, 1942; RG 53.004M, Reel 2, Folder 152, 2–27, "Reports from the Grodno Police," October–November 1942.

275   This Nazi thoroughness was evident . . . USH, RG 18.002 M84, Reel 11, Folder 122, 7–10, Himmler Order, Kommando Order No. 42, "Concerning Fight against Partisans."

275–76 When a report from the OKW propaganda . . . Cooper, *Nazi War*, 50. Dallin, *German Rule in Russia*, 518; USH, RG 18.002 M84, Reel 11, Folder 80, 25–26, "OKH Notice," June 8, 1942.

276   The guidelines issued by the Higher SS and Police Leader's office . . . USH, RG 18.002, Reel 11, Folder 133, 5–11, "Guidelines for

Combating Partisans," from Ostland Higher SS and Police Leader, September 25, 1941.

276   Keeping too, with their policy of collective . . . Kahn, *No Time to Mourn*, 128; CMH, *Partisan Movement*, 70; AI, Peter Silverman.

276   In the Ukraine, for example as punishment . . . Cooper, *Nazi War*, 53.

276   Any action, whether it was burning a village . . . Ibid., 50–51; CMH, *Partisan Movement*, 71.

276   This was the way Hitler wanted . . . Cooper, *Nazi War*, 79.

276   Months later, in December 1942 . . . Nuremberg Documents, v. 7, Testimony, February 15, 1946, 488–89 citing, "The Combating of the Guerrillas," December 16, 1942, signed by Keitel. See also Cooper, *Nazi War*, 80–81; Nuremberg Documents, v. 15, June 5, 1946, 407; v. 2, Document 3713-PS, 477–79, "Affidavit by General of the Panzer Rottiger," December 8, 1945.

277   They prepared their troops with simulated training . . . USH, RG 18.002, Reel 11, Folder 121, 34–63.

277   "The goal of these partisans . . ." USH, RG 18.002 M84, Reel 11, Folder 121, 1–2. See also RG 18.002 M84, Reel 11, Folder 122, 37A, "Fighting the Bandits," RSHA, Berlin, September 1942.

277   An order from Himmler . . . USH, RG 18.002, Reel 11, Folder 121, 9, "Directive from Commander of Order Police," Riga, July 30, 1942; RG 18.002 M84, Reel 11, Folder 121, 8, "Directive from the Commander of the Order Police for Ostland," (undated).

277   In January 1942, the following announcement . . . Cooper, *Nazi War*, 55.

277–78 "The Germans were afraid to enter the woods . . ." Temchin, *Witch Doctor*, 37.

278   Similarly, in late December 1942, the gendarmerie . . . USH, RG 53.004M, Reel 12, Folder 146, 33–34, "Report from Grodno Gendarmerie," December 25, 1942.

278   To achieve this goal, he gave Himmler . . . YVA, Nuremberg Documents, 66B, No. 1919-PS, Speech of Reichsführer-SS Himmler, October, 1943; Cooper, *Nazi War*, 94–95.

278   Regarded by Hitler . . . Cooper, *Nazi War*, 95; "Bach-Zelewski," *EH*, vol. 1, 136.

279   If anything, the brutality intensified . . . YVA, Nuremberg Files, JM 2085, no. 1666; Cooper, *Nazi War*, 94.

279   Public executions of suspected . . . USH, RG 53.004M, Reel 3, Folder 277, 125–28, "Announcement from Grodno Kreiskommissar, re: Public Executions in Bialystok," September 18, 1942.

279   One Belorussian policeman who accompanied . . . Cooper, *Nazi War*, 82–83.

279   After reading a detailed report . . . YVA, Nuremberg Files, N11/1021/E, no. 2607, Lohse to Rosenberg (the Reich Minister for the Occupied Eastern Territories), June 18, 1943.

280   Commenting to Himmler on the same operation . . . YVA, Nuremberg Files, N11/1201/E, no. 2608, Bach-Zelewski to Himmler, June 23, 1943.

280   Enraged by the inability of the police and army . . .USH, RG 18.002, Reel 7, Folder 72, 261–62, "Secret Telegram to the Reichskommissar in Riga," July 27, 1943; 266, "Directive re: Evacuation," August 3, 1943; 278–79, "Reichskommissar for Ostland to Berlin," August 5, 1943; Cooper, *Nazi War*, 97.

280–81 "We walked day and night . . ." Silverman et al., *Victims to Victors*, 257–58.

281   "It was our experience that Russian forces . . ." Cooper, *Nazi War*, 89.

281   Operation Hornung, which was carried out . . . Ibid., 87.

281   A police report on the action . . . USH, RG 18.002 M84, Reel 11, Folder 191, 53–53b, "Report on Operation Hornung," April 4, 1943. See also RG 18.002, Reel 8, Folder 20, 18, "Report on Air Surveillance," March 1943.

282   More than 3,000 Jews, for example, perished . . . Cooper, *Nazi War*, 87; Ainsztein, *Jewish Resistance*, 264–65.

282   From August 1 to December 1, 1942, for example . . . YVA, Nuremberg Document No. 1128, "Directive from Higher SS and Police Leader in Southern Russia, the Ukraine and the North East," December 27, 1942, 1–3.

282   In Nazi reports and communiques . . . USH, RG 18.002 M84, Reel 11, Folder 184, Pamphlet: "Fighting the Bandits," September 1942; RSHA, Berlin, 4; RG 15.034, Reel 5, Folder 63, 26b, Report of March 24, 1943; RG 53.002, Reel 4, Folder 5, 4–4b, Report of February 2, 1944.

282   There were, claimed Alfred Jodl . . . Nuremberg Documents, v. 15, June 5, 1946, 403; June 7, 1946, 566.

282–83 "In all the clashes with the partisans . . ." Arad, *Ghetto in Flames*, 411–13; YVA, Nuremberg Documents, No. 3943, Translation of Chief of Security Police and SD, Reports from the Occupied Eastern

Territories, Excerpt Report no. 7, n.d.

283   The goal was nothing less than destruction . . . Cooper, *Nazi War*, 136–37.

283–84 "Within two nights . . ." Ibid., 135.

284   But far from being defeated, the Nazis . . . Ibid., 137; CMH, *Partisan Movement*, 205–6.

284   Unwilling to accept partisan interference . . . Ilya Kuzin, *Notes of a Guerrilla Fighter* (Moscow, 1942), 28; CMH, *Partisan Movement*, 69. On the German railway police, see USH, RG 53.002, Reel 1, Folder 217, 19, "Report by the Railway Management at Minsk," September 25, 1942; Reel 2, Folder 400, 8–9, "Order No. 53 Minsk, re: Railways," May 1, 1943; Silverman et al., *Victims to Victors*, 166; AI, Peter Silverman; Cooper, *Nazi War*, 138.

284   In another example of partisan ingenuity . . . Armstrong, *Soviet Partisans*, 500.

285   The Nazi police also tried spraying . . . Kahn, *No Time to Mourn*, 130; AI, Leon Kahn.

285   While the Germans became quite competent . . . Armstrong, *Soviet Partisans*, 495.

285   Official passes were required . . . CMH, *Partisan Movement*, 70.

285   By this time, however, as Peter Silverman . . . Silverman, et al, *Victims to Victors*, 167. See also Albert, *Slonim Jewry*, 319; Cooper, *Nazi War*, 132.

285   "As we always worked in the dark . . ." Kahn, *No Time to Mourn*, 134.

286   They would order a group of men . . . Cooper, *Nazi War*, 132.

286   In the central sector, 841 operations . . . Ibid., 138; CMH, *Partisan Movement*, 206.

286   In the spring, more than 18,000 partisans . . . Cooper, *Nazi War*, 139; CMH, *Partisan Movement*, 154–55.

286   In the district of Lublin . . . USH, RG 15.034, Reel 5, Folder 12, 5–116b, SS Reports for Lublin District, May 1944.

287   In one bold action, they put . . . Cooper, *Nazi War*, 138; Arad, *Partisan*, 168.

287   If Himmler realized the end . . . USH, RG 15.034, Reel 5, Folder 63, 165–70, "Memorandum," May 3, 1944.

CHAPTER 12: A PERILOUS LIBERATION

289   "We found it hard to accept the fact . . ." Cholawski, *Soldiers from the Ghetto*, 177.

290   On January 18, 1945, ten days before . . . Gilbert, *Holocaust*, 771–73.

290   Hitler reportedly responded . . . Ibid., 711.

290   In June 1944, in eastern Galicia . . . Trunk, *Jewish Responses*, 226.

290   In the Parczew Forest, the Germans ran . . . Krakowski, *War of the Doomed*, 97–98.

291   From Stalin's point of view . . . Alexander Werth, *Russia at War 1941–1945* (London: Barrie and Rockliffe, 1964), 759, 764–65.

291   On July 17, as a sign of power, the Soviets . . . Ibid., 862.

291   One young partisan . . . FVA, Ralph F., T-110.

291–92 Jacob Greenstein, one of thousands of fighters . . . AI, Jacob Greenstein.

292   "Long columns of German trucks and tanks . . ." Werner, *Fighting Back*, 223.

292   "Returning to our liberated city . . ." Smolar, *Minsk Ghetto*, 148.

292   Of the 80,000 Jews in Minsk . . . Ainsztein, *Jewish Resistance*, 485; "Minsk," EH, vol. 3, 974–77.

292   Soon Minsk resembled . . . Smolar, *Minsk Ghetto*, 150.

293   "The destruction in the cities was appalling . . ." Werth, *Russia at War*, 864.

293   "For the first time since the Germans . . ." Sutins, *Jack and Rochelle*, 137.

293   At one family camp in the Lipiczany Forest . . . Trunk, *Jewish Responses*, 302.

293   Many more young Jews like Bebale Weisman . . . Werner, *Fighting Back*, 227.

293   As historian Martin Gilbert states . . . Gilbert, *Holocaust*, 732.

294   Days before the Soviet liberation . . . Ibid., 733.

294   The Soviet partisans, following orders . . . Tadeusz Piotrowski, "Kielce and the Postwar Years," in *Kielce*, 29–31.

294   In early 1944, the Polish Home Army wiped out . . . Gutman and Krakowski, *Unequal Victims*, 130–31; YVA, Testimony of Leib Reiser, 016/621.

294   Yitzhak Arad recalls one particular confrontation . . . Arad, *Partisan*, 161. See also Librant, "Family Camp," 83.

294 Farther west, in Warsaw in August . . . Gilbert, *Holocaust*, 717.

295 In April, the Bielski Jews . . . Tec, *Defiance*, 195–97.

295 Among those who joined the Bielski *otriad* . . . AI, Willy Moll.

295 At the Bielski camp, guards apprehended three young SS soldiers . . . Tec, *Defiance*, 196–97.

296 "I will never forget it . . ." YVA, Testimony of Eliezer Englestern, 3249/233. Ibid., 197.

296 A Jew named Pupko . . . Tec, *Defiance*, 197.

296 According to Liza Ettinger, who witnessed this . . . Ettinger, "From the Lida Ghetto to the Bielski Partisans," 67.

297 "Everyone started beating them . . ." Sutins, *Jack and Rochelle*, 142–43.

297 "Suddenly thousands of Germans are upon us . . ." Yonson, "I Avenged Our Blood," 361.

297 In the early morning of July 9 . . . Tec, *Defiance*, 197.

298 Later he was taken to a Minsk hospital . . . Sutins, *Jack and Rochelle*, 144–45.

298 "Dear friends, we were together for a long time . . ." Ibid., 145.

298 "Our joy was indescribable . . ." Yonson, "I Avenged Our Blood," 361.

298–99 And yet, as Shalom Cholawski . . . Cholawski, *Soldiers from the Ghetto*, 176–77.

299 The Soviets demanded that the Jews destroy . . . Tec, *Defiance*, 199.

299 The anticipation of the march to freedom . . . AI, Grunya Ferman, Ruchel Wolfe, Moshe Bairach, Anna Goldsmith.

299 "Our great hour had come . . ." Ettinger, "From the Lida Ghetto to the Bielski Partisans," 67–68.

299–300 A Jew named Polonecki . . . Tec, *Defiance*, 200–1.

300 "When the liberation occurred, we knew . . ." AI, Peter Silverman.

300 Their Polish and Ukrainian neighbours . . . AI, Grunya Ferman, Jerry Seigel, Gitel Morrison, Faye Druk; FVA, Frances B., T-959; Silverman et al., *Victims to Victors*, 221.

300 In Slonim, Lisa Derman found . . . USH, RG 50.030.300, Video testimony of Lisa Nussbaum Derman; AI, Lisa Nussbaum Derman.

300–1 Faye Schulman walked out . . . Schulman, *Partisan's Memoir*, 192.

301 Shalom Cholawski described his return . . . Cholawski, *Soldiers from the Ghetto*, 179.

301 "For days after that I wept . . ." Kahn, *No Time to Mourn*, 173.

302   Jerry Seigel, who had been with the Bielski *otriad* . . . Seigel, "My Mother's Dream," 23–28.

302   At first, Peter Silverman was given . . . Silverman et al., *Victims to Victors*, 227–30.

302   Asael Bielski was not as lucky . . . Tec, *Defiance*, 202; AI, Chaya Bielski.

302   Tuvia and Zus Bielski avoided conscription . . . Tec, *Defiance*, 201.

302   As Sam Gruber remembered . . . Gruber, *I Chose Life*, 155.

303   Meyer Itzkovitch, for instance, worked . . . AI, Meyer Itzkovitch.

303   In Pinsk, Faye Schulman became the official photographer . . . Schulman, *Partisan's Memoir*, 196–222.

303   Leon Kahn was appointed a policeman . . . Kahn, *No Time to Mourn*, 175–206; AI, Leon Kahn.

303   After wandering for several months . . . Sutins, *Jack and Rochelle*, 156–60; AI, Jack and Rochelle Sutin.

303   During the summer and fall of 1945, pogroms . . . Gilbert, *Holocaust*, 815–18.

303   The most notorious act of treachery . . . Ibid., 819; *Kielce*, 9.

304   In the aftermath of the Kielce . . . Gilbert, *Holocaust*, 819.

304   At precisely the same moment that the Red Army . . . Ibid., 699; Arad, *Ghetto in Flames*, 446, 460.

305   Abba Kovner, the young resistance leader . . . Gilbert, *Holocaust*, 703–4.

EPILOGUE

307   "I am a man with two lives . . ." Kahn, *No Time to Mourn*, 208.

309   Though I did not visit Parczew's former Jewish cemetery . . . Martin Gilbert, *Holocaust Journey: Travelling in Search of the Past* (Vancouver: Douglas and McIntyre, 1997), 269.

310   There was a young teenage girl . . . AI, Gitel Morrison.

310   One among thousands was Philip Weiss . . . AI, Philip Weiss. See also Allan Levine, "Survivor gives students glimpse into Nazi hell," *Winnipeg Free Press*, June 2, 1995.

310–11 Not surprisingly, the survivors' ability to successfully adapt . . . "General Survey, Psychology of Survivors," *EH*, vol. 4, 1426–32.

311   After they had left the forest, Gitel and her family . . . AI, Gitel Morrison.

311   Jack and Rochelle Sutin and their new baby daughter . . . Sutins, *Jack and Rochelle*, 480–81; AI, Jack and Rochelle Sutin.

312   "During [the fifties] we met with a number of American Jews . . ." Cited in *American Jewish World*, May 5, 1995.

312   Fruma (or Frances) B., a Bielski survivor . . . FVA, Testimony of Frances B., T-960.

312   Looking back, it is clear . . . Schulman, *Partisan's Memoir*, 192.

313   The Nazis found an ally . . . Kahn, *No Time to Mourn*, 209.

313   Even the soldiers of the Soviet Red Army . . . CMH, *Partisan Movement*, 203, 209.

313   This myth deeply troubled former partisan . . . Fyodorov, *Underground Committee*, 509.

313   In the whirlwind that seized them . . . Tec, *Defiance*, 205.

314   "All I went through to survive . . ." Schulman, *Partisan's Memoir*, 162.

314   "Today, when I think about it . . ." AI, Yitzhak Arad.

315   "Without Tuvia, what would we be . . ." AI, Sulia Rubin. See also "The Bielski Brothers," Film for the Humanities and Sciences.

315   There are probably more than 13,000 . . . D. J. Ficke, "He took on the Nazis," *Our Town* 27 no. 7 (September 21, 1995); 12.

315   "I will never go back . . ." AI, Gitel Morrison.

315–16 More than fifty Bielski camp survivors . . . AI, Chaya Bielski; See also "The Bielski Brothers," Film for the Humanities and Sciences.

316   Peter Silverman and David Smuschkowitz . . . AI, Peter Silverman and David Smuschkowitz.

316–17 Fugitives like Alex Levin . . . AI, Alex Levin.

GLOSSARY

Aktion (pl., *Aktionen):* A Nazi raid or assault on Jews, especially in a ghetto, for deportations or killings.

Armia Krajowa (AK): Poland's Home Army, organized in the fall of 1939 and linked with the Polish government-in-exile based in London.

Bambioshka (pl., *bambioshki):* A slang Russian term, used mostly by Jews, for a partisan food-gathering expedition.

Betar: The youth section of the right-wing Zionist Revisionist movement led by Vladimir Jabotinsky. Many "Betarists" participated in the resistance in the ghettos and the forests.

Einsatzgruppen (sing., Einsatzgruppe): Mobile Nazi death squads. During the Nazi occupation of the Soviet Union, the Einsatzgruppen were responsible for murdering hundreds of thousands of Jews.

Endecja: A Polish right-wing and anti-Semitic political party that had much success in the late 1930s.

Fareynegte Partizaner Organizatsye (FPO): The United Partisan Organization in English; the Jewish underground established in the Vilna ghetto in late December 1941.

Gwardia Ludowa (GL): The People's Guard, the partisan organization of the left-wing Polish Workers' Party. In January 1944, the GL changed its name to Armia Ludowa, or People's Army. In many forest regions, GL fighters allied themselves with Soviet and Jewish partisans.

Ha-Shomer Hatsair: In English, the "Young Watchman," a popular left-wing youth Zionist group in eastern Europe that attracted many middle-class Jewish teenagers. The powerful spirit and friendship established by Ha-Shomer Hatsair before the war laid the foundations for the underground movement in such ghettos as Vilna and Bialystok.

Judenrat (pl., Judenrate): Jewish councils. Established by the Nazis, the Jewish-led organizations were to govern their own ghetto communities.

Narodowe Sily Zbrojne (NSZ): The National Armed Forces, the right-wing and anti-Semitic Polish underground. Beginning in the summer of 1942, many units of the NSZ were allied with the Armia Krajowa.

Oblava (pl., oblavy): A Russian term meaning a round-up of suspected persons. In the context of the partisan movement, it referred to a German blockade of the forest.

Otriad (pl., otriady): A Soviet partisan detachment, usually consisting of 50 to 200 fighters.

Puszcza: A Polish term used to describe a vast forest wilderness. Local peasants designated a forest as a *puszcza* depending on its size and its jungle-like topography.

Shtetl **(pl., *shtetlach*):** An east European Jewish village.

Ukrainska Povstanska Armyia (UPA): The Ukrainian Insurgent Army, the right-wing and anti-Semitic Ukrainian guerrilla army loyal to Stefan Bandera. The UPA fought against Soviet and Jewish partisans more than it did the Nazis. To the Jews in the forests, the UPA were known as the *Bandera* or the *Banderovtsy.*

Yevrei (pl., Yevrei): The Russian term for Jew.

Zemlianka (pl., Zemlianki): A forest bunker.

Zhyd (pl., Zhydy): In Russian, a derogatory term for Jew.

SIGNIFICANT DATES

August 23, 1939: The Nazi–Soviet Pact is concluded.

September 1, 1939: German invasion of Poland.

September 3, 1939: Britain and France declare war on Germany. The Second World War begins.

October 8, 1939: The Nazis create the first ghetto for Jews in the Polish town of Piotrkow.

June 22, 1941: The Nazis invade Soviet-occupied territory with Operation Barbarossa.

July 3, 1941: Josef Stalin's radio address calling for the organization of a partisan movement.

September 29–30, 1941: More than 33,000 Jews from Kiev are murdered at Babi Yar by the Einsatzgruppen.

December 8, 1941: In an *Aktion* in Novogrudok, 4,000 Jews are killed. Flights to the forest begin.

January 20, 1942: The Wannsee Conference is held near Berlin and details of the Final Solution are worked out.

March 26, 1942: The beginning of large-scale deportations of Jews to Auschwitz.

May 1942: In Moscow, the Central Staff for Partisan Warfare is organized.

September 12, 1942: The battle at Stalingrad starts.

February 2, 1943: The Soviets are victorious at Stalingrad and the tide of the war on the eastern front begins to turn.

April 19–May 16, 1943: The Warsaw ghetto uprising.

September 23–24, 1943: The Vilna ghetto is liquidated and many members of the underground FPO escape to the forests to join Soviet partisans.

July 13, 1944: Vilna is liberated by the Soviet army.

January 27, 1945: The Red Army enters Auschwitz.

April 30, 1945: Hitler commits suicide in his Berlin bunker.

May 8, 1945: The Second World War in Europe ends.

SELECTED BIBLIOGRAPHY

I. AUTHOR'S INTERVIEWS

Arad, Yitzhak. Tel Aviv, June 17, 1996.

Asner, Abraham. Windsor, Ontario, May 12, 1996.

Bairach, Moshe. Tel Aviv, June 13, 1996.

Balinksi, Stephan. Telephone interview, Winnipeg, March 31, 1997.

Bernstein, Ike. Winnipeg Beach, Manitoba, July 20, 1997.

Bielski, Chaya. Haifa, June 9, 1996.

Blutstein, Sarah. Winnipeg, December 20, 1995.

Brancawskaja, Fanya. Toronto, May 8, 1996.

Czuzoj, Luba. Telephone interview, San Bernadino, California, June 23, 1997.

Druk, Faye. Toronto, May 10, 1996.

Feldon, Ignaz. Tel Aviv, June 16, 1996.

Ferman, Grunya. Toronto, May 14, 1996.

Geffen, Aba. Jerusalem, June 5, 1996.

Gelman, Abba. Toronto, May 9, 1996.

Ginaite, Sara. Toronto, May 13, 1996.

Goldsmith, Anna. Toronto, May 14, 1996.

Goldstein, Rachel Szternfeld. Winnipeg, December 21, 1995.

Goldsweig, Kunia. Jerusalem, June 4, 1996.

Goszer, Adam. Winnipeg, October 9, 1997.

Greenstein, Jacob. Tel Aviv, June 14, 1996.

Grynszpan, Chil. Letters to author (from Mario Grynszpan), April 5, 1997, and May 18, 1997.

Gruber, Sam. New York, April 25, 1996.

Ihilchik, Saul. Toronto, May 6, 1996.

Itzkovich, Meyer. Tel Aviv, June 12, 1996.

Johnson, Leah. Hallendale, Florida, April 14, 1996.

Katz, Eugene. Toronto, May 6, 1996.

Kahn, Leon. Vancouver, June 22, 1997.

Kirshner, Morris. Winnipeg, December 22, 1995.

Kremer, Anna, and Alex Kremer. Toronto, May 8, 1996.

Levitt (Yankielewicz), Israel. Telephone interview, Chicago, July 27, 1997.

Levin, Alex. Telephone interview, Toronto, September 21, 1997.

Lungen, Ben. Winnipeg, November 5, 1995.

Moll, Willy. Toronto, May 7, 1996.

Morrison, Gitel. Winnipeg, December 4, 1995.

Ostrinsky, Sonia. Winnipeg, January 8, 1996.

Ozersky, Len. Winnipeg, December 21, 1995.

Pinsky, Rubin. Vancouver, June 21, 1997.

Raber, Leo. Winnipeg, March 26, 1996.

Resnik, Irving. Telephone interview, Montreal, July 16, 1997.

Rubin, Sulia. Upper Saddle River, New Jersey, April 26, 1996.

Seigel, Jerry. Fort Lauderdale, Florida, April 6, 1996.

Shneidman, Norman. Toronto, May 8, 1996.

Schulman, Faye. Waterloo, Ontario, May 11, 1996.

Shutan, Moshe. Tel Aviv, June 17, 1996.

Shiffrin, Yisrael. Tel Aviv, June 12, 1996.

Silverman, Peter. Toronto, May 10, 1996.

Sutin, Jack, and Rochelle Sutin. Minneapolis, August 20, 1997.

Tessler, Ernie. Winnipeg, March 10, 1996.

Wolfe, Harry. Toronto, May 7, 1996.

Wolfe, Ruchel. Toronto, May 14, 1996.

Zelcovitch, Simon. Toronto, May 7, 1996.

II. TESTIMONIES

Fortunoff Video Archive for Holocaust Testimonies, Yale University
B., Frances. T-959.

B., Murray. T-960.

F., Sam. T-582.

F., Ralph. T-110.

F., Irving. T-927.

J., Lois, and Abraham J. T-156.

M., Sonia. T-221.

R., Esther. T-172.

W., Shirley. T-23.

Z., Schifre. T-11.

Simon Wiesenthal Center for Holocaust Studies, Los Angeles

Faber, David.

Frenkel, Benjamin.

Frumkin, Sy.

Hieftetz, Myron.

Peskin, Joseph.

Zuker, Max.

United States Holocaust Memorial Museum Archives, Washington, D.C.

Bielski, Lillian (Lilka). RG 50.030.026.

Bielski, Sonia. RG 50.030.025.

Derman, Aron. RG 50.030.299.

Derman, Lisa Nussbaum. RG 50.030.300.

Gruber, Samuel. RG 50.030.087.

Yad Vashem Archives, Jerusalem

Bielski, Tuvia. 03/3607.

Bazilian, N. 03/2335.

Charni, Zhana Ran. 03/7505.

Czapnik, Liza. 03/2309.

Geler, Shmuel. 03/2103.

Gildenman, Misha. 0-33/522.

Gildenman, Simcha. 03/4250.

Goldfischer, Bella. 0-33/1376.

Grabow, Jakow. 03/2950.

Greenstein, Bella, and Jacob Greenstein. 0-33/459.

Grusscott, Abraham. 0-33/1309.

Hauberenshtok, E. 03/2078.

Heiman, Lucyna. 03/6764.

Kaganowitz, Moshe. 0-33/630.

Koren, Arieh. 03/2019.

Leonard, Rubin. 03/3223.

Lewenbaum, Avraham. 03/2080.

Liberman, Eliahu. 03/1824.

Miller, Tuvia. 03/2078.

Poland, Adolph. 0-33/1317.

Reiser, Leib. 016/621.

Rubinovitch, Sarah. 03/2997.

Rud, Ania. 03/6424.

Sass, Ella. 03/7386.

Szymszonowicz, Yehuda. 0-33/296.

Waldman, Aaron. 03/2794.

Winokur, Rachel. 03/2220.

Private

Kagan, Simon. Interview January 30, 1984. In possession of family, Winnipeg.

III. BOOKS

Abramsky, C., M. Jachimczyk, and A. Polonsky, eds. *The Jews in Poland.* New York: Basil Blackwell, 1986.

Agar, H. *The Saving Remnant: An Account of Jewish Survival.* New York: Viking, 1960.

Ainsztein, Reuben. *Jewish Resistance in Nazi-Occupied Eastern Europe.* London: Paul Elek, 1974.

Albert, Nachum. *The Destruction of Slonim Jewry.* New York: Holocaust Library, 1989.

Amarant, Shmuel. *Nivo Shel Adam* (Expressions of man). Jerusalem: Ministry of Culture and Education, 1973.

Arad, Yitzhak. *Ghetto in Flames: The Struggle and Destruction of the Jews in Vilna in the Holocaust.* New York: Holocaust Library, 1982.

———. *The Partisan.* New York: Holocaust Library, 1979.

———. *The Pictorial History of the Holocaust.* New York: Macmillan, 1990.

Arad, Yitzhak, Yisrael Gutman, and Abraham Margaliot, eds. *Documents on the Holocaust.* Jerusalem and New York: Ktav, 1981.

Armstrong, John A., ed. *Soviet Partisans in World War II*. Madison: University of Wisconsin, 1964.

Aron, Isaac. *Fallen Leaves: Stories of the Holocaust and the Partisans*. New York: Shengold, 1981.

Ascherson, Neal. *The Struggles for Poland*. London: Michael Joseph, 1987.

Bairach, Moshe. *Vzot Ltuda: Begetaot Vbriarot Belorussia* (And this is to witness). Israel: Ghetto Fighters' House, 1981.

Barkai, Meyer, ed. *The Fighting Ghettoes*. New York: J. B. Lippincott, 1962.

Baron, S. W. *The Russian Jew under Tsars and Soviets*. New York: Macmillan, 1964.

Bauer, Yehuda. *Flight and Rescue: Brichah: Organized Escape of the Jewish Survivors of Eastern Europe 1944–1948*. New York: Random House, 1970.

———. *A History of the Holocaust*. New York: Franklin Watts, 1982.

———. *The Jewish Emergence from Powerlessness*. Toronto: University of Toronto Press, 1979.

Berenstein, Tatiana, and Adam Rutkowski. *Assistance to the Jews in Poland, 1939–1945*. Translated by Edward Rothert. Warsaw: Polonia House, 1963.

Boshyk, Yury, ed. *Ukraine during World War II*. Edmonton: Canadian Institute of Ukrainian Studies, 1986.

Browning, Christopher R. *Ordinary Men*. New York: HarperCollins, 1992.

Bullock, Alan. *Hitler and Stalin*. Toronto: McClelland and Stewart, 1991.

Chant, Christopher, Brig. Shelford Bidwell, Anthony Preston, and Jenny Shaw. *World War II: Land, Sea and Air Battles 1939–1945*. London: Octopus Book, 1977.

Cholawski, Shalom. *Soldiers from the Ghetto*. San Diego: A. S. Barnes, 1980.

Cohen, Asher, and Yehoyakim Cochavi, eds. *Zionist Youth Movements during the Shoah*. Translated by Ted Gorelick. New York: Peter Lang, 1995.

Conquest, Robert. *The Great Terror*. New York: Macmillan, 1968.

Cooper, Matthew. *The Nazi War against Soviet Partisans, 1941–1944*. New York: Stein and Day, 1979.

Dallin, Alexander. *German Rule in Russia, 1941–1945: A Study of Occupation Policies*. New York: St. Martin's Press, 1957.

Davies, Norman. *God's Playground: A History of Poland*. New York: Columbia University Press, 1984.

Davies, Norman, and Antony Polonsky, eds. *Jews in Eastern Poland and the USSR, 1939–46*. New York: St. Martin's Press, 1991.

Dawidowicz, Lucy S. *From That Place and Time: A Memoir, 1938–1947.* New York: W. W. Norton, 1989.

——. *The Holocaust and the Historians.* Cambridge, Mass.: Harvard University Press, 1981.

——. *The War against the Jews, 1933-1945.* New York: Holt, Rinehart and Winston, 1975.

——, ed. *The Golden Tradition: Jewish Life and Thought in Eastern Europe.* New York: Holt, Rinehart and Winston, 1967.

——. *A Holocaust Reader.* New York: Behrman House, 1976.

Dobroszycki, Lucjan, and Jeffrey S. Gurock. *The Holocaust in the Soviet Union.* New York: M. E. Sharpe, 1993.

Dobroszycki, Lucjan., and B. Kirshenblatt-Gimblett. *Image before My Eyes: A Photographic History of Jewish Life in Poland, 1864–1939.* New York: Schocken Books, 1977.

Drukier, Manny. *Carved in Stone: Holocaust Years — A Boy's Tale.* Toronto: University of Toronto Press, 1996.

Druks, Herbert. *Jewish Resistance during the Holocaust.* New York: Irvington Publishers, 1983.

Duker, Abram G. *Studies in Polish-Jewish History and Relations.* New York: Ktav, 1981.

Dwork, Deborah. *Children with a Star: Jewish Youth in Nazi Europe.* New Haven: Yale University Press, 1991.

Eckman, Lester, and Chaim Lazar. *The Jewish Resistance: The History of the Jewish Partisans in Lithuania and White Russia during the Nazi Occupation.* New York: Shengold, 1977.

Ehrenburg, Ilya, and Vasily Grossman, eds. *The Black Book: The Nazi Crimes against the Jewish People.* New York: Holocaust Library, 1980.

Eibeshitz, Jehoshua, and Anna Eilenberg-Eibeshitz, eds. *Women in the Holocaust.* New York: Remember Publications, 1993.

Eilenberg-Eibeshitz, Anna. *Remember: A Collection of Testimonies.* Haifa: Institute for Holocaust Studies, 1992.

Encyclopedia of the Holocaust. 4 vols. New York: Macmillan, 1990.

Engel, David. *Facing a Holocaust: The Polish Government-in-Exile and the Jews, 1943–1945.* Chapel Hill, N.C.: University of North Carolina Press, 1993.

——. *In the Shadow of Auschwitz: The Polish Government in Exile and Jews, 1939–1942.* Chapel Hill, N.C.: University of North Carolina Press, 1987.

Fishman, J., ed. *Studies on Polish Jewry 1919–1939.* New York: YIVO, 1974.

Foot, M. R. D. *Resistance.* New York: McGraw-Hill, 1977.

Friedman, Ada June, ed. *Roads to Extinction.* (Essays by Philip Friedman) Philadelphia: The Jewish Publication Society of America, 1980.

Fuks, Marian, Z. Hoffman, M. Horn, and J. Tomaszewski. *Polish Jewry: History and Culture.* Warsaw: Polish Interpress Agency, 1982.

Fyodorov, Aleksei. *The Underground Committee Carries On.* Moscow: Foreign Languages Publishing House, 1952.

Gefen, Aba. *Hope in Darkness.* New York: Holocaust Library, 1989.

Gelman, Charles. *Do Not Go Gentle: A Memoir of Jewish Resistance in Poland, 1941–1945.* Hamden, Conn.: Archon Books, 1989.

Gilbert, Martin. *The Boys: Triumph over Adversity.* Vancouver: Douglas and McIntyre, 1996.

———. *The Day the War Ended.* London: HarperCollins, 1995.

———. *The Dent Atlas of the Holocaust.* London: J. M. Dent, 1988.

———. *The Holocaust: A Jewish Tragedy.* London: Fontana Press, 1987.

———. *Holocaust Journey: Travelling in Search of the Past.* Vancouver: Douglas and McIntyre, 1997.

Goldhagen, Daniel Jonah. *Hitler's Willing Executioners: Ordinary Germans and the Holocaust.* New York: Alfred A. Knopf, 1996.

Grosman, Chaika. *The Underground Army: Fighters of the Bialystok Ghetto.* New York: Holocaust Library, 1987.

Gross, Jan T. *Polish Society under German Occupation.* Princeton, N.J.: Princeton University Press, 1979.

Gruber, Samuel. *I Chose Life.* New York: Shengold, 1978.

Gutman, Yisrael. *Fighters among the Ruins: The Story of Jewish Heroism during World War II.* Washington, D.C.: B'nai Brith Books, 1988.

———. *The Jews of Warsaw, 1939–1943.* Bloomington, Ind.: Indiana University Press, 1989.

Gutman, Yisrael, and Shmuel Krakowski. *Unequal Victims: Poles and Jews during World War II.* New York: Holocaust Library, 1986.

Gutman, Y., E. Mendelsohn, J. Reinharz, and C. Shmeruk, eds. *The Jews of Poland between Two World Wars.* Hanover, Mass.: University Press of New England, 1989.

Gutman, Yisrael, and L. Rothkirchen, eds. *The Catastrophe of European Jewry.* Jerusalem: Yad Vashem, 1976.

Halecki, Oskar. *A History of Poland.* New York: D. McKay, 1976.

Heiman, Leo. *I Was a Soviet Guerrilla.* London: Brown, Watson, 1959.

Heller, Celia S. *On the Edge of Destruction.* New York: Columbia University Press, 1977.

Hertzberg, Arthur. *The Zionist Idea.* New York: Atheneum, 1976.

Hilberg, Raul. *The Destruction of European Jews.* New York: New Viewpoints, 1973.

——. *Perpetrators, Victims, Bystanders: The Jewish Catastrophe, 1933–1945.* New York: HarperCollins, 1992.

——, ed. *Documents of Destruction 1933–1945.* New York: Quadrangle, 1971.

Hilberg, Raul, Stanislaw Staron, and Josef Kermisz, eds. *The Warsaw Diary of Adam Czerniakow.* New York: Stein and Day, 1979.

Holliday, Laurel. *Children in the Holocaust and World War II.* New York: Pocket Books, 1995.

Ignatieff, Michael. *Blood and Belonging.* London: Penguin, 1993.

Jachimczyk, Maciej, ed. *The Jews in Poland.* Oxford: Basil Blackwell, 1986.

Jewish Resistance during the Holocaust: Proceedings of the Conference on Manifestations of Jewish Resistance, 1968. Jerusalem: Yad Vashem, 1971.

Kahane, David. *Lvov Ghetto Diary.* Amherst, Mass.: University of Massachusetts Press,1990.

Kahn, Leon. *No Time to Mourn.* Vancouver: Laurelton Press, 1978.

Karski, Jan. *The Great Powers and Poland: 1919–1945.* New York: University Press of America, 1985.

Katsh, Abraham, ed. *Scroll of Agony: The Warsaw Diary of Chaim A. Kaplan.* New York: Collier, 1981.

Kielce–July 4, 1946. Toronto: The Polish Educational Foundation in North America, 1996.

Kohn, Nahum. *Voice from the Forest.* New York: Holocaust Library, 1980.

Korbonski, Stefan. *The Jews and the Poles in World War II.* New York: Hippocrene Books, 1989.

Korczak, Janusz. *Ghetto Diary.* New York: Holocaust Library, 1978.

Kovpak, S. A. *Our Partisan Course.* London: Hutchinson and Company, 1947.

Kowalski, Isaac, ed. *Anthology on Armed Jewish Resistance, 1939–1945.* 3 vols. New York: Jewish Combatants Publishers House, 1984.

Krakowski, Shmuel. *The War of the Doomed: Jewish Armed Resistance in Poland, 1942–1944.* New York: Holmes and Meier, 1984.

Kuzin, Ilya. *Notes of a Guerrilla Fighter.* Moscow: Foreign Languages Publishing House, 1942.

Laqueur, Walter. *A History of Zionism.* New York: Holt, Rinehart and Winston, 1972.

Lazar, Chaim. *Destruction and Resistance: A History of the Partisan Movement in Vilna.* New York: Shengold, 1985.

Lendvai, Paul. *Anti-Semitism without Jews.* New York: Doubleday, 1971.

Levin, Dov. *Fighting Back: Lithuanian Jewry's Armed Resistance to the Nazis, 1941–1945.* New York: Holmes and Meier, 1985.

Lukas, Richard. *The Forgotten Holocaust: The Poles under German Occupation 1939–1944.* Lexington, Ky.: The University Press of Kentucky, 1986.

Macksey, Kenneth. *The Partisans of Europe in the Second World War.* New York: Stein and Day, 1975.

Marcus, Joseph. *Social and Political History of the Jews in Poland, 1919–1939.* New York: Mouton Publishers, 1983.

Marrus, Michael. *The Holocaust in History.* Hanover, Mass.: The University Press of New England, 1987.

——, ed. *The Nazi Holocaust: Historical Articles on the Destruction of European Jews.* 9 vols. London: Meckler Corporation, 1989.

Mendelsohn, Ezra. *The Jews of East Central Europe between the World Wars.* Bloomington, Ind.: Indiana University Press, 1993.

——. *Zionism in Poland: The Formative Years, 1915–1926.* New Haven: Yale University Press, 1982.

Mendelsohn, John, ed. *The Holocaust: Selected Documents.* 18 vols. New York: Garland Publishing, 1982.

Mermelstein, Max, ed. *Skala.* New York: Skala Benevolent Society, 1978.

Michel, Henri. *The Shadow War: European Resistance, 1939–1945.* New York: Harper and Row, 1972.

Michelson, Frida. *I Survived Rumbuli.* New York: Holocaust Library, 1979.

Noakes, J., and G. Pridham, eds. *Nazism 1919-1945: A Documentary Reader.* Vol. 3. Exeter, Devon: University of Exeter Press, 1988.

Patterns of Jewish Leadership in Nazi Europe 1933–1945: Proceedings of the Third Yad Vashem International Historical Conference, 1977. Jerusalem: Yad Vashem, 1979.

Pearson, Raymond. *National Minorities in Eastern Europe, 1848–1945.* New York: St. Martin's Press, 1983.

Polonsky, Antony. *Politics in Independent Poland 1921–1939*. Oxford: Clarendon Press, 1972.

——, ed. *My Brother's Keeper? Recent Polish Debates on the Holocaust*. London: Routledge, 1990.

Porter, Jack, ed. *Jewish Partisans: A Documentary of Jewish Resistance in the Soviet Union during World War II*. New York: University Press of America, 1982.

Rescue Attempts during the Holocaust: Proceedings of the Second Yad Vashem International Historical Conference. Jerusalem: Yad Vashem, 1977.

Richmond, Theo. *Konin: A Quest*. London: Pantheon Books, 1995.

Ringelblum, Emmanuel. *Polish-Jewish Relations during the Second World War*. Edited by J. Kermish and S. Krakowski. Jerusalem: Yad Vashem, 1974.

Riwash, Joseph. *Resistance and Revenge, 1939–1949*. Montreal: R and R Distribution, 1981.

Rosner, Mina. *I Am a Witness*. Winnipeg: Hyperion Press, 1990.

Rothchild, Sylvia, ed. *Voices from the Holocaust*. New York: New American Library, 1981.

Rubin, Sulia Wolozhinski. *Against the Tide: The Story of an Unknown Partisan*. Jerusalem: Posner and Sons, 1980.

Rudashevski, Yitzhok. *The Diary of the Vilna Ghetto: June 1941–April 1943*. Western Galilee, Israel: Ghetto Fighters' House, 1972.

Ryan, Michael D., ed. *Human Responses to the Holocaust*. New York: The Edwin Mellen Press, 1981.

Salamia-Loc, Fanny. *Woman Facing the Gallows*. Amherst, Mass.: Word Pro, 1981.

Samuels, Gertrude. *Mottele: A Partisan Odyssey*. New York: Harper and Row, 1976.

Schama, Simon. *Landscape and Memory*. Toronto: Random House, 1995.

Schatz, Jaff. *The Generation: The Rise and Fall of the Jewish Communists of Poland*. Los Angeles: University of California Press, 1991.

Schectman, J. B. *Zionism and Zionists in Soviet Russia*. Zionist Organization of America: New York, 1966.

Schulman, Faye. *A Partisan's Memoir*. Toronto: Second Story Press, 1995.

Sefer Hapartisanim Hayehudim (The Jewish partisan book). Merchavia: Sifriath Poalim, Hashomer Hatzair, 1958.

Shirer, William L. *The Rise and Fall of the Third Reich*. New York: Crest Books, 1962.

Shutan, Moshe. *Ghetto and Woods* (in Hebrew). Tel Aviv: Jewish Partisan and

Fighters Organization, 1985.

Silverman, Peter, David Smuschkowitz, and Peter Smuszkowicz. *From Victims to Victors.* Toronto: Canadian Society for Yad Vashem, 1992.

Smolar, Hersh. *The Minsk Ghetto: Soviet-Jewish Partisans against the Nazis.* New York: Holocaust Library, 1989.

The Soviet Partisan Movement. Washington, D.C.: Center of Military History, 1969.

Spector, Shmuel. *The Holocaust of Volhynian Jews 1941–1944.* Jerusalem: Yad Vashem and the Federation of Volhynian Jews, 1990.

Suhl, Yuri, ed. *They Fought Back: The Story of the Jewish Resistance in Nazi Europe.* New York: Schocken Books, 1975.

Sutin, Jack, and Rochelle Sutin. *Jack and Rochelle: A Holocaust Story of Love and Resistance.* St. Paul, Minn.: Graywolf Press, 1995.

Syrkin, Marie. *Blessed Is the Match.* Philadelphia: The Jewish Publication Society of America, 1947.

Tec, Nechama. *Defiance: The Bielski Partisans.* New York: Oxford University Press, 1993.

———. *In the Lion's Den: The Life of Oswald Rufeisen.* New York: Oxford University Press, 1990.

———. *When Light Pierced the Darkness: Christian Rescue of Jews in Nazi-Occupied Poland.* New York: Oxford University Press, 1986.

Temchin, Michael. *The Witch Doctor: Memoirs of a Partisan.* New York: Holocaust Library, 1983.

Tenenbaum, Joseph. *Underground: The Story of a People.* New York: Philosophical Library, 1952.

Tory, Avraham. *Surviving the Holocaust: The Kovno Ghetto Diary.* Cambridge, Mass.: Harvard University Press, 1990.

Trunk, Isaiah. *Judenrat: The Jewish Councils in Eastern Europe under Nazi Occupation.* New York: Stein and Day, 1977.

———, ed. *Jewish Responses to Nazi Persecution.* New York: Stein and Day, 1979.

Shapiro, Gershon, ed. *Under Fire: The Stories of Jewish Heroes of the Soviet Union.* Jerusalem: Yad Vashem, 1988.

United States Holocaust Memorial Museum. *Historical Atlas of the Holocaust.* New York: Macmillan, 1996.

Vago, B., and G. Mosse, eds. *Jews and Non-Jews in Eastern Europe.* New York: Wiley, 1974.

Vakar, Nicholas P. *Belorussia: The Making of a Nation.* Cambridge, Mass.: Harvard University Press, 1956.

Vital, David. *The Origins of Zionism.* London: Oxford University Press, 1975.

Werner, Harold. *Fighting Back: A Memoir of Jewish Resistance.* New York: Columbia University Press, 1992.

Werth, Alexander. *Russia at War 1941–1945.* London: Barrie and Rockliffe, 1964.

Laska, Vera, ed. *Women in the Resistance and in the Holocaust.* Westport, Conn.: Greenwood Press, 1983.

Yahil, Leni. *The Holocaust: The Fate of European Jewry.* New York: Oxford University Press, 1990.

Zawodny, J. K. *Death in the Forest: The Story of the Katyn Forest Massacre.* New York: Hippocrene Books, 1988.

IV. ARTICLES

Arad, Yitzhak. "Jewish Family Camps in the Forests — An Original Means of Rescue." In *The Nazi Holocaust: Historical Articles on the Destruction of European Jews,* edited by Michael Marrus, vol. 7, 219–39. London: Meckler, 1989.

Armstrong, John. "Collaboration." *Journal of Modern History* 40 (September 1968): 396–410.

Bar-on, Zwi. "The Jews in the Soviet Partisan Movement." *Yad Vashem Studies* 4 (1960): 167–90.

Beinfeld, Solon. "The Cultural Life of the Vilna Ghetto." In *The Nazi Holocaust: The Victims of the Holocaust,* edited by Michael Marrus, vol. 6, 95–115. London: Meckler, 1989.

Bielski, Tuvia. "In the Forests." In *A Tower from the Enemy,* ed. Albert Nirenstein, 352–72. New York: Orion Press, 1959.

Foxman, Abraham. "Not only in Warsaw." *The Maccabean* 1, no. 1 (March 1964): 4–15.

Friedman, Philip. "Two 'Saviors' Who Failed: Moses Merin of Sosnowiec and Jacob Gens of Vilna." *The Nazi Holocaust: The Victims of the Holocaust,* edited by Michael Marrus, vol. 6, 488–500. London: Meckler, 1989.

———. "Ukrainian–Jewish Relations during the Nazi Occupation." *YIVO Annual of Jewish Social Science* 12 (1959): 259–96.

Goldstein, Jaacov. "Mezeritch-Podlaski: Portrait of a City of Refuge and an

Extermination Center." *Publications of the Museum of the Combatants and Partisans* 5, no. 4 (April 1985): 72–84.

Graebe, Herman F. "Testimony of Herman F. Graebe, Given in Israel." *Yad Vashem Studies* 6 (1967): 283–314.

Handlin, Oscar. "Jewish Resistance to the Nazis." *Commentary* 34 (November 1962): 398-405.

Heiman, Leo. "They Saved Jews." *The Ukrainian Quarterly* 17, no. 4 (December 1961): 320–32.

———. "Ukrainians and the Jews." *The Ukrainian Quarterly* 17, no. 2 (June 1961): 3–12.

Hundret, Gershon David. "Some Basic Characteristics of the Jewish Experience in Poland." *Polin* 1 (1986): 28-34.

Kahanowitz, Moshe. "Why No Separate Jewish Partisan Movement Was Established." *Yad Vashem Studies* 1 (1957): 153–67.

Kovner, Abba. "A First Attempt to Tell." In *The Holocaust as Historical Experience*, edited by Yehuda Bauer and Nathan Rotenstreich, 77–94. New York: Holmes and Meier Publishers, 1981.

Kruk, Herman. "Diary of the Vilna Ghetto." *YIVO Annual of Jewish Social Science* 13 (1965): 9–78.

Lestchinsky, Jacob. "Economic Aspects of Jewish Community Organization in Independent Poland." *Jewish Social Studies* 9, no. 1–4 (1947): 319–38.

———. "The Industrial and Social Structure of the Jewish Population of Interbellum Poland." *YIVO Annual of Jewish Social Science* 11 (1957): 243–69.

Lazar, Chaim. "Joseph Glazman: Portrait of a Fighter." *Publications of the Museum of the Combatants and Partisans* 8, no. 9 (September 1994): 65–84.

Levin, Dov. "Lithuanian Attitudes toward the Jewish Minority in the Aftermath of the Holocaust: The Lithuanian Press, 1991–92." *Holocaust and Genocide Studies* 7, no. 2 (September 1993): 247–62.

———. "The Response of the Jews of Eastern Poland to the Invasion of the Red Army in September, 1939." *Gal-ed.* (Journal of the Diaspora Research Institute, Tel Aviv) 11 (1989): 87–102.

———. "Unique Characteristics of Soviet Jewish Soldiers in the Second World War." *The Shoah and the War* (1992): 236–44.

Merin, Yehuda, and Jack Porter. "Three Jewish Family-Camps in the Forests of Volyn, Ukraine, during the Holocaust." *Jewish Social Science* 156, no. 1

(1984): 83–92.

Okunieff, Michael. "Witness to the Execution of Jacob Gens." *Publications of the Museum of the Combatants and Partisans* 8 (September 1993): 83–86.

Rudnikci, Szymon. "From 'Numerus Clausus' to 'Numerus Nullus.'" *Polin* 2 (1987): 246–68.

Schwarz, Solomon. "The Soviet Partisans and the Jews." *Modern Review* (January 1949): 387–400.

Tomaszewski, Jerzy. "Some Methodological Problems of the Study of Jewish History in Poland between the Two World Wars." *Polin* 1 (1986): 163–75.

Wynot, Edward D. "A Necessary Cruelty: The Emergence of Official Anti-Semitism in Poland, 1936–1939." *The American Historical Review* 76, no. 4 (October 1971): 1035–58.

Yonson, Velvke. "I Avenged Our Blood." *Sefer Zikaron Lubcz* (Remembrance book of Lubcz), translated by Esther Nisenholt, 344–63. Tel Aviv: Lubcz Survivors, 1971.

Zawodny, J. K. "Soviet Partisans." *Social Studies* 17, no. 3 (January 1966): 368–77.

V. Unpublished Manuscripts

Bairach, Pessia. "In Their Slashing Claws." Tel Aviv, 1958.

Douglas, Donald M. "Strangers in the Heartland." United States Holocaust Memorial Museum Archives, RG-02.142.

Ettinger, Liza. "From the Lida Ghetto to the Bielski Partisans." United States Holocaust Memorial Museum Archives, RG-02.133, 1984.

Mermall, Gabriel. "Diary." United States Holocaust Memorial Museum Archives, RG-02.008*01, 1986.

Pinsky, Bernard. "Ordinary, Extraordinary: My Father's Life." Vancouver, 1996.

Seigel, Jerry. "My Mother's Dream: The Story of My Personal Survival through the Holocaust." Toronto, 1990.

Zissman, Harold (Cukierman, Hershel). "Torn between Tyrants: Memories about the Holocaust That Linger On." United States Holocaust Memorial Museum Archives, RG-02.135, 1994.

VI. Videos and Films

Herman, David, and Arun Kumar. *The Bielski Brothers.* Princeton, N.J.: Film for Humanities and Sciences, 1996.

INDEX